CRIMINAL CONVERSATIONS

Figure 1. A montage of Victorian periodical and newspaper front pages.

CRIMINAL CONVERSATIONS

―◆○◆―

Victorian Crimes, Social Panic,
and Moral Outrage

Edited by

Judith Rowbotham and Kim Stevenson

THE OHIO STATE UNIVERSITY PRESS
Columbus

This volume is affectionately dedicated to Harold Perkin (1926–2004). A good man and a good historian, he supported and inspired history like this.

Copyright © 2005 by The Ohio State University.
All rights reserved.

Library of Congress Cataloging-in-Publication Data

Criminal conversations : Victorian crimes, social panic, and moral outrage / edited by Judith Rowbotham and Kim Stevenson.
   p. cm.
Includes bibliographical references and index.
ISBN 0-8142-0973-4 (cloth : alk. paper)—ISBN 0-8142-9043-4 (CD-ROM)
1. Crime—England—Public opinion—History—19th century. 2. Deviant behavior—England—Public opinion—History—19th century. 3. Crime in mass media—History—19th century. 4. Deviant behavior in mass media—History—19th century. 5. Criminal justice, Administration of—England—History—19th century. 6. England—Moral conditions—History—19th century. 7. England—Social conditions—19th century. I. Rowbotham, Judith. II. Stevenson, Kim.
HV6950.E5C75 2005
364.941'09'034—dc22
2004024133

Cover design by Laurence Nozik.
Text design by Jennifer Forsythe.
Type set in Adobe Garamond.

The paper used in this publication meets the minimum requirements of the American National Standard for Information Sciences—Permanence of Paper for Printed Library Materials. ANSI Z39.48–1992.

9 8 7 6 5 4 3 2 1

Contents

Acknowledgements — vii
List of Illustrations — ix
List of Tables — x
List of Abbreviations — xi
Table of Cases — xiii
Table of Statutes — xv
Contributors — xvii
Introduction
   Judith Rowbotham and Kim Stevenson — xxi

SECTION ONE: IDENTIFYING THE CAUSES AND IMPACTS OF BAD BEHAVIOR

1. Beyond the Bounds of Respectable Society:
   The "Dangerous Classes" in Victorian and Edwardian England
   David Taylor — 3

2. The Press and the Public Visibility of Nineteenth-Century Criminal Children
   Jane Abbott — 23

3. Religion, Rural Society, and Moral Panic in Mid-Victorian England
   Gary Moses — 40

4. A Victorian Financial Crisis: The Scandalous Implications of the Case of Overend Gurney
   Paul Barnes — 55

5. Larceny: Debating the "Boundless Region of Dishonesty"
   Graham Ferris — 70

SECTION TWO: "EXTERNAL" THREATS TO THE SECURITY OF SOCIETY

6. Criminal Savages? Or "Civilizing" the Legal Process
   Judith Rowbotham — 91

7. Behaving Badly? Irish Migrants and Crime in the Victorian City
   Roger Swift   106

8. Striking at Sodom and Gomorrah: The Medicalization of Male Homosexuality and Its Relation to the Law
   Ivan Crozier   126

9. A Mania for Suspicion: Poisoning, Science, and the Law
   Tony Ward   140

10. A Little of What You Fancy Does You . . . Harm!! (with Apologies to Marie Lloyd)
    Sandra Morton   157

SECTION THREE: THE THREAT FROM WITHIN

11. The Eloquent Corpse: Gender, Probity, and Bodily Integrity in Victorian Domestic Murder
    Shani D'Cruze   181

12. She-Butchers: Baby-Droppers, Baby-Sweaters, and Baby-Farmers
    David Bentley   198

13. Sex, Wives, and Prostitutes: Debating *Clarence*
    Kate Gleeson   215

14. "Crimes of Moral Outrage": Victorian Encryptions of Sexual Violence
    Kim Stevenson   232

15. "Kicked, Beaten, Jumped On until They Are Crushed," All under Man's Wing and Protection: The Victorian Dilemma with Domestic Violence
    Susan Edwards   247

Epilogue
Judith Rowbotham and Kim Stevenson   267

Appendix   273
Selected Further Reading   301
Index   305

Acknowledgments

The editors and chapter authors owe debts of gratitude to the delegates who attended the SOLON "Criminal Conversations" conference in February 2002, out of which this volume has evolved. The contributions made to the thinking that resulted in this collection by speakers and delegates to that conference whose work is not included in this collection have been significant. Throughout, Professor Michael Gunn has encouraged and supported SOLON, and this enterprise. We owe him much. We are grateful, also, to Heather Lee Miller of The Ohio State University Press for her interest, kindness, and support—practical and intellectual—as we have developed and finalized this project from our initial meeting in Chicago. She patiently answered questions both substantial and silly before dashing off on maternity leave!

Thanks are due also to the British Newspaper Library at Colindale: without the help and support of the staff there, the SOLON database and much other research into the Victorian press which has been central to this volume would not have been possible. Special mention must also be made of their help in aiding one increasingly frustrated editor in finding pages which could be photographed—thus providing the bulk of illustrations for this volume. Staff at the British Library at St. Pancras have also aided the editors and individual authors. We must also mention the invaluable assistance of the SOLON Project Manager, Paul Baker, who has kept the editors (reasonably) sane, and provided much help (along with Chris Davis of the Nottingham Business School Technicians in the University), especially with the production of the illustrations. Finally, the editors thank the individual chapter authors for their patience and insights and for being willing to indulge in criminal conversation.

List of Illustrations

Figure 1.	Frontispiece	ii
Figure 2.	Section One Frontispiece:	
	Illustrated Police News, 11 November 1871	xxxiv
Figure 3.	Section Two Frontispiece:	
	Illustrated Police News, 24 May 1870	88
Figure 4.	Section Three Frontispiece:	
	Illustrated Police News, 11 October 1870	178

APPENDIX

Figure 5.	*Illustrated Police News*, July 1871	275
Figure 6.	*Manchester Courier*, 26 January 1850	276
Figure 7.	*Cassell's Saturday Journal*, 1890	277
Figure 8.	*Cassell's Saturday Journal*, 1890	278
Figure 9.	*Cassell's Saturday Journal*, 1890	279
Figure 10.	*Cassell's Saturday Journal*, 1890	280
Figure 11.	*The Times*, 4 March 1875	281
Figure 12.	*The News of the World*, 10 August 1856	282
Figure 13.	*The News of the World*, 17 August 1856	283
Figure 14.	*Daily Telegraph*, 4 August 1859	284
Figure 15.	*Lloyd's News*, 5 June 1870	295
Figure 16.	*Cassell's Saturday Journal*, 1890	295

List of Tables

Table 1. Aggravated Assaults on Women and Children in Courts of Summary Jurisdiction, 1863–1983 — 253

Table 2. Aggravated Assaults at Bow Magistrates Court, 1860–1864 — 255

Table 3. McClaren Return of Sentencing in Violence against Women for 1889 — 262

List of Abbreviations

In an interdisciplinary text of this nature, it has been decided to avoid abbreviations as far as possible, since well-known acronyms to one discipline may not always be more widely familiar. However, the following should be noted, including the designation of judges, in the footnotes mainly, by their judicial rank—hence Lush J means Mr. Justice Lush.

CCR Court for Crown Cases Reserved
CJ Chief Justice
Dtr daughter
GBH Grievous Bodily Harm
Gent Gentleman
HO Home Office
J Justice
Jn Junior
LRO Lancashire Records Office
LB Lord Baron
LCB Lord Chief Baron
LCJ Lord Chief Justice
LJ Lord Justice
MCL Manchester Central Library
MP Member of Parliament
NSPCC National Society for the Prevention of Cruelty to Children
OBSP Old Bailey Sessions Papers
PP Parliamentary Papers
PRO Public Records Office (Kew)

Notes on Sources Used

Much use of newspapers has been made, including those given in the appendix.

A number of the references are available via the SOLON database, at http//solon.law.mmu.ac.uk.

Notes on Legal Terminology

Actus reus refers to the physical elements of an offense, that is, criminal conduct. *Mens rea* refers to the mental elements of an offense, that is, criminal intention.

Deciphering Case Citations for Nonlawyers

Annually, some 2,500 English court cases are fully reported in a variety of law report series, usually where a particular point of law is clarified or interpreted. Every law report has its own mode of citation which includes the abbreviation of the law report series, the year the case was reported, the volume number where appropriate, and the number of the page where the report starts. Hence [1995] 1 All ER 513 refers to the case of *R v Somerset County Council, ex parte Fewings* which can be found in volume 1 of *The All England Reports* for 1995 starting at page 513. The citation will not, however, identify which court the case was heard in. Official reports such as *QB—Queen's Bench Division* do, but equally *AC—Appeal Cases* do not!

Readers will notice in the Table of Cases that sometimes parentheses and sometimes brackets are used in the original citation. This is because the English legal convention is that parentheses are used when a series of Law Report is referred to by volume and number. Brackets are used when the particular series is referenced by year of publication.

From 2001 a form of neutral citation has been used by the House of Lords, the Court of Appeal, and the Administrative Court with a unique number being allocated to each judgment of these courts as in *R v A* [2001] UKHL 25—the 25th numbered judgment of the year 2001 in the House of Lords.

Pre-1865 citations can be particularly disconcerting as there was a proliferation of law reports series during that period. Most of the major series have been gathered together and reprinted to form the *The English Reports* and *The Revised Reports,* for example, (1853) 1 EL & BL 435 refers to the case of *R v Dugdale* reported in the report series of Ellis & Blackburn 1851–1858. Many Victorian criminal cases can also be found in *Cox CC - Cox's Criminal Cases.* An index for all the abbreviations used can be found in Donald Raistrick, *Index to Legal Citations and Abbreviations,* 2nd ed. (London: Bowker-Saur, 1993).

Table of Cases

Andrews v Luckin (1917) 117 LT 726 — 176 n88
Bradley v Wife (1663) 1 Keble 637; 83 ER 1152 — 264 n12
Broad v Broad (1889) LT 687 — 265 n48
Chorlton v Lings (1868–9) LR 4 CP 374 — 246 n10
Fitzpatrick v Kelley (1873) 8 QB 337 — 175 n86
Makin v AG for New South Wales [1894] AC 57 — 214 n58
Moynes v Coopper [1956] 1 QB 439 — 85 n53
Papadimitropoulos v The Queen [1956] 98 CLR 249 — 229 n4
Osman v United Kingdom (2000) 29 EHRR — 264 n24
Otway v Otway (1888) PD 13 — 265 n47
Parker v Alder [1899] 1 QB 20 — 176 n88
R v Ashwell (1885) 16 QBD 190; (1885) 16 Cox CC 1 — 71–73 74, 76–77, 78, 79–82, 83 nn8, 27, 84 nn 28, 30, 34, 85 n58, 66, 69
R v Bazeley (1799) 2 Leach 835; 168 ER 517 — 77, 85 n44
R v Bennett (1866) 4 F & F 1105 — 230 n33
R v Binmore, The Times, 22 March 1875 — 214 n37
R v Boulton and others (1871) 7 Cox CC 87 — 130, 135, 137 n4
R v Brown [1993] 2 All ER 102 — 229 n4
R v Burstow [1996] EWHC Admin 49 — 229 n4
R v Clarence (1888) 22 QBD 23 — 215–16, 220–29, 230 nn24, 30, 34, 37, 231 nn 40, 46, 49–50, 53
R v Cuerrier [1997] 111 CCC (3d) 261 (CACB) — 229 n4
R v Davis (1856) Dears 640; 169 ER 878 — 85 n50
R v Jackson [1891] 1 QBD 671 — 265 n44, 266 n79
R v Justin Harvey (1787) 1 Leach 467; 168 ER 335 — 84 n42
R v Hehir [1895] 2 IR 709 — 72, 79, 80, 81, 83 nn11, 21, 85 nn58, 63, 71
R v Hetherington (1887) PD XX. — 265 n46
R v Humphrey [1898] 1 QBD 875 — 83 n11
R v Lillyman [1896] 2 QBD 167 — 84 n37
R v Linekar [1995] 3 All ER 68 — 229 n4

R v Middleton (1786) 1 Leach 409; 168 ER 306 72, 78–79, 80, 81, 85n51, 86 n72
R v Miller [1954] All ER 529 229 n4
R v Mobilio [1991] 1 VR 339 229 n4
R v Mucklow (1827) 1 Moody 160; 168 ER 1225 86 n72
R v Pear (1786) 1 Leach 409; 168 ER 306 77, 78, 84 n41, 85 n59, 70–71
R v Petrozzi [1987] 35 CCC (3d) 528 229 n4
R v Prince (1868) LR 1 CCR 150 86 n72
R v R [1991] 1 All ER 749 229 n3, 230 n36
R v Richardson [1998] EWCA Crim 1086 229 n4
R v Riley (1853) Dears 149; 169 ER 674 85 n50
R v Sinclair (1867) 13 Cox CC 28 230 n33
R v Thurborn (1848) 1 Den CC 387; 169 ER 293 85 n50
R v Walsh (1812) Russ & Ry 215; 168 ER 767 77
Ruse v Read [1949] KB 377 85 n50
Sidaway v Bethlem Royal Hospital Governors and Others [1984] 1 All ER 1018 229 n4

Table of Statutes

Bubble Act 1720	56
Adulteration of Tea and Coffee Act 1724	173 n4
Adulteration of Tea Act 1730	173 n4
Adulteration of Tea Act 1776	173 n4
Bread Act 1822	175 n77
Beerhouse Act 1830	161
Reform Act 1832	161
Poor Law Amendment Act 1834	149
Joint Stock Act 1844	57–58, 63–65, 69 n37
Summary Jurisdiction Act 1847	33–34, 38 n29
Further Extension of Summary Jurisdiction in Cases of Larceny Act 1850	33–34, 38 n29
Aggravated Assaults Act 1853	252–52, 256m 258
Companies Act 1855	56–58
Joint Stock Companies Act 1856	56–58, 63–65, 69 n37
Divorce and Matrimonial Cases Act, 1857	xx–xxi, xxi n2
Adulteration of Food or Drink Act 1860	169–70, 175 n87
Offences Against the Person Act 1861	219, 221–29, 230 n29, 235–36, 251–52, 253–54
Larceny Act 1861	84 n38, 85 n42
Companies Act 1862	56–58, 63–65, 69 n37
Contagious Diseases Acts 1864	216, 229 n10
Companies Act 1867	64–65
Fairs Act 1871	41
Adulteration of Food, Drink and Drugs Act 1872	170, 173, 175–76 n87
Infant Life Protection Act 1872	207–9, 210, 212, 214 nn 38, 53
Sale of Food and Drugs Act 1875	170–71, 176 n91, 105
Matrimonial Causes Act 1878	256–57
Employers Liability Act 1880	82
Married Women's Property Act 1882	217, 256
Criminal Law Amendment Act 1885	138 n11, 216, 218–19

Infant Life Protection Act 1872	207–9, 210, 212, 214 nn 38, 53
Infant Life Protection Act 1890 (State of Victoria, Australia)	211, 214 n58
Infant Life Preservation Act 1897	211, 214n58
Larceny Act 1901	84 n47
Companies Act 1907	65
Prevention of Crime Act 1908	11, 14–15
Larceny Act 1916	80, 84 n38, 85n47
Adoption of Children Act 1926	200, 213n7
Theft Act 1968	85 n47
Food Safety Act 1990	170
Food Standards Act 1999	170

Contributors

JANE ABBOTT has recently completed her doctoral work on juvenile justice in the nineteenth and twentieth centuries. She has given papers at recent SOLON conferences, and for the future, aims to continue her work within the youth justice service to further research into modern juvenile penal practice.

PAUL BARNES is Professor of Fraud Risk Management at Nottingham Business School. He is a qualified accountant with degrees in Economics and History and has a particular interest in the economic effects of financial crashes, panics, and scandals. He has recently completed a study of one of their twenty-first century forms: Cyber Crime and the demise of "dot coms" (or "cons").

DAVID BENTLEY was appointed QC in 1984. Subsequently, he was appointed Recorder of the Crown Court 1985. He has been a Circuit judge since 1988 sitting mainly in Sheffield, Hull, and York trying crime; and sitting in London as a Deputy High Court judge. Designated Civil Judge for South Yorkshire since 1998. He is also a legal historian and as well as articles and chapters on legal history, is author of four books: *Select Cases from the Twelve Judges' Notebooks* (1997), *English Criminal Justice in the Nineteenth Century* (1998), *Victorian Men of Law* (2000), and most recently, *The Sheffield Hanged* (2002).

IVAN CROZIER is Lecturer in the Science Studies Department at the University of Edinburgh. He was previously a postdoctoral research fellow at the Wellcome Trust Centre for the History of Medicine at University College, London. His interests are the history of sexology, the use of the medical case history, and the history of forensic psychiatry. He is currently completing a book on Havelock Ellis and sexology between 1850–1915.

SHANI D'CRUZE is Reader in Gender and Women's History in the Department of Humanities and Applied Social Studies, Manchester Metropolitan

University, is a Director of SOLON and the Coordinator of the Feminist Crime Research Network. Formerly a co-editor of *Gender and History*, she has published on the history of sexual and physical violence and of the family. She is currently researching the history of gender and crime in the twentieth century.

SUSAN EDWARDS is Professor of Law at the University of Buckingham and Co-Director of the Centre for Multi-Cultural Studies in Law and the Family. A widely respected academic and lawyer, she has been a consultant to the Home Office Crime Reduction Unit on Domestic Violence and to the Crown Prosecution Services on the Expert Witness Project. She has published widely in the field of domestic and sexual violence and is the author of *Female Sexuality and the Law* and *Sex, Gender, and the Legal Process*.

GRAHAM FERRIS is Senior Lecturer in Law at Nottingham Trent University where he specializes in the Law of Trusts. He has published widely in British academic journals in the field of property law and has always been interested in the history of the English legal process. This chapter is his second publication on the history of larceny.

KATE GLEESON is completing a doctorate in the School of Politics & International Relations at the University of New South Wales. Her research concerns modern constructions of sex in political and legal contexts. Her doctoral research has been assisted by an Australian Postgraduate Award, a Chevening Scholarship for study at Nottingham Trent University, and a grant from the Australian Universities European Network.

SANDRA MORTON is a solicitor and Senior Lecturer in the Department of Academic Legal Studies, Nottingham Law School, Nottingham Trent University. She specializes in lecturing in Environmental Law, particularly the topic of contaminated land. She is co-editor of *Blackstone's Statutes on Environmental Law*, currently in its fourth edition.

GARY MOSES is a Prinicipal Lecturer in History at Nottingham Trent University and has undertaken a number of studies regarding farm service and hiring fairs and their broad sociocultural context in nineteenth-century Yorkshire.

JUDITH ROWBOTHAM is a Director of SOLON: Promoting Interdisciplinary Studies in Bad Behaviour and Crime, and Senior Lecturer in History at Nottingham Trent University, a Fellow of the Royal Society of Arts and of the Royal Historical Society. She is also Secretary of the Social History Society, and Managing Editor of *Cultural and Social History*, as well as being a founding member of the Feminist Crime Research Network. She has published on the history of bad behavior and crime, foreign missions, and the history and use of popular writing for historians. She has recently co-edited *Behaving Badly: Visible Crime, Social Panics, and Legal Responses—Victorian and Modern Parallels* (2003) with Kim Stevenson.

KIM STEVENSON is a Director of SOLON and is a Senior Lecturer in Law at the University of Plymouth. She is also a founding member of the Feminist Crime Research Network. Her main research areas are sexual offenses and sexuality, particularly from a historical perspective, and she has published a number of articles in this area. She recently co-wrote the *Blackstones Guide to the Sexual Offences Act 2003* (2004).

ROGER SWIFT is the Director of the Centre for Victorian Studies at Chester College, Visiting Professor in History at the University of Staffordshire, and a Fellow of the Royal Historical Society. He has held research fellowships at the Universities of York, Liverpool, and Cambridge and has published widely in the fields of Victorian crime, policing, and social protest and Irish diaspora studies.

DAVID TAYLOR was educated at Wadham College, Oxford. He is currently Dean of the School of Music & Humanities at Huddersfield University, having previously been Head of History at the universities of Teesside and Huddersfield. He is the author of *The New Police in the Nineteenth Century* (1997) plus *Crime, Policing and Punishment in England, 1750–1914* (1998) and *Policing the Victorian Town* (2002). He has also written articles on various aspects of the history of crime and policing.

TONY WARD is Principal Lecturer in Law at Hull University. He has published papers on the history of coroners, the insanity defense, and infanticide and is co-author with Penny Green of *State Crime: Governments, Violence and Corruption* (2004).

Introduction

JUDITH ROWBOTHAM AND KIM STEVENSON

Criminal Conversations

On 11 August 1859, the *Daily Telegraph* headlined an "Extraordinary Case of Crim. Con.," brought before Mr. Beadon, the stipendiary magistrate of the Southwark Police Court. It is a telling headline in a number of ways. The actual charge (eventually dismissed) was theft of "an old pair of trousers," but the circumstances in which the abstraction of the trousers took place revealed a pretty piece of adultery—and as the reporting indicates, for contemporaries, it was the immoral conduct that provided the real offense in this case.[1] Both headline and content of this report point up the extent to which Victorians saw much that was criminal in the strict legal sense as being also socially criminal; perpetuating the reality that such socially offensive dimensions to law-breaking could be at least as important as the legal dimensions when it came to convicting or acquitting defendants, and to believing or disbelieving witnesses and accusers. Such (often tacit) understandings and conventions formed part of a high profile contemporary debate or "criminal conversation" about the nature of crime and criminality and those who practiced it.

Criminal Conversation, or Crim. Con. in contemporary shorthand, was the term used to describe a husband's civil action for the "crime" of adultery where damages could be claimed against their wives' lovers—though it could not be used in reverse. As well as a legal meaning, it acquired a widespread popular one, with the ubiquitous soubriquet "crim. cons" being used to describe scandalous gossip about illicit relationships, initially in high society.[2] It spread the idea of "criminal conversation" beyond the strict legal definition of the phrase, and this volume takes the idea still further. The concept of scandal-based gossip disseminated through the print media (especially newspapers), of debate and discussion in the press about ideas and people which aroused social panic and moral outrage in a public arena is used to underpin this thematic compilation of surveys of the types of scandal (or would-be scandal) which came before the public gaze of Victorian England, and so helped to shape the Victorian mind, not in its high intellectual dimensions, but in its more everyday preoccupations and worries. After all, Bagehot himself likened London to a newspaper![3] Notice is also taken of ways in which the Victorian experience resonates with present preoccupations.

Such an approach raises issues about ways in which scholars "read" how the Victorians themselves read newsprint and the associated text productions focused on in this collection. As Stewart points out, "discourse analysis . . . is not simply what we practice on the Victorians but what they performed for themselves."[4] Discourse and discourse analysis provide problematic areas for an interdisciplinary collection, because of the differing usages which have become established in individual disciplines of this much used (arguably *abused*) concept. However, despite the apparent laxity of the use of "discourse" in this collection, all the contributors understand it as referring to types of text (with or without illustration) conveying information and ideas, and consciously produced according to the conventions of a particular profession or interest group. Such products were also consciously read by their recipient audiences. There is no intention to claim that Victorians read newspapers without being well aware of the agendas behind their various stances. In fact it was this consciousness which guided the choice of title. There was, after all, no restraint on who bought what beyond that of price.

We have emphasized the term "conversation" in this collection, because this serves to remind us all that the Victorians consciously engaged in debates through the forum of newsprint relating to what may be termed social subjectivity. It was these "conversations" which inspired how and what they wrote and read about bad behavior and crime, shaping the shifting consensus about what constituted unacceptable conduct and its appropriate penalties. Consequently, explorations of this particular theme, of crime and bad behavior, provide wider insights into Victorian society which are not otherwise readily obtainable, promoting a greater understanding of how the internal bonds of that society actually operated. In this, it is not intended to claim an empathy with Victorian perspectives on offensive behavior when echoes of that experience chime with current preoccupations. Darnton's point that figures in the past did not think as we do remains valid, meaning that the nuances of how and why the Victorians reacted to particular situations as they did, and how they interpreted the coded language of Victorian reporting, will always remain a matter of speculation, not knowledge.[5] However, accepting the past as a distant country does not mean that certain features of that other landscape cannot be recognized as elements in a persistent human experience, and fear of the consequences of crime and bad behavior is undoubtedly a constant.

Spreading the Word: The Victorian Press

The Victorians regarded the role of print, especially newsprint, as crucial in promoting and mediating mass consent to the operation of the legal system and the accompanying sociocultural processes of identifying and punishing transgressors. The press proffered, for public appraisal, a daily diet of reports of cases and trials from primarily the summary courts but also the higher courts.[6] Perceptions of what was and what was not acceptable conduct inevitably shifted over time, as a result of a range of socioeconomic changes and a range of imprecise cultural factors. Press conversations helped ensure the maintenance of popular consent to the operation of the legal system, which was in turn dependent upon a sociocultural spirit of agreement which reinforced (or replaced, where strict legal boundaries were not crossed) legal decisions.

That this was not automatically achieved is powerfully indicated by the alarm which the case of the Tichborne Claimant aroused. Bringing to trial Arthur Orton in 1875 for falsely claiming to be Sir Roger Tichborne was intended to signal to the public the unacceptability of varieties of deceit implicated in his claim. Working-class Orton had attempted to pass himself off as a member of an ancient upper-class family, thereby gaining wealth in the shape of both social status and money, and the potential for wielding considerable power, social, economic, and even political. The Claimant's trial sharply divided Victorian Britain along class lines, and the newspapers reflected this. *The Times*, for instance, was profoundly hostile to the Claimant, whereas *Reynolds News* (edited by that ex-Chartist George Reynolds) was vehemently supportive of his claim.[7] This division, though, was significantly different to the general consensus. While there were regular differences, for example over the presentation of trades union disputes when these arrived in the courts, what is far more striking to anyone reading across a range of titles on a daily basis, for any one year, is the degree of conformity about what constituted the kinds of cases which should be reported, and the important aspects of a particular case, in terms of verdicts and comments from judges, magistrates, and counsel.[8]

Victorian newsprint spread gossip about transgressions far beyond local circles and communities, transforming relatively minor incidents into *causes célèbres* of national proportion. Storylines featuring crime and bad behavior, often accompanied by scare-mongering rhetoric, were a major feature of the

Victorian press. From the formal police court and other legal reports, to features and articles of gossipy speculation on wrongdoing and wrongdoers, bad behavior sold well. Titles known to feature these in abundance sold particularly well to audiences across class boundaries, something that the *Daily Telegraph,* the *Illustrated London News,* and the *News of the World,* for instance, understood thoroughly. Justified by claims to expose such conduct for the good of society, as a warning to the respectable and innocent of the perils which beset them, newspapers and periodicals ensured that the reportage of bad behavior and crime appealed across class and gender divisions, and fictionalization of popular real-life dramas enhanced that appeal still further. Thus, the *Daily Telegraph,* noted for its sensational crime reporting, could on the one hand "deplore the effect on the public mind" of their reports of certain types of incident, and on the other, argue that:

> So far as the public is concerned the newspapers must report the proceedings . . . [for] . . . if one paper abstained, twenty others would take its place and nothing would be gained by the public . . . on the broadest grounds of common interest, it is better that society should be occasionally shocked with the report of the most detestable charges than that judicial proceedings should at any time take place in secret, or that crime itself should derive a fatal safety in continuity from the secrecy accorded to it by an abuse of decorum.[9]

This is a very revealing comment, not only because of the claims made but also because of their location, emphasizing the public dimension.

One of the features of British Victorian society was its apparent openness in public reporting of key areas such as crime and its punishment. If, after 1868, the much reduced numbers of executions were removed from the direct public gaze, details were still reproduced in the newspapers, providing assurance of punishment accomplished and justice completed. Views and images of prison life were authentically portrayed reinforcing Foucault's assertion that punishment always has a wider social dimension beyond the specific incident, locating both the crime and its retribution in cultural contexts relating to contemporary social concerns.[10] Focus on both the legally and the socially offensive in any period can therefore provide substantial insights into the broader spirit of that age. The Victorian period was not unique in this, but new technology, new living and working patterns, and the rise of a class-based society obsessed by concepts of respectability combined to bring a genuinely new dimension to popular understandings of, and participation in, the processes whereby a broad consensus was achieved about what constituted acceptable social conduct. This is not to claim it was an easy or a static consensus. It was an age where, as contemporary crime reporting underlines, what can seem agendas of social control were in fact strategies of socialization. There was widespread accord about the desirability of respectability, if not always about the precise methodology to achieve it.[11] It was in this maintenance of consent and debate over methodologies that the Victorian print media played so crucial a part, but despite the growth of scholarship in newspaper history and journalism there has been little substantial investigation into the reporting of crime and the legal process in the Victorian age.

Crime Talking and Crime Reporting

This was the first age of mass-circulation newspapers and periodicals and the beginnings of journalism emerged as a recognizable modern profession. It is not our intention to narrate the history of such developments, going over ground well covered, notably by Lucy Brown in her study of Victorian newspapers, and in the range of discussions included in a number of useful collections on the nineteenth-century media,[12] What this volume sets out to do is locate print conversations about crime and bad behavior in their wider cultural contexts. Despite its importance to the success of Victorian newspaper titles, little sustained attention has been given to the coverage of offensive conduct. Works such as Altinck's *Study in Scarlet* and *Evil Encounters* still set the tone.[13] These highlight the sensational dimensions involved but do not investigate the actual process of reportage, especially the substantial coverage daily given by most national and local titles to proceedings in the courts, summary and higher, where the key interpretation of a particular event, in terms of the decision to convict or acquit defendants, took place. Yet it was, in Foucauldian terms, through such reportage that society worked out the classification to be assigned to a particular offense, with, as W. G. Gilbert put it, making "the punishment fit the crime."[14] What was different about nineteenth-century reporting of legal proceedings, which forms the bulk of Victorian crime reporting, is that the majority of reporters were not the professional journalists considered by scholars such as Nigel Cross, Joel Wiener, or Laurel Brake, but rather legal personnel amplifying their incomes by writing, anonymously, for the press—something explored in more detail by this volume's editors in a previous collection: *Behaving Badly*.[15]

There remains some reluctance to recognize the importance of the Victorian print media as a channel through which popular consensus evolved over issues of offending, partly because in some areas, such as politics, the one-sided nature of the print conversation (except at election times, perhaps) is plain. But the debates surrounding crime and bad behavior were different.

There was a participation in the print conversation which linked to the direct audience participation in the courts themselves. Members of the public served in the higher courts as jurors, of course, but of at least equal importance, they flooded to the summary courts in considerable numbers. The lower courts (police or magistrates courts, as they were variously termed) sat on an almost daily basis, and members of the public were involved as witnesses and as spectators. It was this experience which underpinned the demand for crime news in all the Victorian press, from the respectable titles such as *The Times* to those with a more dubious contemporary reputation, such as *Reynolds News*. Dukes and dustmen all enthusiastically read about crime in a variety of newspapers aimed at such different markets. But the most striking aspect is the similarity of coverage over such a broad range of papers.[16] People's basic ability to read (though not automatically to write) was already high by the midcentury, though levels of competency varied widely. Proportions of men in the population able to read stood higher than those of women: equally the poorer classes constituted the majority of those whose literacy was at best adequate.[17] The reality was that newspapers played a considerable part in sustaining and increasing literacy, acquainting people with a vocabulary that they learned because of its association with thrilling and sensational stories.

Headlines regularly resorted to adjectives such as "shocking," "horrible," or "fearful," and actual incidents could be presented as an "outrage" or a "scandal" if the criminal description (say, a rape or an assault) was either too indelicate or too mild to convey sufficient levels of sensation. The rhetorical language used in newspaper crime stories, especially headlines, sometimes appears to be repetitious, but this was a useful device in a number of ways. It suggested to readers the way in which a report should be read, and could be used to ensure that "big" words which best conveyed the sense of what was going on became familiar at all levels of society and reading competency. Even those unable to read (or read easily) for themselves could receive the benefit of the information through having the tales read aloud to them, as Dickens emphasized in his novels, from Mr. Wopsle's dramatic reading of crime stories in *Great Expectations* to Betty Higden's admiring testament to Sloppy's renditions of "the police" in "different voices" in *Our Mutual Friend*.[18] Both Mr. Wopsle and Mrs. Higden were on the economic margins of respectability, but their frank enjoyment of newspaper reporting of criminal gossip provides not only a fictional reflection of a reality attested to by the numbers turning up at court proceedings, but also reflects one of the cheapest and most accessible forms of public entertainment. Nor did this disappear. At the close of the Victorian age, Sherlock Holmes advertised himself as a regular peruser of the press, often making comment on its usefulness as in *The Hound of the Baskervilles*.[19] It must also be remembered that newspapers offered the opportunity for public response via the space they all provided for letters from readers. While the provenance of some of these may be doubted, particularly those on political topics, it is our judgment that many of those relating to episodes of crime and bad behavior are honest responses, seeking wider engagement with a particular "scandal" or crime. Letters to the *Daily Telegraph,* for instance, on the sentencing of Stephen Holder to two months for participating in a game of "pitch-and-toss" provide addresses which can be checked through local directories.[20] Such correspondence rarely contains criticisms of decisions to publicize particular crime episodes. Instead, letters generally served to enhance and sustain debates over the doling out of justice, and the implications of certain types of offensive conduct, indicating the correspondence element provided a flourishing channel for sustaining a criminal conversation.[21] Of course the process of editorial choice makes it likely that letters would be published which joined in a conversation already featured in their columns. However, practical commercial sense would suggest that they were unlikely to have continued to publish such correspondence if it adversely affected their sales and if it was seen as entirely spurious.

Social Panic and Moral Outrage

Public scandals may be held to be episodes of bad behavior, and may or may not encompass actual legal offenses, but a common feature is their interpretation by key groups in society of the reality of the transgressions involved (including the impact on any "victims"). Where a scandal reaches national proportions, the interpretations of threat (expressed through the rhetoric of moral outrage) strikes chords across a wide range of interested groups and communities because it represents behavior considered detrimental to the health and stability of society as a whole from the perspective of these groups. Thus for what may be very different actual reasons, the result is a sense of shared panic about the wider implications of such episodes. This, clearly, relates to the concept of moral panic as outlined by Cohen, and subsequently modified by other scholars. Cohen's original point was that "Societies appear to be subject, every now and then" to episodes of what he termed "moral panic," where

> A condition, episode, person or groups of persons emerges to be become defined as a threat to societal values and interests: its nature is presented in stylised and stereotypical fashion by the mass media; the moral barricades are manned by editors, bishops and other right-thinking people; socially accredited experts pronounce their diagnoses and solutions.[22]

Aspects of this model can appear, at first sight, to fit much of what is discussed in this volume. However, the contributors to this volume encourage a more complex comprehension of the role of panic, and of the role of the media in promoting manifestations of social alarm through publicizing expressions of moral outrage and suggested remedies to cope with particular types of bad behavior. The historically sensitive work of Alan Hunt, on the issues of moral imperatives, has thus significantly informed the perspectives in this collection.[23]

What periods of panic provide, as Hunt demonstrates, are opportunities for "moral entrepreneurs" to move in. They coalesce inchoate disquiet, and channel it against targets identified by them as the cause of offense to the community, and also suggest the due remedies to eradicate that offensiveness. It has particular resonance in the realm of crime because "honesty" is and always has been a moral, more than a legal, concept, as exhortations, past and present, to potential groups of offenders to police themselves in terms of their "integrity" underline. In other words, it is an enduring expectation that "good" behavior can be achieved as much through sociocultural pressure on the individual tempted toward transgression as through the ponderous operations of the law itself. A measure of the extent of social panic in a society is therefore the number, vehemence, and indications of public support for, demands for actual legislation to deal with crises which are perceived as specific to a "new" scenario involving transgression considered serious enough to pose a threat to social stability. The expressions of moral outrage which accompany a period of social panic involve the argument that something extraordinary needs to be invoked to deal with particular crises, since the "normal" social pressures are deemed to have failed.

We argue that certain key occurrences of Victorian scandal surveyed through the lens of media reporting provide a nuanced understanding of the nature and extent of the enduring sense of social unease and cultural tension which affected the Victorian period, an unease which was readily stirred up into episodes of social panic. A rhetoric of outrage is then disseminated through the media as appropriate and appealing moral entrepreneurs come forward to give shape and focus to a particular set of fears. Newspapers (as now) readily gave airings to the certainties of the moral entrepreneurs as they identified the "real" nature of a problem, and promoted their remedies, and in so doing, the press initiated a series of conversations with the wider public on the issue of the precise nature of the threat and the most suitable coping strategies.[24] In the climate of sustained underlying social insecurity that characterized so much of the Victorian period, such entrepreneurs encouraged consciousness of the threats to social stability posed by a variety of crimes that seemed to contemporaries to be a particular attribute of the nature of Victorian lawlessness and antisocial behavior. As this collection underlines, it was these commentators, driven by their own moral agendas, who regularly engendered a sense of there being something "new" and "unique" about individual manifestations of crime and bad behavior reported in the press.

The use of print to sustain conversations also means that apparently discrete scandals interacted through such media conversations sustaining a series of both large-scale and more minor panics feeding this continuing sense of insecurity in society, and providing key insights into the Victorian age. Contributors therefore reflect on the extent to which such expressions of criminality and bad behavior were, in fact, exclusive to the period in their fundamental characteristics, as well as on the superficial characteristics which enabled Victorian commentators to present such events in ways that made them seem both peculiar to the period and location, and high profile. The cultural hypocrisies and disingenuities which surrounded the shifting boundaries between the merely offensive and actual offenses are also explored, since it was the lack of recognition of these, and so lack of reconciliation of their contradictions, which fueled both the sense of panic and the rhetoric of moral outrage which characterized, then as now, such socially uncomfortable revelations.

Investigations into the media also encourage insights into the ways in which what may seem to contemporaries to be new and "unique" problems, caused by immediate, short term factors in fact have long lasting resonances. Thus at one level, this collection deals with Victorian conversations, or discussions, which demonstrate the processes whereby the criminal nature of particular types of behavior became a matter of public concern, resulting in either new legislation, or significant modifications to existing legislation or legal practice, or to very serious attempts to introduce such. At another level, this collection reveals the confused and opaque nature of a society which defined itself as "modern" and "forward looking," proud of new advances in technology, in political and social culture and which also sought to invoke the past to give itself a degree of legitimacy and a sense of reality. Both have important resonances for a comprehension of the contradictions and hypocrisies of the late-twentieth and early-twenty-first centuries through their investigations into the confusions of the Victorian age.

This collection has been divided up into sections seeking to reflect Victorian comprehensions of how and why crime and bad behavior were a threat. In identifying the causes and impacts of bad behavior, which occupies Section One, the starting point is the emphasis Victorians placed on respectability, something which implied conduct which was both culturally acceptable and innately law abiding. There could be almost comforting reasons why some did not achieve respectability, as debate about the so-called dangerous classes and juvenile delinquency emphasized. But less comfort could be derived from the reality that though individual and national prosperity was, in the eyes of contemporaries, founded upon the collective effects of individual enterprise and self-help which shaped market forces, it was precisely those characteristics which (uncontrolled) produced the scandals which afflicted the age and its sense of self-worth and pride in its achievements. The general truism of the age was that only those the Victorians identified as habitual criminals preplanned their depredations on society, and that such people were in some way set apart from "normal" society. But too many of the offenders highlighted in newspaper crime reports turned out to be "ordinary" members of society in terms of their background and behavior for Victorian comfort. Even more worrying, many had not the excuse of being driven into bad behavior or criminality by the extremes of poverty, but came to it through some impetus of self-indulgence and greed. Where did this leave the great principle of "Self-Help," encapsulated by Samuel Smiles in his best seller?[25] Clearly, there were rather too many people taking self-help to extremes never intended by respectable society.

Examination of what contemporaries sought to identify as "external" threats to the integrity of Victorian British society occupies Section Two. Building on themes raised in Section One, chapters explore the ways in which Victorian moral entrepreneurs gave shape to the inclination to distance the causes and the perpetrators of bad behavior and crime from those possessed of intrinsically "British" (or English) values. This proclivity gave much opportunity for the development of experts to give testimony "proving" difference such as racial or sexual difference. However, the process of Victorian othering was complex and often contradictory, and experts themselves could be seen as alien and external to ordinary daily concerns, making them ready targets for distrust or at least resistance of their conclusions.

Section Three completes the picture of Victorian unease by a discussion of the threats from *within* which were, if reluctantly, admitted to exist. Gender and class issues feature powerfully here, and it is worth remembering that in historical terms, the concept of criminal conversation reveals important aspects of the nature of power equations in this period, as well as the importance of property to a society which, despite its advertised modernity, estimated claims to both respectability and status on the basis of a hierarchy of possessions, animate and inanimate. Originally an ecclesiastical court concern, adultery entered the secular courts initially as a misdemeanor, a classification affecting both men and women. By the late seventeenth century, though, husbands could pursue claims for damages in court against the seducers of adulterous wives, in what amounted to "a common law adaptation of the law of trespass."[26] Until enactment of the Divorce and Matrimonial

Causes Act 1857, it was not a process which directly involved the woman who was the core of the claim. Instead, the men involved fought out the issue in the civilized surroundings of the King's Bench Division of the High Court, but with spectators ensuring that the less restrained process of gossip spread information and ideas about the results. Social security was assured when women, in particular, were shown to conform to expected standards when events conspired to bring them under the attention of the law, and yet in practical terms that conformity was not always possible. As the chapters in this section indicate, the Victorian legal system and the press were at times very conscious of the shifting moral ground on which justice was often delivered, but could see not easy alternative to established practice—thus ensuring a continuance of the criminal conversation.

Notes

1. *Daily Telegraph*, 11 August 1859. The full text of the report is in the Appendix.

2. The Divorce and Matrimonial Causes Act 1857 saw the end of criminal conversation as a legal action, but the popular terminology remained for adulterous incidents.

3. Cited, Michael Wolff and Celina Fox, "Pictures from the Magazines," in *The Victorian City*, ed. J. Dyos and M. Wolff (London: Routledge and Kegan Paul), 2: 559–84.

4. G. Stewart, *Dear Reader: The Conscripted Audience in Nineteenth-Century British Fiction* (Baltimore: Johns Hopkins University Press, 1996), 275.

5. Robert Darnton, *The Great Cat Massacre and Other Episodes in French Cultural History* (New York: Basic Books, 1984), 4.

6. The press is here used to signify the activity, including the people, involved in production of newspapers.

7. For example, see *A Literary and Pictorial Record of the Great Tichborne Case* (London: *The Graphic*, 1875).

8. Judith Rowbotham and Kim Stevenson, "Causing a Sensation: Media and Legal Representations of Bad Behaviour," in *Behaving Badly: Social Panic and Moral Outrage—Victorian and Modern Parallels*, ed. Judith Rowbotham and Kim Stevenson (Aldershot: Ashgate, 2003).

9. *Daily Telegraph*, 23 May 1870.

10. See, for example, *Cassells Saturday Journal*, 1890, 690; Michel Foucault, *Discipline and Punish: The Birth of the Prison* (Harmondsworth: Penguin, 1991), chap. 1.

11. F. M. L. Thompson, *The Rise of Respectable Society: A Social History of Victorian Britain, 1830–1900* (London: Fontana, 1988).

12. Lucy Brown, *Victorian News and Newspapers* (Oxford: Clarendon Press, 1985); Laurel Brake et al., eds., *Nineteenth Century Media and the Construction of Identities* (Basingstoke: Palgrave, 2002); Laurel Brake, Aled Jones, and Lionel Madden, eds., *Investigating Victorian Journalism* (Basingstoke: Macmillan, 1990); Joel H. Wiener, ed., *Papers for the Millions: The New Journalism in Britain, 1850s to 1914* (Westport, CT: Greenwood Press, 1988).

13. Richard Altick, *Evil Encounters: Two Victorian Sensations* (London: Murray, 1987); Richard Altick, *Victorian Studies in Scarlet* (London: Dent, 1972).

14. Foucault, *Discipline and Punish*, chap.1; W. G. Gilbert, *The Mikado* (1885).

15. Rowbotham and Stevenson, eds., *Behaving Badly.*

16. Rowbotham and Stevenson, "Causing a Sensation."

17. D. Vincent, *Popular Literacy and Popular Culture: England, 1760–1914* (Cambridge: Cambridge University Press, 1989).

18. Charles Dickens, *Great Expectations* (1861), chap. 18; Charles Dickens, *Our Mutual Friend* (1865), chap.16.

19. Arthur Conan Doyle, *The Hound of the Baskervilles* (1901), chaps. 2 and 3.

20. *Daily Telegraph* 1870, letters Geo. Groombridge 18 August, 3 September; comment and letters 2 August, 4 September.

21. Stanley Cohen, *Folk Devils and Moral Panics: The Creation of Mods and Rockers* (London: Routledge, 2002), 9.

22. Ibid.

23. Alan Hunt, *Governing Morals: A Social History of Regulation* (Cambridge: Cambridge University Press, 1999).

24. Hunt, *Governing Morals*, 196–201.

25. Samuel Smiles, *Self-Help: With Illustrations of Conduct and Perseverance* (London: John Murray, 1859).

26. Hilaire Barnett, *Introduction to Feminist Jurisprudence* (London: Cavendish 1998), 61–77.

Figure 2. *Illustrated Police News*, 11 November 1871. A typical example of a front page for editions without high-profile crimes to report, highlighting the disorderly nature of Victorian society.

SECTION ONE

◄o►

Identifying the Causes and Impacts of Bad Behavior

This section features the chapters examining Victorian conversations problematizing for respectable society some expressions of both bad behavior and actual criminality. The debates raised in the various chapters focus on different groups within society which felt threatened by some aspect of the "bad" behavior of the age. The conversations range from the broad debates around the dangerous classes through to the concerns surrounding juvenile delinquency in the chapters by Taylor and Abbott, and the micropanic felt by the Church of England over the morality of farm servants in Moses's chapter. Worries about the new shape of society and the new opportunities for crime at all levels of society are also covered in this section in the chapters from Barnes and Ferris. Throughout, the identification of appropriate evidence and judgments about what constituted a competent witness (issues interpreted through established gender, age, class, and racial stereotypes) are emphasized. In addition, there is a highlighting of the suggestions made by the Victorians for dealing with these issues in order to keep them within bounds and so achieve a stable, secure, and harmonious society, something with profound contemporary echoes.

I

Beyond the Bounds of Respectable Society: The "Dangerous Classes" in Victorian and Edwardian England

DAVID TAYLOR

Introduction

In recent years the British media has devoted time and space to the alleged monstrosities lurking on the fringes of respectable society. Britain, at the turn of the twenty-first century, faces a threat from a brutish criminal underclass, containing inadequate parents, existing on "sink estates" who, living by a system of values unrecognizable to "respectable" society, have brought up such dehumanized individuals such as "Spider Boy," "Rat Boy," and "Balaclava Boy" to terrorize respectable neighborhoods from Oxford to Newcastle-upon-Tyne.[1] To compound matters, the sense of crisis is further heightened by references to the inadequacies of the criminal justice system.[2] Moral panic is alive and well! Not for the first time there has been a construction of an alien group, beyond the bounds of respectable society, that not only contains threatening and dysfunctional individuals but which brings into question both fundamental social institutions, notably the family, and the wider codes of behavior that bind society together.

But for the "underclass" of the late years of the second Elizabethan period one could substitute the "dangerous classes" or the "residuum" of the early and late-Victorian years, respectively. This chapter proposes to look more closely at the ways in which these threatening social entities—the "predatory classes" or the "destructive classes" to take two of the more pejorative nineteenth-century descriptions—were constructed through a variety of debates echoed in the media, and the purposes that they served in these conversations through two "snap shots": one of the mid-Victorian period, the other of the Edwardian era.

The variety of terms used to describe the threat "from below" is indicative of both the scale of concern and the extent of uncertainty. There was no agreed or consistent definition of the social composition or geographical location of "the dangerous classes." That they were "out there" and threatening was agreed but it was often left to intrepid social explorers to attempt a more precise delineation of these alien people. Commonly based on direct experience, the journalistic writings of a Henry Mayhew or the scientific findings of a Charles Goring had a commonsense authority that disguises the problematic nature of their evidence. If, as Edward Said has argued in his influential discussion of western conceptions of the orient, "the development and maintenance of every culture requires the existence of another different and competing *alter ego*" and that "the construction of identity . . . involves establishing opposites and 'others' whose actuality is always subject to the continuous interpretation and re-interpretation of their differences from 'us,'" then the constructed "other" of the "dangerous classes" throws more light on the thinking and perceptions of the "respectable classes," that is the observers, than it does on the observed.[3] In addition to casting light on "respectable" values, social enquiries served a variety of functions. In part they were intended to (and did) create a sense of fear, acting as a wake-up call to society but in part they were also writings of reassurance. However, these writings did not exist independently of contemporary beliefs about the causes of criminal behavior, and it will be argued that changing explanations of criminality significantly reduced the element of reassurance and simultaneously heightened the sense of fear.

The "Dangerous Classes" in Early and Mid-Victorian England

While the notion of the criminal as an "outsider" threatening the health of the body politic is to be found frequently in eighteenth- and early-nineteenth-century accounts of crime, there was a shift to a language of class and conflict that emerged as urbanization and industrialization proceeded apace. The burgeoning working-class quarters of urban Britain were seen as the natural environment of the criminal. Further, it was commonly believed that the criminal, exercising his or her free will, chose a life of crime, for whatever reason, and in so doing set him/herself beyond the bounds of respectable society. It was this wilful desertion of the standards of respectability that dominated the criminal conversations about the dangerous classes.

Interestingly, some of the earliest influential writings that contributed to these criminal conversations in Britain were produced by French social enquirers. Flora Tristan's *Promenades dans Londres* (1840) described St. Giles's in terms of its "extreme poverty . . . [and] total degradation." Here was a population that lived "by prostitution and theft," for whom entry to Coldbath Fields prison was a red-letter day of improved living standards.[4] Eugene Buret in *Of the Distress of the Working Classes in England and France*, published the same year, spelled out more clearly the danger because

> in the very heart of the busiest centres of industry and trade [in England and France] you see thousands of human beings reduced to a state of barbarism by vice and destitution. . . . The governments are rightly apprehensive. They fear lest formidable dangers may some day burst forth from amid these degraded and corrupted people.[5]

A third author from that same year, though focusing on France, coined a phrase that, for all its imprecision, captured the growing sense of imperilment. M. A. Frégier concluded that

> the poor and vicious classes have always been and will always be the most productive breeding ground of evildoers of all sorts; it is they whom we shall designate as the dangerous classes. For even when vice is not accompanied by perversity, by the very fact that it allies itself with poverty in the same person, he is a proper object of fear to society, he is dangerous.[6]

Frégier's notion of "the dangerous classes" was quickly taken up by English commentators and achieved considerable currency as it moved from specialist academic literature to more generalist periodicals during the next two decades. Thomas Beames, for example, popularized the notion that demoralization and moral contamination were to be found in the slums of London while Mary Carpenter made a series of high-profile appeals to rescue destitute children from a life of crime.[7] In England the elision of working classes and dangerous classes may not have been so common as in mid-nineteenth-century France (Paris in particular) but there was a common feeling that within the working masses of the nation, particularly among its poorer sections, there lurked such "dangerous classes," which in turn were largely synonymous with, and hosted, the indubitably threatening criminal classes.

Nowhere is this clearer than in the writing of Henry Mayhew who was at pains to ensure that his readers "should no longer confound the honest, independent working men, with the vagrant beggars and pilferers of the country," but rather that they should appreciate that "the one class is as respectable and worthy, as the other is degraded and vicious."[8] Mayhew conceded that the binary division was misleading because there were some "*casual*" criminals, responsible for "accidental crimes, arising from the pressure or concomitance of a variety of circumstances" and "the professional criminals [or] habitual ones."[9] It was the latter who were both morally and physically threatening. Mayhew's description was graphic. Using language not dissimilar to that used by Dickens in his portrayal of Bill Sikes in *Oliver Twist* (1839), he described one of his ventures into criminal London:

> On entering into a public-house in another alley near Union Street we came to see one of the most dangerous thieves' dens we have visited in the course of our rambles. As we approached the door of the house we saw a dissipated-looking man stealthily whispering outside the door to the ruffian-looking landlord, who appeared to be a fighting man, from his large coarse head and broken nose. . . . We went to another outhouse beyond, where some thirty and forty persons were assembled around a wooden enclosure looking on, while some of their dogs were killing rats. They consisted of burglars, pickpockets, and the associates of thieves, along with one or two receivers of stolen property. Many of them were coarse and brutal in their appearance, and appeared to be in their element as they urged their dogs to destroy the rats. . . . The men apparently ranged from twenty-two to forty years of age. Many of them had the rough stamp of the criminal in their countenances, and when inflamed with strong drink, would possibly be fit for any deed of atrocious villainy.[10]

Alongside such formidable characters co-existed "common thieves . . . often characterised by mental imbecility and low cunning . . . lazy in disposition and lack[ing] energy both of body and mind," but the threat they posed to "decent" society was equally beyond dispute.[11]

Mayhew was at pains to stress that criminals, "such strange members of the human family," needed to be studied closely:

> We have thought the peculiarities of their nature as worthy of study in an ethnological point of view, as those of the people of other countries, and we have learnt to look upon them as a distinct race of individuals, as distinct as the Malay is from the Caucasian tribe. . . . An enumeration of the several natural orders and species of criminals will let the reader see that the class is multifarious, and surely, in a scientific point of view, as worthy of being studied as the varieties of animalcules.[12]

True to his claim, Mayhew presented a detailed analysis that produced, for example, a threefold categorization of thieves (based on the means whereby they operated) each of which was then duly subdivided. The reader is presented with an ordered but also a mysterious world with its own language to describe its nefarious specialisms: "rampsmen," "bludgers," "prop nailers," "thimble screwers," "sawney hunters," and "dead lurkers" were terms intended to send a frisson of fear down the back of respectable readers.

However, one needs to pause and consider the effect of such a representation. Behind the seemingly objective classification of the criminal classes were a variety of messages. Emsley has argued that the "elite" constructions of a criminal class "gave the reader a sense of superiority over criminals" but also "alleviated at least some of the uncertainty and fear about crime."[13] In other words, it was a rhetoric of reassurance. This is, undoubtedly, the case with much of Dickens's writing, contrasting the almost comic inadequacies of the criminal with the moral and physical strength of the policeman:

> [c]oiners and smashers droop before him; pickpockets defer to him; the gentle sex (not very gentle here) smile upon him. Half-drunken hags check themselves in the midst of pots of beer, or pints of gin, to drink to Mr. Field. . . . One beldame in rusty black has such admiration for him, that she runs a whole street's length to shake him by the hand; tumbling into a heap of mud by the way, and still pressing her attentions when her very form has ceased to be distinguishable through it.[14]

Having painted a grim picture of Rats' Castle, Dickens was able to reassure his readers with the conclusion that

> Before the power of the law, the power of superior sense—for common thieves are fools beside these men—and the power of a perfect mastery of character, the garrison of Rats' Castle and the adjacent Fortress make but a skulking show indeed when reviewed by Inspector Field.[15]

The threat from below is less than we (poor, frightened readers) might imagine; the forces that protect us stronger and in control. Sleep easy, gentle reader; sleep easy as Inspector Field and his men guard the streets and houses in which you live!

On the surface, Mayhew is less reassuring. At one level, the sheer detail of his analysis gave force to the belief, encouraged by much popular literature, that there was a separate world in which the criminal class lived.[16] This was a frightening thought, especially as there was, in the words of the 1863 Royal Commission on Penal Servitude, "a class of person . . . so inveterately addicted to dishonesty and so averse to labour that there is no chance of their ceasing to seek their existence by depredations on the public."[17] The phasing out of transportation added to this sense of fear because the hardened criminal was now to live in the midst of respectable society. There was now present, as Lord Kimberley observed, "a great army—an army making war on society."[18] And yet, at another level, there was a sense in which Mayhew's analysis was comforting, insofar as the criminal districts were, first, clearly defined in geographical terms, and, second, contained, and controlled by the police. While never eulogizing the Metropolitan Police as Dickens did, Mayhew nonetheless painted a reassuring picture, as in the description of the police in action in Bluegate Fields. The district was "nothing more or less than a den of thieves, prostitutes and ruffians of the lowest description," and yet

> the police penetrate unarmed without the slightest trepidation . . . we proceeded to Brunswick Street, more generally known in the neighbourhood and to the police as "Tiger Bay." . . . We entered No 6, accompanied by two policemen in uniform, who happened to be on duty at the entrance to the place. . . . We afterwards searched two houses on the opposite side of the way. . . . When the magic word "Police" was uttered, the door flew open, as the door of the robbers' cave when Ali Baba exclaimed "Sesame."[19]

However, there is something more going on. Mayhew's criminal world (that of Dickens likewise) was inhabited by grotesque figures, scarred both physically and morally; they wear the badge of crime on their very faces.

The language used to describe this world emphasizes both physical squalor and lack of orderliness ("sickening smells," "heaps of filth," "noisome and offensive," "tumbling houses," "lairs and holes") and moral failings ("most improvident manner," "unprincipled parents," "indiscriminate admixture of the sexes," "gross depravity or impropriety"). The "underworld" mirrors the "over-world" in its highly complex structure but in that mirror world the moral order has been subverted and "good" replaced by "evil." There has been a process of transference whereby all that is seen to be immoral, all that is feared in respectable bourgeois society, has been ascribed to the inhabitants of the slums and rookeries. In so doing, not only has an "other" or "nether" world been constructed but also the superiority of "respectable" values has been confirmed. Those intrepid domestic explorers discovering the East End of London were effectively involved in the same process of discovery and definition that Said associates with the West's contact with the Orient.

Mayhew was not alone in identifying distinct criminal districts. James Greenwood, a prolific journalist and master of disguise, whose direct observations informed his social commentary, was well aware that criminals were to be found in many parts of London, but nonetheless stressed the concentration of "desperate criminals" in one quarter "around the alleys of the Borough." These were men whose "life is one continuous conspiracy against the usages of property and safety of society," but there were specific areas, such as "the quarter around Kent Street, in the Borough [that were] almost wholly tenanted by them."[20] Similarly, Gustav Doré and Blanchard Jerrold associated the criminal class with specific localities. It was in the "maze of courts and narrow streets of low houses" and "in the hideous tenements" in Whitechapel and Shadwell that were to be found "the densely-packed haunts of poverty and crime."[21] But, as with Dickens and Mayhew, these districts and their inhabitants were under the gaze and control of policemen such as the "intelligent, reflective and professional" detective sergeant Meiklejohn.[22]

The simple binary division—good/evil or respectable/rough—conceived in moral, physical, and geographical terms, provided an analysis from which the worried reader might draw comfort; but not all writers shared this view. The distinction (moral and geographical) between "the criminal or predatory class" and other elements of working-class society was not always seen to be clear-cut. In a major academic discourse, Thomas Plint, writing at the same time as Mayhew, saw the terms "criminal classes" and "dangerous classes" as synonymous. This segment of society included "not only the professional thief or burglar" in his "criminal or dangerous classes" but also "the whole rabble of the vagrant and dissolute classes, who labour by fits, and eke out subsistence by pilfering, and who are ever on the verge of a more serious breach of the law."[23] While constructing the criminal class as "other" in moral and religious terms, Plint did not see the geographical distinction between the criminal and the respectable working class. Worryingly,

> the Criminal classes live amongst, and are dove-tailed in, so to speak, with the operative classes, whereby they constitute so many points of vicious contact with those classes—so many ducts by which the virus of a moral poison circulates through and around them. They constitute a pestiferous canker in the heart of every locality.[24]

In other words, there was no physical separation between decent operatives and dissolute criminals; one important boundary had been breached.

Plint described the criminal class as being "in the community, but neither of it, nor from it" and thus "isolated from the other classes" but this strengthened, rather than weakened, his earlier observation that this "pestiferous canker" has the effect of

> revolting the sensibilities, and lowering, more or less, the moral status of all who come in contact with them. Their very presence, and the daily commission of offences by them, is an evil, because it so habituates society to the loathsome spectacle of the one, and the constant recurrence of the other,

that the sensibilities become blunted, and the judgment benumbed and stupefied.[25]

Other influential writers of the 1850s shared this concern about the intermixing of respectable and criminal elements and the resultant blurring of the lines between different elements of working-class society. Mary Carpenter, for example, proposed a more complex (and not always clearly defined) fourfold model of society that encompassed a working class, a ragged class, and a perishing class as well as a dangerous class. On certain occasions she wrote of the "perishing and dangerous classes" as if they were a single, continuous social entity.[26] This worrying fluidity between boundaries was well captured by John Hollingshead. Another investigative journalist, Hollingshead was commissioned by the *Morning Post* to report on the distress that beset ordinary Londoners in the severe winter of 1860/1. The series of articles, entitled "Horrible London," were reprinted later as *Ragged London* in 1861. Recognizing the "many different degrees of social degradation and unavoidable poverty," he noted how "daily . . . one or more [of these outcasts] drop through into the great pit of crime."[27]

Although there were differences in expert analysis, there was a general feeling in mid-Victorian England that there was a definable and distinct category of people, the "dangerous classes," that posed a threat to moral well-being and social stability. In particular, the great towns (London specifically) were seen to be scarred by criminal districts in which men and also women chose to live a life outside the law of the land. The reality, even in London, was significantly different. Many criminals, overwhelmingly drawn from the working classes, and especially the less skilled elements therein, were scarcely distinguishable from the population at large. But the construction of a category of threatening "others," which was to be found in specific geographical areas, gave both a sense of moral superiority and a sense of security, not least from the knowledge that there were increasingly professional and efficient police forces that protected the law-abiding majority from the depredations of the law-breaking minority.[28]

Heredity, Feeble-Mindedness, and the Criminal in Edwardian England

Concern with the presence of a demoralized and criminal class did not disappear in the late nineteenth century. Fears were probably at their greatest in the 1880s.[29] George Sims expressed concern at the "mighty mob of famished, diseased and filthy helots . . . [whose] lawless armies" threaten to bring to London "a taste of the lesson the mob has tried to teach now and again in Paris" and bemoaned the fact that there was no longer a physical gap between "respectable" and "dangerous" classes.[30]

Jones argues that fear of the "lawless armies" peaked in the 1880s but was undermined, partly by the events surrounding the Dock Strike of 1889 (which revealed the residuum as a "small and hopeless remnant" rather than an invading army), partly by the findings of Charles Booth in the following decade and partly by the long-term decline in the recorded crime rate, which led *The Times,* for example, to claim that "at the present rate of decrease the professional burglar and pickpocket will soon disappear." But not everyone was comforted. The *Pall Mall Gazette* dismissed Booth's report as "too much like a complacent and comforting bourgeois statement of the situation." Class A might be small but it was not totally disassociated from the numerically larger Class B and, as Booth himself conceded, the members of these classes threatened to contaminate more respectable members of working-class society. Second, one should not overlook a potentially more worrying finding of Booth's, namely that "every social grade has its criminal": a conclusion that strengthened the fear that there was an "enemy within."[31]

The late-Victorian and Edwardian debate about crime, while sharing certain features in common with earlier discussions, took a distinct turn. This was partly a product of the growing awareness of the problem of recidivism and the existence of a class of persons for whom crime was a way of life; in part, it was the product of new "scientific" explanations of criminal behavior which cast doubt on classical explanations of criminality based on the notion of free will. More specifically, the problem of the professional or career criminal was at the heart of the late-Victorian and Edwardian concern. From this concern emerged the Prevention of Crime Act 1908, which introduced onto the statute book the idea of preventive detention.

Perhaps the most prolific writer on the career criminal and the most high-profile (though not the most sophisticated) campaigner in the "crusade" against professional crime, was Sir Robert Anderson who, although best known as an experienced policeman, came from a legal family and was himself a trained lawyer. He first made his name when he was transferred to the Home Office as adviser on Fenian affairs in 1876 and was subsequently appointed to Scotland Yard, heading the Criminal Investigation Department from 1888 to 1901. Pessimistic in outlook, he believed that without "statutory morality" men had no "incentive to virtue" and nothing to hold them "back from vice." This was particularly the case with "the hopelessly depraved" for whom Anderson's solution was "social tutelage," which meant placing habitual criminals "permanently under police supervision." After he left the force,

Anderson produced a series of highly publicized articles (subsequently brought together in book form) in which he sought to foreground the victims of crime and further "the protection of society" through the introduction of indeterminate sentences, which, notwithstanding the emotive arguments of "the humanity-mongers" in society, was the only way (in his mind) to tackle the problem.[32]

Anderson's ideas were not universally welcomed at the time (he was variously described as simplistic, crude, and sensationalist) and have received little praise from later historians ("a hotchpotch of old and new theories . . . embroidered with religious quotations and written in a highly inflammatory way").[33] This is not the place to attempt a resurrection of Anderson's reputation. There was much about the man that jarred. Many contemporaries (let alone later historians) found him an unsympathetic character while his beliefs and mode of expression antagonized many. However, that does not mean that his ideas did not resonate in certain important quarters, nor that he lacked influence both in the general sense of shaping the public perception of the career criminal and in the specific sense of influencing legislation.

Anderson never doubted there was a general decline in crime ("the judicial statistics afford indisputable proof") but constantly reiterated that "professional crime is on the increase." Like Mayhew, Anderson acknowledged a larger group of "weak" professional criminals, "those who are so utterly weak or so hopelessly wicked that they cannot abstain from crime," but he focused his attention on the "hard" professional criminals "who pursue a career of crime deliberately, with full appreciation of its risks."[34] These were the men responsible for the increase in burglary and housebreaking and for inflicting suffering upon "honest and peaceful citizens," and who were ignored by his pet hate, "the humanity-mongers." Such "professionals" were numerous enough "to keep the inhabitants of our large cities in a state of siege." To give substance to his general contention, he paraded before the reading public the likes of Henry Marchant, as a typical example of the desperate, professional burglar:

> The prisoner under several aliases, has had a remarkable criminal career. In 1869 he had four months' imprisonment for theft; in 1872 two months'; in 1874, twelve months' for housebreaking; and in 1879, seven years' penal servitude for larceny. Soon after his release on ticket-of-leave he was captured in the act of breaking into a house in Canning Town, when he tried to use a revolver on his captor. Liberated on heavy bail, he absconded, and when re-arrested at Manchester he was in possession of a revolver, a complete burglar's outfit, numberless skeleton keys, and articles of jewellery, the proceeds of robberies in Manchester and Liverpool. He was tried at the Old Bailey and sentenced to ten years' penal servitude. By good conduct in gaol

he again obtained a remission of sentence, and in 1896 he was caught housebreaking at Bow for which offence he was ordered twelve months' hard labour and sent back to complete his former sentence. When released again . . . he obtained employment and worked regularly for the greater part of the week, but carried out marauding expeditions on Saturday and Sunday evenings. . . . [Arrested February 1901] in his pocket he had a powerful jemmy and some skeleton keys, and in his room were found jewellery and other stolen property.[35]

Such men were self-professed "outlaws" who had by their actions forfeited their right to liberty. Challenging conventional wisdom, of "measuring his sentence by his latest offence," Anderson argued that "the question should not be what the prisoner did . . . but *what he is*."[36] Only by introducing indeterminate sentences could society be protected: only such incarceration of the hardened criminals would create the necessary geographical separation that would offer general protection to respectable society and also ensure that the criminal's trade was not taught to the next generation. Anderson's construction of the career criminal was intended to exploit fears of an increase in serious crime but, as with Mayhew, there was a message of reassurance in his writing. The hard core of career criminals, he was telling his audience, was known to the astute detective, such as Anderson. These men, who held society to ransom, could be apprehended and (with a change in the law) dealt with effectively. Society could be kept secure by the indeterminate incarceration in a single prison of the few hundred "outlaws."

It would be tempting to dismiss this as the ranting of an embittered and isolated policeman with but a crude grasp of Lombrosian criminology, tempting but not wholly accurate. Anderson received support from and was quoted with approval by a number of eminent figures. Major Arthur Griffiths, a former soldier and prison inspector, with considerable experience of the prison system, adopted a very similar line of argument. Concerned with "the extraordinary number of reconvictions that constantly occur," he located "the essence of the criminality of the country" in that group of habitual criminals, "the outlaws, overt and undisguised against society . . . who persistently defy the law and refuse to abide by the rules and regulations that society makes, and which are respected by honest people." For such people, who wage such "ceaseless warfare" against society, the only answer was "indefinite detention."[37] Dr. R. F. Quinton, a eugenicist also with direct experience of the prison system as governor and medical officer of Holloway prison (and also a defender of Edmund Du Cane), was another to inveigh against the "person who deliberately adopts crime as his profession" and demanded indeterminate sentences.[38]

Support was not confined to the "professionals" from the prison service. Mr. Justice Wills wrote to *The Times* in 1901 supporting Anderson, and later referred to his "remarkable work." Faced with the threat of the calculative repeat offender, the "ideal system of punishment . . . would be the indeterminate sentence." Wills looked to the Home Office "to hold its own against the outcry which at present seems sure to be evoked by any wholesome severity, however well deserved and however necessary for the protection of those amongst us who neither murder, steal, nor knowingly receive stolen goods."[39] Similar sentiments were echoed by Mr. Justice Darby (notably in the case of *R v Woodman*) while Hugh Gamon, who had written an extensive and (from a working-class perspective, largely sympathetic) study of the London Police Courts, financed by the Toynbee Trust, painted a more alarming picture than Anderson. Focusing on the serious crimes of burglary, housebreaking and shop breaking, he noted that the "ratio of apprehensions to crime is lowest," a result of such criminals being "more skilful in eluding arrest," and argued that "these are emphatically the crimes of the professional criminal."[40] Thus, an early-twentieth-century Bill Sikes was recreated, through the writings of senior policemen, prison officers, and judges. But whereas Bill Sikes was duly punished (though not through the courts), his latter-day counterpart was effectively encouraged and nurtured by the "absurd system of punishment."

It is difficult to assess the precise impact of these writers on opinion in the early twentieth century. Their analysis of the problem, and more so their prescription for it, aroused considerable opposition. The correspondence columns of *The Times,* as well as the pages of such publications as *The Law Times, The Law Magazine and Review, The Law Journal, The Law Quarterly Review, The Nineteenth Century and After, The Edinburgh Review,* and *The Humane Review* contained a vigorous debate with strongly expressed arguments on both sides. Nonetheless, a concern with the hardened professional criminal and the perceived need for a new form of punishment gained momentum and resulted in an important piece of legislation, the Prevention of Crime Act 1908.

Herbert Gladstone, the Home Secretary, introducing the bill with examples that could have been drawn from Anderson, laid great emphasis on "formidable offenders, men who are physically fit, who take to crime by preference, decline work when it is offered them, and refuse the helping hand."[41] Later, Gladstone sought to shock the House of Commons with a list of men who had chosen crime as their profession:

> A., thirty-eight years of age, received his first conviction at twenty-five; had served sentences of two and six years' penal servitude; time actually spent in prison, seven and a half years; a well-educated man, a professional forger.

> B., forty-five years of age, received his first conviction at twenty-nine; served three terms of penal servitude and eleven sentences for stealing; now undergoing three years penal servitude for stealing and receiving; eleven and a half years in prison; C., forty years of age, received first conviction at twenty-seven; served thirteen sentences for stealing and housebreaking, now serving five years for larceny; nine years actually in prison. D., thirty-one years of age; first conviction eighteen; served nineteen sentences for stealing and shop breaking; now serving three years penal servitude for stealing; seven and a half years in prison.[42]

Thus, Gladstone gave official sanction to the construction of the career criminal, a small but threatening band of men, who at relatively mature ages and in an apparently calculating manner chose a life of burglary or shop-breaking, thereby terrorizing the law-abiding property owners of any class.

Gladstone accepted (or exploited) other elements in this construction, for he asserted, in a manner that would have pleased Anderson, that such men mocked the present "absurd system" of punishment. There was a "large number of hardened, determined, persistent criminals, who rejoiced at only getting three years, because in two years and eight months they would be on the job again with health recruited and able to enjoy themselves again."[43] Herein lay the basis for the introduction of the new principle: "long-continued persistency in crime," by men capable of earning an honest living, if they chose, was to be "punishable by indeterminate seclusion." In other words, the most dangerous of the dangerous classes were to be taken out of respectable society and incarcerated "until the man gives *bona fides* and sufficient assurance that he will take to an honest life, or until by age or infirmity he becomes physically incapable of resuming a life of crime."[44]

Despite Gladstone's eloquence the bill was not accepted in its entirety. The notion of the indeterminate sentence was rejected, in part, for in its place was substituted preventive detention for a specified period of between five and ten years. Nonetheless the Act recognized both the existence of (and endorsed the concept of threats to the safety of respectable society posed by) the "professional" criminal and the need for special punishment for such distinctive criminals. Gladstone had reassured parliament that preventive detention was intended for the *danger* to society rather than the *nuisance* but, in so doing, he (like others in the ongoing debate) drew attention to the fact that the habitual criminal could not be simply characterized as a strong-minded and calculative individual. There were also a large number of criminals whose lifestyle was the product of weakness rather than strength. In many respects, the habitual criminal as an inadequate individual, suffering from both physical and mental weaknesses (probably inherited), was a more widely recognized figure. Concern with the degeneration of the country's urban population dated back into the last third of the nineteenth century but received further stimulus during and after the problematic second Anglo-Boer war when a significant minority of would-be recruits were shown to be physically unfit to fight and die for their country. The subsequent growth of the "national efficiency" movement in the 1900s strengthened the concern with and fear of the "weak" habitual criminal who seemed literally to embody the very physical and moral deficiencies undermining the standing of the nation.[45]

Even Anderson, for all his preoccupation with the hardened, professional criminal, had recognized the existence of "the poor wretch who, begotten and born and bred in crime, has not the moral stamina to resist when opportunity for theft presents itself," for whom the proper institution was "the asylum prison, where his life can be spent in useful labour, with every reasonable alleviation of his lot."[46] Similar views could be found among his critics. For a growing number of commentators this was the more important element in the problem, not simply because of their greater numbers (Gladstone estimated there to be 5,000 calculative professional criminals compared with the 60,000 weak-willed habituals "wandering about the roads and cities in a state of semi-vagrancy and crime") but also because of the more insidious threat they posed. The concern of people such as Anderson with the "calculative" professional criminal chimed with mid-Victorian commentators in the sense that they too claimed to have identified a distinct and threatening group preying on respectable society. While such predators no longer inhabited a separate geographical location, they were a definable "other," set apart. With the weak-willed habitual the situation was less clear cut.

From the 1870s onward growing numbers of social commentators had noted the increase of urban degenerates, particularly in the great cities. The Reverend Osborne Jay had no doubt that in places like Shoreditch there were to be found a "submerged and semi-criminal class" who were in that position precisely because of their "physical, mental and moral peculiarities." These were "drunken, besotted" creatures with "inherited defects of will and taints of blood," existing in squalid conditions, little better than animals.[47] "Skilled criminals" were not recruited from the "mentally inferior stocks of the proletariat," as the medical officer of Holloway Prison wrote, but "some criminals are of bad or degenerate stock."[48] The presence of such human flotsam and jetsam, incapable of work but outbreeding respectable, law-abiding society, was an ever increasing source of worry in a country whose economic and imperial dominance appeared yearly under yet greater threat. But (not for the first time) a process of displacement is evident, whereby Britain's relative economic decline and challenges to its imperial power, were seen as the product of a defective and criminal residuum. Fears about the health of the nation were focused on the most visible manifestation of degeneration: the physically and mentally weak habitual criminal.

Given their threat it was imperative to identify clearly these problem groups and to prevent them from contaminating the rest of society. While rejecting Lombrosian ideas of the born criminal, the biometrician and Broadmoor doctor, Charles Goring, talked in his monumental study of the need for "a crusade against crime":

> To modify inherited tendency by appropriate educational measures; or else to modify opportunity for crime by segregation and supervision of the unfit; or else—and this is attacking the evil at its very roots—to regulate the reproduction of those degrees of constitutional qualities—feeblemindedness, inebriety, epilepsy, deficient social instinct, etc.—which conduce to the committing of crime.[49]

There is much in this to ponder, but the contemporary preoccupation with feeble-mindedness is particularly worthy of attention. Goring was not alone in this focus. Mary Dendy observed that "hooligans, or corner-lads, criminals, paupers and drunkards—all are these frequently only because they are feeble-minded." Sullivan identified the criminally inclined "bad or degenerate stock" were a specific group "within the great pathological class of the feeble-minded."[50] What was particularly disturbing was the fact that much (especially much seemingly purposeless) crime was committed by those "semi-insane intellects" who inhabited the "borderland." The desire to categorize and compartmentalize (never far from the surface) was particularly strong among a scientific community that saw identification and classification (via new scientific and statistical methods) as a necessary step in the battle against degeneration. But the confidence that allowed such men and women to distinguish between morons and imbeciles was undermined by the discovery of a "borderland" of feeble-mindedness wherein identification was highly problematic.[51] The worry that this could engender is captured in an article by the medical superintendent of the Birmingham Education Committee.[52] Auden cited a number of cases of youthful offenders, whom he identified as "moral imbeciles." He then quoted approvingly Sir J. Crichton-Browne's definition in a manner that might be taken to imply that the dangerous "moral imbecile" is a definable and hence detainable individual who can be identified and removed before inflicting damage on others.

However, one highly problematic case was described in detail.[53] The background was the murder by some person or persons unknown of a fifteen-month "little toddling mite" who had been found half-buried in rubbish on waste ground in an unspecified part of the north of England. A week later, a mother missed her own baby, who had been playing on the door-step, and, on instituting a search found him in the arms of an eight-year-old boy, who had almost reached the fateful waste patch, the scene of the previous murder. He was accompanied by another small boy who was known to be mentally deficient. The [first] boy then made the following statement:- He had been in the street a week previously, and seeing the little boy crying, had picked him up. As he carried the child about it fell asleep in his arms. He carried it into the field and laid it down while he made a hole with his hands in the débris from the disused ironworks. As he laid the baby on its back in the hole it woke and cried "Mummy! Mummy!" He described how it struggled and kicked while he piled the rubbish, brick ends and a large stone upon the living grave. Having done this, he went home, totally unconcerned, to his tea.

The sense of shock created by this "youthful fiend" was magnified by the fact that

Every detail of this tale of horror was retailed without the slightest sign of compunction or regret, and he admitted that it had been his intention to repeat his exploit with the baby now found in his arms, though he said that he and his companion (the mentally-deficient child . . .) had discussed whether they should bury this one or vary their method by drowning it.[54]

The most worrying feature of this whole case was the fact that the would-be double child-killer "had as yet shown no such signs of mental deficiency as had already marked out his companion of his second and fortunately unsuccessful attempt." If there was any consolation to be found in the case it resided in the police officer's report on the boy. Recognizing that the prisoner, though "not very bright" was "not insane," he noted that the boy was illegitimate and had a mother who led "a very immoral life." Clearly such indicators offered some *prima facie* evidence of feeble-mindedness in the family.

For Auden, the case highlighted a real dilemma for those grappling with the problems of "diagnosing the border-line of cases of feeble-mindedness." To "commit an individual who shows no very clearly marked signs of mental defect to a semi-penal institution would be a gross infringement of the liberty of the subject." But "it cannot be too strongly impressed upon our notice that every imbecile, especially the high-grade imbecile, is a potential criminal, needing only the proper environment and opportunities for the development and expression of his criminal tendencies."[55] The enemy was in the midst of society and sufficiently well camouflaged to escape detection. The threat of crime was taking on a new and deeply disturbing form. War was being waged on decent society, not only by self-evident villains, with the marks of infamy on their faces, but also by the seemingly innocent. In the days of Mayhew, or even Booth, there was a relative comfort to be derived from the fact of having a clearly identified group of "barbarians," at the gates of, or even encamped within, respectable society. In the early twentieth century this was being replaced by a growing anxiety generated by the fifth-columnist (had the term been invented) who passed her or himself off as a normal member of society whereas in reality s/he was a criminal time bomb just waiting to go off.

Conclusion

Over the past two centuries in Britain there has been a recurring series of social or "moral" panics. While writing this essay, the media has returned to the problem of juvenile crime and resurrected the careers of those dehumanized "boys" mentioned in the introduction, often using language that would not have been out of place in the 1850s.[56] The threatening, law-breaking, and immoral young male is but one (often the most prominent part) of a wider construction of an "other" criminal class beyond the bounds of respectable society. The persistence of such a construction (notwithstanding important variations in details) across a long period of time raises questions about its purpose. From a Whiggish perspective such incursions into "alien" territory and the call for reform can be seen as evidence of a progressive desire to discover, understand, and ultimately civilize the less fortunate in society. Alternatively, such activities can be seen as a more complex process whereby a "criminal class" (the precise terminology varies over time) was constructed that was an inversion of "respectable" society. Such a construction reasserted "respectable" values but did (and does) add little to the understanding of the realities of the life of this "criminal class." Despite drawing attention to threatening "others," it also operated as a rhetoric of reassurance, in two ways. It was comforting to know that there was a distinct minority who were criminally inclined and a majority who were law abiding. Conversely, it was very worrying and difficult to accept that large sections of seemingly respectable society were, on some occasions at least, lawbreakers. Second, it was reassuring to know that the police were acting as a thin blue line, offering effective protection to the law-abiding majority against the law-breaking minority. In the specific period under review, from Mayhew and Dickens to Anderson, there was a dominant view in which the criminal threat was both identifiable and containable. The latter may have demanded change to the law but, nonetheless, remained confident that the police could control the threat of the professional criminal in a manner not dissimilar from Mayhew.

However, the effectiveness of such a construction was challenged by uncomfortable evidence and, perhaps even more so, by new ways of thinking about criminality from the late nineteenth century onward. Despite repeated attempts to construct a simple binary division (both moral and spatial) between criminal and noncriminal, it was apparent to successive social observers that "reality" was more complex. The "strong" criminal, choosing a life of crime, was to be found but so too was the "weak" criminal, constitutionally incapable of resisting the temptation to turn to crime. More worrying was the recognition that the "criminal" was to be found within respectable society and that the distinction between the respectable working man or woman and the criminal was blurred. Indeed, the respectable of today could be the criminal of tomorrow, particularly if today was relatively prosperous and tomorrow, not. Thus, criminals could no longer be seen as constituting a clearly identifiable and containable group. The enemy was within the camp and, in a nightmare scenario that was intensified by the growing concern with degeneration in general and feeble-mindedness in particular, increasingly difficult to distinguish from ordinary, law-abiding citizens.

Notes

1. See *The Observer* and *The Independent on Sunday*, 19 May 2002. Perusal of the websites of major newspapers (tabloid and broadsheet) and the BBC reveals the extent to which the media has been preoccupied with the threat of violent crime in the past four years.

2. Most recently Sir John Stevens, the Metropolitan Police Commissioner, castigated the "appalling" criminal justice system, which, in his view, shielded and encouraged criminals. *The Guardian*, 7 March 2002.

3. Edward Said, *Orientalism: Western Conceptions of the Orient* (Hammondsworth: Penguin, 1995), 332.

4. Flora Tristan, *The London Journal of Flora Tristan* (London: Virago, 1982), 157–58.

5. Cited, Louis Chevalier, *Labouring Classes and Dangerous Classes in Paris during the First Half of the Nineteenth Century* (London: Routledge and Kegan Paul, 1973), 139.

6. M. A. Frégier, *Des classes dangereuses de la population de la grande villes*, 1840, cited, Chevalier, *Labouring Classes*, 141.

7. Thomas Beames, *The Rookeries of London: Past, Present, and Prospective* (London: Thomas Bosworth, 1852); Mary Carpenter, *Reformatory Schools for the Children of the Perishing and Dangerous Classes and for Juvenile Offenders* (London: Gilpin, 1851); M. Carpenter, *Our Convicts* (London: Longman, 1864).

8. Henry Mayhew, "London Labour and London Poor," vol. 4, 1862, in *London's Underworld*, ed. P. Quennell (London: Hamlyn, 1969), 204–5; Henry Mayhew and J. Binney, *The Criminal Prisons of London and Scenes of Prison Life* (1862; reprint London: Cass, 1968), 87.

9. Ibid.
10. Mayhew, *London Labour,* 204–5.
11. Ibid., 134.
12. Mayhew, *London Prisons,* 45.
13. Clive Emsley, *Crime and Society in England, 1750–1900* (London: Longman, 1996), 175.
14. Charles Dickens, "On Duty with Inspector Fields," in *London Crimes,* ed. N. Aisenberg (Boston: Rowan Tree Press, 1982), 61. It is not possible in these confines to discuss Dickens's construction of the criminal underworld, but this forms part of the larger project on which the author is currently engaged.
15. Ibid.
16. J. Davis, "Law Breaking and Law Enforcement: The Creation of a Criminal Class in Mid-Victorian London" (Ph.D. diss., Boston University, 1984, reprinted, UMI Dissertation Services, 1994), 7.
17. Ibid., 11.
18. Ibid., 15.
19. Mayhew, *London Labour,* 63.
20. James Greenwood, *The Seven Curses of London* (London: Stanley Rivers, 1869), 82.
21. Gustave Doré and Blanche Jerrold, *London: A Pilgrimage,* 1872 (New York: Dover, 1970), 145.
22. Ibid., 138.
23. T. Plint, *Crime in England: Its Relation, Character, and Extent As Developed from 1801 to 1848* (London: Gilpin, 1851), 144.
24. Ibid., 146.
25. Ibid.
26. Carpenter, *Reformatory Schools.*
27. J. Hollingshead, *Ragged London in 1861* (London: Dent, 1986), 23–24.
28. Clive Emsley, *The English Police: A Social and Political History* (London: Longman, 1996); David Taylor, *The New Police in Nineteenth-Century England: Crime, Conflict, and Control* (Manchester: Manchester University Press, 1997).
29. G. S. Jones, *Outcast London: A Study in the Relationship between Classes in Victorian Society* (Harmondsworth: Penguin, 1976), chap.16.
30. G. R. Sims, *How the Poor Live* (London: Chatto and Windus, 1889), 44.
31. Jones, *Outcast London,* 321.
32. See Robert Anderson, "Our Absurd System of Punishing Crime," in *Nineteenth Century and After,* 1901; "The Punishment of Crime," in *Nineteenth Century and After,* 1901; "More about Professional Criminals," in *Nineteenth Century and After,* 1902; "The Crusade against Professional Criminals," in *Nineteenth Century and After,* 1904; *Criminals and Crime: Some Facts and Suggestions* (London, 1907); "Criminals and Crime," *Law Magazine Review,* 1908; "The Prevention of Crime Act," in *Nineteenth Century and After,* 1909.
33. S. Petrow, *Policing Morals: The Metropolitan Police and the Home Office, 1870–1914* (Oxford: Clarendon, 1994), 105.
34. Anderson, "Absurd System," 271.
35. Ibid., 274–75.
36. R. F. Quinton, *Crime and Criminals, 1876–1910* (London: Longman, 1910); R. F. Quinton, "The Need for Preventive Detention," *Edinburgh Review* (1914).

37. Major A. Griffiths, *Fifty Years of Public Service* (London: Cassell, 1905), 385–86.
38. Quinton, *Crime;* Quinton, "Preventive Detention."
39. Justice Wills, "Criminals and Crime," in *Nineteenth Century and After,* 1907, 893.
40. Hugh R. P. Gamon, "The Punishment of Crime and the Indeterminate Sentence," *Law Magazine and Review* (1910): 192–93.
41. *Hansard,* 1908, col. 1122.
42. Ibid., col. 247.
43. Ibid., col. 498.
44. Ibid., col.1122.
45. G. R. Searle, *The Quest for National Efficiency: A Study in British Politics and Political Thought, 1899–1914* (Oxford: Blackwell, 1971), is the essential starting point.
46. Anderson, "Absurd System," 278–79.
47. Rev. Osborne Jay, "The East End and Crime," *New Review* (1894). A. Morrison, *A Child of the Jago* (London: Methuen, 1986), provides a fictionalized account of the Old Nicol where Jay worked.
48. Dr. W. C. Sullivan, "Eugenics and Crime," *Eugenics Review* (1909): 120.
49. Sir Charles Goring, *The English Convict* (London, 1910), 373.
50. Ibid.
51. Cited, M. Jackson, *The Borderland of Imbecility: Medicine, Society, and the Fabrication of the Feeble Mind in Late Victorian and Edwardian England* (Manchester: Manchester University Press, 2000).
52. G. A. Auden, "Feeblemindedness and Juvenile Crime," *The Medical Officer,* 31 December 1910.
53. There are obvious parallels with the high-profile Bulger case almost a century later, in 1993.
54. Ibid.
55. Ibid.
56. See *The Observer,* 19 May 2002; *The Independent on Sunday,* 19 May 2002; David Taylor, *Crime, Policing, and Punishment in England, 1750–1914* (Basingstoke: Macmillan, 1998), 62–64.

2

The Press and the Public Visibility of Nineteenth-Century Criminal Children

JANE ABBOTT

Introduction

Few are now unaware of the media-fueled public outrage surrounding the 1993 murder of James Bulger by two children, Robert Thompson and Jon Venables. British newspapers and television branded the two killers as "evil." When the accused children were brought to trial, television images showed impassioned adults attacking the van they were in. The emotional media reporting of the case has been heavily criticized for generating the impetus for a witch hunt. Certainly public commentary surrounding the case generally failed to provide any defensive reasoning for why two children had turned into killers; they were simply presented as highly dangerous and a liability to society. The trial, verdict, sentence and the furor surrounding their release eight years later can only be described as ongoing "trial by the public." But though it has been suggested that this type of criminal conversation was unique to the twentieth century, there was similar media-induced public outrage surrounding juvenile crime in the Victorian era.[1]

This chapter examines debates fueled by moral outrage and public concern about juvenile criminality in the mid-nineteenth century. Its focus will be upon the public disclosure of juvenile criminals, to make an assessment of the impact of such on society's understanding of childhood delinquency. Analysis of contemporary crime reporting shows that many children were branded criminals after committing what now appear to have been very slight misdemeanors. The incidence of child-performed crime was generally seen as high, and to Victorian alarm, it ranged from petty theft to murder. Twentieth-century consideration of child criminality remains centered on its total unacceptability, but what is not recognized is that twentieth-century debates simply continue a dialogue which took its modern form in the Victorian age, when juvenile criminality was first legally set apart from adult offending.

The reality of childhood for Victorian society was significantly different to that of today. If childhood for the middle and upper classes has close modern echoes, it was not so for the working classes. Most of these children were expected to help earn an income from seven or eight years of age. Crime was for many the only means to that end, with children starting a criminal career by lifting small items of clothing. Victorians considered something such as handkerchief theft or shawl robbery as serious crimes, not just because of the principle of thievery involved, but also because the act may have robbed a hard-working poor citizen of a precious symbol of respectability. The combination ensured that these crimes often generated harsh sentences. While the Victorian period saw new legislation specifically intended to deal with juveniles, and reduce the threat to society by lowering levels of child crime, a great amount of confusion and ambiguity remained, as regular debates in the print media underline.

Juvenile criminality was not a new phenomenon. However, increased use of publicly accessible written material during this period provided a platform on which individual crimes were reported on a mass scale, promoting a greater uniformity of debate and consequent national consciousness of levels of child crime. Through print, social commentators were able to voice their concerns to a national audience, making theories on the reform and treatment of child criminals very accessible to the increasingly literate Victorian audience. The contemporary impression was that juvenile crime rates were extremely high, and yet statistical evidence modifies this image, suggesting that as a proportion of total Victorian crime, juvenile crime was not dramatically elevated.[2] This suggests it was media constructions which provoked public anxiety.[3] While this is by no means a comprehensive study, it is hoped it will demonstrate some aspects of the "conversations" this subject initiated.

The "Moral" Concern Raised by the Criminal Child

It has been suggested by many writers and thinkers throughout the nineteenth and twentieth centuries that the twin processes of industrialization and urbanization concentrated the social problem of "lawlessness" in Britain by the mid-nineteenth century.[4] As the chapters from Taylor and Swift indicate, "classes" of offender were identified and labeled as "dangerous" or "criminal" and generated associated public concern.[5] Thus the middle-class law reformer and social commentator generated a classification of persons who could be easily identified as responsible for the majority of criminal activity.[6] To further compound identification of these groups, the "dangerous," "criminal" or "perishing" classes, were singled out as predominantly part of the working classes, with criminality promoted by the dense, overpopulated conditions in which they existed. There was a popular belief that most, if not all, children who lived in these appalling conditions were inexorably, even inevitably, drawn into a criminal lifestyle, thereby increasing the size of the established criminal classes. So identified, they provided a coherent group that could be directly targeted for investigation by concerned social reformers.

The "causes" of criminality in children were heavily debated in a variety of venues including Parliament, and presented to a wider public via the media. It was the print media which effectively popularized and fixed the stereotypes associated with juvenile criminality. The background for this conversation was predominantly urban, because increasing population density made crimes committed by children more visible to greater numbers of concerned adults:

> The enormity and amount of juvenile depravity is a subject which now most painfully engages the public mind. The mature and headstrong character which it exhibits has been unveiled and presented to the public eye in colours, fearful, because true, by various recent publications, which must make every Christian heart shudder and tremble.[7]

So what was the agenda of those producing these publications and reports, the people responsible for the level of publicity generating such strong feeling? Did they create a level of anxiety that was not warranted by the numbers involved, or the types of crime committed?

Promoting the Visibility of Juvenile Crime

Victorian society featured many social commentators who concentrated some or all of their efforts on the plight of working-class children, and the issue of juvenile criminality. Among the most prominent was Mary Carpenter who pioneered the introduction of Ragged Schools. She was in many ways typical, in that her interest in this area resulted from a wider concern with the ills of Victorian society and a belief that long-term remedies depended on reforming the young, including their living and working conditions. Her interest in a range of measures associated with education provided the path through which her focus on their criminality developed. In her contributions to this criminal conversation, she described two classes from which, in her experience, juvenile criminals came. There were the "perishing classes," those who "have not yet fallen into actual crime, but who are almost certain, from their ignorance, destitution, and the circumstances in which they are growing up, to do so, if a helping hand is not extended to raise them." There were also what she dubbed in 1851 as the "dangerous classes," those "notoriously living by plunder, who unblushingly acknowledge that they can gain more for the support of themselves and their parents by stealing than by working."[8] Her research and published comment established Carpenter in the Victorian public mind as an expert in the field of juvenile crime.

Another well-known contributor to the debate was Henry Mayhew, journalist and social explorer, who produced comprehensive studies of working-class London society in the 1850s, including his renowned social study on *London Labour and London Poor*, first published as a series of articles in the *Morning Chronicle*. Indications of public interest in the living conditions of the urban poor prompted Mayhew to suggest that the newspaper carry out an investigation into the actual condition of the laboring classes to "bring before the public the social iniquities rife both abroad and throughout England."[9] Their success in that format encouraged the incorporation and expansion of the articles into book form. Mayhew portrayed children who often had no alternative but crime to survive, being "Untaught, mistaught, maltreated, neglected, regularly trained to vice, or fairly turned to the streets to shift for themselves."[10] Mayhew was primarily a journalist, reporting the ills he saw as part of a vague philanthropy, while Carpenter was more of an activist, using her writings to stimulate particular reforms.

They represent two types of commentators writing on this topic in a range of outlets, with writings based on some form of personal experience, but also on other information available in the public domain, who significantly raised the profile of juvenile criminality in the public consciousness. Newspapers, and police and court circulars, contained a multitude of stories detailing further criminal activities of children, underlining the visibility of child crime and explaining also why such commentators found a ready audience for their pronouncements. These reports interspersed accounts of child criminality with those of adult men and women committing a range of indictable offenses. The reporting structure of newspapers such as *The Times* and the *Manchester Guardian* thus created an atmosphere of public opinion which agreed that children who committed crimes had to be held, tried, and punished in the same courts, if not always quite under the same legislation as their adult counterparts, because of the level of threat they posed to the stability of the community.

The *Nottingham Review* can be used to demonstrate the vast scale of disclosure of juvenile criminality: all the following cases were reported on the same day, 3 February 1854. Further examination of local and national newspapers indicates that juvenile petty theft was similarly common and widely reported throughout the country, national papers often echoing reports in the provincial press, and bringing them together in a way that emphasized the countrywide spread of such offending:

> Sarah Smith, aged 17 years, a servant in the employ of Mr. Pearson, pork butcher, Hockley, was apprehended by Inspector Raynor at 5 o'clock last evening, charged with stealing 8d from her Master's shop. The prosecutor however, not wishing to press the case further against the girl, discharged the case.
>
> William Ratcliff, aged 17 years, lace-maker, Fyre-street, was apprehended by Sergeant Taylor for attempting to steal cotton yarn. Radcliff was committed to the House of Correction to be kept to hard labour for one month.
>
> George Litchfield, 14-years-old of Montford-street was charged with attempting to pickpocket some ladies standing near a shop window in Wheelergate. Lichfield denied the charge but was committed to the House of Correction to be kept to hard labour for 14 days.
>
> Ann Smith, aged nine years, a child of very sickly appearance, stole a piece of beef weighing about 6lbs. She was sentenced to 14 days imprisonment with hard labour.[11]

All these cases (except the first, where the prosecutor dropped the case) indicate that children were regularly committed to prisons, often with hard labor, for a range of petty offenses. Why did Victorian society react so strongly to the evidence of relatively minor wrong-doing, especially when, as in the case of Ann Smith for example, it was often clearly driven by economic necessity?

Juvenile Criminals

A twentieth-century view of the nineteenth-century child criminal depicts an Artful Dodger–style figure embroiled in some organized underworld, run by a fearful Fagin-like character who trained and forced his pupils onto the streets to prey on the unsuspecting majority. This modern view is not far removed from many of the stereotypes afflicting Victorian society, stereotypes which Mayhew promoted, though other commentators such as Carpenter sought to mitigate them with more measured insights. However, the dramatized view of child criminality remained an appealing part of media reporting despite efforts to argue that, in the majority of cases, it was far from the truth of the real children who, through circumstance, had resorted to crime.[12]

The expectation was that males would provide the majority of criminals brought before the courts, and boys did commonly form the majority of perpetrators. However, girls did engage in criminal activity, often involving peculation from employers (though not all automatically prosecuted). In one case, alarmingly headlined "Juvenile Depravity," Elizabeth Atkins was convicted of stealing clothes and money from a tenant of her former employer. The seriousness with which the case was viewed, however, had as much to do with the fact that she was eventually arrested after seeking out an actress of her acquaintance, Miss Neal (who had declined to take her in!). Given the popular association made between actresses and prostitutes, this indicated the depths of Atkins's moral danger, and explains her commitment to a Reformatory for five years.[13] Contrast this with the experience of Mary Ann Dible, aged ten or eleven, found guilty in 1853 of stealing a pair of shoes and a pair of trousers from her master, which she had attempted to sell to a Mrs. Ford. Mary was sentenced to three months, but interestingly enough, Mrs. Ford was also cautioned, on the grounds that buying from a child so young could tempt her to steal again (no hint of sexual impropriety was involved here).[14]

Girls regularly committed petty theft in public places, possibly because they were the less obvious suspects and so were able to move through crowds and market areas quickly with less danger of immediate detection. Although their crimes might appear of an opportunistic nature, there was often skill and premeditation involved, as in the example of Elizabeth Coggar, thirteen, imprisoned for three months for stealing a purse containing two shillings. The arresting policeman stated she was continuously picking pockets and stealing, and actually had a lining in her petticoat to hide the stolen items. Worse, she often took her younger brother along to screen her actions, showing she was capable of detailed planning and application in her criminal activities.[15] Equally worrying were examples such as Caroline Driscoll, sixteen, described as a "notorious thief" when brought before Westminster police court charged with "a series of robberies." She picked the pockets of shopkeepers whose attention was temporarily distracted by young accomplices accompanying her on her larcenous sprees. Caroline was remanded for a week "in order that other charges may be exhibited," then sent to the Assizes and transported.[16] Louisa West and Eliza Cranstone, both seventeen, were found guilty of breaking and entering a dwelling to steal gowns and other items. In the same session they had both been previously charged with stealing and receiving stolen trousers. For both crimes they were sentenced to a total of six months.[17]

Not all juvenile "crime" was obviously criminal. Two reported incidents of "sliding" in Trafalgar Square and snowballing by children under seventeen years resulted in convictions, fines, and warnings to the "offenders," because these juvenile high jinks were presented as a serious disturbance to the comfort of passersby.[18] Clearly, the variety of "criminal" activity engaged in by juveniles was complex, ranging from organized felonies to nuisance behavior. But reportage of all under similar labels combined to ensure that the incidence of juvenile crime was portrayed as a frequent and real threat to society.

Crimes of Murder and Assault

Children were also the perpetrators of more serious crimes including murder and assault.[19] Two contrasting, yet similar cases, demonstrate the levels of pressure from the public gaze. One example explored here is dated before the period under main focus in this chapter, however it has been utilized to emphasize the channeling of such public pressure through the forum of the media. As a comparative model it is invaluable in demonstrating the development in the application of public concern over a thirty-year period in the mid-1800s.

The first example, from 1831, was the trial at the Summer Assizes in Maidstone of the curiously named John Any Bird Bell, fourteen, for the murder of little Richard Faulkner Taylor. The motive was money; John knew that Richard would be walking to collect the family Parish Relief, and joined him, accompanied by his brother James. According to written accounts of the event, John said to his brother, "There goes young Taylor, James, let us kill him and take his money and let us lay him under these stones that we can't count over." The murder was bloody:

> The little boy lay down crying and while the boy was lying down, he cut his throat. He took the money from the boy's glove and gave part to his brother. His brother gave him his knife to cut the boy's throat. The boy squeaked when his throat was cut as a rabbit squeaked.

Thirty years later came a murder as brutal and shocking as the above. At Chester Assizes on 9 August 1861, Peter Barratt and James Bradley were placed at the bar for their trial of the murder of George Burgess, aged two.[20]

The murder was described by the judge as a "most extraordinary case, almost unparalleled in the annals of crime." The accused, who came from poor homes, and were neglected, uneducated and "accustomed to brutal sports and habits," took their little victim from his minder. The following day, George's drowned body was discovered in a pond. He was badly battered, with injuries inflicted while he was still alive. When questioned, the boys revealed a litany of brutality. They had undressed him, ducked him several times in the water, and then begun to beat him:

> Morley (the arresting police officer) then said, "Where did you hit it?" Bradley said, "Over the back," and Barratt added, "Yes, and over the head." Morley said, "How long did you hit it with the stick?" Bradley said, "Until it was dead." Barratt said nothing then, but upon Morley saying, "Then it was quite dead before you left it?" he said, "Yes."[21]

But while such cases made Victorian headlines and heightened perceptions of the dangers of juvenile criminality, they were relatively uncommon when compared to the bulk of cases dealt with at summary levels. Even the majority of those referred to the higher courts featured lesser offenses than murder or serious assault.

A Real Nuisance?

Was it the actual volume of petty theft reported which frightened and concerned the public rather than the seriousness of the crime, or were there other factors involved? The issue of opportunism versus premeditation was one such factor. The thought of preplanned organized crime was (and still is) more terrifying than the image of crimes committed on the spur of the moment by those down on their luck. Actual evidence of gang activity on the lines of that organized by Fagin was relatively scanty, but the fact that there were some examples ensured a continuing fear of organized child crime. Suggestions of repeat offending by juvenile criminals also fulfilled the stereotype of the hardened and irredeemable offender, the more terrifying because of their youth and the consequent time their subsequent career could offer for further depredations.

Cases involving children suggest that Victorian contemporaries readily extrapolated a vision of organized criminality from regular petty thefts, regardless of their economic and social circumstances. Consider the case of Henry Tibbetts, ten, charged with stealing two loaves of bread in London. Henry's mother attempted to excuse this behavior by stating that since the death of his father, he had taken to running around the streets with a lot of "bad boys." This vague statement was heavily capitalized on by the magistrate, Mr. Newton, and the newspaper reporting implicitly approved this through the choice made to highlight the magistrate's comments, without qualification or criticism. *The Times* reproduced Newton's comments that it was "bad company" which was to blame, and that this was a common cause of criminal behavior by children. Although Newton did not suggest an organized gang culture existed, he did indicate that these incidents were a major problem, giving his opinion that there was need for drastic action: sending these children to prison and/or whipping them.[22] It seems probable that Henry's crime was opportunistic, and while it remains possible his actions were committed under the influence of others, there was no substantial evidence of this having been a serious and malicious incident.

This was certainly true for Dennis Collins, fourteen, also charged with "stealing a half-quatern loaf" by Shoreditch baker and churchwarden, Jeremiah Death. Death announced that "the charge would not be pressed . . . but for the fact of incessant petty robberies of this character" in the neighborhood. Supporting police evidence described a "gang" of juvenile shoeblacks who resorted to stealing food "when the dry weather afforded but little occasion for their polishing avocations." With the implication of gang involvement hanging over the case, it is not surprising that Mr. D'Eyncourt sent Collins to the House of Correction for a month.[23] Vagrancy and begging on the streets by children were also technically criminal activities, and the Victorian legal system took such incidents seriously. In Nottingham, George Leggat, thirteen or fourteen, was charged with being "one or two nights in a state of destitution," bordering on starvation. He had absconded from the local Workhouse but was promptly sent to the Union until his proper abode could be identified.[24] As their reporting underlines, the suggestion in such cases was that the infringement of the law involved in vagrancy would inexorably lead to a criminal career.

Such cases demonstrate the apparent disregard, certainly in the mid-Victorian period, of the circumstances of the individual child, something that aroused the particular indignation of philanthropists and reformers, who sought to use print to correct the stereotype of naturally bad children wilfully taking to offending, and moving from begging to thievery. Their argument was that if children did so develop, it was the system which created the criminal career, not the initial offending, which was anyway often not performed out of choice. One philanthropist, Thomas Guthrie, reported the case of John Sullivan described as "a little bare-footed boy" who was brought before a magistrate, charged with begging "with great activity" in Regent Street. His mother had sent him out begging, where he sometimes "earned" as much as two shillings a day, used to buy "much gin and ale" for his mother. Sending Sullivan to the workhouse to separate him from his mother, the magistrate commented upon the frequency of like cases, recounting details of a little girl he had discharged only a couple of days before, to witness her begging at the door of some public houses the next day.²⁵

Any regular reader of crime reporting would have known that cases like these were part of the daily diet of the provincial and national press. Reporting regularly depicted children sent out by parents too inebriated to beg for themselves, to bring in enough money for the family to survive on, as the case of Charles and Emily Palmer, "two wretched-looking children" of eleven and nine, charged with begging. It was "one of those cases, unhappily too common, in which the benevolent feelings of the public are imposed upon by an appearance of fictitious distress." The father was regularly employed but "took very little care of his children." The mother "sent them out every day begging, while she watched them" and "speedily disposed" of the proceeds on gin.²⁶ All too often, when caught in the act of "supporting their families" in this way, children were in danger of being branded as criminals. Instances such as these generated great concern not only from philanthropists like Guthrie but also among some of the urban stipendiary magistrates, like Sir Robert Carden. They were aware that established responses to this activity punished a child who (having criminal or destitute parents) had no moral example on which to base their behavior, and who had not voluntarily taken to offending. As Mary Carpenter pointed out in 1853, "The law as it now stands punishes the obedient child, and lets the disobedient parent go free!"²⁷

Thus juveniles involved in this type of offending were not seen as bearing sole responsibility for their crimes. Attitudes to certain types of theft were also complex, with temptation by irresponsible shopkeepers being blamed in reports of shoplifting, for instance. Newspapers regularly reported magistrates' criticisms of owners who allowed their goods to be displayed openly at the front of their establishments, so providing an almost irresistible temptation for destitute children.²⁸ While comments mitigating the responsibility of the children for their lawbreaking may imply that the community at large was beginning to recognize the need for change, not all child crime was viewed so sympathetically. Even where some level of mitigation or responsibility was admitted, the Victorian judicial process often failed to respond adequately to demands for better strategies to deal with juvenile offenders, for a complex mix of factors.

Reform?

From the 1840s on, there was impetus for judicial reform in a number of areas, including juvenile criminality and appropriate sentencing practice for child criminals. Part of the publicity generated by the incidence of juvenile crime promoted debates on the vexed question of the efficacy of the contemporary legislation and the utility of using the same legislation as adults to deal with child criminals. Early reformers of the legal system and philanthropists identified dangerous flaws in the old system. Their arguments promoted development of a discrete juvenile criminal process by the end of the 1840s, with the introduction of the Summary Jurisdiction Act 1847. This made it possible for certain offenses to be tried quickly in magistrates' courts, and was held to be particularly beneficial for children because it did away with the need to incarcerate vulnerable children in dubious surroundings before trial.[29]

The Times followed the debate which led to the enactment of this legislation, reporting, among others, the opinion of the Attorney General in his capacity as Recorder in Bristol:

> it had long been considered, he said, that there were cases which might be decided by the magistrates without coming before the judges at assizes or sessions . . . persons, especially the youthful, were sent to prison before trial, when the same discipline cannot be administered as after; they became contaminated by conduct with hardened criminals, and came out worse than they went in.[30]

Yet there was also dissent about the usefulness of this legislation. One letter to *The Times* described the proposed legislation as a "two-edged sword doing all kinds of mischief" because it would take away the rights of law (i.e., the judgment of a jury) from children and leave them to the dubious mercy of justices of the peace.[31] Such debates formed part of the mass of material produced on the nature, causes, and treatment of juvenile criminals which stimulated the wider public conversation, courtesy of the print media.

For instance, in the absence of alternatives, penal sentencing regularly continued to be utilized despite the recognition of the failure of traditional methods in reforming child criminals. Magistrates themselves found the law challenging to apply and often used discretion; their reservations were widely publicized. Thomas Paynter, a Metropolitan Police Magistrate, in his evidence to the 1852 Select Committee on Criminal and Destitute Juveniles, agreed that the law was "ambiguous" and that punishments available to the magistrates were ultimately ineffective in diminishing crime and reforming individuals. He referred to the new provisions for juveniles in the Summary Jurisdiction Act 1847 and its 1850 amendment; where the 1850 Act stated that children under fourteen years and over sixteen years could not be whipped. Paynter commented that this was a useless tool where (as was common) a group of boys of mixed ages were found guilty. He referred to the uselessness of short sentences for juveniles, merely "exposing the criminal to the contamination of the gaol" without having the intended "deterrent effect." Paynter admitted to using a large amount of discretion when hearing cases of juvenile crime. Rather than committing children to short terms in jail, he preferred to release them to sureties of their families if at all possible.[32]

Paynter was not alone. In the Palmer children case, for instance, Sir Robert Carden was reported as observing that "an Act of Parliament" to enable the offense and punishment to be shifted to the parents was "almost required."[33] A similar "sad tale of castaway children" featured in the *Pall Mall Gazette* in 1865. Taken into custody for begging, they admitted that their idle father "flogged them" if they "did not bring home as much money as he thought they should get." Consequently, "the magistrate remanded them for a little while to see if anything could be done for them." They were eventually removed from their father's care and sent to an industrial school, at the father's expense.[34]

Sentencing in Practice

Despite such examples, however, the practical dilemma of what to do with convicted juveniles exercised reformers, philanthropists, magistrates, and many members of the public. The post-1840s period witnessed an increased use of more humane punishment regimes, shifting away from the earlier concentration on transportation, and so forth, to a focus on rehabilitation and reform. New Utilitarian thinking on prisons and punishment promoted public discussion and a general opinion that children should not be automatic candidates for the traditional "prison," especially if there was a chance of rehabilitating them into useful members of society. Pressure for reform of the conditions in which juveniles were held generated the creation of alternative forms of incarceration, including Industrial Schools and other reformatory establishments.

The *Daily Telegraph*, for instance, reported the 1856 public meeting in Manchester on the need for a juvenile reformatory there, where "a strong sentiment seemed to be entertained generally, that there was a necessity for something being done"; but it was agreed that it was a national problem, and could not be dealt with efficiently by "any voluntary effort," requiring the intervention of the state. They argued for a national system of reformatories, supported at the public expense.[35] However, such a system was never properly established, despite the setting up of numbers of reformatories and industrial schools, largely as a result of interested local endeavor. It meant that, all too often, convicted juveniles ended up in adult prisons, especially (but never exclusively) where the conviction was for more serious offenses, ensuring a criminal record with all the implications that had for them on release. For the panicmongers in the media, therefore, there was a sustained base of recidivist juveniles to fuel the construction of the deviant and outlawed children running through society, and the continuation of harsh sentencing. But severity was not automatic, as legal and reporting reactions even to more serious crimes indicates.

Henry Crewe, twelve, William Cody, fourteen, and Peter Butler, eleven, along with other boys, were charged with breaking and entering a shop and stealing a quantity of earthenware. The named boys all appeared to have previous convictions. Butler's "career" appears to have started at nine, and he clearly knew a great deal about the legal system. Given the opportunity to cross-examine the witness, Butler did so with "remarkable shrewdness," protesting his innocence until he was given the option of being committed for trial at the Old Bailey, or pleading guilty and being dealt with under the Summary Jurisdiction Act 1847. He then unhesitatingly chose the second option, with its lesser sentences. This crime was demonstrative of a rarer, more organized class of crime and criminal. The main perpetrator, Butler, appeared to have gained not only criminal expertise in relation to his actual crimes but also knowledge of the criminal justice system. He could handle himself on the streets and in the courtroom, unfortunately influencing others along the way: a character not unlike a fledgling Artful Dodger. Was Butler born with these "talents" or had he been subjected to a thorough training process in the prison system? Interestingly, however, the boys were awarded a sentence of fourteen days imprisonment, followed by five years at a reformatory school, indicating that despite their previous offending, they were seen as potentially reformable. The prisoners were reported to have been "astonished" and "pleased" on hearing the sentence.[36] Should this have been the desired effect of the prescribed sentence?

It is also instructive to examine the reaction to girls involved in burglaries and more organized crimes. As girls were less frequent perpetrators and expected, according to Victorian stereotypes, to be purer creatures, their sentencing often seems to have been more severe in relation to their crime when compared to a boy committing the same offense. In the Old Bailey Session papers for just one year, 1853–1854, convicted girls were all sentenced to confinement, suggesting a greater severity of reaction against deviant girls.

It is also interesting to examine the sentences allotted in response to the serious crimes examined earlier. Back in 1831, Bell was not shown any leniency. He stated he knew he should be hanged and showed no remorse or emotion during the trial. In passing the death sentence, the judge commented on the amount of interest the case had excited and the "excessively crowded state of the court, by all classes; of the fair sex there was a vast assemblage, all well dressed, and some fashionably."[37] But the case was not widely reported by the newspapers of the day, and Gatrell has pointed out that the newspapers which did report the trial failed to mention the age of the boys, only referring to the atrocity of the crime.[38] There appeared to be no humane reasoning or excuse voiced in defense for this young offender and during all procedures he was treated as an adult. In the mid-Victorian atmosphere promoting rehabilitation, the widely reported trial of Bradley and Barratt saw a different result. Their defense counsel had argued that the accused "were mere babies," with no idea of the consequences of their actions, asking the jury "not to let the brand of felons fall upon such infants as they saw before them." Convicted only of manslaughter by the jury, the judge endorsed their conclusions by sentencing the boys to a month's imprisonment, followed by five years in a reformatory.[39]

When such a slight sentence and willingness to understand the actions of these child killers are compared to reactions to cases of handkerchief theft and begging, the levy of Victorian sentencing appears truly unrepresentative of the crime. These examples do suggest, however, that sentencing policies did appear to have one thing in common. If the public witnessed, were everyday victims of, or were inconvenienced by, a relatively petty action classified as criminal, it potentially carried far greater consequences than another act which only affected a few and so could be seen as atypical or unrepresentative. Cases of child killing, generally headlined in the media as "unique" in their horror, were more condonable because of that supposed uniqueness. Society was more concerned with sentences which reflected their desire to rid the streets of nuisance crimes, condoning harder sentences as means of control, instead of focusing on scales of punishment appropriate to the actual crime. Newspaper reporting ensured that the public were more aware of their potential to become victims of petty crime, and their consequent outrage was expressed in demands for punishment for commonplace, rather than unusual, crimes.

Thus sentences continued to be mixed, ambiguous and, according to reformers, often inappropriate for the children, and public debate raged on, with the conversation arguing for and against punishment or for and against reform. No happy medium was apparent. In theory, the emphasis was plainly on the side of the reformers and their powerful print expressions. Benjamin Waugh argued that "Our convict prisons, it is believed by persons who at once have authority to speak and lack the liberty to do so, are supplied with a large proportion of their inmates from the juvenile victims of fatally unsuitable proceedings of law."[40] Hesba Stretton used Waugh's book in a powerful novel, well reviewed in the press, about David Fell who started on a life of crime after initial incarceration on being convicted of begging.[41] She finished with a postscript in which she argued the solution to "the problem of juvenile crime" lay in Waugh's argument that there should be "no gaol for children," and at worst, institutions which would "serve not only for the purpose of punishment, but also provide for the education of the wards; the neglect of education being recognized as one of the chief sources of crime." She concluded, "'The Gaol Cradle: Who Rocks It?' You and I."[42] In practice, sentencing continued to take more account of more immediate pressures on magistrates and judges.

Conclusion

What effect did this amount of printed comment have on Victorian understandings of the criminal child? Whether it was the increased visibility of juvenile crime itself which prompted this production or whether the increasing use of material available to the public brought the criminal child and associated concerns into the public gaze, the fact remains that the phenomenon of juvenile delinquency gave rise to great public concern and outrage. The mass reporting of petty theft, for example, portrayed a scenario where children ran like uncontrollable savages through towns and cities threatening the health and happiness of the law-abiding.[43] The horror of juvenile crime was thus established at a very real and personal level, with tales of the theft of personal property predominating in the reportage and being equated to an infringement of an individual's rights to security within the community.

Print productions also spread the idea that lawbreaking led to a child's inevitable downfall and misery.[44] The concept of the criminal child was a powerful stimulus to the generation of cheap, widely available print material, and few were oblivious to the idea that juvenile criminality was a "real" moral evil, in danger of spreading through society. The legal system struggled to address these concerns while legislation, generated in this new politicization of juvenile crime, was often considered ineffective and confused, for a range of equally confused reasons arising out of individual agendas and fears. Media conversations constructed highly contradictory images of juvenile criminals, depicting both violent, unruly urban savages and forlorn neglected "innocents" in need of care and susceptible to reform, with both categories capable of performing the same crimes. The confusion inherent in the increased visibility of child criminals ensured a continuing moral outrage in Victorian England.

Notes

1. For a further discussion of this aspect, see Judith Rowbotham, Kim Stevenson, and Samantha Pegg, "Children of Misfortune: The Parallel Cases of Thompson and Venables, Bradley and Burgess," *Howard Journal of Criminal Justice* 42, 2 (2003): 107–22.

2 PP VII.I, Select Committee Report on Criminal and Destitute Juveniles (1852). Criminal returns for 1848 demonstrate the fairly erratic nature of juvenile crime statistics: *The Friend,* 1 October 1849, 149.

3. Heather Shore, "The Idea of Juvenile Crime in Nineteenth Century England," *History Today* (June 2000): 21–27.

4. See W. G. Carson and Paul Wiles, eds., *Crime and Delinquency in Britain: Sociological Readings* (London: Martin Robertson,1971), containing studies examining social perspectives on juvenile crime from the nineteenth century onward.

5. L. Radzinowicz, *Ideology and Crime* (London: Heinmann, 1966), 38.

6. "Dangerous Classes," *Lectures Delivered Before the Church of England Young Men's Society for Aiding Missions at Home and Abroad in St. Martins Hall* (London: Nisbet, 1850).

7. Fredrich Engels, "Crime and Condition of the Working Class," in *The Condition of the Working Class in England,* ed. Karl Marx and Friedrich Engels, (Moscow: Progress Publishers, 1953), v.

8. Mary Carpenter, *Reformatory Schools for the Children of the Perishing and Dangerous Classes* (London: Woburn Press, 1968), 2.

9. Henry Mayhew, *Selections from London Labour and London Poor,* ed. J. L. Bradley (London: Oxford University Press, 1965), xxxiii.

10. H. Mayhew, *London Street Folk,* vol. 1, *London Labour and London Poor* (London: Frank Cass, 1967), 468.

11. *Nottingham Review,* 3 February 1854.

12. Heather Shore, "Cross Coves, Buzzers, and General Sorts of Prigs," *British Journal of Criminology* 39, 1 (1999): 10–24.

13. *Daily Telegraph,* 22 April 1856.

14. *OBSP,* 1853, London and Middlesex Session, Session 5, 107.

15. *OBSP,* 1853, Kent Session, Session 4, 271.

16. *Daily Telegraph,* 1 January; 2 March 1856.

17. *OBSP,* 1853, Surrey cases, Session 4, 401.

18. *Illustrated Police News,* 19 January; 26 January 1867.

19. *OBSP,* 1853, London and Middlesex cases, Session 5, 594.

20. *The Times,* 10 August 1861; *News of the World,* 11 August; 21 August 1861.

21. *The Times,* 10 August 1861.

22. *The Times,* 5 January 1870. Ann Smith, also convicted of stealing food, was awarded the same punishment as the boy, seventeen, convicted of stealing lace.

23. *Daily Telegraph,* 31 January 1856.

24. *Nottingham Review,* 10 February 1854.

25. Thomas Guthrie, *The City: Its Sins and Sorrows and Pleas for Ragged Schools* (London: Daldy, Isbister, 1877), 162.

26. *Daily Telegraph,* 6 January 1861.

27. Mary Carpenter, *Juvenile Delinquents: Their Condition and Treatment* (Patterson, NJ: Smith, 1970), 25.

28. PP VII.I, *Select Committee Report on Criminal and Destitute Juveniles* (1852), Evidence, W. J. Williams, 15.

29. The Summary Jurisdiction Acts 1847 and 1850 enabled trial by magistrate of cases of simple larceny under the value of five shillings. If the cases involved a greater amount but the juvenile pleaded guilty, the magistrate had powers to sentence up to six months' imprisonment.

30. *The Times,* 6 November 1855.

31. *The Times,* 10 August 1840.

32. PP VII.I, *Select Committee Report on Criminal and Destitute Juveniles* (1852), Evidence, T. Paynter, 85.

33. *Daily Telegraph,* 6 January 1861. Emily, eleven, went to a reformatory school; Charles was returned to his mother's care.

34. *Pall Mall Gazette,* 25 July; 2 August 1865.

35. *Daily Telegraph,* 5 June 1856.

36. *The Illustrated Police News,* 2 February 1867.

37. *The Times,* 30 July 1831.

38. V. A. C. Gatrell, *The Hanging Tree–Execution and the English People, 1770–1868* (Oxford: Oxford University Press, 1994), 1–5.

39. *The Times,* 10 August 1861.

40. Benjamin Waugh, *The Gaol Cradle—Who Rocks It?* (London: Strahan, 1873), 64.

41. Hesba Stretton, *In Prison and Out* (London: Religious Tract Society, 1887).

42. Ibid., 186.

43. PP VII.I, *Select Committee Report on Criminal and Destitute Juveniles* (1852), Evidence, M. Davenport Hill, 43.

44. J. O. Springhall, *Youth, Popular Culture, and Moral Panics: Penny Gaffs to Gangsta-Rap, 1830–1996* (Basingstoke: Macmillan, 1998).

3

Religion, Rural Society, and Moral Panic in Mid-Victorian England

GARY MOSES

Introduction

This chapter examines a campaign of criticism, reform, and abolition directed at hiring fairs and farm service by Church of England clergymen in the East Riding of Yorkshire during the mid-Victorian period. Hiring fairs were the traditional venue for the creation of annual contracts between farmers and the various categories of farm servant, male and female. Farm servants were hired on yearly contracts and "lived in" on the farm.[1] Though in decline by the Victorian period in much of southern England, farm service and hiring fairs remained important in many northern and midland counties. In the East Riding, for example, farm servants constituted 33 percent of the male agricultural labor force in 1851.[2] Wherever farm service remained important these fairs continued to exhibit vitality. They also tended to become the focus for moral outrage, and the East Riding of Yorkshire provides a salient example of this tendency during the mid-Victorian years. Here, a predominantly Anglican attempt to undermine the hiring fairs, and the farm service system that underpinned them, began in the early 1850s and lasted until the mid-1870s.[3] This campaign, which has interesting echoes for modern campaigns aimed at young people and their social practices, was conducted through print outlets in particular.

Hiring Fairs

In the 1850s the campaign centered on introducing a new form of contract as the basis of relations between masters and servants. Farmers were urged to hire only those servants who possessed a written testimony of their moral character and conduct over the past year. In seeking to emphasize the importance of such criteria at the point of engagement, the campaign hoped to reassert a moral dimension into relations between farmers and servants. The clerical view was that this dimension had become neglected and was in urgent need of restoration. This ideal of replacing verbal with written contracts remained throughout the campaign but was never fully realized. There is some evidence that written "characters," or references, gained currency among female farm servants, but virtually all male and many female servants consistently rejected the new practice.

A second phase of attack, developed from the early 1860s, focused on measures designed to compete with and erode the carnivalesque excesses associated with hiring fairs. Their absence of restraint and the opportunities they offered for the public and promiscuous mingling of the young of both sexes was a source of great anxiety. Their supposed effect upon the moral characters of female servants was considered especially regrettable. In attempting to draw servants away from the market places, streets, and public houses, reformers offered alternative hiring facilities in nearby rooms. They also attempted to compete with the commercial entertainment provided by publicans and showmen by offering alternative "rational recreations" in the form of, for example, brass bands and indoor concerts. The provision of indoor hiring rooms and the alternative rational recreations was predominantly aimed at female servants. It was designed to remove women from the dangers that prevailed in the "public sphere" of the hiring fair and to segregate male and female hiring. From the early 1860s segregation by sex gradually established itself as the norm at most of the East Riding's larger hiring fairs. This was the major long-term achievement of the campaign.

For some opponents, however, this was far from being sufficient. Hiring fairs continued to be popular, and though most females no longer stood in the open market to be hired, once hiring was finished they rejoined male servants in enjoying the excesses of the day. The continued vitality of the East Riding's hiring fairs and the passing of legislation facilitating easier abolition of fairs (in the form of the Fairs Act 1871) stimulated a final flurry of activity by their opponents in the 1870s. This phase of agitation involved an attempt to mobilize support for separate hirings for men and women or the legal suppression of hiring fairs in the East Riding. This final phase had little support and enjoyed no success. Although rural clergymen continued to complain of the iniquitous influences of hiring fairs and farm service, there was a gradual decline of their antipathy to them from the 1870s. This chapter will now explore further the meaning and nature of this campaign by analyzing it through reference to the concept of moral panic.

Immoral and Corrupt?

Cohen, in the first systematic use of the concept of moral panic in Britain, focused on an episode in the 1950s that emerged around a few minor gatherings and gang fights at seaside resorts. He demonstrated a process of amplification, construction of a stereotypical image of young adolescents that portrayed them as deviant "folk devils." This labeling then served to motivate and legitimize repressive and counterproductive responses from the police and the courts.[4] For Cohen, panics were likely to occur at times of social change, and part of their function was to act as a spontaneous safety valve for the cultural unease generated by social change.[5] However, within this process, the media and "moral entrepreneurs" who utilize the media play a pivotal role in amplifying these anxieties, giving them greater focus and mobilizing support for control and the restoration of traditional values.[6]

Encouraged by Cohen's suggestion that moral panics were a persistent feature of societies over time, a number of historians have transported the concept of moral panic and used it in their interpretation of public anxieties about street disorder and crime and the censorious campaigns that these generated.[7] These studies have indicated that the concept, and its associated methodology, may prove instructive for the examination and analysis of the campaign against hiring fairs in the East Riding.[8] This chapter will now attempt to utilize to this end the classic Cohen-type model of moral panic.

Cohen's social anxiety approach model suggests that panics begin with a discourse defining something or someone as constituting a threat to the values and interests of society.[9] Hiring fairs were portrayed in letters, tracts, and sermons as cockpits of corruption which attracted the young and exposed them to temptations that were extreme in their scale and intensity. A hiring fair was, according to a memorial issued by the York Diocesan Board of Education, "an assembly from which all moral control is simply excluded" and in which "the very force of numbers aids the work of corruption."[10] Because custom demanded that young men and women had to attend the fairs in order to get hired, it was suggested that this meant that the innocent and unwary who otherwise would not have chosen to visit them were exposed to their excesses. One leading opponent, the Reverend James Skinner of Driffield, claimed for example that "Many we know have gone to the statutes only for the purpose of being hired, their passions have been excited at the dancing saloon and their senses dulled by intoxicating drinks, and thus they have gone home divested of all self-respect, too often to begin a life of sin and wickedness."[11] Clergymen also attacked the hiring practices of farmers who, they alleged, neglected considerations of moral worth and "hired servants, of both sexes, solely on the recommendations of brute strength."[12]

It was often at this point that the moral threat of the hiring fairs was linked to a perceived problem within living-in farm service. For many rural clergymen, behavior at the fairs was regarded as a reflection of the degenerate condition of farm service as a social institution. The clerical ideal was that farm service should act as a regime of moral superintendence and social control. They expected farmers to exercise discipline over their servants, care for their moral welfare, and encourage regular attendance at church.[13] Their critique of contemporary practice suggested that farm service had deviated from this paternalistic ideal and lost its moral dimension. East Riding farmers, it was alleged, now treated their servants as "mere machines who must get through a certain amount of work" and took little or no interest in their character and conduct.[14] This absence of care and control was regarded as having bred a sense of alienation which manifested itself in fractious and defiant behavior. It was claimed that farmers faced "the constant misconduct of their servants, and the total want on their part of any means of control over them" and that servants were "showing by their insubordination and wilfulness that the hand of authority sits lightly upon them."[15] The sexual promiscuity that many clergy believed rife within farm service was ascribed to farmers allowing servants to "associate together without any moral restraint" and dismissing "open and habitual fornication" among them as "mere sweethearting."[16] For many, therefore, the critique of hiring fairs was also a critique of farm service. Because farm service was no longer informed by paternal control and Christian morality, it had become a fallen institution generating sin and disorder.[17]

Churchmen were especially irritated by the consequences that the custom of hiring farm servants at fairs and boarding them on farms had for what was termed "village morals."[18] In systemic fashion, this combination presented them with an irritating visitation each November when a clutch of new farm servants was hired into their parish. Clergymen came to regard the young farm servants (generally not born in the parishes into which they were hired) as disruptive and demoralizing influences. They were often perceived and portrayed by clergymen as rootless delinquents whose "deep degradation," "ignorance," and "sensuality and drunkenness" served to make them a source of moral corruption and social disorder.[19] For some, this was the most "injurious" consequence of the system of hiring fairs and farm service: "by its means, bad and profligate persons are disseminated over the country far and wide, to work as much evil as a bad example can work in a year's time in one parish and then move on to pursue the same work of corruption in another."[20]

Thus the campaign against hiring fairs did largely conform to aspects of the model outlined above. Within the discourse of panic, farm servants were presented as "folk devils" who, having been demoralized by hiring fairs and farm service, threatened the morality of rural society. The campaign also called for remedial action in the form of the restoration of control within farm service and an end to hiring fairs. The first phase of the campaign, for example, in advocating contracts based upon character references sought to reassert moral considerations at the point of their creation. It also hoped that this would continue throughout the duration of the contract, and beyond, as farmers came to realize the advantages of greater discipline. Advocates emphasized, for example, the "additional authority and power" a master would enjoy:

> by having it always in his power in the event of wilful negligence, disobedience, or misconduct, to threaten that he should, at the year's end, decline giving a satisfactory account of his behaviour; for were this system universally adopted as it ought to be, servants would soon discover the loss of having only an indifferent character to show to a person wishing to engage them.[21]

Clergymen also hoped to undermine the hiring fairs by promoting this alternative system of contracts. Because they were to be administered through a network of register offices located in East Riding villages, without the need for attendance, hiring fairs, it was hoped, would wither away.

Cohen suggested the moral panic discourses were heavily reliant on the media for their transmission and diffusion: the media depicts the threat to societal values in an easily recognizable form and mobilizes opinion against the folk devils. In the East Riding, editors of local newspapers such as *The Yorkshire Gazette*, the *York Herald*, the *Hull and Eastern Counties Herald*, *The Driffield Times*, and *The Beverley Guardian* were supportive and gave it considerable publicity. Arguably the campaign was launched in local newspapers when, in January and February of 1854, several East Riding clergymen used their letter pages to voice their concerns and outline proposals for reform.[22] The positive local press response provided the campaign with publicity and moral support for much of the mid-Victorian period. Editorial columns condemned the excesses of hiring fairs and the demoralized condition of farm servants; critics of the system were also given space for extended pieces detailing its evils. Newspapers also sent correspondents to report on hiring fairs and "reveal" their practices and character to their readers.[23]

Some of this coverage was detailed and investigative, but there was also a tendency to offer a stylized and stereotypical representation of hiring fairs, farm service, and farm servants that served to label them as deviant. Hiring fairs were compared to "an Oriental Slave-market" with farm servants "huddled together . . . like so many cattle."[24] They were criticized for offering "powerful enticements and seductive temptations" and for encouraging "reckless debauchery" (males) and "vice and infamy" (females).[25] Seemingly mundane and factual reporting of hiring fairs, and court cases involving farm servants, was also informed by this conversation.[26] Although comparisons between the regional press of the nineteenth century and the national media of the later twentieth century need to remain tentative, the threat to society posed by hiring fairs and farm service was depicted in an easily recognized form in local newspapers. Some of this coverage was designed to mobilize opinion against them.

Another characteristic of moral panics is that as opinion is mobilized there is a rapid build-up of public concern. There is evidence of this in the East Riding, although only in a limited form. Local newspapers were primarily aimed at an upper- and middle-class readership, and the tracts, pamphlets, and letters issued by clergymen were aimed predominantly at fellow clergymen, landowners, and farmers; they tended to talk *about* farm servants, not *to* them. The language and tactics employed indicate that clergymen sought to mobilize what they regarded as their traditional constituency of support, landowners and tenant farmers, and effect change from above. Despite this qualification (which indicates that the discourse of panic was aimed at mobilizing a limited public opinion), the response in the East Riding did conform to Cohen's model in that the moral barricades were literally "manned by editors, bishops and other right-thinking people."[27] As indicated above, the editors of local newspapers supported the campaign. William Thomson, Archbishop of York (1863–90), was also a supporter. In his primary Visitation Charge, for example, he suggested that:

> The whole system of contracts with farm labourers in this county is so unfavourable to religion and good morals that I do not suppose there is one minister of religion who does not desire to see it altered. I trust the time will come when people will hear with incredulity that farmers used to take into their houses, where their wives and children dwell, young servants of both sexes without the slightest enquiry into their character; that so arranged the work of the Sunday that it should be impossible for some of their dependants to enter a place of worship from the beginning of the contract to the end of it; that they did not attempt to exercise any influence over their character or general behaviour.[28]

Other "right-thinking people" included Charles William Strickland, Chairman of the East Riding Magistrates who, at the April 1854 meeting of the Quarter Sessions, drew attention to the demoralized character of the farm servant population and attacked "the reckless carelessness of employers as to the character of their employees."[29] Lieutenant-Colonel B. Granville Layard, the

Chief Constable of the East Riding Police, was a critic of hiring fairs and provided police assistance to the reformers.[30] E. B. Portman, who reported on the East Riding for the Royal Commission on Children, Young Persons, and Women in Agriculture in the 1860s, drew attention to the campaign and its concerns.[31] Support also came from several prominent East Riding landowners, including the region's largest landowners, the Sykes family, who worked alongside rural clergy to promote registration societies in villages on their Sledmere estate.[32] Gatherings of Church Congresses and the Social Science Association held at York in the 1860s also provided an opportunity for "experts" to pontificate at length as to the evils of hiring fairs and farm service and to "pronounce their diagnoses and solutions."[33]

There is, therefore, evidence for a degree of panic and associated public concern. However, it remained confined to a rather narrow band at the top of the rural hierarchy. In part, this reflected the aims and tactics of the Church campaign which concentrated upon sharpening the awareness of its "traditional" supporters and marshalling their influence. But it was also an indication that this particular conversation found only limited resonance within even those sections of East Riding society that the campaign had sought to mobilize. Local farmers, for example, were often indifferent and (at times) openly hostile to the campaign: in 1876 at a public meeting in York, Jonathan Dunn of the York Chamber of Agriculture dismissed those who opposed hiring fairs as "sentimental" and "mistaken"; he was applauded when he advised farmers to "quietly take no notice of them."[34]

Panics are also said to provoke remedial action in the form of a more regulatory and coercive mode of control toward the identified deviant practices and individuals. Despite the support already discussed, the main response continued to be the direct measures initiated by rural clergy from parishes close to hiring fairs and with a substantial farm servant population. They were at the center of the campaign throughout, and it was they who, along with their wives, daughters, and other Anglican laity, attempted to regulate, reform, and abolish hiring fairs and, in doing so, reshape the institution of farm service. Only the second phase of the campaign, centering on providing indoor hiring accommodation for women, can be regarded as having produced significant remedial action. Establishment of segregated hirings was a substantial reform in its own right, and it provided a platform for other attempts to reshape the internal character of the hirings. The establishment of indoor hiring at Driffield, for example, was accompanied by the introduction of brass-band music in the hiring rooms and in the market place outside.[35]

It could also be argued that this panic, in helping to draw attention to the excesses of the fairs, encouraged local authorities to adopt measures to make them more orderly and disciplined. York's City Council, for example, actively supported attempts to end the combined hiring of men and women by issuing regulations that forbade the practice and using the police to enforce them.[36] The police were also instrumental in the implementation of segregated hiring at other East Riding fairs. The following reflection from the Reverend M. C. F Morris, son of the Reverend F. O. Morris (one of the campaign's leading lights), implied a direct correlation between the change in hiring practices effected by the campaign and the emergence of a more orderly hiring fair:

> Happily the worst part of the old system is now done away with. The statties go on as of yore, but they are conducted in an altogether improved fashion. Both clergy and laity combined to get rid of the worst phases of the institution . . . rooms are now hired in every town, in which the girls are assembled by themselves, and can be engaged by the farmer's wives in an orderly and befitting manner; the Girls' Friendly Society and other kindred institutions all help in the same general cause, and although occasional brawls and disturbances take place, yet there is no comparison between the state of things now and what it was thirty years ago.[37]

Although hiring fairs did continue to exhibit carnivalesque characteristics there is more than a grain of truth in Morris's view. The major riot that occurred in Driffield in 1875 was remembered in the twentieth century as the last of its kind.[38] It may be, as Morris suggests, that this decline in the scale of disorder was the result of the Church of England campaign. Possibly its efforts were sufficient to render the problem less visible and this explains why the panic receded from the late 1870s. Equally likely, given that the campaign failed to achieve its more ambitious aims of abolishing or even fundamentally reshaping hiring fairs and farm service, is that the panic receded due to exhaustion and frustration.

An Ideal Breeding Ground?

This chapter has demonstrated ways in which the concept of moral panic has some value to those interested in nineteenth-century popular culture. The model is useful in facilitating identification of the salient aspects of what might otherwise seem to be a sprawling and incoherent mass of opinions and actions. Valuable though this process of analytical mapping is, the major reason why historians have turned to this concept and the theories with which it is associated is their potential for explaining why panics occur. It is to this dimension that the chapter will now turn.

According to the classic "social anxiety" model of moral panics their fundamental cause is anxieties about social change and the cultural strains that it brings about. As a predominantly rural area the East Riding might seem an unlikely setting for such a panic. In fact, however, the Riding had experienced a significant degree of social change from the late eighteenth century as it experienced a transformation from an agricultural backwater into one of the most advanced and productive arable farming regions in England. At the heart of this process was a two-phase agricultural revolution promoting the emergence of large-scale, capital-intensive "high" farming.[39] This process of economic transformation was accompanied by, and in many respects caused, changes in the settlement pattern. Basically, more farms were now located away from village centers as a nucleated settlement pattern gave way to a mixture of dispersed and nucleated settlements.[40] This process of economic and spatial change had a significant impact on the nature of East Riding society as it encouraged population growth, class formation, and more overt capitalist social relations.

These changes also affected the nature of farm service. Farm service is sometimes regarded as a traditional, precapitalist form of labor organization, but in parts of Britain it was integral to the development of modern large-scale capitalist agriculture.[41] The East Riding is a prime example of this symbiosis: the expansion of high farming also saw an increased reliance on the labor of farm servants. The larger, more capital-intensive farms associated with high farming practices were the most likely to hire and board large numbers of farm servants.[42] Although the Church of England's vision of what farm service had once been was informed by an imagined "golden age" of order, as farms became larger and more capitalist in their ethos, the system did witness a decline in its familial and paternalist character. Farmers were less likely to have much contact with their servants in their working lives as they delegated their control to supervisory workers. They were also less likely to share space and time with their servants after work, as they increasingly boarded and housed them away from their own families.[43] Male and female farm servants on these farms led an increasingly proletarianized and alienated existence as the ties that bound them to their employers became predominantly economic.[44] The larger farms also tended to be outside of village centers and their churches, which facilitated the perception of the young farm servants as outsiders and interlopers.[45]

Farm servants were, therefore, at the heart of the region's economic and social changes. Within the framework of the social anxiety model that has informed much of this chapter, the panic over hiring fairs and farm service might be interpreted as a product of social change. Because of their independent lifestyle, and the fact that they were often located within a reshaped form of farm service associated with the larger capitalist farms, farm servants were well placed to act as a symbol of social change. Possibly the stress that social change had brought about found release in the critical panic directed at them. This model might, then, usefully lead us to interpret the panic as an example of pent-up tensions within rural society being channeled at the young farm servants and their deviant way of life.

The empirical referents' deviations from the model suggest a degree of caution, however. The narrow social base of those active in the campaign and the limited response that it engendered within society in general are two examples of such dissonance between the model and the case study. More recent work might help to explain this divergence. McRobbie and Thornton have criticized Cohen and other early studies for their neglect of "counter discourses" which are able to resist and thereby limit the impact of moral panics. They have suggested that these pioneering studies were too monolithic and functionalist and, therefore, inappropriate for the analysis of contemporary panics: the complexity of modern society and its media means that responses are equally complex. Media opportunities provide space for other opinion formers to engage with moral panic discourses and negate their influence.[46] Nineteenth-century East Riding society and its media were undoubtedly less complex than the modern multimedia world discussed by McRobbie and Thornton, but it was a society characterized by increased plurality and an expanding local media. Both farmers and farm servants used local newspapers and publishers to contest the discourse of panic.[47] This resistance combined with the fact that the campaign enjoyed only limited support within the East Riding suggest that an explanation based solely upon the existence of anxieties within society at large is less than credible. It also suggests that a more convincing interpretation might emerge from a fuller consideration of the motivations of those most active in the campaign: Church of England clergymen.

Cohen's social anxiety approach identified the importance of "moral entrepreneurs," though in his interpretation they are probably less significant than the media. Other recent interpretations have given them greater prominence. Goode and Ben Yahuda, for example, have argued that sectional interests try to generate panics because they offer a means through which they may further their own interests.[48] Other post–Cohen approaches have emphasized that individuals and institutions who feel that their status and position have been recently eroded have a propensity to become moral entrepreneurs and launch crusades: either as a means of reasserting their status or, alternatively, as a way of exorcising their anxieties and frustrations.[49] Given the central role played by Anglicans in the crusade against hiring fairs, these more conspiratorial variations of the original panic model are worthy of fuller consideration.

The first half of the nineteenth century was a time of crisis for the Church of England.[50] Interpretation of this crisis often centers on the Church's difficulties in adapting itself to the challenges posed by urban and industrial society, but Anglicanism also experienced problems in rural society, difficulties which were especially pronounced in parts of northern England. There, the parochial system was weak and struggled to cope with agricultural change, population growth, and rural industrial development.[51] Nonconformist churches (especially the "New Dissent" of the Wesleyan and Primitive churches) proved more adaptable, thriving at the expense of the established church. In contrast, the mid-Victorian period is often regarded as a time of relative revival for the Anglican church.

Much of this revival took place at the local level and involved a vigorous effort to reengage with society and counter the influence of rural Methodism. At its heart was a determination to reinvigorate the role of the parish clergyman and restore the Anglican parish to its supposed former glory: a determination combining modernity and tradition. It sought to promote a sense of professionalism among its clergy: every parish needed a resident clergyman actively engaged with his parishioners' daily lives. But it also envisaged that this would be realized within the context of the preservation and, in some cases, reinvention of traditional society: a society characterized by stability and paternalism.[52] This parochial revival was most suited to, and successful in, southern England where the Anglican tradition and its parochial system were much stronger. Nevertheless, a similar effort was made in northern counties including the East Riding of Yorkshire where, after decades of relative decline, the Church of England sought to reassert itself in its rural parishes.

Conclusion

The campaign against hiring fairs can be interpreted as a reflection of this attempted revival in that it involved a renewed determination by clergymen to engage with, and refashion, ways of life that were a barrier before the recreation of the parochial system.[53] In many respects, however, the East Riding proved not to be ideal terrain for this effort. The settlement pattern placed a substantial proportion of its population away from the immediate influence of clergy. The emergence of a more class-orientated society was also a problem: Anglicanism was uneasy with horizontal identities and social relations. In contrast, Methodism, with the flexibility of its circuit system (and especially Primitive Methodism with its use of working-class preachers), was able to reach out and resonate with the rural population in ways that were beyond the ideological and organizational conservatism of the Established church.[54]

The religious census of 1851 demonstrates the strength of Methodism in the East Riding with the Methodist churches recording a combined percentage share of attendance of 47.3 compared with the Church of England's 37 percent.[55] The problems that clergymen experienced with farm servants in some of the more remote areas of the East Riding provide a concentrated example of this adverse situation. The recent expansion of high farming in areas such as the Wolds and Holderness meant that a substantial proportion of the population outside village centers were farm servants. Unreachable, unruly, and, even worse, susceptible to the dubious attractions of the Primitive Methodists, these young proletarians were the bane of many rural clergymen's lives: a symbol of many churchmen's parochial difficulties.[56]

When placed within this wider context, the Church critique of farm service and hiring fairs, and the crusade that flowed from it, correlates with the interpretations offered by the more conspiratorial post-Cohen interpretations of panics. The Anglican critique was based upon a genuine concern for the moral and spiritual health of those supposedly exposed to demoralizing influences, but it was also a response to the relative weakness of the Church in many East Riding parishes. To further the practical political end of reasserting their role and status, clergymen became moral entrepreneurs. This offered an opportunity for them to project themselves and their concerns within civil society. In doing so, they revealed themselves to be adept and prescient users of an expanding and increasingly important media: the provincial press. The anxieties and criticisms articulated in this and other media combined outrage and panic with a discourse of nostalgia rooted in anxieties about recent social change. This conversation sought to secure consent for action designed to restore order and control through the scapegoating of hiring fairs and farm service. The iniquities of both were presented as a threat to society in general, but it was the Church of England which experienced the greatest contradiction between its interests and the lifestyle of the farm servants. Confronting this contradiction created an opportunity for the Church to assert the values of deference and paternalism, to work toward their restoration, and to engage with the challenges posed by social change and Nonconformity.

Finally, as well as functioning as a vehicle for the practical political objective of advancing the role and status of the Anglican Church, the panic and its expressions of moral outrage also served as a form of symbolic politics. The critique of farm service and hiring fairs allowed clergymen to vent their spleen at a specific problem that symbolized other broader frustrations. Farm service and the farm servants' way of life were symbolic of broader difficulties facing the Church of England in the East Riding of Yorkshire: its failure to respond to social change with the same degree of flair and success as the Methodist churches. Ultimately the farm servants were scapegoats, not for anxieties within society in general, but for the failure of the Established Church to achieve a contemporary relevance.

Notes

1. East Riding farm servants are discussed more fully in M. G. Adams, "Agricultural Change in the East Riding of Yorkshire, 1850–1880: An Economic and Social History" (Ph.D. diss., University of Hull, 1977); Stephen Caunce, *Amongst Farm Horses: The Horselads of East Yorkshire* (Stroud: Alan Sutton, 1991); and Gary Moses, "Proletarian Labourers? East Riding Farm Servants, c. 1850–75," *Agricultural History Review* 47 (1999): 78–94.

2. J. A. Sheppard, "East Yorkshire's Agricultural Labour Force in the Mid-Nineteenth Century," *Agricultural History Review* 9, 48 (1961): 43–51. In parts of the Riding where isolated farmsteads were common the proportion of farm servants in the labor force rose to over 50 percent.

3. For a more detailed examination of this campaign and its outcomes see Gary Moses, "'Rustic and Rude': Hiring Fairs and Their Critics in East Yorkshire, c. 1850–75," *Rural History* 7, 2 (1996): 151–75; Gary Moses, "Reshaping Rural Culture? The Church of England and Hiring Fairs in the East Riding of Yorkshire, c. 1850–80," *Rural History* 3, 1 (2002); G. Moses, "Popular Culture and the 'Golden Age': The Church of England and Hiring Fairs in the East Riding of Yorkshire, c. 1850–75," in *The Golden Age: Essays in British Social and Economic History, 1850–1870*, ed. Ian Inkster et al., 184–98 (Aldershot: Ashgate, 2000). These and related themes are developed in greater depth in Gary Moses, "Social Relations in the Victorian Countryside: Hiring Fairs and Their Critics in the East Riding of Yorkshire, c. 1840–1880" (Ph.D. diss., Nottingham Trent University, 2000).

4. Ibid., 9.

5. Ibid., 9.

6. Ibid., 8–10.

7. See, for example, Rob Sindall, *Street Violence in the Nineteenth Century: Media Panic or Real Danger?* (Leicester: Leicester University Press, 1990); J. O. Springhall, *Youth, Popular Culture, and Moral Panics: Penny Gaffs to Gangsta-Rap, 1830–1996* (Basingstoke: Macmillan, 1998).

8. For a discussion of the use and influence of the various approaches to the study of moral panics see Keith Thompson, *Moral Panics* (London: Routledge, 1998).

9. Stanley Cohen, *Folk Devils and Moral Panics: The Creation of the Mods and Rockers* (London: Routledge, 2002), 9.

10 "Memorial of the York Diocesan Board of Education," *The Yorkshire Gazette*, 18 October 1856.

11. Rev. J. Skinner, "A Letter to the Masters and Mistresses of Farm Houses in the East Riding of Yorkshire." This was distributed to farmhouses in the Riding and reprinted in newspapers. See, for example, the *York Herald*, 10 November 1860.

12. Rev. G. Chester, *Statute Fairs: Their Evil and Their Remedy* (York: John Sampson, 1856), 7.

13. For an early articulation of these arguments see Rev. R. I. Wilberforce, *A Letter to the Gentry, Yeomen, and Farmers of the Archdeaconry of the East Riding* (York: J. Furby,

1842); see also Rev. J. Eddowes, *The Agricultural Labourer as He Really Is; or, Village Morals in 1854* (Driffield, 1854).

14. Rev. D. Legard, "The Education of Farm Servants," in *More about Farm Lads*, ed. F. D. L., 1 (London, 1865).

15. Rev. F. Simpson, Letter, "Hiring of Farm Servants," *The Yorkshire Gazette*, 28 January 1854; Legard, "Education of Farm Servants," 3.

16. Letter, "Nemo," *The Yorkshire Gazette*, 6 December 1863.

17. Simpson, "Hiring of Farm Servants."

18. Eddowes, *The Agricultural Labourer*, 1.

19. Ibid., 6–15.

20. Chester, *Statute Fairs*, 15.

21. Simpson, "Hiring of Farm Servants."

22. For examples of theses early proposals see *The Yorkshire Gazette*, 28 January 1854.

23. See, for example, Editorial, *The Yorkshire Gazette*, 28 January 1854; Editorial, *Hull Advertiser*, 7 April 1854; "The Evils of Public Hirings," *The Yorkshire Gazette*, 18 November 1854. The latter is an extended piece.

24. *Hull Advertiser*, 11 November 1854; *The Yorkshire Gazette*, 25 November 1854.

25. *The Yorkshire Gazette*, 25 November 1854; Editorial, *The Yorkshire Gazette*, 9 June 1855.

26. *York Herald*, 4 May 1875.

27. Cohen, *Folk Devils*, 9.

28. Archbishop W. Thomson, *Work and Prospects: A Charge to the Clergy of the Dioceses of York Delivered at His Primary Visitation in October 1865 by William Lord Archbishop of York* (London, 1865), 11.

29. *Hull Advertiser*, 7 April 1854.

30. See, for example, Chief Constable's Reports to the East Riding Quarter Sessions, reported in *The Hull and Eastern Counties Herald*, 5 January 1865; 4 January 1866; 3 January 1867; 2 January 1868; 7 January 1869; and 6 January 1870.

31. PP XVII, First Report from The Commissioners on The Employment of Children, Young Persons and Women in Agriculture, 1867–68, 1, 98–100.

32. *The Yorkshire Gazette*, 3 December 1854; 10 December 1859.

33. "Report of the Eighth Annual Social Science Congress at York," *York Herald*, 1 October 1864; "Report of the Annual Church Congress at York," *York Herald*, 13 October 1866.

34. *York Herald*, 14 July 1876.

35. *The Yorkshire Gazette*, 16 November 1863.

36. For details of the gradual success of this policy see *York Herald*, 29 November 1866; 28 November 1868; 29 November 1869; 26 November 1870.

37. Rev. M. C. F. Morris, *Yorkshire Folk-Talk with Characteristics of Those Who Speak It in the North and East Ridings*, 2nd ed. (London: A. Brown, 1911), 209–10.

38. Susan Parrott, "The Decline of Hiring Fairs in the East Riding of Yorkshire: Driffield, c. 1874–1939," *Journal of Regional and Local Studies* 16, 2 (1996): 19–31.

39. This transformation is examined in O. Wilkinson, *The Agricultural Revolution in the East Riding of Yorkshire*, East Yorkshire Local History Series: No. 5 (1956); and Adams, "Agricultural Change."

40. M. B. Gleave, "Dispersed and Nucleated Settlement on the Yorkshire Wolds, 1770–1850," *Institute of British Geographers Transactions and Papers* 30 (1962): 105–28;

Alan Harris, *The Rural Landscape of the East Riding of Yorkshire, 1700–1850* (London: Oxford University Press, 1961).

41. This symbiosis between farm service and modern farming practices is discussed in T. M. Devine, ed., *Farm Servants and Labour in Lowland Scotland* (Edinburgh: Donald, 1984); Brian Short, "The Decline of Living-in Servants and the Transition to Capitalist Farming," *Sussex Archaeological Collections* 122 (1984): 147–64; Alan Howkins, "Reply: Peasants, Servants, and Labourers: The Marginal Workforce in British Agriculture," *Agricultural History Review* 42 (1995): 65–66; Stephen Caunce, "Farm Servants and the Development of Capitalism in English Agriculture," *Agricultural History Review* 45 (1997): 49–60; and Moses, "Proletarian Labourers."

42. Harris, *East Riding*, 99; C. Hayfield, "Farm Servants' Accommodation on the Yorkshire Wolds," *Folk Life* 33 (1994): 7–28.

43. Caunce, *Farm Horses;* Moses, "Proletarian Labourers," 86–87.

44. Caunce, *Farm Horses*, 86.

45. On the contradictions between the Anglican parochial ideal and farm service in the East Riding, see also Moses, "Popular Culture and the 'Golden Age'"; Moses, "Social Relations."

46. Angela McRobbie and Sarah L. Thornton, "Rethinking 'Moral Panic' for Multi-Mediated Social Worlds," *British Journal of Sociology* 46, 4 (1995): 559–74.

47. For a farmer's response to clerical criticisms see W. Barugh, *"'Master and Man,' A Reply to the Pamphlet of the Rev. John Eddowes, Entitled 'The Agricultural Labourer As He Really Is'"* (Driffield: James Blakeston, 1854). A reporter from *The Yorkshire Gazette* spoke to servants congregated at York's Martinmas Fair and found that they were opposed to change: *The Yorkshire Gazette*, 25 November 1854.

48. Erich Goode and Nachman Ben-Yehuda, *Moral Panics: The Social Construction of Deviance* (Oxford: Blackwell, 1994).

49. Stuart Hall, C. Critcher, T. Jefferson, J. Clarke, and B. Roberts, *Policing the Crisis: Mugging, The State, and Law and Order* (London: Macmillan, 1978); Philip Jenkins, *Intimate Enemies: Moral Panics in Contemporary Great Britain* (New York: Aldine de Gruyter, 1992).

50. For a succinct overview of the fortunes of the Anglican Church in the nineteenth century, see Gerald Parsons, "Reform, Revival, and Realignment: The Experience of Victorian Anglicanism," in *Traditions*, vol. 1, *Religion in Victorian Britain*, ed. Gerald Parsons (Manchester: Manchester University Press, 1988), 14–66. .

51. B. I. Coleman, *The Church of England in the Mid-Nineteenth Century: A Social Geography, The Historical Association* (London: The Historical Association, 1980), 9–25.

52. For fuller discussions of this revival of paternalism see James Obelkevich, *Religion and Rural Society: South Lindsey, 1825–1875* (Oxford: Clarendon, 1976); Alan Howkins, *Reshaping Rural England* (London: HarperCollins, 1991), chap. 3.

53. Moses, "Rustic and Rude," 164.

54. Colemen, *Social Geography*, 40.

55. Ibid.

56. Moses, "Rustic and Rude," 160–62.

4

A Victorian Financial Crisis: The Scandalous Implications of the Case of Overend Gurney

PAUL BARNES

Introduction

Underpinning the Industrial Revolution was the ease by which limited liability companies could be established from 1855 onward, something which both fascinated and alarmed the Victorians, as a variety of contemporary print conversations demonstrate.[1] This development facilitated not only a "new breed" of entrepreneur but also a "new breed" of "pure" investor. The rise in popularity of limited liability companies was accompanied by increasing, publicly expressed skepticism by investors about the claims made by their promoters about the future profitability of these companies and the returns to be made. The bubble burst on "Black Friday," 14 May 1866 when the highly reputable bill-broking company of Overend Gurney Ltd. collapsed among claims of fraud against its promoters and directors. The press gave this much attention, as it had done for financial scandals in the previous decade. The resulting newspaper conversations helped to create an atmosphere of panic and moral outrage surrounding the financial sector, rooted in the feeling of insecurity that the collapse of Overend Gurney engendered. As a result limited liability suddenly became unpopular.

Ironically the impact of this conversation lasted much longer than either the initial enthusiasm or the immediate panic, and only finally abated at a point well into the following century, when investors had been given more protection in law and companies were forced to provide necessary financial information. This chapter examines the nature of and circumstances surrounding the first financial "Black Friday" crisis, thereby also touching on the implications for the working of similar mechanisms today, notably the mechanized stock markets and our own "information technology revolution," the internet and the rise (and fall?) of e-commerce and cybercrime.

The Role and Importance of Limited Liability

An important aspect of the Victorian financial landscape, lasting into the twentieth century, was the creation of the limited liability company, enabling entrepreneurs to set up large businesses by means of finance from investors with little involvement in their business. This made the creation of much larger businesses much easier; it also enabled them to limit their losses to the amount of capital invested (as opposed to an ordinary business or partnership in which the proprietor or partner was personally liable for his/her business debts, and could be taken to the Bankruptcy Court in pursuit of a debt). In fact, limited liability came relatively late in the Industrial Revolution. Despite this, capital had been raised and, overall, industrial production was not hindered by its absence. Individual ownership and partnerships financed by their own savings were the framework within which most businesses, certainly manufacturing, raised the finance that they required:

> By the time the acts of 1855 and 1862 gave the company law its present form, a single national market for long-term investment was functioning almost as smoothly as that for short-term loans. . . . A social base to the capital market of the mid-century was provided by the new class of "pure" investors, the people who had learned to put their money into profitable use, and to decide that use by the sole criterion of interest and whose expectations of income were very largely a matter of yields and quotations. It is their activities that imparted to the behaviour of capital all its characteristics of a perfect capitalist factor of production.[2]

In other words, the capital market was remarkably efficient and well developed, providing a mechanism to limit the risks of investment.[3]

The delay in the development of companies with freely transferable shares was caused by the Bubble Act 1720, a criminal statute which had been passed as a result of the South Sea Bubble scandal, aimed at preventing just this kind of transaction. After its repeal and the passing of the 1855 and 1856 Companies Acts, allowing entrepreneurs freely to set up limited liability companies, the benefits were quickly recognized. New businesses were formed; existing ones converted and expanded as a result of offerings of shares to the public, such as the Vale of Belvoir and Newark Plaster, Cement and Mineral Co. Ltd.[4]

Effectively, general limited liability started under the 1856 Act. The initial impact was slight, but rapidly began to increase. Between 1856 and 1862 nearly 2,500 companies were registered and 3,500 more between 1863 and 1866 (of which 900 offered shares to the general public). By 1865, *The Times* was sufficiently impressed to exclaim that "the whole country, if not the world, was growing every day into 'one vast mass of impersonalities.'"[5] Crucial to the development was that it was led by the promotion of limited liability banks and finance companies in which Parisian fashions in finance blossomed. As *The Times* remarked:

> There arose a new institution . . . the Finance Company, or Discount Company, or General Trading Company, or simple Bank, emerging from the straight-laced chrysalis into the gaudy and volatile butterfly, in the form of a Company (limited, and for the express purpose of sharing the profits of trade, [combined] in one the Bank, the discounter, the railway, the iron master, the merchant, the stock-jobber, and that specious form of limited liability which induces the hope of profits on a very large sum with the risk of a very small one.[6]

However, as with most innovations, there are risks and problems as people learn to understand them. Limited liability was potentially a device by which honest businessmen and financiers could be exploited and defrauded without the necessary protection. This was what happened in England. It was introduced and, quite innocently immediately, its benefits were trumpeted in the press, but without the implications being fully addressed or the necessary protective controls put in place. Quite naturally a disaster soon occurred: the Overend and Gurney scandal. As a result, what was seen to be a very good idea was then seen to be a very bad one in a public perspective, with the press taking a leading role in explaining its failings to its readership, as it had initially taken a leading role in publicizing it. It was only gradually, with the introduction of the necessary safety precautions (company law and regulations) that its popularity recovered so that a century later, it had become the main form of business organization.

It is necessary to distinguish "limited liability companies" and "joint-stock companies." The former relates to a firm's legal status, that is, incorporated under the relevant Companies Acts: the latter refers to a firm based on accumulated capital fund whose membership took the form of a freely transferable share. In other words, the former term refers to legal form whereas the latter refers to economic form. At the time of the first major Companies Act in 1844, there were few companies; most joint stock companies were unincorporated, legally partnerships, and so subject to partnership law. Entitled

"An Act for the Registration of Joint Stock Companies," the 1844 Act was directed at unincorporated joint stock companies which were often fraudulently exploited, so creating considerable legal problems. It forced all associations with transferable shares and all associations of twenty-five or more persons, whether or not their shares were transferable, to incorporate. A further Act in 1855 extended the facility to all partnerships of twenty-five or more members to convert to companies *with* limited liability status.

Within a year, the Joint Stock Companies Act 1856 had increased the availability of limited liability to ordinary and small businesses enormously. It not only dispensed with the minimum capital requirements but enabled also associations of merely seven persons to incorporate. Apparently (ironically) it was not intended by its Parliamentary proponents to facilitate small businesses incorporating. For example, in his guide to the Act, its original legislative draftsman, Henry Thring, expressed regret at the failure to pass Partnership Amendment Bills because of the "gap" it left in the law, by preventing the ordinary trader from benefiting from funds provided by capitalists as a result of limited liability compared with larger firms which could incorporate.[7] Nevertheless, some opposed the development and pointed to the potential abuse by fraudsters and the usage by small businesses in which an individual merely had to give a single share to six others.[8] Its broad application was recognized by many outside Parliament. Barrister Edward Cox was highly critical, commenting that the improvements to the law were "at the price of enormous evils" in which limited liability, "immoral in itself," permitted a trader to speculate for unlimited gain without being liable for more than a small and definite loss.[9]

This chapter first depicts events leading up to the creation of Overend Gurney Ltd. and its subsequent crash, along with the immediate effects. Second, the implications of the crash for the future of limited liability as a business form are discussed through a focus on the contemporary print conversation over the affair. Finally, the rise and fall of Overend Gurney and the longer-term implications are briefly discussed, and parallels drawn with the information technology revolution and the internet, with implications for the growth of e-business and cybercrime.

The Rise and Fall of Overend Gurney and Co. Ltd.[10]

The old and highly reputable private bill-broking firm Overend and Gurney fell on bad times during the 1850s. In an attempt to resolve their problems, it was decided in July 1865 to float off the firm as a limited company and sell the shares to the public by way of a prospectus. Because of its reputation, the invitation was fully subscribed and raised £1,500,000 as new capital. This was described by *The Bankers Magazine* at the time as "the greatest triumph which limited liability has yet achieved," being not only "an additional illustration of the soundness of the new principle" but also a mark of "the confidence with which it may be regarded by every class of investors."[11] *The Economist* was suspicious, recognizing the difference between good bills of exchange and bad. It offered a guarded welcome to the change as it would compel the house to publish accounts, distinguishing between its legitimate bill-dealing business and its "other" business, as it was "a matter of public notoriety" that for some time the house had been involved in "business not at all in general of an illegitimate or unprofitable character, but still of a sort different from those conducted by bill brokers 'pure and simple.'"[12]

King has described the public reaction:

> It was announced that Overend Gurney and Co whose name had long been uttered "with that curious solemnity, almost under, almost under the breath"; which in the minds of old men was the "best that could be thought of"; that this great house was to be transformed into "the worst they could think of"—a limited company. Surprise, however, quickly gave place to satisfaction, and a sort of wonder that a benevolent deity should have decreed that even the humblest might share in the great riches and power of so mighty an institution.[13]

However, the prospectus failed to disclose bad debts and the fact that the old firm was insolvent. All that was revealed was that the new company would take over Gurney's business for £500,000; half would be paid in cash, the other half in shares, "the vendors guaranteeing the company against any loss on the assets and liabilities transferred." Three of the nine owners of the old business (J. H. Gurney, H. E. Gurney, and R. Birkbeck) would retain "a large pecuniary interest" and join the Board of Directors, the others being all famous bankers. Managing Directors would be H. E. Gurney and R. Birkbeck. The capital of the new company was to be 100,000 £50 shares, of which £15 was to be paid. No details were given of past profits or even the value of the assets and liabilities to be transferred.

By October 1865 shares had almost doubled in price, despite problems in the foreign exchange market and huge increases in the Bank rate (from 3 to 7 percent) to try and correct it. A number of crashes, unrelated to Overend Gurney, then occurred which eventually brought it down. The first were a firm of railway contractors, Watson, Overend and Co. and the Contract Corporation, with which it was closely tied, followed by Joint Stock Discount, a discount house which supported them. These events forced the bank rate even higher, to 8 percent, causing grave concern in the securities and money markets. Many "bubble" companies collapsed. Overend Gurney was particularly affected by these events, not least by the similarity of its name with Watson Overend. This was a coincidence. It was able to meet the large amount of withdrawals during the early months of 1866.

However, the collapse of Pinto, Perez and Co., a firm of Spanish merchants it was known to be heavily supporting, put on huge pressure. An active bear market, a fall in all finance companies' shares, and the short selling of its shares, brought them to a heavy discount and led to a huge run by depositors.[14] The final straw occurred on 9 May 1866, when the value of its holdings of railway company shares was wrecked by a widely reported court ruling.[15] It was forced to apply to the Bank of England for support. The Bank could not assist and the crash came the following day.[16] *The Bankers' Magazine* described the panic which ensued:

> [It was like] the shock of an earthquake. It is impossible to describe the terror and anxiety which took possession of men's minds for the remainder of that and the succeeding day. No man felt safe. A run immediately commenced upon all the banks, the magnitude of which can hardly be conceived.[17]

The Times continued: "about mid-day the tumult became a rout. The doors of the most respectable Banking Houses were besieged and throngs heaving and tumbling about Lombard Street made that narrow thoroughfare impassable."[18]

The Bank of England acted to stem the panic by first raising the bank rate to 9 percent and then to 10 percent. Although this worked in the short term, there were more failures. In the next few weeks, ten banks suspended payment, only three of which ever resumed business. The rapid rise in the bank rate caused not only losses on the discount business but fresh failures of firms in Overend Gurney's other business. The vendors were called upon under their guarantee to the limited company, forcing them to sell their own properties, which attracted public attention. Overend Gurney was paid £650,000 during the first few months of its existence. By August 1866, it was established that creditors amounting to £5,228,000 would rank for a first dividend but only £660,000 was available. It was decided to make a call of £10 per share as only £15 had been paid on the £50 shares at the time of their allotment. Shareholders objected, a Defence Association formed, and a legal battle commenced, all this well reported by the Victorian press. Shareholders argued that the Board had acted fraudulently, misleading investors by not informing them of its insolvency. Their case was that there were two deeds to the transfer of business. The first, available for inspection, made no mention of these facts. The second, revealing the insolvency, was secret.

In court, the judge commented that, while the directors could not "on principles of morality and justice" justify the concealment, acknowledging that "if the public by this prospectus had been told what those issued it knew, no one share would have been taken," nevertheless he held that there had been no misstatement of fact and no intention to defraud. Hence, shareholders could be released from claims by the directors, but not from claims by the public.[19] This ruling was upheld by the Lord Chancellor and shareholders had no alternative but to pay the call. The delay had the effect of increasing the losses. It had forced the liquidators to sell assets during unfavorable market conditions and made the creditors restless. When a second call of £10 (secured by a creditors' application to the Court) proved insufficient to meet immediate claims, the threat of enforcing the full £15 outstanding on the shares forced the issue of interest-bearing certificates of indebtedness. These were eventually discharged in the autumn of 1869, after a further call of £5, making £40 paid on the shares. As a result, creditors received twenty shillings in the pound on their debts plus interest, bringing the total loss to shareholders, including the original share capital, to over £3.5m despite the sale of the Gurney family estates and properties.

On 13 December 1869 began the nine-day trial of the former Gurney directors, charged with wilful conspiracy to defraud. The judge's summing up was wholly favorable to the defendants and a verdict of "not guilty" reached in less than ten minutes. The reasons for the failure were shown as a massive accumulation of bad business over many years together with fraud by one of its directors. The beginnings went back to 1853 and a foolish decision by senior partner David Chapman. Discovering fraudulent pledges against advances which the firm had made, instead of taking proceedings against the offenders Chapman had decided to ask for new security. Eventual uncovering of the frauds brought widespread prejudice both against him and the firm. He had left, and neither of his successors was the soundest of bankers. Other associates brought more bad business and, as a result, the firm had become partners in various speculative businesses, most of which had had no prospect of success. Friends of Chapman and Edwards had been appointed to well-paid positions in these speculations, and an important aspect of these appointments had been the commission that had been paid to Edwards (both from the borrowers and from Gurneys) in addition to his salary. Chapman had probably been unaware of some of these transactions, but it was argued that the "double commissions" to Edwards were the principal reason for the huge losses leading to the collapse.[20]

By 1861, despite sound and profitable dealing in its discounting business, Gurneys had been hard pressed for funds and had had to resort to extensive accommodation finance. Assets had been mortgaged to London banks to obtain this. In 1864 Edward's responsibility for the losses and "double commissions" had been discovered and he had been dismissed. In 1865 the partners had called a meeting and discussed reorganization schemes; including for example, the introduction of new capital from friends and the admission of new partners. All were refused. There was only one alternative to liquidation: the formation of a company.

The Immediate Effects of the Crash

Fortunately, belying the surrounding press publicity, the crisis remained mainly financial in character.[21] It caused enormous discredit to the security markets and limited companies, but financial failures were surprisingly few. The bank rate remained at 10 percent for the next three months. It was then followed by "a period of prolonged quietude and 'sobering discipline' that took the Bank rate down to 2 percent by 25 July 1867, at which level it remained for nearly sixteen months."[22] In this, the failure of Overend Gurney was unlike most bank crashes (for instance, the City of Glasgow Bank in 1878).[23] These, past and present, have huge economic and social effects, beginning with depositors and customers of the bank and extending out into the local business community and beyond, creating further panic and business failures in their path. There was no such socioeconomic impact, as, quite surprisingly, the creditors were paid in full, plus interest where appropriate.

Ironically, the danger of trading with a limited company (or depositing with, if a financial institution) is the limited liability of its main providers of capital, its shareholders. It was this which, in 1866, caused the panic associated with the failure. Because of the issue of shares on which there were huge outstanding calls, Gurney's creditors could be paid off by making these calls. In these early limited liability companies, there was effectively no limited liability provided to shareholders. Although the convention must have been established because of prudence and a provision for unforeseen disasters, its implications could not have been recognized, since this was the first major case in which potentially unlimited calls had to be made. The possibility of this occurring again immediately made shares unmarketable. Contemporaries estimated that between £20m and £30m invested in shares was "in a state of suspended animation" because those with a large amount unpaid could not be sold.[24] Shareholders would not knowingly have agreed to the possibility of large calls simply to help creditors. The understanding about this potential for huge unpaid calls had been that it was simply a theoretical scenario which would not be invoked.

The failure of Overend Gurney raised wide ranging questions about that new type of company which had been quick to take advantage of limited liability, the "finance" company, questions which fuelled a lively public debate through the media. As one widely read Victorian periodical put it,

> It was an evil day for this country when the word "finance" and the undertakings known as "Finance Companies" became known in this country . . . almost invariably those investments of which the public understood least that were most sought after, namely, the shares of the finance companies.[25]

The panic did not spread further because fortunately, "the belief in their stability has been confined mostly to City men, who ought to have known better, and has hardly been shared in at all by country gentlemen, or by that numerous body of the middle classes who have a fixed but small income to live upon."[26] Lord Redesdale, in an extensively reported speech to the House of Lords on 14 May 1866, echoed this anonymous author as he described a number of reckless transactions.[27] One of these had involved establishment of a contracting company to construct a railway for £300,000. The proposed capital was to have been £300,000 of which £29,000 was subscribed (the balance liable to be paid by shareholders on call by the directors). Soon afterward the directors raised a further £960,000 to finance the project by means of issuing preference shares and loan stock. *Temple Bar* commented,

> The question will naturally arise, first as to what became of the balance of the money raised, and secondly, how will the subscribers to the original £29,000 feel at being thus swamped by the increased capital? Were these gentlemen consenting parties to the drowning of their own property, or had the directors the power to make ducks and drakes of their money?[28]

The Longer-Term Effects on Limited Liability

The crash and subsequent disclosures of promotional fraud and financial irregularities among limited companies significantly reduced the rate of company formation. There were only 799 formations between 1867 and 1869, for "Limited liability suddenly became extremely unpopular; it had 'palpably and plainly intensified a panic,'" stimulating a "universal outcry against all joint-stock companies."[29] Yet the increase in company enterprise after 1856 and the rising trade prosperity until the 1860s must not be attributed wholly to the introduction of limited liability. Although an incentive to increased enterprise, economic optimism would itself be an incentive to company formation. Indeed economic historians look on the development as largely unfavorable.[30]

Yet when a Parliamentary Committee of Inquiry was set up, many witnesses believed that the effects of the Limited Liability Acts were almost wholly good; so immediate efforts were made to repair those aspects which were responsible for the current problems.[31] Unsuccessful companies may be divided up between the purely speculative, the badly managed, and those which were purely or largely fraudulent. The latter may be separated between fraudulent formations and liquidations (or, of course, the two combined) and fraud during the actual operation of the company. An immediate effect of the freedom to form limited liability was the creation of companies that were never intended to come into existence but through which their promoters could make money selling their shares.[32] The defrauding of creditors by the establishment of companies with a very small amount of capital was also common.[33] Both types increased enormously after the passing of the 1862 Act.

Probably the single largest reason for the Overend Gurney "fraud" was the misleading prospectus. In 1865 this was common, prospectuses regularly "consisting of 'hypothetical' future profits" as, from 1847 to 1867, they were not subject to statutory controls.[34] The Joint Stock Act 1844 did require registration of prospectus, advertisements, and so forth, relating to the formation of a company; but, because it was "found to be very burdensome to the promoters of such companies," the requirement was repealed three years later. The Select Committee on the Limited Liability Acts examined the regulation of the prospectus, identifying two problems from testimonies before it: an inconsistency of material facts between a prospectus and a company's memorandum of association; and undisclosed contracts between a company and its promoters, effectively diverting funds raised by the share issue. Although the latter was at the heart of the Gurney "fraud," the committee made no recommendations. The final report hardly mentioned the prospectus.[35] However, Parliament did act, hastily drafting an amendment to the Companies Act 1867 requiring prospectuses to list all contracts made prior to its issue, together with names of the relevant parties and dates. There was considerable confusion over what constituted a contract and some promoters evaded the new requirement by means of a waiver clause.[36] The Act also made provision for companies to have the option of *un*limited liability for their directors. However, this had little effect as it was they who decided a company's constitution!

The Committee considered how to eradicate other types of fraud. Various remedies were suggested by witnesses; in particular, increasing the liability of directors and increasing the amount of publicly available information. The provisions of the 1856 Act, under which it was unnecessary to file annual accounts with the Registrar of Joint Stock Companies, were considered to be inadequate. Amending the 1867 Act allowed companies to reduce their nominal capital, thereby eliminating the threat of unmade calls. Unfortunately, the law requiring the publication of accounts and the required contents was not radically changed. Not until the Companies Act 1907 were disclosure requirements introduced.[37]

However, the problem of fraud largely cured itself within the next ten to fifteen years, when limited liability became effective (i.e., when the practice of leaving a large proportion of the nominal share capital uncalled ceased) and a higher level of commercial morality and a better quality of entrepreneur emerged.[38] The unlimited liability of a partner (partnerships were far the most common legal form of business entity) had always been a threat. There was a desire to eliminate this and create a fairer constituted business entity. It was probably the economic difficulties of the so-called Great Depression of 1873–96 that provided a change of attitude toward, and an increased incentive for, limited liability and its eventual acceptance.[39]

The Historical Perspective of the Crash

Clearly, the events surrounding the collapse of Overend Gurney may be seen to be a classic illustration of what is often described in print conversations as the bursting of a "speculative bubble," a phenomenon first publicized in 1852.[40] The theory has since been refined and developed, Minsky's "Financial Instability Hypothesis" being one of the more recent formulations.[41] This theory goes further than the simple irrationality of financial markets to whole economies and economic sectors.[42] Kindleberger has documented these crises globally, to argue that they occur about once every ten years.[43] They essentially take the following form: boom (probably fed by bank credit); overestimation of expected returns; euphoria and bandwagon effect; profit taking and the recognition that previous expectations were unjustified.[44] Finally, as price falls occur, panic sets in (again, the irrational herding instinct), revulsion and overall discrediting of the item, the subject of the boom in the first place. There are certain necessary conditions. The object (say, a tulip bulb) must be capable of making money (or thought to be), and visible on a sufficiently large scale to attract popular attention. It should be available to everyone or almost everyone.[45] The proponents of the theory identify fraud, swindles and other forms of dishonesty as being an important component: "In a boom, fortunes are made, individuals wax greedy, and swindlers come forward to exploit that greed."[46] It is not surprising that the most common items subject to manias and panics have been stocks, financial schemes and property, and that (given the easily induced sense of economic vulnerability at times of such crises) it should give rise to associated expressions of moral outrage.

The 1988–92 UK property boom-crash is a good recent example. People tried to borrow by way of mortgage as much as they could possibly obtain. How much they could borrow determined how much profit they could make. Many attempted to falsify details in their mortgage applications as banks and building societies (savings and loan associations) were swamped and often did not bother to check applications. It was estimated that four out of five mortgage applications were fraudulent in some way. Nor were just ordinary people involved. Estate agents, and other professionals involved in housing transactions were also involved in larger, more complex mortgage frauds.[47] The full "horrors" of this crisis, as with the Overend Gurney affair, were revealed to the public through the medium of the press, which readily acted as a channel for competing rhetorics of moral outrage, from professionals and experts to those from "ordinary" people fearing they were affected. This forms the heart of the "conversations" surrounding such crises, and sustains the panic and moral outrage associated with it.

Fraud also occurs during the final stage of the cycle, adding to the sense of popular outrage and betrayal. Kindleberger commented: "sheep to be shorn abound, and need only the emergence of effective swindlers to offer themselves as sacrifices." When corporations or individuals find themselves financially overstretched, they need to conceal the problem and fulfill expectations. For instance the late 1980s UK boom was followed by a recession in which companies tried to maintain their impression of growth and cover up losses by means of creative accounting and financial statement fraud. In Britain, Robert Maxwell's failure was the classic case; in the United States, developments surrounding Enron seem likely to encapsulate the typical case. The looting of a company's funds by its top executives and main shareholders when they realize its "time is up" is, of course, a rational act, and therefore expected to occur.[48] It also, equally rationally, arouses great rage among many observers when informed of the details via media presentations.

In Kindleberger's terms, the Overend Gurney crisis related to general limited liability. Its speculative peak occurred in July 1865 and the crisis in May 1866. Although it was not the first relating to securities, it affected the way in which businesses did business because of the way in which they were constituted, how they were viewed by a wider populace, and how the affair was reported. Since the 1860s the way in which business has been transacted has largely remained the same since that time, or at least until the 1990s and the beginnings of the information technology revolution. The latest product of this is the internet, which has profoundly affected how we communicate and do business. What is currently known as e-business is thought to become the norm for normal business in the foreseeable future.

The parallels between the Overend Gurney scandal and the development of the internet, e-business, and the rise and fall of dot-com stocks are obvious. About two years ago, business commentators in the developed world were openly wondering whether high-tech stocks were overvalued. The following comment is typical: "I know that the bubble in IT company stocks will burst. I just don't know when." Of course, it did, little more than days after this outburst from Hamish MacRae. Many dot-coms and high-tech stocks collapsed, others shrank enormously both in size and stock market value. Almost overnight, Silicon Valley in Northern California changed to an economically depressed region with high unemployment, rapidly falling property prices, and increasing negative equity. Its history parallels that of the Gold Country, which led to one of the greatest population movements in world history, but now mainly comprises "ghost towns" relying on the new industry of tourism.[49]

E-business has been remarkably slow to take off. Over three-quarters of businesses still either conduct no e-business or it accounts for less than 5 percent of their total. The reason, according to them, is fear that the internet is an unsafe medium.[50] For Victorians, it took twenty years before capital raised through company promotion again reached the level of the mid-1860s, much longer than the period of the original boom.[51] How long will it take for the internet to be seen to be safe and used for business as it could? As in the Victorian period, the media is likely to ensure that the original panic will remain part of the public consciousness by regularly reminding consumers of it, whenever an echo can be identified.

Notes

1. Novels also drew from discussions in contemporary newspapers. See Mrs. Henry Wood, *Oswald Cray* (London: Richard Bentley, 1871).

2. M. M. Postan, "Recent Trends in the Accumulation in Capital," *Economic History Review* (1935): 1–12.

3. Ibid.

4. Unfortunately, partly because of the Overend Gurney scandal and the sudden loss of popularity of limited liability the flotation was unsuccessful. See Paul Barnes and R. Firman, "The Vale of Belvoir and Newark Plaster Companies, Nottinghamshire 1864–73: A Case Study in Business History and Finance," *Transactions of the Thoroton Society of Nottinghamshire* (1994): 112–25; Paul Barnes and R. Firman, "The Loss of Popularity of Limited Liability Companies in Great Britain in 1866 and the Role of Financial Information: A Case History," *Financial History Review* 8, 1 (2001): 143–61.

5. *The Times,* 19 May 1865.

6. *The Times,* 14 May 1866.

7. H. Thring, *The Joint Stock Companies Act 1856* (London, 1856).

8. For an account of the debate see P. W. Ireland, "The Rise of the Limited Liability Company," *International Journal of the Sociology of Law* 12 (1984): 239–60.

9. Ibid.

10. This account is largely based on W. C. T. King, *History of the London Discount Market* (London: George Routledge, 1936), 238–63.

11. *The Bankers Magazine,* 1865, 25: 907–9

12. *The Economist,* 1865 845–46.

13. King, *London Discount Market,* 238–39.

14. "Short selling" is the selling of a company's shares and buying them later in that account and enables a dealer to make a profit in a bear market.

15. *The Times,* 10 May 1866.

16. H. A. Shannon, "The Limited Companies of 1866–1883," *Economic History Review* 4 (1933): 290–316, wittily refers to it as "that Black Friday when strong men were paralyzed and rich men fancied they were poor in an hour."

17. *The Bankers' Magazine,* 1866, 639.

18. *The Times,* 12 May 1866.

19. *The Bankers' Magazine,* 1867, 100–105; 239–44; 894–99, contain full reports of the proceedings.

20. See Stephanos Xenos, *Depredations; or, Overend Gurney & Co., and the Greek & Oriental Steam Navigation Company* (London, 1869). The author was one of Overend Gurney's largest creditors.

21. See, for example, *Pall Mall Gazette,* 22 December 1868.

22. King, *London Discount Market,* 244.

23. This involved fraud and mismanagement on a huge scale in which its directors had lent millions to family and friends with little regard for security. See George Robb, *White Collar Crime in Modern England: Financial Fraud and Business Morality, 1845–1929* (Cambridge: Cambridge University Press, 1992), 72–75; L. Rosenblum, "The Failure of the City of Glasgow Bank," *Accounting Review* 8 (1933): 285–91.

24. See Shannon, "Limited Companies."

25. Anon., "Finance, Frauds, and Failures," *Temple Bar,* June 1866, 381–95.

26. Ibid.

27. For example, *The Times,* 15 May 1866, 8.

28. Anon., "Finance, Frauds, and Failures."

29. B. C. Hunt, *The Development of the Business Corporation in England, 1800–1867* (London: Russell and Russell, 1969; first published 1936), 154.

30. H. A. Shannon, "The First Five Thousand Limited Companies," *Economic History Review* 3 (1932): 396–424.

31. Similar views were repeated in an 1877 inquiry. G. Todd, "Some Aspects of Joint Stock Companies, 1844–1900," *Economic History Review* 3 (1932).

32. Many companies were deliberately set up so that after a short fictitious existence they could be wound up, the "birth and burial expenses" going to their promoters and professional allies. See Wood, *Oswald Cray.*

33. Todd, "Joint Stock Companies."

34. Hunt, *Business Corporation*, 327. A typical prospectus is discussed in Paul Barnes and R. Firman, "Vale of Belvoir and Newark Plaster Companies"; Paul Barnes and R. Firman, "Limited Liability Companies."

35. *Sessional Papers*, House of Commons, 1867, Report of the Select Committee on Limited Liability Acts.

36. Robb, *White Collar Crime*, 98.

37. The accounting and auditing provisions introduced by the Joint Stock Companies Act 1844 were extended in 1856 but relegated to an optional appendix and later reproduced as Table A to the 1862 consolidating act. The effect was that no legal requirement existed for the remainder of the century to provide accounts, either for shareholders or public inspection, although many companies used Table A, thereby imposing directors to provide shareholders with them. See L. W. Hein, *The British Companies Acts and the Practice of Accountancy, 1844–1962* (New York: Arno Press, 1978).

38. Ibid. However, although the occurrence of frauds clearly did fall during this period, Todd does not justify these assertions.

39. Although the magnitude of the severity of the depression is debated, "the economic problems of the last quarter of the nineteenth century led to a serious decline in the confidence of the British businessman." See W. G. Hynes, *The Economics of Empire: Britain, Africa, and the New Imperialism, 1870–95* (London: Longman, 1979), 8.

40. C. Mackay, *Memoirs of Extraordinary Popular Delusions and the Madness of Crowds* (London: L. C. Page, 1932).

41. H. P. Minsky, "The Financial Instability Hypothesis: Capitalistic Processes and the Behaviour of the Economy," in *Financial Crises: Theory, History, and Policy*, ed. C. P. Kindleberger and J-P. Laffargue, 13–29 (Cambridge: Cambridge University Press, 1982).

42. Ibid.

43. C. P. Kindleberger, *Manias, Panics, and Crashes: A History of Financial Crises*, 3rd. ed. (New York: Wiley, 1996).

44. In Keynes's terms, the "biggest fool." J. M. Keynes, *The General Theory of Employment, Interest, and Money* (London: Macmillan, 1978), particularly chapter 12, 147–64.

45. For a more recent analysis of this see P. M. Garber, "Tulipmania," in *Speculative Bubbles, Speculative Attacks, and Policy Switching*, ed. Robert P. Flood and Peter M. Garber (London: MIT Press, 1994).

46. Kindleberger, *Manias, Panics, and Crashes*, 69.

47. Michael Clarke, *Business Crime: Its Nature and Control* (London: Polity Press, 1990).

48. For a "rational economic man" analysis, see G. A. Ackerlof and P. M. Romer, "Looting: The Economic Underworld of Bankruptcy for Profit," *Brookings Papers on Economic Activity* 2: 1–73.

49. Increasing California's population from 7,000 nonnative inhabitants in 1848 to 100,000 four years later. See Mick Sinclair, *Essential Explorer: California* (Basingstoke: AA Publishing, 1993), 26.

50. See CBI and The Fraud Advisory Panel, *Cybercrime Survey, 2001: Making the Information Superhighway Safe for Business* (CBI, 2001).

51. J. H. Clapham, *An Economic History of Modern Britain: Machines and National Rivalries (1887–1914)*, 2 vols. (Cambridge: Cambridge University Press, 1951), 2: 358.

5

Larceny: Debating the "Boundless Region of Dishonesty"

GRAHAM FERRIS

Introduction

This is an essay bringing together different contemporary reports of legal events, in order to throw light upon several questions that a focus on either set of reports alone may leave in shadow.[1] The two sets of reports concerned are legal reports and newspaper reports. The legal event is the trial for larceny of Thomas Ashwell at the Leicester Winter Assize in 1885 and subsequent legal proceedings. The issues that are illuminated are the invisibility in newspaper reports of such issues as the bounds of legitimate judicial behavior and the desirability of legal development; and the obscuring of the importance of the individual judge's actions in legal reports.

The Reports

Reports of legal proceedings produced for the specialist audience of legal practitioners are among the oldest printed works in Britain.[2] Law reports were originally commercially published; in 1865 an official series of law reports was inaugurated. The official series of law reports has never displaced private market law reporting, though. The systematic publishing of reports of criminal trials for the general public dates from the early eighteenth century, with the most important eighteenth-century series of such reports, the proceedings of the Old Bailey Sessions, currently being made available on the internet.[3]

The coverage of the local criminal justice system was a mainstay of the provincial press in the second half of the nineteenth century, regularly feeding into the national press.[4] The local assize was a major social occasion, as well as being a legal ritual with powerful overtones of social control.[5] It was the local manifestation of the "circuit" system, under which the London-based High Court Judges toured the country to preside over trials for serious crimes. The Grand Jury and petty juries which were part of the assize ritual also provided opportunities for respectable men of sufficient wealth to take their part in dispensing criminal justice in their locality. Local (and national) newspapers would have agents at the assize (usually trained barristers), and the report of the assize was a regular feature of their coverage.[6]

Invisible Issues and the Invisible Judge

Leicester had two local newspapers in 1885, the *Leicester Daily Mercury* and the *Leicester Journal*. Both covered the assize (including Thomas Ashwell's trial) and generally coverage in each publication was extremely similar. Both gave prominence to the congratulatory speeches given by the presiding High Court Judge to the Grand Juries for the County and Borough. Both listed the Grand Jury memberships and then reported the presiding Judge's speech; which commended the jurors for their attendance and the relative absence of serious crime from the lists. In 1885, for instance, the trial of a father for the negligent manslaughter of his daughter was the most prominent case reported in terms of column inches.[7]

As the law reports of the Ashwell case show, the High Court Judges of England and Wales could not reach even a majority agreement over the case.[8] The case opened up issues of the limits of appropriate judicial activity in criminal law, and of the very nature of larceny, the key offense against property in the substantive criminal law. Despite the local connection and extensive reporting of the original trial, these issues simply did not break the surface of the newspaper reporting.[9] Criminal trials may have been ready copy, a source of entertainment, or even of morality tales, for the local press. However, they clearly were not seen as a source of insight into conflicts within the criminal justice system. Even when the local Recorder was unceremoniously rebuffed, for treating *R v Ashwell* as a legal authority that could be used to punish what must have been a fairly common piece of opportunistic dishonesty by a workman, the newspaper reports merely recorded the voices of the law's oracles without question.[10] Neither open and unresolved judicial disagreement on matters of principle, nor the slighting of local authority by London, could elicit any curiosity over of the nature of the central judiciary's role in local newspaper reports.

Just as the local reports obscured questions about judicial lawmaking in criminal law, so law reports obscured the active judicial preparation of the "case" of *R v Ashwell* from the raw material of Ashwell's indictment. The trial judge, Mr. Justice Denman, reserved the case for the Court for Crown Cases Reserved (henceforth CCR). By so acting he was referring the question of law to the court that had the greatest power (bar the House of Lords), to make a declaration of the criminal law.[11] If we are to understand the dynamics of judicial lawmaking in the Victorian criminal law we will need to examine very closely how Denman came to his decision to refer *R v Ashwell* to the CCR. To this end the newspaper accounts of the trial have been vital in recreating the events that led to the creation of the "case."

The Place of *R v Ashwell* in the History of Larceny

R v Ashwell has been identified as the epitome of developments in the offense of larceny, and of the barren nature of the classic law of larceny.[12] The case concerned a dispute over a sovereign, and yet saw the fourteen judges of England and Wales divided equally. Seven thought Ashwell's conduct constituted larceny, and seven thought it did not. This judicial discord was extremely unusual. It is unique in the 273 decisions of the CCR reported in the official law reports between 1865 and 1908 and the author is aware of only one other example in the nineteenth century.[13] The vast majority of decisions of the CCR were decided by the usual bench of five judges (250 out of the 273), and the majority of these were unanimously decided (239).[14] The legal issues raised by *R v Ashwell* had already caused notable judicial disagreements in *R v Middleton* twelve years earlier, and would lead to the Irish Court for Crown Cases Reserved dividing five to four ten years later in *R v Hehir*.[15]

To understand the nature of the judicial disagreement here, and thus the different conceptions of larceny and of the role for judges as lawmakers that this disagreement indicated, it is necessary to start with a conception of the nature of larceny. Larceny was a very old offense in England, dating back at least to the twelfth century. Larceny was a felony, and for most of this long history, larceny of property worth a shilling or more (grand larceny) was a capital offense.[16] Until 1916 there was no statutory definition of larceny, just the words found in indictments, learned books, and the reported judgments of the courts.[17] From these sources the elements of the old common-law offense of larceny can be identified. There had to be property capable of being stolen, and that property had to belong to someone other than the thief. The property must have been taken and carried away by the thief. The thief had to have taken the property against the will of the owner, and the taking had to have been in bad faith.

Probably the most influential explanation of the historical development of larceny has been that of Fletcher, first advanced in 1976.[18] Fletcher advanced the thesis that there had been a shift in juristic understanding of the law of larceny in the late eighteenth and early nineteenth centuries. He identified the impetus for this shift in the eighteenth-century Enlightenment, which introduced a subjective understanding of the nature of the offense.[19] The triumph of a newer subjective approach left the older approach, based on manifest criminality, incomprehensible to jurists. Subsequent changes were largely the working out of the consequences of the new principles of liability.[20] For nineteenth- and twentieth-century jurists the old law of larceny was merely chaotic.[21] The rational principles that lay behind the old law were invisible to jurists, equipped as they were with conceptual tools and preconceptions that were incompatible with that law.[22]

In Fletcher's narrative, *R v Ashwell* was a part of the uncomprehending remaking of the law of larceny by courts engaged in a major expansion of criminal liability.[23] Nineteenth-century courts lost sight of the rationale behind the old law of larceny, which distinguished sharply between public harms (amenable to criminal sanction) and private harms (amenable to civil redress).[24] The deprivation of property rights was not the primary organizing principle that lay behind the old distinctions between larceny and kindred crimes of dishonesty. The organizing principle was rather the nature of the relationships violated, or endangered.[25]

The Origins of the Case of *R v Ashwell*

Friday was payday for Edward Keogh, and when he left the gasworks on Friday 9 January 1885 he made for the Avenue Inn, where he could warm his body and revive his spirits. Thomas Ashwell was also in the Avenue Inn on that night, and he called Edward into the yard. There, he asked Edward to lend him a shilling until the next day. Edward, his wages in his pocket, agreed and passed him a coin. Thomas always insisted that the coin he received that night was the shilling Edward had agreed to lend him; but Edward lost a sovereign that night, and became convinced that he had given it to Thomas in the darkness of the yard.

When Edward got home that Friday night he realized his loss. That same night, he hurried back to the pub, but the landlord, Mr. Wortley, convinced him that he had handed over only a shilling and not a sovereign in payment for his drink. The next morning Edward called on Thomas, and offered to allow him to keep five shillings out of the sovereign if he would only let Edward have the rest of it back. Thomas was infuriated by this approach and denied having received more than the shilling he had asked for. That afternoon

Edward saw Thomas extremely drunk, and felt convinced that it was at his expense. He contacted the police and reported Thomas for stealing the sovereign.

When Police Constable Cox questioned Thomas about the events of 9 January he insisted that he had not received a sovereign from Edward. However (as related at the trial), PC Cox was lucky enough to overhear Thomas confessing to a man named Hodges, while he was crouched behind a low wall. When, like a jack-in-the-box, Cox popped up from behind the wall and confronted Thomas with his admission, Thomas was speechless. There was other evidence that cast suspicion on Thomas. Mrs. Wortley, the landlady of the Avenue Inn, remembered Thomas returning and changing a sovereign on the night of 9 January. Her report was supported by one Scotton, who had been with Thomas when he came into the public house on the second occasion. Scotton testified that Thomas had repaid him a shilling loan, with sixpence interest that night.

On 23 January 1885 Thomas was indicted and tried for larceny at the Leicester Winter Assize. Denman, the judge presiding over Crown business (criminal trials), took an interest in Thomas's case *before* the trial, an interest sparked by the allegations contained in the bill of indictment, which was presented to the Grand Jury. Denman "recommended" the Grand Jury to find the bill true (so that Thomas would have to face trial) "as it was a curious case and involved a point of law which he thought should be decided."[26] The judge requested a barrister, Mr. Sills, to watch the case for the prisoner and argue the case on the point of law. Thomas still denied ever having received a sovereign from Edward, and in conducting his own defense he called a witness, a young man by the name of Ludd. But Ludd did not appear, and the jury had only the unsworn word of Thomas that he had a sovereign in his pocket when he borrowed the shilling from Edward. The jury did not believe him. The judge put three questions to the jury, and upon hearing their answers, declared that they amounted to a guilty verdict. However, the judge felt that the case raised "a very nice and delicate point" of law, which he intended to reserve for consideration by the CCR in London. Therefore, he ordered that Thomas be released, bound over to appear for judgment if so called.[27]

R v Ashwell came up for consideration before five judges on 21 March 1885.[28] The judges could not agree whether the case as stated amounted to larceny. Therefore, the case was heard again on 13 June 1885, before fourteen judges.[29] The judges were still divided, full judgments were written, and delivered on 5 December 1885. The result was seven judges in favor of the conviction standing, and seven judges in favor of quashing the conviction.[30] This meant that the conviction stood, as there was no majority in favor of overturning it. Thomas was guilty of larceny because there was no majority of the judges willing to hold that he was *not* guilty.

Thomas was called to appear at the Winter Assize in Leicester, and he duly presented himself for sentence.[31] The presiding judge was Justice Manisty, who had held that Thomas was not guilty of larceny at the CCR, and had consulted with Mr. Justice Denman over the appropriate sentence to award. His speech was recorded in the *Leicester Journal* on 29 January 1886:

> Considering that it was a very doubtful point, and that the temptation was put in prisoner's way by the sovereign being handed to him instead of a shilling; considering also that the case had been hanging over him a considerable time, and must have caused him some annoyance and anxiety; considering further the great difference of opinion there was as to whether or not he had come under the criminal law—although he certainly did what was not honest, as he could easily have returned the 19s.—and considering also that he had conducted himself in a satisfactory manner, under all the circumstances of the case he thought justice might be done by binding him over in his own recognisance in £20 to appear to receive judgment when called upon.

However, Thomas had one more question to ask of the law before he disappeared from the historical record: would the conviction interfere with his pension? Justice Manisty (no doubt having no idea as to the answer to this question) fell back on the majesty of his position as the human representative of the law and replied: "You are now at liberty, and had better stand down." Thomas understood the implied threat and left with his question unresolved.

The Legal "Issue"

The point of law that had attracted Denman's attention lay in the requirement that property be taken by someone who had the necessary bad faith at the time he took it. Consider the three questions that he put to the jury at Thomas's trial. The first question was: had Edward Keogh given Thomas Ashwell a sovereign?[32] If the jury believed Thomas's account then they clearly would have concluded that he had not stolen anything. The second question was: "did the prisoner, at the time he received the money, know it was a sovereign and that the prosecutor handed it to him in mistake?" The third question was: "did he discover it was a sovereign soon enough to restore it to the prosecutor without any difficulty, and did he apparently appropriate it to his own use, knowing that the prosecutor only intended to lend him a shilling?" The jury had answered:

that prosecutor handed prisoner a sovereign by mistake, but [they] had a doubt as to whether prisoner knew what coin it was exactly at the time . . . [and] that prisoner appropriated the money, having found what it was early enough to have returned it without difficulty.[33]

On the basis of these answers there were two possible reasons why Thomas Ashwell might not have been guilty of larceny.

First, he had not *taken* the sovereign from Edward Keogh. Thomas had received the coin *from* Edward.[34] Although Edward had not realized which coin he was handing over, it was far from apparent that Thomas had acquired the coin against the will of Edward. Second, even if such a receipt of a coin was a "taking," at law the jury had not found any bad faith at the time of the taking, unless the act of taking could be deferred to apply to Thomas's actions after the physical transfer of the coin.[35] Thomas seemed to have taken innocently, and been in bad faith only after he discovered that he had been given a sovereign rather than a shilling by mistake.

R v Ashwell and Judicial Lawmaking

The events of January 1885 are of special interest, beyond the inherent interest that they hold for the history of social attitudes to the police, and the operation of the criminal justice system of the late nineteenth century, revealing a complex layer of criminal conversation in which the press played a significant role. The procedure for the reservation of a case for the CCR needs explanation. There was no right for a defendant to reserve a case to the CCR, the process was not by appeal. The decision to reserve a case for the CCR was made by the judge. A case would only be reserved following a conviction, and it was common practice to request a jury to give a "special verdict," by which was meant a jury would specify what facts it had found to be proved by answering questions asked by the judge.[36] This procedure clearly allowed a judge to select and prepare cases for the CCR with a view to encouraging legal development in an area of law in a particular direction.[37]

A role for judges as creators of law is recognized by the English legal system, but as a secondary duty. The primary duty of judges is to resolve whatever dispute is brought before them, and it is generally assumed that legal development is a by-product of the execution of this duty. The system for referral to the CCR allowed a more active role to a judge interested in legal development. He still needed a suitable case to be brought before him. However, given the raw material of accusation, the bill of indictment, and cooperative grand and petty juries, a judge could select and refine a case for referral to the CCR. The period 1875–1900 was largely one of legislative quiescence in the field of larceny.[38] One possibility opened up by an examination of *R v Ashwell* is that during this legislative lull, some members of the judiciary were actively seeking to reformulate the law of larceny.

The Historical Background

The legal development identified by Fletcher as the metamorphosis of larceny began in the courts. In 1779 the precursor of the CCR[39] decided, in *R v Pear,* that the hirer of a horse who had entered into a contract of hire with the intention of not returning the horse could be convicted of larceny.[40] This type of larceny became known as "larceny by a trick." The importance of *R v Pear* for the future of larceny was threefold. First, it marked a very considerable extension of capital criminal liability by judicial decision.[41] Second, it created apparent anomalies in the law of larceny where the new form of liability did not extend.[42] Third, it created a problem of demarcation between the crime of larceny and the crime of obtaining property by false pretences, a misdemeanor created by statute in 1757.[43]

In the nineteenth century Parliament created offenses of dishonest retention of property, complementary to larceny's prohibition of the dishonest acquisition of property. In *R v Bazeley* in 1799 it was held that an employee who received property from a third party on behalf of his employer and kept it for himself was not guilty of larceny of that property.[44] Within months Parliament responded by the passage of a statute that made such an employee's actions criminal as embezzlement.[45] In *R v Walsh* in 1812 it was held that a stockbroker who absconded with bank notes, obtained by cashing a check written by his principal for the purpose of funding the purchase of stock, was not guilty of larceny.[46] Again the legislative response was effected within months.[47] In 1857 the legislature made the conversion of property by bailees generally criminal.[48] These legislative changes, while respecting the integrity of the common law of larceny, made the requirement of a taking in larceny seem anomalous.

The judiciary was also active in the nineteenth century. In the seventeenth century Hale had been clear that a person who found lost property could not be liable for larceny.[49] A finder of lost property did not take the property from the owner, because the owner had already lost possession of the property concerned. By 1848 the judges had decided that if at the time of finding property a person realized that it would be possible to trace the owner and return the property, then that person could be found guilty of larceny for a dishonest finding of lost property.[50]

Chapter 5

The Context of *R v Ashwell*

In 1873 the CCR decided the case of George Middleton, who had gone to the Post Office with the intention of withdrawing ten shillings from his account at the Post Office Savings Bank.[51] To enable him to do this, George had obtained a warrant for the payment of the ten shillings. The clerk mistakenly put £8 16s. 6d. on the counter, which George picked up and kept. George was tried, and convicted, for larceny, but the presiding judge reserved the case for the CCR. There were obvious difficulties with holding that George had taken the money against the owner's will, as required for a conviction of larceny, because the clerk had deliberately given him the money. George Middleton's case was referred by the original court of five judges to an enlarged court of fifteen judges. The conviction was upheld by a majority of eleven to four. However, of those eleven three decided the case on the ground that a Post Office clerk's authority was limited in a peculiar manner by statute, and one took the view that George had taken the money from the clerk when he picked it up from the counter, a view not shared by any other judge. Thus only seven of the fifteen judges held that generally in such circumstances there was a "taking" for the purposes of larceny. Furthermore, the joint judgment of these seven judges indicated that it was essential that an accused acquire possession of the property allegedly stolen with the required bad faith. To quote from their joint judgment:[52]

> We admit that the case is indistinguishable from the one supposed in the argument, of a person handing to a cabman a sovereign by mistake for a shilling; but after carefully weighing the opinions to the contrary, we are decidedly of opinion that the property in the sovereign would not vest in the cabman, and that the question whether the cabman was guilty of larceny or not, would depend upon this, whether he, at the time he took the sovereign, was aware of the mistake, and had then the guilty intent, the *animus furandi*.

Denman was one of the judges who subscribed to this judgment.

As described by Fletcher, the cases of *R v Middleton* and *R v Ashwell* are the contribution of the last quarter of the nineteenth century to the metamorphosis of larceny. The joint judgment of the seven judges in *R v Middleton* did extend the law of larceny in the manner described by Fletcher.[53] However, the dissenting judgments do not suggest a judiciary that had lost all understanding of the rationale of the old law.[54] The vital role of *R v Pear*, and the cases that followed it, in extending the boundaries of larceny was both recognized and subjected to criticism.[55] The key distinguishing features of the old law of larceny, as identified by Fletcher, were defended by Baron Bramwell for essentially the same reasons as those urged by Fletcher.[56]

Larceny: Debating the "Boundless Region of Dishonesty" 79

This defense was not the last gasp of a traditional understanding that was almost lost; four of the fifteen judges in *R v Middleton* dissented in defense of the old law, and four delivered judgments based on reasoning that did not accept the reasoning in the joint judgment.[57] Furthermore, Bramwell's reasoning would be adopted by judges in both *R v Ashwell* and *R v Hehir*.[58] In addition to reasoning based on the nature of larceny, three other reasons were advanced for rejecting the reasoning of the majority in *R v Middleton*. First, that the judges did not have the authority to implement such a change.[59] Second, that the general rule of the common law was that it did not assist those that put themselves in harm's way.[60] Third, that larceny was restrictively defined because historically the punishment for grand larceny was death, and the statutory change in the punishment did not alter the common law definition of the crime.[61]

The Law after *R v Ashwell*

There was no majority judgment in *R v Ashwell*. Those judges who refused to affirm the conviction acted on the basis that they were following established authority. The impact of *R v Ashwell* could not be known until an opportunity arose for the questions raised by the judicial deadlock to be answered. Providentially Leicester provided such a case within weeks of the decision in *R v Ashwell* being delivered. The recorder of Leicester, reserved *R v Flowers* for the CCR in January 1886.[62] Charles Flowers had received his wages from his employer's clerk, and discovered they were threepence short. Charles had taken his empty wage packet to the clerk, and requested the three pennies he was owed. The clerk mistakenly handed him another man's wage packet, which contained 7s. 11½d., and put in Charles's hand the three pennies he had asked for. The jury found that Charles had not realized he was being given another man's wage packet, and wages, when the clerk had handed it to him. However, upon realizing the mistake he had decided fraudulently to appropriate the money. The recorder directed that this amounted to a verdict of guilty of larceny. He relied upon *R v Ashwell*, which he held decided that an innocent receipt of property followed by a fraudulent appropriation of that property was larceny at common law. However, given the uncertain status of *R v Ashwell* he reserved the case for the CCR.

When *R v Flowers* was heard by the CCR in February 1886, this treatment of the decision in *R v Ashwell* was decisively and unanimously rejected by a court of five judges, two of whom had given or subscribed to judgments confirming Ashwell's conviction three months previously. The CCR quashed Flowers's conviction on the grounds that it was not larceny to receive property innocently and subsequently fraudulently appropriate the same. There had to be a simultaneous taking of possession with a guilty mind, and that had not happened in Charles Flower's case. The difficulty, not touched upon by the CCR in *R v Flowers*, is to identify any relevant difference in the facts of *R v Ashwell* and *R v Flowers* which could justify treating the cases differently. In both cases the accused received an object, when it was intended that some other object should have been given to him. In both cases he accepted the object, without realizing there had been a mistake. In both cases when he subsequently realized what had happened he kept the object. In both cases the accused acted in bad faith in keeping the object. Clearly, those judges that had confirmed Thomas's conviction but quashed Charles's conviction did not wish to take advantage of Charles's case to consolidate any extension of the law effected by *R v Ashwell*.

An innocent receipt due to a mutual mistake followed by a dishonest appropriation was considered once again, by the Irish Court for Crown Cases Reserved in *R v Hehir* in 1895.[63] The judges were divided, and a majority held that there was no larceny in these circumstances. The case is notable for the force of statements by Mr. Justice O'Brien in support of the traditional concept of larceny, and against any aspiration to transform the law of larceny into a law forbidding dishonest appropriation:[64]

> It [Hehir's behavior] remains in that category of moral transgression, as to which the law has not hitherto given effect to the views of such as think to compass the sea by undertaking the impossible task of trying to push out the confines of crime into the boundless region of dishonesty.

However, his judgment was not characteristic of the judgments in *R v Hehir*. The most important factor for the five judges in the majority was judicial reluctance to undertake a reform of the law so radical that it was more appropriately performed by the legislature.[65] That *R v Ashwell* did not effect an extension of liability for larceny was confirmed, *sub silentio*, by the legislature in 1916. The Larceny Act 1916 confirmed the correctness of the joint judgment of seven judges in *R v Middleton*, but not the further extension which was necessary to confirm Ashwell's conviction.

Conclusion

It has been established that the "case" of *R v Ashwell* was created by Denman, and that he must have been aware that by reserving the case he was inviting the CCR to extend larceny beyond its traditional boundaries. None of the judges who supported the conviction even proposed that the basis of liability for larceny should be dishonesty. All suggestions that a desire to criminalize dishonest conduct *per se* was at work were made by those opposing any extension of larceny's boundaries to meet the case.[66] This disinclination to ground their judgments upon the moral equities of the case may have had its origin in the castigation of such an approach to criminal liability by Baron Bramwell in *R v Middleton* when he asserted: "There is more doubt in the case than has appeared to some, who seem to me to reason thus: The prisoner was as bad as a thief (which I deny), and being as bad as a thief ought to be treated as one (which I deny also)."[67]

This judicial reticence in the CCR is all the more remarkable in Denman, a subscriber to the joint judgment in *R v Middleton*, who was reported in the *Leicester Daily Mercury* 23 January 1885 as telling the Grand Jury that the charge:

> Raised a point in the criminal law which had never been decided.... There was no evidence so far as he could see, that Ashwell knew at the time he received the money that it was a sovereign, but his conduct afterwards was very bad. He could not find any case to meet it, but in his judgment it ought to be a criminal offence, although he thought it very doubtful that it was according to the law.

In contrast to this newspaper report, in his judgment in the CCR Denman remembered that at the trial: "if I had been compelled then and there to give a decision, I was inclined to think that the case was covered by authority."[68]

In his statement of the case to the CCR Denman attributed to the jury the opinion that "if it were competent to them consistently with these findings and with the evidence to find the prisoner guilty, they meant to do so."[69] However, there is no mention in the newspaper reports of the jury indicating any such sentiment. It is tempting, in the light of the reported address to the Grand Jury, to view the judge as foisting his own moral judgment and resulting inclination to punish onto the jury. Several judges opposed to extensions of larceny in the late nineteenth century ascribed exactly such a motive to their brethren.[70] In both *R v Middleton* and *R v Hehir* some of the judges advocating an expansive approach to larceny accepted that such a motivation was an appropriate one for judicial decision making.[71]

On the basis of a more careful consideration of *R v Ashwell*, and *R v Middleton*, it seems the last quarter of the nineteenth century did not evidence the loss of understanding of the old law of larceny argued for by Fletcher.[72] Fletcher's thesis is persuasive over a broad historical perspective. However, a more detailed consideration of the developments in the late nineteenth century suggest the theory needs refining, or maybe even reformulating. In particular Fletcher has mischaracterized *R v Ashwell* as part of a linear development of ever increasing liability. A consideration of the case within its context suggests it should rather be viewed as a conversation resulting in the drawing of a line beyond which the judiciary were not willing to extend liability.

The newspaper reports never hint at any disquiet over the process of justice to which Thomas Ashwell was an unwilling party. His guilt appears to be as unproblematic an issue as the astounding good fortune of PC Cox in overhearing exactly the conversation he required to arrest and charge the uncooperative suspect. Certainly, those theories of legal change that look to moral or social panic as the motor of extensions of the criminal law receive at best negative support from *R v Ashwell*.[73] There is no evidence of any social anxiety either being created or reflected in the newspaper reports. When the result of the CCR's consideration was reported in the *Leicester Journal* it was headed: "A Curious Appeal Case," and was immediately followed by a report headed: "Important Appeal Case."[74] The second case concerned the application of the Employers Liability Act 1880 to subcontracting miners under the "butty" system. Thus, the reporting of the case reveals moral or social aplomb, rather than moral or social panic, over Thomas's behavior. In this instance a lack of any moral or social panic correlated with a judicial refusal to extend criminal liability.

No punishment was inflicted on Thomas Ashwell. In *R v Flowers* the CCR decisively rejected the opportunity to endorse any extension of liability suggested by the confirmation of the conviction in *R v Ashwell*. Perhaps the case should be seen as a triumph for the rule of law over a judicial urge to chasten wrongdoers. More ominous is the possibility that the case supports the view that such a judicial urge exists, and has an impact upon the development of the criminal law.

Notes

1. Thus, a similar technique to that used by Oldham who compares manuscript notes with published law reports in James Oldham, "Detecting Non-Fiction: Sleuthing among Manuscript Case Reports for What Was Really Said," in *Law Reporting in Britain*, ed. C. Stebbings, 44–80 (London: Hambledon Press, 1995), but with the hope of the illumination being reciprocal.

2. See J. H. Baker, *An Introduction to English Legal History*, 4th ed. (London: Butterworths, 2002), 181; 192–93.

3. http://www.oldbaileyonline.org/.

4. Following removal of punitive taxation on newspapers in 1853 and 1869.

5. See for example the comments on the impact of the local assize in Mrs. Henry Wood, *Mrs. Halliburton's Troubles* (London: Richard Bentley, 1865).

6. Judith Rowbotham and Kim Stevenson, "Causing a Sensation: Media and Legal Representations of Bad Behavior," in *Behaving Badly: Visible Crime, Social Panics, and Legal Responses—Victorian and Modern Parallels*, ed. Judith Rowbotham and Kim Stevenson, 31–46 (Aldershot: Ashgate, 2003).

7. *Leicester Daily Mercury,* 23 January; 24 January 1885; *Leicester Journal,* 30 January 1885.

8. *R v Ashwell* (1885) 16 QBD 190; (1885) 16 Cox CC 1.

9. *Leicester Journal,* 11 December 1885.

10. See discussion of *R v Flowers* below; *Leicester Journal,* 5 March 1886.

11. The precise force of a CCR decision within the doctrine of precedent was never adequately determined: see *R v Humphrey* [1898] 1 QBD 875 and *R v Hehir* [1895] 2 IR 709 at 756.

12. G. P. Fletcher, "The Metamorphosis of Larceny," *Harvard Law Review* 98, 469 (1976): 449–530; Eighth Report of the Criminal Law Revision Committee, 1966, "*Theft and Related Offenses,*" (Cmnd. 2977) at paras. 15, 23–24.

13. *R v Palmer,* an unreported case considered in 1827.

14. In a very small number of cases (seven), and for no apparent reason, four or six judges sat. Five cases were determined by a bench of six judges on a single day on 11 November 1865, one case was decided by a bench of six judges in 1898, and one case was decided by a bench of four judges in 1904. Therefore, between 1865 and 1908 (when the CCR was abolished) the full bench was considered necessary only on sixteen occasions.

15. (1873) LR 2 CCR 38 and [1895] 2 IR 709.

16. The distinction between grand and petty larceny was abolished and replaced by "simple larceny" in 1827: see 7 & 8 Geo. 4 c. 29 ss. 2 and 3.

17. Larceny Act 1916 s. 1.

18. See Fletcher, "Metamorphosis of Larceny," 472, 474, 481, 483, 497. Fletcher has defended his thesis in G. Fletcher, "Manifest Criminality, Criminal Intent, and the Metamorphosis of Lloyd Weinreb," *Yale Law Review* 319 (1980): 413–29; and in G. Fletcher, *Rethinking Criminal Law* (Boston: Little, Brown, 1978).

19. Fletcher, "Metamorphosis of Larceny," 502–3.

20. Ibid., 473.

21. Ibid., 469–70. See also J. Gibson on the law of larceny in *R v Hehir* [1895] 2 IR 709 at 722.

22. Ibid., 473.

23. Ibid., 514.

24. Ibid., 473.

25. Ibid., 474.

26. *Leicester Journal,* 30 January 1885. The report continues: "His own conviction was that the case was one of larceny, because when the prosecutor parted with the sovereign, he did not mean to do so, and therefore he never had the sovereign intentionally out of his possession."

27. *R v Ashwell* (1885) 16 QBD 190 is inaccurate in reporting the date of the trial as January 1883, the report in Cox's Criminal Law Cases at (1885) 16 Cox CC 1 gives the correct date for the trial. I have preferred the *Leicester Journal*'s report to the case as

stated by Denman J. and reported at (1885) 16 QBD 190 at 191 because the case stated makes it appear that the receipt of the sovereign was not disputed at the trial. Ashwell based his entire defense on this point. Mr. Sills argued that even if the prosecution proved its entire case there would still be no larceny.

28. The five judges were Lord Chief Justice Coleridge, Justice Grove, Justice Lopes, Justice Stephen, and Justice Cave. See *R v Ashwell* (1885) 16 Cox CC 1 at 3. The report in Cox gives the dates of the two hearings and the membership of the first court; the report at *R v Ashwell* (1885) 16 QBD 190 omits any reference to the first hearing.

29. The fourteen judges were Lord Chief Justice Coleridge, Justices Cave, Day, Denman, Field, Grove, Hawkins, Manisty, Mathew, Smith, Stephen, and Wills, and Barons Huddleston and Pollock.

30. The headnote in *R v Ashwell* (1885) 16 Cox CC 1 omits Justice Mathew from the list of judges in favor of quashing the conviction.

31. *Leicester Journal*, 29 January 1886.

32. *Leicester Journal*, 30 January 1885.

33. Ibid. The ellipse is an interjection by Justice Denman: "That is just the difficulty in the case."

34. *R v Ashwell* (1885) 16 QBD 190; Sills in argument at 192 and 195, Smith J. at 196, Cave J. at 200, Matthew J. at 205, Stephen J. at 206.

35. This was the effect of the reasoning of those judges who affirmed Thomas's conviction: see ibid., Cave J. at 203–4; and Coleridge C. J. at 225.

36. The practice of judicial interrogation of juries upon the grounds of their verdict has long been discontinued. However, there is a recommendation in Lord Justice Auld, *The Review of the Criminal Courts* (2001), to reinstate a version of the special verdict to allow appeals from "perverse" jury verdicts; see chap. 5 para. 97; and chap. 11 paras. 43–45, recommendations 249 and 250.

37. This ability of the judiciary to reserve cases in order to allow a disputed point to be resolved was recognized and acted upon by the judiciary in an open manner: see *R v Lillyman* [1896] 2 QBD 167 at 168 n. 1, 173–74, 177, 178, in which Hawkins J. successfully used the reservation of a case to effect a change to the law of evidence and thereby overturned sixty years of judicial "usage" on the point.

38. Larceny Act 1861 (24 & 25 Vict. c. 96) and the Larceny Act 1916 (6 & 7 Geo. 5 c. 50) were both major pieces of legislation. However, they were both primarily consolidating statutes, concerned to restate rather than alter the law.

39. For the formation of the precursor of the CCR (which had its origin in the statute 11 & 12 Vict. c. 78) see Baker, *English Legal History*, 521–23.

40. Violating what Fletcher terms the principle of "possessorial immunity," Fletcher, "Metamorphosis of Larceny," 472. See Foster's Crown Law at 123; 168 ER 61.

41. For George Charlewood at least it seems the risk was not theoretical: see E. H. East, *A Treatise of the Pleas of the Crown* (London, 1803), reprinted in P. R. Glazebrook., ed., *Blackstone's Statutes on Common Law*, 2 vols. (London: Blackstone, 1972), 689. The case is reported at *R v Pear* (1786) 1 Leach 409; 168 ER 306, where it is recorded "the prisoner received sentence accordingly." However, death sentences did not necessarily lead to execution even in the eighteenth century.

42. For example, see *R v Justin Harvey* (1787) 1 Leach 467; 168 ER 335.

43. 30 Geo. 2, c. 24. The original statute was repealed in 1827 by 7 & 8 Geo. 4, c. 27 but reenacted in the same session of Parliament by 7 & 8 Geo. 4, c. 29, s. 53. At the

time of *R v Ashwell* the relevant statute was the Larceny Act 1861 (24 & 25 Vict., c. 96), ss. 88, 89, and 90.

44. *R v Bazeley* (1799) 2 Leach 835; 168 ER 517.

45. 39 Geo. 3 c. 85.

46. (1812) Russ. & Ry. 215; 168 ER 767.

47. 52 Geo. 3 c. 63. The offense created by this statute became the germ of the Theft Act 1968 definition of theft. See Cmnd. 2977 at para. 35. 52 Geo. 3 c. 63 was repealed and effectively reenacted in 1827 (7 & 8 Geo. 4 c. 27 and 7 & 8 Geo. 4 c. 29, ss. 49–52); which was in turn repealed in 1861 (24 & 25 Vict. 95) and replaced by s. 75 of the Larceny Act 1861 (24 & 25 Vict. c. 96); which was replaced by the provisions of the Larceny Act 1901 (1 Edw. 7 c. 10); which was replaced by s. 20(1)(iv) of the Larceny Act 1916 (6 & 7 Geo 5 c. 50).

48. 20 & 21 Vict. c. 54.

49. M. Hale, *History of the Pleas of the Crown*, reprinted in P. R. Glazebrook, ed., *Blackstone's Commentaries*.

50. *R v Thurborn* (1848) 1 Den CC 387; 169 ER 293. In one isolated case the judiciary was even willing to extend larceny until it encompassed a person who was subjectively innocent at the time of a taking because the taking was tortuous; see *R v Riley* (1853) Dears. 149; 169 ER 674; which was followed in *Ruse v Read* [1949] KB 377.

51. *R v Middleton* (1873) LR 2 CCR 38.

52. Ibid., at 45.

53. Fletcher, "Metamorphosis," 515–17. The joint judgment received statutory endorsement in the Larceny Act 1916 s. 1(2): see *Moynes v Coopper* [1956] 1 QB 439 at 444.

54. Fletcher, "Metamorphosis of Larceny," 472, 474, 515–17.

55. *R v Pear* (1873) LR 2 CCR 38 at 43, 53.

56. Ibid., at 54; 56–57; 59. Fletcher, "Metamorphosis of Larceny."

57. The joint judgment was a minority judgment. However, there were eleven judges in favor of affirming the conviction for various reasons, and the authority of the joint judgment stems from its being delivered on behalf of seven of those judges.

58. *R v Ashwell* (1885) 16 QBD 190 at 199; and *R v Hehir* [1895] 2 IR 709 at 748.

59. *R v Pear* (1873) LR 2 CCR 38 at 64; 71.

60. Ibid., at 54.

61. Ibid., at 57.

62. *Leicester Journal*, 8 January 1886.

63. *R v Hehir* [1895] 2 IR 709.

64. Ibid., at 745; 746; 747. See also Johnson J. at 745.

65. Ibid., at 738; 759; 745; 752.

66. *R v Ashwell* (1885) 16 QBD 190 at 199; 204–6; 221.

67. *R v Pear* (1873) LR 2 CCR 38 at 59.

68. Ibid., at 222. Note the report in the *Leicester Journal*, 30 January 1885, quoted in footnote 25 above, which supports Denman J.'s recollection that he always inclined to holding Ashwell's conduct larcenous.

69. *R v Ashwell* (1885) 16 QBD 190 at 191.

70. *R v Pear* (1873) LR 2 CCR 38 at 54; 56–57; 59; *R v Ashwell* (1885) 16 QBD 190 at 199; 204–206; 221; *R v Hehir* [1895] 2 IR 709 at 738; 745; 747; 751;754.

71. *R v Pear* (1873) LR 2 CCR 38 at 42–43; 46; 49; 51; *R v Hehir* [1895] 2 IR 709 at 722; 731; 734.

72. Also note *R v Mucklow* (1827) 1 Moody 160; 168 ER 1225, *R v Davis* (1856) Dears. 640; 169 ER 878, *R v Prince* (1868) LR 1 CCR 150 as examples of larceny refusing to undergo metamorphosis. Also, a leading work on the criminal law refused to accept the correctness of the decision in *R v Middleton* and subjected the judgments in *R v Ashwell* in favor of the conviction to withering criticism well into the twentieth century. See J. W. Cecil Turner in *Russell on Crime,* 11th ed. (London: Sweet and Maxwell, 1958), 1099–1106, appendix 1.

73. Such as S. Cohen, *Folk Devils and Moral Panics: The Creation of Mods and Rockers* (London: MacGibbon and Kee, 1972).

74. *Leicester Journal,* 11 December 1885.

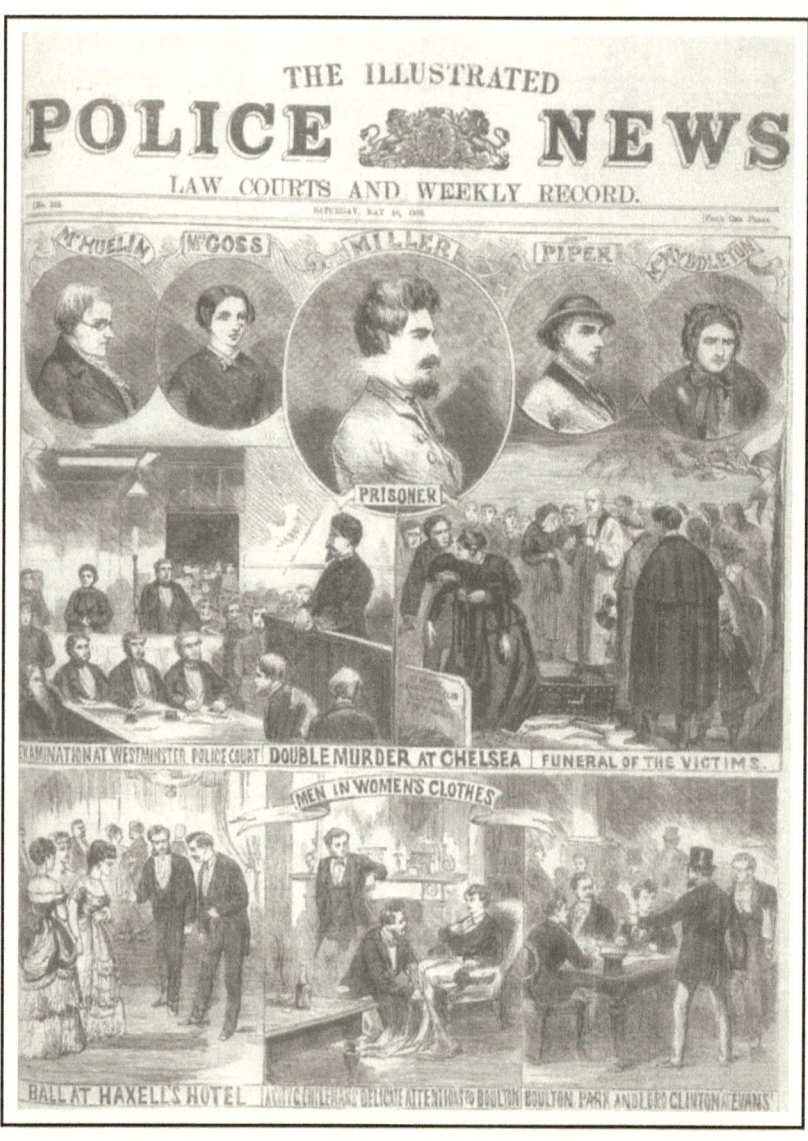

Figure 3. *Illustrated Police News*, 24 May 1870. As well as depicting the interior of Westminster Police Court, the bottom three illustrations depict the early reporting of the Boulton and Park case.

SECTION TWO

"External" Threats to the Security of Society

This section features the chapters examining Victorian conversations around the threats from those considered "other" within respectable Victorian society on some basis of difference. This includes those identified as "different" on relatively predictable grounds, such as race (in chapters by Rowbotham and Swift), or the evidence of their sexual practices, as in Crozier's chapter. Well-established fears associated with Ireland's capacity for spawning revolutionary feeling to trouble England's happiness were readily increased by the regular reports of Irish men and women featuring in court cases for brawling, for drunkenness, and so forth. As with the examples provided in Rowbotham's chapter, this concerned petty crime for the most part, but it assumed sinister proportions because of the xenophobic overtones of popular stereotyping.

The issue of the threat by those felt to have demonstrated the "uncivilized" and "primitive" aspects of their nature by their use of poison is also dealt with in Ward's chapter. However, this section also explores wider aspects of "otherness" within Victorian society, such as the expressions of discomfort and consequent alienation voiced by many ordinary Victorians when faced with new professions and practices that seemed dangerously unfamiliar, or when evidence indicated that aspects of daily life which seemed secure were, in fact, threatening to health and happiness. Thus the new medical experts touched on by Crozier both comforted and alarmed contemporaries, and the extent of distrust of the conclusions of such "new" experts and their methodologies is demonstrated in Morton's chapter on food adulteration. The conversations here point to the tensions caused by the impact on domestic Victorian society of intrusions from "outside," whether those external factors were in some senses familiar (as in the case of the Irish and even denizens of the British Empire) or products of the industrial urban age and its need for professionals. This section thus points to the commonalities, quite as much to the discontinuities between these various external threats to the stability and happiness of Victorian society, highlighting the need to conflate types of "other" often examined in isolation.

6

Criminal Savages?
Or "Civilizing" the Legal Process

JUDITH ROWBOTHAM

Introduction

The focus here is on the development of a kind of rhetoric invoked in reporting crime and bad behavior, one which interpreted the "seriousness" of types of crime against a standard of "civilization." A habit evolved where use was made of coded language to locate the cultural seriousness of cases according to a hierarchy ranking offenders and their transgressions against presumptions about their place on the "ladder" of civilization. The higher up the ladder an individual could be placed, the more serious the "crime" in a sociocultural sense, with consequent implications for the ways in which the legal process dealt with it. Thus one of the major concerns of Victorian society, expressed in the columns of the press and other forms of print media, was the working out of strategies to deal with physical expressions of bad behavior, especially violence, both individual and communal.

This print conversation had its effect on the ways in which the legal process itself regarded types of offending. For instance, violence was, for the law, always a notoriously difficult area. At what point did violence cease to be an acceptable, even necessary, part of daily life and the adjustment between individuals, to become instead a threat to the happiness of the individual and the security of society as a whole? Everyday violence was thus very much a part of the daily life of courts also. Most expressions of violence which reached the level of official attention were dealt with in the petty courts, but were no less widely reported for that. The press reporting of offenses involving violence, however, increasingly featured comments which indicated that the legal strategies being pursued in reaction to public opinion were far more complex than they had been in earlier periods. Specifically, this shift was associated with the takeoff of the great modern missionary enterprise and, associated with that, the development of the so-called home missions, all intending to eradicate "heathen" customs from regions under the civilities of British rule. The British foreign missionary enterprise began to acquire a high public profile from the 1830s on, with key societies including the Church Missionary Society, the Baptist Missionary Society, and the London Missionary Society. From the 1840s on, philanthropic endeavor at home began to use the terminology of foreign missions.[1] This left its mark on newspaper headlines and the reporting of crime for all audiences, and not just an educated elite one, as a glance at the front pages of the *Illustrated Police News* underlines. Horrid depictions of domestic brutality were regularly intermixed with illustrations of heathen savagery in action, and views of British heroism included pictures of missionary valor.[2]

Stereotypical Depictions

This development reflected the extent to which unrestrained physical violence, that seen as "inappropriate," had come to be associated with non-British peoples and increasingly to be identified as a racial characteristic which marked such peoples as inferior, or "uncivilized," to a greater or lesser degree. Women were a particular focus of concern, because of the ways in which they were identified as major markers of civilization in any society on the one hand, and on the other, as the major proponents in the daily duties of any civilizing mission.[3] It was not that women set the standards of civilization, but rather that, once set by God and interpreted for human living by men, women had the responsibility assigned to them of living out those standards.[4] It was, after all, easy to assign a fairly comprehensive disapproval of female violence (including chastisement of children) in any society at any time, whereas attitudes to male physical violence were complicated by the positive stereotyping of a more physically aggressive masculinity. True, masculine physical violence that was aimed at the categories identified as "vulnerable," notably women and children, was condemned unequivocally. But male physical violence that was "disciplined" by rules such as the Marquis of Queensberry rules, or military expectations, was not just desirable—it was essential to the success of any nation, including the British nation.[5] This meant it was difficult to be too dogmatic in using masculine conduct as practical daily markers of civilization, turning the focus more strongly upon women and their everyday behavior. Thus the presence in colonies of native women reportedly given to regular violent outbursts provided an affirmation of their lower standards, but the reality of women in British daily life also was a real challenge to the complacency of this "advanced" civilization.

This situation resulted in an increase not just in the levels of disapproval leveled at uncontrolled and unnecessary violence in Britain and her empire generally, but also a strongly disapproving focus on female violence. Of course this needs also to be placed in the broader context of the reality that from the 1820s on, the legal system faced a challenge from the dominant (in terms of power, if not absolute numbers) social values of the period to find a way of restraining violence among those elements of the population which would, or could, not learn the lessons of respectability and civilization through gentler social pressures. Such "gentler" pressures included the dissemination of behavioral guides through the discourse surrounding the reporting of cases of violence in the summary and the higher courts, which led to development of a complex set of categories comprising behavior which was "acceptable"; that which was "unacceptable but understandable as a result of human frailty"; and that which was "unequivocally unacceptable." Particular types and actual incidents of violence were readily slotted into these categories in their media depictions.

For a variety of reasons associated with the visibility of empire in everyday life in Victorian Britain, in talking of violence, language codes governed by imperial consciousness were increasingly prevalent. Judges, magistrates, barristers, and media commentators all made use of a range of terminology that characterized unacceptable violence as "savage," while acceptable violence was "civilized" because justified as forceful retribution (as in the present debates surrounding the twenty-first-century "War" against Terrorism). In an interesting reinterpretation of Victoria's many small colonial wars, one missionary handbook for domestic audiences advised that though "War is an awful thing," some wars such as the various campaigns against the Asanti "have been made to stop blood-shedding . . . in the interests of humanity," adding the rider "Who can say it was not better for English soldiers to enter the country and put a stop to such despotism, than to allow it to continue slaughtering innocent men and women to please the whims of a Heathen monster."[6]

It is easy to presume that Victorian condemnation of uncontrolled violence was part of a long English tradition; after all similar rhetorical devices can be found in Shakespeare, for example. Yet the Victorian rhetoric of violence did have a wider set of implications for auditors. In terms of popular understanding of the nuances involved, that rhetoric was mediated increasingly through the consciousness of empire and, arising out of that, the concept of what was "civilized" and what was "uncivilized" in terms of individual and communal behavior. And other metaphors used to signify uncivilized conduct, including "primitive," "barbaric," and "savage," acquired prominent new layers of meaning as a result of the regular dissemination of information about the indigenous peoples of Britain's secular and spiritual empires. This imperial dimension had a significant effect within Britain itself; indeed (given the claim of some African and Asian historians that the imperial episode left little mark on them) a case can be made that empire had its strongest impacts on the Mother Country and its attitudes and beliefs.[7]

Disinterestedly Promoting "Civilized" Standards?

The realities of running an empire, combined with a range of widely available reading matter (especially missionary material) interpreting the empire for a mass domestic British audience, had a profound effect on British perspectives on the world around them. In terms of the standards of daily conduct expected of Britons, it added extra pressures to established expectations of appropriate gender behavior, as well as that expected of individuals and groups defined on class and age grounds. Definitions demarcating the boundaries of what even constituted violence, and then the subdivisions of that violence into the right and the necessary (civilized) versus the unnecessary and wrong (primitive, savage, barbaric, and uncivilized) related very strongly to Britain's (or rather, England's) perceptions of its place in the global hierarchy. But increasingly, any separation in this area between a purely domestic vision and this global one became blurred, partly because of the constant cross-referencing at all levels of society to situations which in a wide range of locations were perceived by certain interest groups, from Colonial Office officials to missionaries and newspaper editors, to have lessons to teach the British about their own self-management, both personal and communal.

This consciousness had a strong resonance for practitioners in the legal world, because the British legal system and British legal personnel played a crucial part in maintaining empire. Large numbers of colonies were actually formally acquired in the first place because of the interruptions to trade caused by local disorderliness of some kind (after all, a disorderly empire is an unprofitable empire). Once formal empire was established, among the most immediate developments would be the setting up of a colonial legal establishment to help run that colony by keeping the peace, communally and individually.[8] Missionaries also had an interest. The exporting of British law to the colonies was frequently mediated through moral pressure by missionary societies to reform "primitive" and "unacceptable" customary law in India, say, or Nigeria, and the eradication of *sati* (widow burning) or twin murder.[9] The effects at home, including the explicit depictions of the barbarous abuses associated with the uncontrolled continuation of customary law in the colonies, intensified negative attitudes to cultural practices sanctioned in common law (seen as the British version of "customary" law in the colonies).[10] This was particularly true of behavior associated in some way with unrestrained or undisciplined violence. There continued to be an acceptance of officially and legally sanctioned violence such as, for example, policing and military action and "reasonable" corporal punishment within the domestic or educational context. But such behavior could only be tolerated where the means of violence could be publicly identified as being governed by clear rules, and where its ends promoted the interests of respectability and an orderly and stable society.

England was then at the heart of two overlapping and increasingly cooperative global empires, one secular and one spiritual. Substantial information about both, but especially the latter, was available to a mass audience via the print medium. Direct experience of secular empire was predominantly an elite affair.[11] But contact with the moral empire created by missionary endeavor was more substantial and personal across class, age, and gender audiences. Large numbers acquired a knowledge of "empire" through the widespread missionary information (or propaganda) that was disseminated to the British public from the 1820s in print and via personal delivery from missionaries on leave from the field. There was a shared knowledge that empire was there as a formal territorial presence, and (particularly at times of crisis such as colonial wars) there was a shared majority of support for its territorial continuation. But on the whole, most Britons were less concerned than the various British official elites with precise boundaries, or with the political and economic realities of empire, for instance. They were more interested in the moral images of empire presented to them by the missionary movement and its supporters, images in which women increasingly played a crucial role. British women as supporters of the missionary movement at home and, increasingly, abroad featured prominently, as did their unfortunate "sisters" depicted in all their "uncivilised degradation."[12]

The missionary societies and the commercial publishing houses collaborated from the 1830s on in producing a steady stream of specialist missionary periodicals as well as pamphlets, tracts, and hagiographic biographies, and responded readily to technological advances in printing to make their texts ever more widely and cheaply available.[13] But the excitement associated with exotic tales of missionary endeavor also ensured that reports of their activities found their way into the newspapers and nonspecialist periodicals. A survey of Victorian newspapers, from *The Times* to the *News of the World* or *Reynolds Weekly*, highlights the regularity of reports on missionary activity in all these outlets. Discussing "How to excite and maintain a missionary spirit," the Reverend Whiting of the Church Missionary Society commented that "Newspapers afford a very powerful means of spreading widely missionary information. Incidents and facts introduced into newspapers would catch many an eye which would never look upon a missionary periodical."[14] Stories and novels also played an important part, according to Whiting, and the widespread consciousness of this is further underlined by Dickens (not a missionary supporter), who could satirize the popular appeal of missions in the character of Mrs. Jellaby and her love for the natives on the banks of the Borrioboola-gha.[15]

In terms of the images depicted, including those of the miserable state of heathen women, a particular authority was ascribed to the "facts" sent home by missionaries as part of their reports, because they were held to be honest and disinterested observers and the ones who (because of their work) knew the various indigenous peoples most intimately and accurately. As a result, their reports were rarely subjected to any sustained contemporary critical scrutiny in terms of the accuracy of their depictions. The critical scrutiny was reserved for the implications of their conclusions for behavior at home in Britain. Working from a starting premise that British/English was best, missionaries sought to depict various heathens in ranking inferiorities within a human hierarchy that was divinely ordained. Why, if not to permit Britain to disperse its cultural and economic influences as part of a civilizing mission aimed at the "primitive" and "barbaric" heathen races? As the Bishop of Bombay claimed in 1872:

> We did not seek this Empire. We scarcely wished for it. It rather came to us and was forced upon us than deliberately sought for and conquered by us. We found ourselves here in a position out of which this Empire has grown, as if by a kind of fate and pre-destined necessity.[16]

After all, one justification of this, and proof both of that divine ordination and the British people's leading role as God's chosen people, was the very existence of this large global empire for such a small island.[17]

Experience rapidly taught that the most popular reports were those depicting the various types of "heathen" in their differing locations, "proving" how they were in so much need of the ministrations of the British to improve their lot. The most palatable way of doing this was through stories and pictures of various kinds in which what were held to be the distinguishing characteristics of a particular race or ethnic group were imparted in a comparative fashion, with the end object being to show that it was better to be a scullery maid in London (or Liverpool, etc.) than a king in Fiji—note the gender inversion here![18] The effect was the creation of a hierarchy of racial types with the civilized British at the top and the primitive, supposedly barely human Australian aboriginal at the bottom.[19] Certainties about this hierarchy were widely disseminated to a popular readership via the print media, with some nice underlining illustrations.[20] Great emphasis was laid on what can seem to be a fairly crude process of stereotypification, yet there was an underlying and profoundly gendered sophistication to the process, with its complex motivation ranging from a justificatory process for the missionary crusade to a desire to make the categories memorable for a mass audience by keeping them simple (or perhaps simplistic). The various "distinguishing" characteristics allotted to the different races were accumulated in a series of formulae which gave them "scores" on the civilization ladder. There was within Western cultures a traditional heavy reliance on appearance, including dress (or lack of it) as a clear external measure. In missionary propaganda, the symbolic importance of appearance was further amplified and explained by linking it to heathen behavior. While certain things could be joked about (such as eating habits), others were taken extremely seriously. Violence, especially violence toward or by females, was a key theme in interpreting the acceptability or not of non-British behavioral patterns, in a highly intricate equation.[21]

Militant Civilization

Given that this presentation of racial stereotyping was Christian in origin, it might be expected that there would be a general disapproval of violence. There was not. As indicated earlier, the tradition of Christian pacifism played little part in this exercise. This is hardly surprising. The British secular empire was neither peacefully acquired nor maintained, on the whole, and neither was the spiritual empire pioneered by missionaries. Not for nothing was it common, from the start, to use military terminology to describe the great Christian conversion enterprise. Missionaries, both male and female, were "soldiers of Christ" (men were the officers, though) and violence against missionaries was widely publicized. The greatest missionary icons were figures like Bishop Hannington, in what later became Uganda, facing hostile, spear-waving hordes before being bloodily and violently martyred or the Girl Martyrs of Fuh-Kien, holding hands as they were cut down before the altar of their mission chapel. Such narratives of moral victory made exciting news.[22] More significantly, they "proved" beyond all doubt the lower moral standards of these un-Christian savages with their "primitive" and unreasoning resort to violent expression of their emotions, with that expression usually aimed at the most vulnerable and most in need of protection: the single missionary, and the women and children of their own race.

Thus when the English ranked non-European indigenous peoples in some order of relative merit, a race's capacity for violence was an important indicator and one that was readily assimilable into popular discourse, in newspaper reporting, in fiction, and in the courts. It was undoubtedly a positive factor for the men to have an inclination that way. For instance a race considered to have "brave" (i.e., disposed to aggression) males such as the Zulus ranked higher than that disparate group rather disparagingly referred to by British Victorians as the Hottentots, where the men were stereotyped as cowards communally and individually because of a supposed dislike of direct engagement in face-to-face violence identified by the missionaries.[23] Stereotypically, they were supposedly inclined to either run away in the face of superior force, or to seek (treacherously) to deal with an opponent by literally attacking him from behind.[24] However, a propensity for violence in a race had to be accompanied by an equal propensity for discipline. Thus, again, the Zulus ranked higher than, say, the Asante of West Africa, because of their respective fighting methods. Worst of all on this list were those races like the Usagara of East Africa, who were quite willing to fight, but "If there were danger, these same husbands would set their wives and children in the front, and display much appearance of valour at a safe distance in the rear," according to the missionaries.[25]

For purely practical reasons, the inclination to "undisciplined" violence was considered a serious racial defect, one that was likely to spill over into daily life and affect, among other things, the running of the territorial empire. Much disapproving comment was expended, therefore, on males of races who indulged in unprovoked or extreme types of violence toward those less able to defend themselves, notably women and children. This was particularly so because such habits were likely to be accompanied by what was seen as a barbarity of attitude among women and children which robbed them of any claims to civilized ranking. Missionary texts indicated, for instance, the unwomanly tendency to child murder among the Yoruba, which in turn supposedly encouraged the men into wife kicking. The violent lack of tender emotion displayed by the women was matched (even incited) by male violence toward them. In all these, the use of intoxicating liquors (native or imported) was also implicated.[26]

A susceptibility to the effects of liquor, combined with a tendency to such overindulgence among the men and (worse) the women of a race, was increasingly seen as a negative factor by both missionaries and colonial legal authorities. Thus Zulu and Masai males, it seemed, were notoriously hardheaded and also, stereotypically, relatively "respectful" in their attitudes to their wives, who were not notorious consumers. By contrast, Hottentots were weak headed, and nasty to their domestic accessories, who were in turn inclined to various forms of child abuse from infanticide to beating.[27] The carefully packaged comments, backed up by the authority of the missionary voice, established enduring racial stereotypes, but also had significant implications for self-identification in the domestic British sphere. The British firmly believed that Britain (essentially England) represented a beacon of civilization and that its inhabitants were, at best, the most civilized people in the world. Within this perspective, unmanaged and undisciplined violence was identified as a negative characteristic associated with "lesser" races. Further, it was linked to unwritten forms of law, in turn identified alongside native/indigenous law, which itself thus became implicitly associated with a lack of what were identified as the standards of "civilization" among those (non-British) groups who clung to it.

This stance had considerable implications for those individuals and communities in Britain itself who justified types of behavior on the grounds of custom and tradition. But at least, unlike the example of the majority of indigenous peoples, an affection for such forms of "bad" behavior among the British was associated with the working classes rather than any elites. No British king would be guilty of the kind of savage and undisciplined brutality of, say, familiar imperial villains such as Cetewayo, king of the Zulus, or Mtesi, king of the Baganda. As earlier chapters in this volume have underlined, the undisciplined violence of the working classes in Britain was identified as a threat to the overall social stability of society and the nation, as being essentially anarchic. Linked to this, the lessons learned from empire fired the determination of those entrusted with the daily regulation of behavior, especially through the legal process, to eradicate, or at least severely curtail, such expressions of savagery as had earlier been largely taken for granted as part of the overall process of self-regulation within a community. The effects of this relentless stereotyping on British attitudes becomes apparent through an examination of the reporting of the workings of the legal system back in Britain, including the reasons judges and magistrates ascribed to their sentencing policy, as well as the editorial comments of the various crime reporters, many of whom were themselves barristers as well.

Legal Contributions to the March of Civilization

Many prominent figures in the legal world had an interest in empire that was both practical and moral, attested to, for instance, by regular appearance of legal names such as Baron Bramwell's on lists of missionary supporters. It is reasonable to infer that their interest in foreign missions would have exposed them to missionary propaganda, which in turn would have an effect on their attitudes to the stereotypes of race as well as gender and class existing in England. This would infuse their work where they had to make decisions and pronouncements upon the social context in which law operated, quite as much as on the letter of the law. Consider the comments of Mr. Beadon on the case of "A Savage Biting," as it was headlined. In a fight a "tall powerful young black fellow," identified as a "native of Central Africa," with a face "tattooed as the distinctive mark of his tribe," had committed what Beadon described as "an act of cannibalism." The evidence showed that he (a highly educated man, speaking five or six languages) had been infuriated by racist taunts and had thrown a punch at one of his hecklers, Henry Cooper, and that they had then fallen to the floor, trading blows, and scratching and gouging at each other. In the fight, the "black fellow" had bitten off, and presumably swallowed since no trace was subsequently found, a small bit of Cooper's ear. Punches had also been thrown at another participant, Mr. Good. Mr. Beadon stated that the prisoner had rushed at Cooper "in a very savage manner," adding that "When a man so far forgot himself as to become a cannibal he must be treated as a brute; and if the practices of savages was tolerated in the country from whence he came, it could not be in this." He fined the prisoner £5 for the assault on Cooper, £5 for the assault on Good, in order to make an example of him, with one month's hard labor consecutively for each offense in default.[28]

One prominent jurist who was also an imperialist and missionary supporter (though he abandoned his personal allegiance to formal religion at the end of his life) was Sir James Fitzjames Stephen, creator of the Indian Criminal Code of 1872. Stephen, one of Britain's leading Victorian legal figures, was a son of the famous Colonial Office official known as "Mr. Mother Country Stephen" because of his devotion to the interests of the metropolitan power in the imperial relationship.[29] Fitzjames Stephen's mother was the daughter of Henry Venn, the charismatic and influential Secretary of the Church Missionary Society. The influence of essentially Anglican thinking on "right" and "wrong" was central to the Criminal Code that Stephen developed for use in Indian courts at all levels, as indeed to the thinking of other colonial administrators like Eric Stokes, charged with developing codes for other colonial areas such as Jamaica.[30] Even on returning to Britain after establishing the Indian Criminal Code, Fitzjames Stephen's continued commitment to civilizing India by means of legal improvements was underlined by the regular and heavy correspondence he maintained in the 1870s with Lord Lytton, when Viceroy of India. Lytton sought his advice on legal developments and reforms in India.[31] Among the Victorian legal figures who appeared at missionary meetings were Bramwell and Mr. Justice Lush, both noted for their magnificently stereotypical comments on acceptable behavior and their rhetoric, which can easily be shown to be in line with the thinking promoted by both foreign and home missions. Bramwell, for example, compared in court the conduct of an aggressive wife to that of a savage dog, lamenting only that such "uncivilized" females, who took advantage of a Briton's "natural repugnance" against striking women, were less readily disposed of than the dog.[32]

Thus it can be said that the exporting of British law to the colonies, in suitably modified form, was a significant industry, occupying considerable numbers who made it a point to sustain contact with their metropolitan base—for example, one of Fitzjames Stephen's brothers was a judge in Australia, and a very regular contact was kept up between the domestic and colonial branches of the family.[33] The practical result of this sustained contact was that ideas came back to Britain quite as much as they went out from it. Of particular concern to those adjudicating on acceptable levels of violence, and those reporting it, were the types of incident which seemed to indicate a lack of civilized standards among individuals and groups in society. The general expectation was that the majority of those encountering the legal system would be members of the working class. Class-based stereotyping included a belief that the British working classes were more regulated by their "passions" or emotions than those of higher social rank. This meant that the working classes were consequently less "advanced," or "civilized," than their social betters, who had had the advantage of training which included learning self-discipline through a variety of educational strategies. An inclination toward social conformity and "respectability" was increasingly relied on as a mark of individual "improvement," accompanied by an ability to control the inclination toward undisciplined expression of emotion and a lessening taste for the sensational and the gaudy—both so "primitive." But even so, the British working classes as a whole were supposed to be less at the mercy of ungovernable and immoral passions than were members of other races.

Class, Race, and Gender

These presumptions had a significant effect on the language used to describe reactions to particular types of lawbreaking, especially where they involved violence. The *Daily Telegraph* hoped, "for the sake of civilisation," that something could be done about that section of the population "seemingly composed of human baboons" when referring to the "ruffianism" of the "young brutes" whose idea of Sunday evening recreation was "to insult, hustle and outrage respectable females."[34] Generally, transgressions linked to undisciplined conduct like this were regarded with increasing disfavor and described in terms which underlined their very un-Britishness. More than that, the level of disapproval was directly linked to the social standing of the offender. On 22 January 1880, for instance, the *Pall Mall Gazette* noted the comments made at the Lancaster assizes by Lord Justice Brett when sentencing to two months' imprisonment a young farmer who had hit his opponent "below the belt," saying that "It was hard to believe that a human English man" could behave in so cowardly and degrading a fashion.³⁵ It was the worse for the farmer that he came from that level of society who, through education, could have been presumed to have more self-control. In January 1861, a working-class man was hauled up for kicking his wife, who subsequently died (though medical opinion on the contribution of the kicking to her demise was ambiguous). Sir Robert Carden commented disapprovingly on the "heathen" nature of the husband's behavior, including kicking her when she had fallen, saying it was conduct he would expect of a Hottentot, but not a Briton. However, given that the man was "an un-educated brute," he was more leniently treated than the young farmer, being awarded a mere six weeks' imprisonment.³⁶

Unacceptably passionate behavior by women was an even more horrifying puzzle for British legal and newspaper comment. Child abuse by African or Asian mothers was a major theme in missionary literature and used regularly as an indication of the "primitive" level of such women. Thus British examples of perverted and unnatural maternity, unless justified by lunacy, were particularly problematic for magistrates, judges, and juries in ways that are illuminating of the hidden conventions and expectations surrounding the shifting boundaries between "acceptable" and "unacceptable" expressions of violence. Popular rhetoric surrounding gender stereotyping identified women as markers of civilization. A pacific and domesticated womanhood was a feature of an advanced civilization on the one hand, and on the other, women's presumed susceptibility to the morality of civilization meant that they were seen as the main channels through which (heathen) men would be effectively and lastingly civilized.³⁷ As already indicated, a violent woman was an uncivilized woman, unless insane. Increasingly, therefore, the violence of women, toward men and especially toward other women, was identified as a particular concern, with instances treated with increasing disapproval and severity. Mr. D'Eyncourt, stipendiary magistrate at Worship Street Police Court, commented to one working-class woman who had reacted to husbandly provocation by hitting him, hard, with a heavy hammer, that she had acted "abominably." He committed her for trial for attempted murder, somewhat to the reported disconcertment of the slightly bruised husband who had merely wished her to be bound over to keep the peace.³⁸

Considerations of race as well as class and gender in the home context point up still further the impact of widespread popular knowledge of accepted racial hierarchies on the daily workings of the legal system, and the associated social expectations as expressed in Victorian newspapers. As Roger Swift's chapter demonstrates, the Irish working-class migrants to Britain were, *en masse,* identified with a range of uncivilized and undisciplined (even immoral) behavior, including foul fighting,[39] domestic violence, and so forth. The Irish, with their supposed racial propensity for drink shared by women and men, were particular targets for negative sentencing and comment. In British perceptions, the Irish were not the same as the British, something which affected attitudes at the highest and lowest levels. It was, for example, quite common for politicians and civil servants running the Colonial Office to have served an apprenticeship in Ireland, and (especially in policy development relating to the legal regulation of behavior) to invoke that Irish experience when deciding how to deal with a bunch of, say, recalcitrant Chinese in Singapore.[40]

The un-Britishness of feminine violence was further emphasized by the media reporting of one type of female violence, that involving Irish working-class women. Giving such incidents a comic thrust, through use of Irish "dialect," was part of an exercise in alienating such disruptive forces from British society by stressing the foreignness of such women.[41] After all, foreigners could not really be blamed for their violence, and the British could afford to laugh at it since the foreigners knew no better and lacked the inbred racial inclination toward self-control and peacefulness.

Conclusion

The visibility of working-class lawlessness at a time when the "uncivilized" aspects of so much of previously acceptable conduct was being brought out by imperial propaganda about African and Asian races had a significant effect on the descriptors used to characterize and stereotype it in Britain quite as much as in the Gold Coast or Punjab. It was important to differentiate between Britons and others by defining what a Briton could not do, more than what he or she could. Thus, a will to leave groups of street brawlers to fight themselves to a standstill, and so sort out their differences, was replaced by a will to remove such behavior altogether by invocation of statute law to conquer customary regulation, because it was more British. Bluntly, it had become impossible to turn a blind eye to types of behavior that could now be so visibly seen as primitive and undisciplined—acceptable (or at least understandable) because of their association with the kind of behavior that might be accepted of an aboriginal of some kind. Respectable society demonstrated their realization of this "truth" in their increasingly determined attempts to regulate "wrongheaded" expressions of violence from their fellow citizens, enthusiastically aided by the legal system. What was presented as acceptable was for the British, individually and communally, to respond to the violent provocation of others with an expression of appropriate and measured force, sufficient to restore order. It meant that, increasingly, officially sanctioned violence was not presented as such in the media. Force was a concept with associations with power and authority, exercised in the interests of peace and order—so unlike the home life of a native on the banks of the Borrioboola-gha.

Notes

1. Andrew Porter, "Religion, Missionary Enthusiasm and Empire," in *The Nineteenth Century: The Oxford History of the British Empire*, ed. Andrew Porter (Oxford: Oxford University Press, 1999), 3: 222–46; F. K. Prochaska, *Women and Philanthropy in Nineteenth Century England* (Oxford: Clarendon, 1988).

2. See, for example, *Illustrated Police News*, 22 July 1870; 11 November 1870.

3. Preface, Baroness Burdett Coutts, ed., *Woman's Mission: A Series of Congress Papers on the Philanthropic Work of Women by Eminent Writers* (London: Sampson Low Marston, 1893).

4. Maria Charlesworth, *India and the East: Or, a Voice from the Zenana* (London: Seeley, Jackson and Halliday, 1860), 4.

5. Judith Rowbotham, "'Only When Drunk': The Stereotyping of Violence in England, c1850–1900," in *Everyday Violence in Britain, c1850–1950: Class and Gender*, ed. Shani D'Cruze, 155–69 (London: Longmans, 2000), .

6. F. D. Thompson, *A Deputation Handbook for Speakers, Preachers, and Others in Connection with Bible Society and Missionary Meetings* (London: Charles Thynne, 1912), 104–5.

7. For example, Adu Boahen, *African Perspectives on Colonialism* (Baltimore: Johns Hopkins University Press, 1987).

8. Diane Kirby and Catherine Coleborne, eds., *Law, History, Colonialism, the Reach of Empire* (Manchester: Manchester University Press, 2001).

9. Judith Rowbotham, "'Hear an Indian Sister's Plea': Reporting the Work of British Women Missionaries, c1870–1914," *Women's Studies International Forum*, Summer 1998, 247–61.

10. Edwin T. Atkinson, *A Manual of Criminal Procedure for British India, for the Magistrate, the Justice of the Peace and the Police Officer* (Calcutta: Barham Hill, 1870).

11. Porter, "Missionary Enthusiasm"; David Cannadine, *Orientalism: How the British Saw Their Empire* (London: Allen Lane, 2001).

12. Rowbotham, "Indian Sister's Plea"; Judith Rowbotham, "Minstering Angels, Not Ministers, Reporting Nineteenth Century Women Missionaries," in *Women, Religion, and Feminism in Britain, 1750–1900*, ed. Sue Morgan (London: Palgrave, 2002).

13. Judith Rowbotham, "Hagiographic Biography and the Creation of Masculine Stereotypes, c1850–1870," in *The Golden Age: Essays in British Social and Economic History, 1850–1870*, ed. Ian Inkster et al., 262–79 (Aldershot: Ashgate, 2000).

14. Rev. T. B. Whiting, "On the Best Means of Exciting and Maintaining a Missionary Spirit," in *Conference on Missions Held in 1860 at Liverpool: Including the Papers Read, the Deliberations, and the Conclusions Reached, Edited by the Secretaries to the Conference* (London: Nisbet, 1860), 61.

15. Ibid., 61–62; Charles Dickens, *Bleak House* (1856). Borrioboola-gha was a real

location, made familiar through reports from the Niger missions.

16. H. Douglas, *Indian Missions: A Letter Addressed to His Grace the Archbishop of Canterbury* (London: Rivingtons, 1872), 12.

17. *Mission Work for All* (London: Society for the Propagation of Christian Knowledge [SPCK] 1880), 12; John Wolffe, *God and Greater Britain: Religion and National Life in Britain and Ireland, 1843–1945* (London: Routledge, 1994).

18. FML, *Recitations for Missionary Meetings* (London: Robert Culley, 1903), 49–50.

19. See Bessie Rayner Parkes, *Peoples of the World* (London, 1863).

20. *Illustrated Police News,* 11 November 1871, for example.

21. Amy Carmichael, *From Sunrise Land: Letters from Japan* (London: Marshall Bros., 1895).

22. *The Times,* 14 August 1895. See also *Illustrated Police News,* 17 August 1895, reporting (with illustrations) the Fuh-Kien "atrocities."

23. Rayner Parkes, *Peoples;* Henry Rider Haggard, *King Solomon's Mines* (1886); Georgina Gollock, *Africa and Missions* (London: Church Missionary Society–[CMS], 1890).

24. A. Brigg, *"Sunny Fountains" and "Golden Sand": Pictures of Missionary Life in the South of the "Dark Continent"* (London: T. Woolmer, 1888). See also characters such as Hans in Rider Haggard's Allan Quartermain novels.

25. Rev. G. Ensor, *Mission Martyrs: Or, Night on the Nyanza* (Bury St. Edmonds: A Lankester, 1878), 16.

26. Rev. A. Robb, *The Gospel to the Africans: A Narrative of the Life and Labours of the Reverend William Jameson in Jamaica and Old Calabar* (Edinburgh: Andrew Elliot, 1890).

27. Brigg, *"Sunny Fountains,"* 49–50.

28. *Daily Telegraph,* 3 August 1859.

29. Judith Rowbotham, "Edward Knatchbull Hugessen, 1st Lord Brabourne, and the British Empire, 1868–1893" (Ph.D. diss., University of Wales, 1982).

30. Judith Rowbotham and Kim Stevenson, "Utopian Visions? The Dream of the Code Victoria in Criminal Law," *Nottingham Law Journal* (Autumn 2000): 25–38.

31. University of Cambridge, Stephen Papers, ADD 7349 (C)14 Lytton–Stephen, 1876–1891.

32. *News of the World,* 3 February 1861.

33. This has interesting echoes for Bentley's chapter in this volume.

34. *Daily Telegraph,* 9 November 1870.

35. *Pall Mall Gazette,* 22 January 1880.

36. *News of the World,* 7 January 1861. See also Martin Wiener, *Men of Blood: Violence, Manliness and Criminal Justice in Victorian England* (Cambridge: Cambridge University Press, 2004).

37. Christopher Wordsworth, *Christian Womanhood and Christian Sovereignty* (London: Rivingtons, 1884); Rowbotham, "Indian Sister."

38. *News of the World,* 22 April 1875.

39. This was a regularly used expression that denoted unfair or "foul" tactics on the part of a protagonist.

40. Rowbotham, "Knatchbull Hugessen."

41. *News of the World,* 24 February 1880. The full text is in the appendix, with the spelling exactly as given in the original.

7

Behaving Badly? Irish Migrants and Crime in the Victorian City

ROGER SWIFT

Introduction

The first half of the nineteenth century witnessed a substantial increase in the pace and scale of Irish migration to Britain. The 1841 census enumerated the Irish-born population of England, Wales, and Scotland at 419,000. By 1851, in consequence of the massive exodus during the Great Famine, this figure had risen to 727,000. In 1861 the Irish-born population peaked at 806,000, when it comprised 3.5 percent of the total population. Thereafter, as this migration declined, the number of Irish-born migrants in Britain also fell, declining to 550,000 in 1911 (or 1.3 percent of the population). In essence, this process involved the positive movement of people in search of better economic opportunities in Britain and, accordingly, the Irish presence was concentrated overwhelmingly in the towns and cities of "the workshop of the world."

These migrants were by no means an homogeneous group. Their ranks contained rich and poor, middle and working class, skilled and unskilled, Catholics and Protestants (and unbelievers), Nationalists and Loyalists, and men and women from a variety of distinctive provincial rural and urban cultures in Ireland. The majority were young, single, and disproportionately male. They were also notoriously transient, and the urban districts they inhabited experienced continual in- and out-migration, with only a relatively small number of migrants establishing permanent settlements. The vast majority of these Irish people were poor and Roman Catholic. It is their story, a story in many cases of triumph over adversity, that looms large in the history of the Irish in Britain.[1] This chapter focuses on some aspects of the varied and complex conversations that surrounded the concept of the Irish and crime, but can only touch upon some of the main themes in such an intricate area.

Irish Representation in Crime Rates

The Irish presence was generally unpopular, as its print presentation underlines. Even before the Famine, British social investigators and commentators perceived Irish migration as little short of a social disaster which, it was argued, exacerbated urban squalor, constituted a health hazard, and increased the burden on poor rates. It was also argued that the Irish constituted a threat to law and order. The 1836 Report on the State of the Irish Poor devoted four pages to the examination of Irish criminality, noting that "the Irish in the larger towns of Lancashire commit more crimes than an equal number of natives of the same places."[2] The 1839 Report of the Constabulary Commissioners concluded that:

> when large bodies of Irish of less orderly habits, and far more prone to the use of violence in fits of intoxication settled permanently in these towns [of South Lancashire], the existing police force, which was sufficient to repress crime and disorders among a purely English population, has been found, under these altered circumstances, inadequate to the regular enforcement of the law.[3]

That same year, Carlyle, the intellectual hero of the age, was moved to comment: "Crowds of miserable Irish darken all our towns . . . as the ready-made nucleus of degradation and disorder."[4] Similar observations were expressed by visitors to England during the 1840s.[5] These are random examples, but they are illustrative of a popular belief in the innate criminality of the Irish poor which formed part of the negative side of the Irish stereotype. To many middle-class observers, Irish migrants augmented a challenge by the "dangerous classes" to authority and order.

Relatively few detailed analyses of the Irish contribution to Victorian crime rates have been conducted. This said, the chief conclusion to be drawn from selective local studies (which may therefore be unrepresentative) of crime in some early and mid-Victorian towns, including York, Manchester, Liverpool, Preston, Bradford, Wolverhampton, Chester, and Middlesbrough, is that the Irish-born were not only well represented in the statistics of crime but that their capacity for breaking the law was disproportionate to their numbers in the community.[6] These studies conclude that the Irish-born were almost three times as likely to face prosecution as their English neighbors, endorsing the evidence of policemen, prison officers, and magistrates in the 1836 Report.[7] However, these statistics deserve further scrutiny.

First, they refer only to the Irish-born and do not include children of Irish immigrants born in Britain, who, though perceived by the host society as

Irish, were variously classified as English, Scottish, or Welsh. Thus the contribution of the Irish to local criminality was probably higher than these figures suggest. Second, the Irish proportion of the working-class population of these towns was obviously far higher than its proportion of the population as a whole, and the statistics reflect to some extent the relative proportion of Irish in that sector of society most likely to be prosecuted.[8] Third, many of the second- and third-generation Irish would have been Roman Catholic, hence the proportion of Catholics in crime statistics would have been higher than those of the Irish. Fourth, these localized surveys suggest that the proportion of Irish-born enumerated in crime statistics gradually declined toward the end of the century. This does not imply that the Irish were less likely to face prosecution (for they continued to be overrepresented); it merely reflects, in relative terms, the decline in immigration from Ireland and the consequent reduction in the number of Irish-born in Britain during the period.

Finally, it is important to recognize that incidence of crime, Irish and non-Irish, was much higher than the (notoriously unreliable) criminal statistics suggest, for they represent only those offenses reported to the police which resulted in prosecutions and convictions, as opposed to all offenses committed, many of which went unreported or unprosecuted (the so-called "dark figure of crime"). The Irish-born were also overrepresented in committals to prison. The Judicial Statistics for 1861–1901 indicate that while the proportion of Irish-born prisoners gradually declined, the Irish-born were five times as likely to be committed to prison as the English.[9] Thus, on the surface at least, criminal statistics suggest that the Irish were more likely to be prosecuted and convicted for lawbreaking than their neighbors.

The evidence suggests that it was not just a case of men behaving badly: Irish women also figure disproportionately in the statistics.[10] Taking but one example, in Chester between 1851 and 1871, Irish women comprised 67 percent of female convictions for assaults on the police, 28 percent for assault, 33 percent for obtaining goods by false pretences, 33 percent for begging, and 23 percent for drunkenness and disorderly behavior.[11] A notable figure was Mary Ann Glynn of Boughton, with 101 convictions for drunkenness, disorderly behavior, vagrancy, and petty thefts. Sentenced to twelve months' imprisonment in July 1869, she continued to defy authority in Chester Gaol, using "obscene and violent language" and subsequently destroying "13 panes of glass, 2 cell stools, 1 lamp, 8 beds, 10 jackets, 12 petticoats, 19 capes, 2 blankets, 6 chemises, 2 flannel ivylets, 6 tin-cans and 2 chamber utensils." A muff (restraining jacket) was deployed to control her, but to little effect.[12] Even Glynn's record pales into insignificance with that of one Liverpool Irish woman, a street trader, who by 1897 boasted a national record, having been held 356 times for drunkenness, assaults, damage, and begging.[13]

However, these patterns require further qualification. There is much evidence to suggest that Irish criminality was concentrated largely in less serious or petty categories. The 1836 Report concluded that "Crimes against the person, committed after long premeditation and with unrelenting cruelty, by several persons, such as murders, nightly attacks on houses, beatings, vindictive rapes, and so forth, which are unhappily so frequent among the Irish in their own country, scarcely ever occur among them in Great Britain."[14] Police superintendents in Liverpool and Manchester told a similar story.[15] Some local studies of Irish crime confirm this impression, showing that whereas the Irish were overrepresented in summary prosecutions, they were less frequently committed to the Quarter Sessions and Assizes.[16] Second, the evidence suggests that the Irish were not overrepresented in all categories of petty crime. Irish criminality was highly concentrated in the often interrelated categories of drunkenness, disorderly behavior, and assault (including assaults on the police) and, to a lesser extent, petty theft and vagrancy.[17] On average, almost one-third of all prosecutions in these categories involved Irish people. Yet the supposed predilection of the Irish for such offenses is deserving of closer scrutiny.

Consider drink-related crime. In British eyes, the terms "drink" and "Irish" were synonymous.[18] Drink, it was argued, was the Irishman's weakness, and drunkenness was the precursor of disorderly behavior, breaches of the peace of all kinds, and assaults. It was also held that drink had a markedly more extreme effect upon the Irish. In 1877, a Cardiff magistrate, referring to excessive drunkenness among Irish dockworkers, claimed "they are not all bad fellows, but they have all the peculiarities of their forefathers."[19] This is perhaps indicative of the way in which contemporaries resorted to stereotype and conveniently ignored the drunken violence that distinguished English, Scottish, and Welsh working-class *mores*. However, even John Denvir, an Irish nationalist, was moved to comment that whereas the Irish did not drink more than other nationalities, "being naturally demonstrative, they put themselves in evidence when under the influence of intoxicants, where the Englishman would go and sleep off their effects."[20] Of course, the Irish were far from being all inveterate imbibers.

Located as they were in marginal employments, most Irish people could not afford to drink throughout the week; those who drank confined the practice to the weekend. And while the public houses and beer shops that proliferated in working-class districts populated by the Irish poor provided plenty of opportunities for drink, they also served important social, cultural, and economic functions for them.[21] Moreover, it was a common practice for contractors to pay Irish laborers their wages in public houses, which not only encouraged them to spend their wages on drink but also promoted disputes, between laborers and contractors, and among laborers themselves. Public houses were not the only focus for Irish drinking practices. Some migrants brought alcohol with them from Ireland and sold it, without license, in local lodging houses. These "wabble shops" were illegal, but were very difficult for the police to detect.[22] So were illegal whiskey stills, usually located in lodging houses. It was reported in 1836 that in Manchester these houses were "crammed with Irish the whole of Saturday night; parties of men come mad drunk out of these places."[23]

The realities of Irish drinking were more complex and varied than this imagery suggests. Drink was a key element of leisure culture in rural Ireland, playing a central role in the main rituals of life: birth, marriage, and death. Consumption of whiskey ("water of life" in Gaelic) was fundamental to this.[24] In Ireland, patterns of drink consumption were variously influenced; rural drinking was irregular, confined largely to weekends and special occasions, whereas urban drinking was more regular and, in some instances, daily. Nevertheless, the persistence of the Irish reputation for drunkenness was based partly on the assumption that expatriate (migrant) drinking habits were also characteristic of Ireland, which was not wholly true. Arguably, the key questions which should be addressed should not be "Why Paddy Drank" (which assumes the validity of the stereotype) but rather "Did Paddy Drink?" (suggesting both "yes" and "no") and "Which Paddy Drank?"[25] After all, the efforts of temperance crusaders such as Father Mathew met with some success in both Ireland and Britain. Mayhew noted the presence of mutual aid societies, including temperance groups, among London's Irish Catholics in the 1840s, while one of the motives for Mathew's visit to Glasgow in 1842 and to other English towns in 1843 was to raise the reputation, soiled by drink, of the Irish in Britain, sometimes administering the pledge in Gaelic. Thus "Teetotal Paddy" reflects the other side of the coin.[26] It is worth noting that between 1841 and 1871 Irish spirit consumption was actually below the annual United Kingdom average, while beer consumption in England, Scotland, and Wales was almost four times higher than in Ireland.[27]

Consider, too, the link between the Irish and disorder. A closer analysis suggests that incidents were essentially multicausal, coming in various shapes and sizes. Sometimes they comprised disturbances among the Irish themselves; on other occasions they involved collective violence, either by or against the Irish, or a combination of both. Moreover, they operated on both intra- and intercommunal levels within specific communities, revealing different types of behavior according to time and place. Disorders confined to Irish districts consisted largely of drunken brawls, quarrels between neighbors and domestic disputes, mainly between rather than against Irish people. When combined with the drunkenness, noise, and casual violence associated with Saturday night saturnalia in so-called "Little Irelands," these disorders made the Irish more visible, reinforcing popular perceptions of the Irish predilection for drink and disorder.[28] Yet these "Irish rows," as the press described them, which so horrified "respectable" opinion, were generally of little interest to the police or magistrates unless they spilled over into the public domain.

By contrast, violence bred of sectarian rivalries sometimes spilled over into the public domain in cities with substantial Ulster Protestant and Irish Catholic populations, most notably in Liverpool and Glasgow. Here, communal conflicts were compounded by the activities of the Orange Order. Orange marches, important in Protestant working-class culture, were frequently accompanied by sectarian violence well into the Edwardian period.[29] In mid-Victorian west of Scotland, sectarian violence also erupted in smaller towns with Irish populations, including Airdrie, Port Glasgow, Greenock, Dumbarton, Kelso, Coatbridge, and Paisley, where, in 1857, three members of the local night police, once off-duty, joined an Orange procession in their uniforms, carried flags, and led an assault on a body of Irish Catholics, one of whom was stabbed to death.[30] In England, sectarian violence also disfigured community relations in the industrial townships of late-Victorian Cumbria.[31] Nevertheless, sectarian conflict appears in general to have been less evident in most Irish communities in nineteenth-century Britain.

Clashes between the Irish and the police had a character of their own. At such points, distinctions between intra- and intercommunal violence becomes blurred.[32] Whole Irish communities often stood shoulder-to-shoulder in face of what they popularly held to be police harassment. The overrepresentation of Irish people in statistics pertaining to assaults on the police, of frequent occurrence during these disorders, could be seen as partly an index of Irish hostility to police interference. It is not surprising to discover that Irish people comprised 33 percent of all prosecutions for assaults on the police in Liverpool and Manchester between 1841 and 1871.[33] In Birmingham, 1862–77, it was 20 percent, although they comprised only four percent of the local population.[34] It is difficult to lay exclusive blame on either side during some of these intercommunal disorders. There were some famous battles between Irish and English railway navvies during the 1830s and 1840s, which were partially rooted in the harshness of that kind of life.[35] Yet navvy riots were also multicausal. In some instances they involved violence by the Irish as a protest against their exploitation by contractors and gangers; in others they may be ascribed to English or Scottish xenophobia.[36]

In contrast, intercommunal disorders which, on the surface at least, were rooted in religious differences between the Irish and the host society were frequently the product of violence directed against Irish Catholics. This was particularly evident during the mid-Victorian period, when the resurgence of popular Protestantism in the wake of the reestablishment of the Catholic hierarchy provided an additional cutting edge to Anglo-Irish tensions and contributed to a number of serious anti-Catholic and anti-Irish disorders, notably at Stockport in 1852. The homes of Irish Catholics in Rock Row were besieged by a Protestant mob and the local Roman Catholic Church was desecrated.[37] The activities of anti-Catholic lecturers also fomented communal violence. William Murphy, a member of the Protestant Evangelical Mission and Electoral Union, became the apostle of popular anti-Catholicism between 1867 and 1871. Until his premature death from injuries inflicted upon him by Irish miners as he prepared to address Whitehaven Orangemen in the Oddfellows Hall in 1871, his lectures sparked serious disorders in the Irish districts of many towns.[38] Thus variety was hallmark of the disorders in which Irish migrants became embroiled, many reflecting purely local and regional tensions. Yet the extent to which disorder invariably accompanied the Irish presence in the Victorian city remains problematic. Studies of the Irish experience in Coventry, Chester, and Leicester paint a different picture.[39] Here, the relative absence of disturbances involving the Irish signifies a measured degree of accommodation into local society. Victorian towns were far from monochrome, and accordingly, the Irish urban experience was itself characterized by diversity.

Outcasts and Scapegoats?

So why were the Irish poor generally overrepresented in certain categories of criminal behavior? Any examination of Victorian Irish crime and disorder needs to be placed in the broader context of English attitudes to the Irish, with its complex history.[40] Although hostility to the Irish had ancient roots, the growth of anti-Hibernian sentiment during early and mid-Victorian years was a consequence of the economic, social, political, and religious currents of the period, and intimately linked to the scale of immigration from Ireland during the Famine.[41] This exacerbated hostility to the Irish poor by raising the profile of contemporary social ills for which the Irish emerged as convenient scapegoats.[42] The effects of the restoration of the Catholic hierarchy in England and Wales in 1850 has been mentioned. Over the next twenty years both public and government went through a phase of anti-Catholicism in response to perceived "Papal aggression." Most anti-Irish disorders belong to this period, notably in South Lancashire.[43] There, the situation was compounded by the activities of the Orange Order.[44]

Political factors also fanned the flames of anti–Irish feeling, particularly between 1865 and 1868 when Fenian activities on the mainland brought a sense of fear of Irish nationalist violence to the host population. Dramatic events in 1867, including the abortive Fenian raid on Chester Castle, the case of the "Manchester Martyrs," and the Clerkenwell bombing, all served to raise Anglo-Irish tensions, albeit temporarily. In the latter incident, a barrel of explosives, placed outside the exercise-yard wall at Clerkenwell Gaol in an abortive attempt to release Fenian prisoners, exploded, killing twelve civilians and injuring 120. It resulted in popular outrage and panic, witness Tenniel's famous *Punch* cartoon, *The Fenian Guy Fawkes,* which not only condemned the Fenian dynamiter but also played on old anti-Catholic prejudices in a new version of the Gunpowder Plot.[45] It has also been argued that economic competition between English and Irish workers exacerbated native reactions to the newcomers because the Irish threatened to undercut wage levels and were prepared to work as strikebreakers.[46] Thus, it might appear that poor working-class Irish Catholic immigrants were in some respects the "outcasts" of mid-Victorian society because of their poverty, ethnicity, religion, and politics.

In fact, the Irish experience in the Victorian city was more diverse and complex.[47] Nevertheless, Irish nationalists claimed that the perceived association between the Irish, crime and disorder was only one manifestation of the sustained hostility, rooted in English prejudice, directed toward the Irish. In June 1868 *The Nation,* a Dublin weekly newspaper, observed that "Nowhere in England can our countrymen consider themselves safe from English mob violence."[48] In 1892 John Denvir noted, "We know how, by studied insults to his creed and country, the hot-blooded Irish Celt is often made to appear the aggressor."[49] More recently, this theme has been developed further by work pointing not only to the overrepresentation of the Irish in the statistics of crime and disorder, but also to violence in the workplace. There, psychological terror, small-scale brawls, attacks on individuals, and a routine diet of discrimination were common means by which the non-Irish vented their aggressions on Irish migrants.[50]

Of greater importance was the widely held perception that Irish peasant society was inherently brutal, demonstrating a fundamental weakness of the Irish national character. The stereotype of the brutalized "Paddy" was entrenched in the public mind even before the Famine, and the subsequent experiences of the pauper Irish, who brought rural traditions with them and yet had to adapt to the *mores* of urban industrial society, served only to reinforce these ingrained perceptions. Thus, Irish districts were *expected* to be hotbeds of crime, and antisocial behavior by the Irish merely confirmed preconceived notions regarding the irresponsibility and criminality of the Celt.[51] It also, of course, influenced the attitudes of police and magistrates in their attempts to maintain law and order in urban Britain.

Irish criminality in Victorian Britain also needs to be examined and understood in the context of patterns of crime in Ireland which, fluctuating in time and place, were in some ways different from those of England and Wales. With the exception of Dublin and Cork, crime was overwhelmingly rural, and convict records shed some light on the nature of Irish criminality. Approximately 160,000 convicts were transported to Australia between 1788 and 1868.[52] Of the quarter of all Irish transported to Australia who were transported direct from Ireland, the mix contained both those convicted for ordinary offenses and social and political protesters. They comprised 62 percent of all persons transported from Ireland and Britain for crimes of protest during the period, but while a minority of these were political prisoners (United Irishmen, Young Irelanders, and Fenians), the majority were the representatives of various Irish agrarian movements.[53]

Thus to many contemporary observers, Irish peasant society appeared inherently lawless, violent, and brutal. Faction fights provide one illustration of this. Observing the proceedings at Waterford Assizes in July 1835, Alexis de Tocqueville commented:

> These assizes gave us the very clear impression that the lower classes of this county are very prone to quarrelling and fighting; that nearly every village forms a kind of faction. . . . Factions that began nobody knows when and continue nobody knows why, without taking on any political significance. When men of these different factions meet each other at a fair, a wedding, or elsewhere, it is rare they do not come to blows for the sole pleasure of the excitement that a fight gives. These quarrels very often end in the death of someone.[54]

Faction fights proliferated in nineteenth-century Ireland.[55] Although motives varied, they could also be regarded as an illustration of violence as sport in nineteenth-century Ireland. Such fights were distinguished by clearly defined rules, willing participants, a sense of pleasure and an absence of malicious intent. Their scale was underreported in crime statistics because parties were rarely arrested; even when serious injuries and fatalities resulted. In the case of brawls, characterized by the use of fists, feet, teeth, stones, and even knives, severe punishment of offenders was unlikely because there was usually an absence of malice.[56] The strength of this tradition, which provided further evidence in British eyes of the inability of the Irish to govern themselves (thereby endorsing the value of the Union), explains its maintenance by some Irish migrants in British cities. Given the violent nature of so much "crime" in Ireland it is somewhat surprising that Irish crime in Britain was not more violent than was actually the case.

The realties of Irish criminality were therefore at odds with British perceptions, a theme examined in the *Dublin Review* in 1857:

> There are some people who live and die in the belief that everything Catholic is inferior to anything Protestant. They have always been told so, everybody says so, and of course it must be so . . . on the particular subject of crime the phrase commonly adopted and circulated will be flavoured with Protestantism and love of country, two very acceptable ingredients, and thus of course become the reigning belief of general society . . . and doubtless every English foolometer will repeat that the people in Catholic countries are far more criminal than in Protestant countries, and especially that Ireland is very black indeed when compared with England.[57]

In seeking to challenge this, Gainsford compared and contrasted the Criminal Returns for England and Wales with those for Ireland and observed that "Ireland is more addicted to crimes of personal violence and England to crimes of fraud or of violence arising from motives of lucre."[58] His concluding remarks are interesting, if not entirely surprising:

> These returns vindicate the character of poor and Catholic Ireland, when compared with rich and Protestant England; . . . the convictions for crime, and especially for the more heinous crimes, are considerably less in proportion to the population in Ireland than in England and Wales. The greater poverty of Ireland would prepare us to expect a greater number of invasions upon property there; the contrary is the fact. . . . The lesson which these returns teach to Ireland is, that her character, though bearing on the whole an advantageous comparison with that of England and Wales, yet does not shine with that degree of superior brightness which would otherwise distinguish her, because so many of her sons are yet slaves to passion, and revenge, and drink, for to these causes . . . may be attributed the assaults and riots which form one-sixth of all the crimes for which Irishmen are convicted. . . . [D]ishonesty and fraud, in all the forms in which they can develop themselves, seem peculiarly to preponderate in England and Wales.[59]

Another context concerns contemporary efforts to combat crime and disorder in Victorian British cities and, in particular, the impact of developments in provincial policing. The practices of the "new police" forces represented an intrusion into working-class districts not previously kept under regular surveillance. The targets of these provincial forces were, essentially, varieties of "street crime," including drunkenness, disorderly behavior, petty theft, vagrancy, and unruly forms of popular leisure.[60] Police forces were sometimes under considerable local pressure to achieve results to justify their expense to ratepayers. Since Irish migrants tended to live in the most intensively policed inner-city districts and were distinguished in the public mind by an unenviable reputation for the very offenses that the police were directed to control, they were doubly vulnerable. There is evidence to suggest that the Irish districts of some towns were deliberately targeted by the police, which partly explains the high level of prosecutions of the Irish-born in specific criminal categories in so many towns.[61]

This raises the question of the extent to which the police were prejudiced against the Irish *per se*. It has been suggested, for example, that police prejudice was evident in Birmingham during the 1867 Murphy Riots of 1867, when police did little to prevent the rioters' entry into the Irish quarter or the destruction and ransacking of Irish houses. However, a majority of those prosecuted after the riot bore Irish names and were charged with throwing stones at the police from *inside* their houses.[62] It is thus possible that many assaults by the Irish on the police represented a response by the Irish to a perceived victimization, although it is important to acknowledge that an antipolice culture was prevalent among many in Ireland before they migrated to Britain. Clashes with British policemen in Victorian towns could therefore be regarded as partly an extension of a traditional dislike of police authority in Ireland.[63] It also possible that the deliberate policing of the Irish, as well as other outcast groups, enhanced local police popularity. In an echo of Taylor's chapter, it could be argued that by creating scapegoats (the habitual criminal, or drunkard, the disorderly Irish), Victorian anxieties were displaced and focused on the enemy within.[64] But many policemen were themselves Irish. Of forty-seven chief constables appointed between 1839 and 1880, fourteen possessed previous experience in the Royal Irish Constabulary.[65] There was a significant proportion of Irish policemen, Catholic and Protestant, in some provincial forces, including Manchester.[66]

Despite evidence of intensive policing in Irish districts in some towns (often counterproductive as it fomented more serious clashes between the police and the Irish), many provincial policemen were afraid of executing their duties in volatile Irish districts without considerable support. When provided, this only fuelled Irish suspicions that they were being discriminated against. Police "prejudice," therefore, might perhaps be better explained in terms of a general discrimination against the "dangerous" or "criminal" sections of working-class society, a category within which the Irish were particularly vulnerable, rather than as prejudice against the Irish *per se*. Of greater significance, as Taylor points out, is the fact that more forms of behavior were being criminalized during the Victorian period. The overrepresentation of the Irish in committals to prison also requires further qualification. It cannot be explained simply in terms of a general prejudice by provincial magistrates against the Irish when determining sentences. It may well be that the petty offenses for which the Irish were largely prosecuted carried a greater likelihood of successful detection and prosecution, making imprisonment a more likely scenario for those convicted, although further research on this subject is necessary before any conclusions may be drawn in support of either claim.

Finally, there is the context of Irish poverty, which many British Protestants ascribed to the deleterious effects of Roman Catholicism. Much Irish criminality was clearly the by-product of a poverty-ridden and brutalizing urban slum environment, although even here it is important to acknowledge that many poor people, Irish and non-Irish, were law-abiding. *The Tablet* observed in 1846,

> there are two classes of Irish labouring people who differ about as widely as light and darkness. There are many who are industrious, methodical, orderly, thrifty and generous in the highest degree. But ask anyone to show you where "the Irish" live. He will take you to a miserable cul-de-sac, which you are afraid of penetrating, and which, bad as it is physically, bears a moral character even worse. There are times when no policeman who is careful of his life dare show himself within that sacred enclosure.[67]

Thus the worst-off Irish poor were associated in the public mind with crime and disorder. In a sense this mirrors the more negative attitudes of the period toward the poorest sections of the English working class.

Vagrancy, a constant nineteenth-century problem, offers another illustration of the relationship between Irish poverty and crime. Vagrants were placed firmly within the "dangerous classes" category.[68] The 1839 Constabulary Commission argued that much crime was the product of migratory criminals in general and vagrants in particular, noting that many of the latter were Irish.[69] Although research has shed considerable doubt on the "migratory thesis," it was nonetheless a powerful force behind contemporary perceptions of criminality, and the transience of Irish migrants made them particularly vulnerable to it.[70] While the stereotype of the Irish beggar was firmly fixed, much so-called "vagrancy" was in fact the seasonal movement of Irish harvesters and the migration of Irish navvies to new construction projects.[71] However, movement of thousands of poor Irish into British towns during the 1840s reinforced popular perceptions of the Irish vagrant as the carrier of crime and disease.

Vagrancy laws were often applied against Irish paupers, particularly for begging. The *Bath Chronicle,* for instance, gleefully reported such cases between 1847 and 1852. John Williams, "an Irishman and his wife, destitute and two children" applied for relief. On being searched, "a bottle of whiskey and 10d" were found in their possession. Williams was "discharged with a caution to leave the city immediately."[72] More harshly, the *Yorkshire Gazette* claimed that "there is no doubt that our gaols obtain a large amount of their inmates from the class of vagrant children who infest our streets." Preston Gaol's chaplain reported that twenty out of twenty-four Irish juveniles who had been imprisoned during the previous twelve months had been convicted of begging, although he acknowledged that they had been driven to Britain by pressure of extreme want and were in a state of great wretchedness. He added he knew of "several exceptional cases in which Irish families have turned out the most industrious and in every way praiseworthy."[73] In reality the actual scale of Irish vagrancy was generally at a lower level than contemporary perceptions allowed. Allegations that that the Irish threw themselves disproportionately on local poor relief were based on prejudice not fact. Even public concern with the subject was in many respects transient, evaporating with the gradual decline in migration from Ireland toward the end of the century.[74]

This provides some possible explanations for the overrepresentation of the Irish poor in the statistics of crime. Fundamental to these, however, were the problems of adaptation faced by newcomers to British society at a time of acute social and economic transformation, given the social tensions arising from this process. Much of the evidence pertaining to Irish criminality relates to the early and mid-Victorian years and is limited, selective and highly subjective, representing the views of the non-Irish and, in particular, those of the "authorities." By contrast, relatively little is actually known of the relationship between Irish migration and crime during the late Victorian period, though the reputation persisted. This subject needs proper investigation to assess how far patterns of Irish criminality characteristic of the earlier period persisted into the 1880s, and beyond. Quite simply, we don't know. This said, it does appear that from the 1870s onward, public concern with Irish criminality in British cities was less urgent than during the mid-Victorian years, reflecting the changing social, economic, political, and cultural contexts of the late Victorian period as well as the growing stability, consciousness, and adaptability of Irish Catholic communities themselves. The nature and pattern of urban crime, and attitudes toward it, were also changing, which had some bearing on the perceived link between the Irish and crime. The marked decline in the incidence of major disturbances involving the Irish (which, as we have seen, were often "anti-Irish" disorders) during the late-Victorian period offers one illustration of change.[75]

Decline of disorders involving the Irish needs to be placed in the broader context of the general decline of violence and disorder and the emergence of a more orderly society during the late Victorian period, where improved policing and techniques of riot control played their part.[76] This was a reflection of the changing face of protest in the context of the growth of more organized and institutional procedures for expressing working-class grievances, the impact of social reform, the extension of the franchise, and the distinctive cultural influences which shaped late Victorian society.[77] It has been generally assumed that the sudden increase in anti-Irish violence was a consequence of the Famine influx coupled with mid-Victorian fears of Catholicism. So, with a subsequent decrease in Irish immigration, newcomers and hosts reached an accommodation, while the Catholic Church became less of a perceived threat and more part of the national religious fabric. Thus Irish immigration was no longer contentious in the same way. The Irish were drawn into the institutions and social life of the areas where they lived, although sectarian rivalries persisted in Merseyside and Clydeside.[78] Ironically, the perceived threat to society in the 1880s and 1890s came not from the Irish but from the thousands of poor Jewish immigrants fleeing from persecution in Eastern Europe who received almost as hostile a reception from the host society as that earlier accorded to the pauper Irish.[79] Finally, the tendency of the Irish, as a dynamic rather than a static group, to disperse within and between late Victorian towns and to integrate into urban society over time made them less visible. This reduced their exposure to riots and other expressions of ethnic conflict, although anti-Irish sentiment may well have been expressed in more subtle and less public ways within working-class communities.[80]

Conclusion

Systematic studies of the statistics of Irish crime are required if further light is to be shed on the precise relationship between Irish migration and settlement and urban crime.[81] The relationship between Irish women and crime (a vastly underresearched subject) is certainly worthy of attention.[82] There is evidence that the Irish-born figured disproportionately in prosecutions for intimate homicide (of female spouses, in particular) between 1835 and 1905.[83] This also opens up the whole question of how far the Irish-born were overrepresented in prosecutions for certain categories of serious crime. Finally, there is need to place Irish crime in urban Britain in a wider comparative context, by reference to Irish criminality in the countries of the Irish Diaspora, most notably the United States and Australia.[84]

In short, much remains to be done if we are to assess adequately the Victorian criminal conversations about the extent to which the Irish were guilty of "behaving badly" in the Victorian city. If "behaving badly" is defined simply in terms of committing an action which violates the criminal law at a specific time and suffering the consequences, the answer, on the evidence to date, is both "yes" and "no." Some Irish migrants did break the law, for some of the reasons explored here. So too did many more English, Scottish, and Welsh people. By contrast, countless Irish were essentially law-abiding and faced the day-to-day difficulties and uncertainties of life in the Victorian city without coming into formal contact with the law. Nevertheless, the study of the relationship between Irish migrants and crime offers insights into contemporary debates about "the other" in Victorian society.

The very presence of the Irish poor in British cities enabled contemporary tensions in society to be deflected onto external factors, thereby helping to define English, or Welsh, or Scottish identities.[85] The particular emphasis on the capacity of the Irish for breaking the law served also to highlight in British eyes the relative orderliness of the non-Irish (even if it was little more than a myth). Pearson, for instance, argues that even the derivation of "hooligan" as a term, coined by the popular press to describe the behavior of rowdy youth gangs during the August Bank Holiday celebrations, was not without significance. It was "most ingenious of late Victorian England to disown the British hooligan by giving him an Irish name."[86] Print reportage of Irish lawlessness provides a window on the complex and diverse experience of Irish migrants, and attitudes toward them, not least in terms of their relationship with the police and the criminal justice system. In a sense, that experience, influenced as it was by issues of identity, community, and nationality, and involving processes of alienation, regulation, adaptation, and accommodation, provides an historical exemplar which is not without relevance to the study of immigrants and minorities in a pluralist society today. But that is another story.

Notes

1. See especially Roger Swift and Shandan Gilley, eds., *The Irish in the Victorian City* (London: Croom Helm, 1985); Roger Swift and Shandan Gilley, eds., *The Irish in Britain, 1815–1939* (London: Pinter, 1989); Graham Davis, *The Irish in Britain, 1815–1914* (Dublin: Gill and Macmillan, 1990); Donald MacRaild, *Irish Migrants in Modern Britain, 1750–1922* (Basingstoke: Macmillan, 1999); R. Swift and S. Gilley, eds., *The Irish in Victorian Britain: The Local Dimension* (Dublin: Irish Academic Press, 1999); Paul O'Leary, *Immigration and Integration: The Irish in Wales, 1798–1922* (Cardiff: University of Wales Press, 2000).

2. PP XXXIV, Report on the State of the Irish Poor in Great Britain, 1836, 20–23.

3. PP XIX, Report of the Royal Commission to Inquire into the Best Means of Establishing an Efficient Constabulary Force in the Counties of England and Wales, 1839, 169, 89, S.97.

4. Thomas Carlyle, *Chartism*, 1839 (London: Everyman, 1972), 182–83.

5. See Flora Tristan, *Promenades dans Londres* (Paris, 1840), 134–35; Leon Faucher, *Manchester in 1844: Its Present Condition and Future Prospects* (London, 1844), 28.

6. See, for example, Frances Finnegan, *Poverty and Prejudice: A Study of Irish Migrants in York, 1840–75* (Cork: Cork University Press, 1982), 132–154; C. Richardson, "The Irish in Victorian Bradford," *The Bradford Antiquary* 9 (1976): 294–316; 311; Roger Swift, "Another Stafford Street Row: Law, Order, and the Irish Presence in Mid-Victorian Wolverhampton," in *Immigrants and Minorities* 3 (1984): 5–29; H. Peavitt, "The Irish: Crime and Disorder in Chester, 1841–1871" (Ph.D. diss., University of Liverpool, 2000); David Taylor, "Policing and the Community: Late Twentieth-Century Myths and Late Nineteenth-Century Realities," in *Social Conditions, Status, and Community, 1860–1920,* ed. Keith Laybourn, 104–22 (Stroud: Alan Sutton, 1997).

7. Report: Irish Poor, 1836, 40–41.

8. Frank Neal, *Sectarian Violence: The Liverpool Experience, 1819–1914* (Manchester: Manchester University Press, 1988), 110–15.

9. *Judicial Statistics, England and Wales, 1861–1901,* House of Commons Papers, 16. The Irish comprised 15 percent of all committals in 1861 (an index of overrepresentation of 4.9), 14 percent in 1871 (5.7), 12 percent in 1881 (5.7), 8 percent in 1891 (5.3), and 7 percent in 1901 (5.6).

10. For example, in Carlisle gaol in 1861, 23.4 percent of males were Irish-born, 12.6 percent female; in 1871, 18.9 percent males were Irish-born, 16.6 percent female: MacRaild, *Irish Migrants,* 163.

11. Peavitt, "The Irish, Crime, and Disorder in Chester, 1841–1871," 182.

12. *Chester Chronicle,* 2 January; 9 January; 13 February; 3 July 1869; Chester City Gaol, Matron's Daily Report Book, 4 February 1870.

13. P. J. Waller, *Democracy and Sectarianism: A Political and Social History of Liverpool, 1868–1939* (Liverpool: Liverpool University Press, 1981), 25.

14. Report: Irish Poor, 1836, 19.

15. Ibid., 19–20; 57; PP., Board of Health, Report on the Sanitary Condition of Wolverhampton, 1849, 28–29.

16. See David Jones, *Crime, Protest, Community, and Police in Nineteenth Century Britain* (London: Routledge and Kegan Paul, 1982), 117–43; T. Dillon, "The Irish in Leeds, 1851–61," *Thoresby Miscellany* 16 (1979): 1–28; Finnegan, *Poverty and Prejudice,* 132–54.

17. Roger Swift, "Crime and the Irish in Nineteenth Century Britain," in *Irish in Britain,* ed. Swift and Gilley, 163–82; see also Roger Swift, "Heroes or Villains? The Irish, Crime, and Disorder in Victorian England," *Albion* 29, 3 (1977): 399–421.

18. B. Harrison, *Drink and the Victorians: The Temperance Question in England, 1815–1872,* 2nd ed. (Keele: Keele University Press, 1994), 156–58.

19. PP XI, Second Report of the Select Committee on Intemperance, 1877, 418, 159, S.5158.

20. John Denvir, *The Irish in Britain* (London: Kegan Paul, 1892), 253.

21. The Chief Constable of Wolverhampton observed: "many are tempted to spend their time and money in these places from the total want of comfort at their own houses," that failing the public house, "they would rather remain out in the open air if the weather was not severe": Sanitary Condition of Wolverhampton, 1849, 28–29.

22. PP XXXVII, Report of the Select Committee on Public Houses, 1852–53.

23. Report, Irish Poor, 1836, appendix I, 40–41.

24. MacRaild, *Irish Migrants,* 164; see also J. R. Barrett, "Why Paddy Drank: The Social Importance of Whiskey in Pre-Famine Ireland," *Journal of Popular Culture* 11 (1977): 1–22.

25. Elizabeth Malcolm, *"Ireland Sober, Ireland Free": Drink and Temperance in Nineteenth Century Ireland* (Dublin: Gill and Macmillan, 1986), 329–34.

26. Harrison, *Drink and the Victorians,* 155–58.

27. W. J. Lowe, *The Irish in Mid-Victorian Lancashire* (New York: P. Lang, 1989), 217–18.

28. Report: Irish Poor, 1836, 23.

29. For further details of the Orange Order, see Hereward Senior, *Orangeism in Ireland and Britain, 1795–1835* (London: Routledge and Kegan Paul, 1966); Elaine McFarland, *Protestants First: Orangeism in Nineteenth Century Scotland* (Edinburgh: Edinburgh University Press, 1990). For Liverpool, see Swift and Gilley, eds., *The Irish in the Victorian City,* 106–29; J. Belchem, ed., *Popular Politics, Riot, and Labour: Essays in Liverpool History, 1790–1940* (Liverpool: Liverpool University Press, 1992). For Glasgow, see Tom Gallagher, *Glasgow, the Uneasy Peace: Religious Tension in Modern Scotland* (Manchester: Manchester University Press, 1987).

30. *Glasgow Herald,* 13 July 1857.

31. For further details, see Donald MacRaild, *Culture, Conflict, and Migration: The Irish in Victorian Cumbria* (Liverpool: Liverpool University Press, 1998).

32. Sanitary Condition of Wolverhampton, 1849, 28.

33. Lowe, *The Irish,* 102.

34. B. Weinburger, "The Police and the Public in Mid-Nineteenth Century Warwickshire," in *Policing and Punishment in Nineteenth Century Britain,* ed. Victor Bailey, 65–93 (London: Croom Helm, 1982).

35. Terry Coleman, *The Railway Navvies* (London: Hutchinson, 1965), 83–90.

36. Swift, "Stafford Street Row," 5–29.

37. See especially P. Millward, "The Stockport Riots of 1852: A Study of Anti-Catholic and Anti-Irish Sentiment," in *The Irish in the Victorian City,* ed. Swift and Gilley, 207–24. These disorders offer an illustration of the extent to which interplay of a variety of factors influenced violence against the Irish. Thus riots may have arisen from antagonism between Irish immigrants and hard-pressed English cotton workers resenting incursion of cheap Irish labor. Insufficient in itself to cause initial violence, the actual spark was restoration of the Catholic religious hierarchy, fanned to a flame by local Anglican clergymen and electorally vulnerable Tory politicians playing the Irish card.

38. Including: Wolverhampton, Rochdale, Ashton, Oldham, Bury, Blackburn, Hanley, Stalybridge, Tynemouth, and Whitehaven. See Walter Arnstein, "The Murphy Riots: A Victorian Dilemma," *Victorian Studies* 19 (1975): 51–71; Roger Swift, "Anti-Catholicism and Irish Disturbances: Public Order in Mid-Victorian Wolverhampton," *Midland History* 9 (1984): 87–108; Donald MacRaild, "William Murphy, the Orange Order, and Communal Violence: The Irish in West Cumberland, 1871–84," in *Racial Violence in Britain, 1840–1950,* ed. Panikos Panayi, 44–64 (Leicester: Leicester University Press, 1993).

39. P. Mulkern, "Irish Immigrants and Public Disorder in Coventry, 1845–1875," *Midland History* 21 (1996): 119–35; K. Jeffes, "The Irish in Early Victorian Chester: An Outcast Community?" in *Victorian Chester: Essays in Social History, 1830–1900,* ed. Roger Swift, 85–118 (Liverpool: Liverpool University Press, 1996).

40. Shendan Gilley, "English Attitudes to the Irish in England, 1780–1900," in *Immigrants and Minorities in British Society,* ed. Colin Holmes, 127–39 (London: Allen & Unwin, 1978).

41. Alan O'Day, "Varieties of Anti-Irish Behaviour in Britain, 1846–1922," in

Racial Violence, ed. Panayi, 26–43; Roger Swift, "Anti-Irish Violence in Victorian England: Some Perspectives," *Criminal Justice History* 15 (1994): 127–34.

42. Graham Davis, "Little Irelands," in *Irish in Britain, 1815–1939,* ed. Swift and Gilley, 106–33.

43. See, for example, N. Kirk, "Ethnicity, Class, and Popular Toryism, 1850–1870," in *Hosts, Immigrants, and Minorities,* ed. Kenneth Lunn, 64–106 (Folkestone: Dawson, 1980).

44. See, for example, Neal, *Sectarian Violence,* 37–79; 151–75; Frank Neal, "Manchester Origins of the English Orange Order," *Manchester Region History Review* (1990–91): 12–24.

45. Patrick Quinlivan and Paul Rose, *The Fenians in England, 1865–72* (London: Calder, 1982), 43–94; Catherine Hall et al., eds., *Defining the Victorian Nation: Class, Race, Gender, and the Reform Act of 1867* (Cambridge: Cambridge University Press, 2000).

46. Arthur Redford, *Labour Migration in England, 1800–1850,* rev. ed. (Manchester: Manchester University Press, 1964), 159–64. Some evidence suggests the Irish impact on wage rates has been exaggerated and competition between English and Irish workers was essentially a product of the pre-Famine period; that there was relative harmony and some political and trades-unionist cooperation between English and Irish workers. See J. Williamson, "The Impact of the Irish on British Labor Markets during the Industrial Revolution," *Journal of Economic History* 46 (1986): 693–720; John Foster, *Class Struggle and the Industrial Revolution* (London: Weidenfeld and Nicolson, 1974), 333.

47. Swift and Gilley, eds., *The Irish in the Victorian City,* 1–12; also B. Collins, "The Irish in Britain, 1780–1921," in *An Historical Geography of Ireland,* ed. B. J. Graham and L. J. Proudfoot, 366–98 (London: Academic Press, 1993).

48. *The Nation,* 6 June 1868.

49. Denvir, *The Irish,* 157–59; 460–62.

50. O'Day, "Varieties of Anti-Irish Behaviour," 26.

51. Finnegan, *Poverty and Prejudice,* 153.

52. Robert Hughes, *The Fatal Shore: A History of the Transportation of Convicts to Australia, 1778–1868* (London: Collins Harvill, 1987).

53. George Rudé, *Protest and Punishment: The Story of the Social and Political Protesters Transported to Australia, 1788–1868* (Oxford: Clarendon, 1978), 8–10; 27–41; 103–12.

54. Emmet Larkin, ed., *Alexis de Tocqueville's Journey in Ireland, July–August 1835* (Dublin: Wolfhound, 1990), 53.

55. See Samuel Clark and James S. Donnelly, eds., *Irish Peasants: Violence and Political Unrest, 1780–1914* (Manchester: Manchester University Press, 1983).

56. Carolyn Conley, "The Agreeable Recreation of Fighting," *Journal of Social History* 33, 1 (1999): 57–72.

57. R. J. Gainsford, "English and Irish Crime," *Dublin Review* 42 (1857): 142–43.

58. Ibid., 151.

59. Ibid., 156.

60. R. D. Storch, "The Plague of the Blue Locusts: Police Reform and Popular Resistance in Northern England, 1840–57," *International Review of Social History* 20 (1975): 61–91.

61. Roger Swift, "Crime and Ethnicity: The Irish in Early Victorian Wolverhampton," *West Midlands Studies* 13 (1980): 1–5; David Taylor, *The New Police in Nineteenth-Century England: Crime, Conflict, and Control* (Manchester: Manchester University Press, 1997), 123.

62. Weinburger, "Police and the Public," 69–71.

63. See Brian Griffin, *The Bulkies: Police and Crime in Belfast, 1800–1865* (Dublin: Irish Academic Press, 1997).

64. David Taylor, "Policing and the Community: Late Twentieth-Century Myths and Late Nineteenth-Century Realities," in *Social Conditions,* ed. Laybourn, 56–87

65. Carolyn Steedman, *Policing the Victorian Community* (London: Routledge and Kegan Paul, 1984), 48.

66. S. Davies, "Classes and Police in Manchester, 1829–1880," in *City, Class, and Culture: Studies of Cultural Production and Social Policy in Victorian Manchester,* ed. Alan Kidd and K. W. Roberts, 30–44 (Manchester: Manchester University Press, 1985), 34. Of 275 Irish policemen recruited 1858–69, a slight majority (148, or 54 percent) were Protestants.

67. *The Tablet,* 24 January 1846.

68. The classic study on vagrancy and crime is David Jones, "The Vagrant and Crime in Victorian Britain: Problems of Definition and Attitude," in *Crime, Protest,* ed. David Jones, 81–103.

69. Constabulary Commission, 1839, 67. It was noted of migratory criminals that "three parts of those who are travelling now throughout the kingdom have Irish blood in them, either from father, mother, or grandmother."

70. See Clive Emsley, *Crime and Society in England, 1750–1900* (London: Longman, 1987), 48–77; R. Swift, "Urban Policing in Early Victorian England, 1835–56: A Reappraisal," *History* 73 (1988): 211–38.

71. Lionel Rose, *"Rogues and Vagabonds": Vagrant Underworld in Britain, 1815–1985* (London: Routledge, 1988), 6–7.

72. Graham Davis, *Bath beyond the Guide Book: Scenes from Victorian Life* (Bristol, 1988), 13.

73. Criminal and Destitute Juveniles, 1852, 197, S.1695–97.

74. Jones, *Crime, Protest,* 183.

75. J. Parry, "The Tredegar Anti-Irish Riots of 1882," *Llafur* 3 (1983): 20–23.

76. John Stevenson, *Popular Disturbances in England, 1700–1870* (London: Longman, 1979), 316–23; Clive Emsley, *Policing and Its Context, 1750–1870* (Basingstoke: Macmillan, 1983), 132–47.

77. Roger Swift, "Anti-Irish Violence in Victorian England: Some Perspectives," *Criminal Justice History* 15 (1994): 127–39.

78. O'Day, "Anti-Irish Behaviour," 37.

79. See Colin Holmes, *John Bull's Island: Immigration and British Society, 1871–1971* (Basingstoke: Macmillan, 1988), 56–83; Vivian Lipman, *A History of the Jews in Britain since 1858* (Leicester: Leicester University Press, 1990), 43–88.

80. O'Day, "Anti-Irish Behaviour," 40.

81. Roger Swift, "The Historiography of the Irish in Nineteenth-Century Britain: Some Perspectives," in *Irish in British Labour History,* ed. Buckland and Belchem, 11–18.

82. See M. Kanya-Forstner, "Defining Womanhood: Irish Women and the Catholic Church in Victorian Liverpool," in *The Great Famine and Beyond: Irish Migrants in Britain in the Nineteenth and Twentieth Centuries,* ed. Donald MacRaild, 168–88 (Dublin: Irish Academic Press, 2000).

83. I am indebted to Professor Martin Wiener for this information. Referring to a range of sources, he has identified 1,050 convictions for domestic homicide during the

period, noting the Irish were represented disproportionately (at least 10 percent of the whole). M. Wiener, "Intimate Homicide in Nineteenth-Century England," unpublished paper, "Crime and Violence in Nineteenth-Century England," unpublished paper, University of Keele, July 1999.

84. See Donald Akenson, *The Irish Diaspora: A Primer* (Belfast: Inssitute of Irish Studies, 1996), 118–19; 181–82.

85. O'Leary, *Immigration and Integration,* 184–85.

86. Geoffrey Pearson, *Hooligan: A History of Respectable Fears* (London: Macmillan, 1983), 74.

8

Striking at Sodom and Gomorrah: The Medicalization of Male Homosexuality and Its Relation to the Law[1]

IVAN CROZIER

Introduction

Social panics were rife in the Victorian period. This is understandable; there were, after all, rapists, poisoners, murderers, prostitutes, and kidnappers to be brought to justice, as the newspapers constantly emphasized. And the newspapers were backed up by a range of other publications, from the specialist to the popular. A formidable list of perpetrators could be assembled, including Thomas Neill Cream, Jack the Ripper, and Dr. Pritchard. There were many others whose names were writ large in the moral fears of Victoria's citizens, and the possibility of meeting such bogeys kept women at home at night, and police on their toes. Another topic that provided prime material for a Victorian social panic with its accompanying expressions of moral outrage was (male) homosexuality, with the famous cases of Boulton and Park and Oscar Wilde, or the Cleveland Street Scandal, providing the targets around which widespread social unease and moral indignation could coalesce. As with so many other episodes of panic, the demand was for solutions. The important questions were: who should be the expert to decide the nature of the problem, and how to deal with "perpetrators"? There were two main candidates: lawyers and doctors. Of course, the lawyers had a stronger position; they worked within the law, and it was the law that had made same-sex practices illegal between 1533 and 1967 (it should be noted that some same-sex practices, such as with minors or involving sadomasochistic group practices, and so forth, still are illegal in England). Doctors, on the other hand, had to struggle to gain some foothold in court, and in society at large. There are contextual reasons for this struggle. Medicine in the nineteenth century was still trying to define itself as a "profession," and doing so partly by trying to limit those who could legitimately practice medicine, and to set standards for the training of doctors.² But what it also needed was public acknowledgment of its professional status. Although medical practitioners coveted the lawyers' power and influence and professional status, based in public acceptance of these factors, there was no obvious way of obtaining it, so far as medicine was concerned. Medical authority over moral issues was then not obvious, and it is only medicine's strong social position that gives it such authority today. This chapter examines one aspect of the way in which medicine asserted its right to authoritative pronouncements in the public sphere, via the publicizing in the media of its activities in the courtroom.

Some Contextual Aspects

As Sandra Morton's chapter in this volume demonstrates, medicine was taking an initiative in the field of adulteration of food and its prosecution. Medicine was also already being called on by law to back up prosecution or defense cases, especially in serious crimes. The advance of science provided real opportunities here. Doctors, especially those with a forensic bent, and others who found themselves in the courtroom giving evidence, had to manage legal knowledge in order to be heard on their own terms. It was exploitation of this legal knowledge that doctors used to enhance their own status. How was this done? By managing the kinds of expert knowledge about legal issues and the publicizing of this. In rape cases, this consisted of producing detailed medical descriptions of defloration, of virginal breasts, and of the "normal" state of the body; in cases of poisoning, it meant biochemical analysis and physiological experience. In the writings with which this chapter is concerned—discourses about male same-sex acts—this also relied on different strategies of producing narratives of expertise by relying on medical knowledge which was too esoteric for even most doctors, based on the reading of specific anatomical, psychological, or biological signs.

This analysis is facile, however. As this chapter shows, there were several different strategies for positing medical expertise in relation to the law which were available, from supporting lawyers in their hunt for sodomites, to constructing psychological ideas about homosexuals which were outside the ambit of legal practice (such as men who loved men, but who had not committed sodomy), to biological, historical, and anthropological standpoints on the nature of same-sex desire which argued that it was natural, and therefore should not even be considered illegal, thus challenging the law directly on the matter. It cannot be argued too strongly that there was no single medical voice, but myriad different medical discourses that had something to say about same-sex practices and were seeking outlets to say it. In all of these types, the law acted as a motor for change in medical knowledge. It was an antagonistic force against which medical practitioners framed their arguments, either in a supportive or a challenging way. The panic in medicine around the discussion of homosexuality was not so much about the morality of same-sex practices, as about who should be the voice of authority.

While this chapter is concerned chiefly with the history of medicine, it fits into a larger historiography of the history of sexuality. Historians of homosexuality have paid much attention to the law of England, and particularly to sodomy trials, in order to gauge both what was generally thought of same-sex practices in the past, and how the law framed such practices as illegal.[3] A great deal of historical attention has been directed toward the law, and especially to the many existing court records, in order to understand homosexual subcultures of the past.[4] Scholars have also addressed the presuppositions about homosexuality that were held by the legal profession.[5] Furthermore, historians of homosexuality have regularly considered medical discourses in order to establish the "official" view of homosexuality that was held in England; these sources often consider English sexologists such as Havelock Ellis.[6] Most attention has been paid to Continental sexology, however.[7] Both Continental and English medical discourses about same-sex practices changed from the focus on physical signs of sodomy used to convict "perverts" to the construction of a "homosexual type." What was happening in England was not different to Continental sexology, although it is usual to think of the importation of Continental theory as a "watering down" of this knowledge for the English medical palette.

There are, however, other important historiographical issues to recognize before embarking on a history of the relationship between the law and medicine with regard to same-sex practices, and the media conversation presenting these to a wider public. These include the idea of fields and the idea of boundary construction.[8] To identify a field, it is important to consider the specific set of dispositions possible for a particular individual. These dispositions are essential for identifying members of a field by constraining what they do, what they write, and how they act. Other actions are the products of other fields. For this reason, it should be emphasized that there were several different medical fields of writing on homosexuality that should not be conflated to suggest that a coherent body of medical thought about same-sex practices existed. These *sui generis* fields of discourse had their own "rules" of construction, even though they all existed under the ægis of medical practice. Here, the fields are forensic medicine, venereology, psychology, and sexology. That venereology and sexology are both medical fields does not mean that practitioners in these specialties have corresponding ideas about human sexuality, and indeed, it is the different dispositions that they adopt which identifies them as venereologists, sexologists, or another type of doctor. For instance, practitioners of sexology formulated a position whereby the law should be revoked, and homosexuality would be an issue for psychologists rather than lawyers, whereas venereologists formulated more specific tests for the forensic expert to aid in the detection of sodomy.

The other idea running through this chapter is that although there was some cooperation between doctors and lawyers, and although some medical evidence was coopted into trials, there was also much antagonism as medicine tried to secure a position for itself.[9] It gained this secure position by constructing boundaries between medical and legal approaches to same-sex practices, by utilizing different ideas and practices; basically, by maintaining the differences between the fields. Boundary working is a specific part of operating within a field; it only comes to the fore when the practitioner has to address the law directly. These boundaries are constructed around where "proper" expertise should lie. When the venereologist is addressing the work of other people in the same field, he constructs specific discourses that either support or challenge the positions held by other workers in the same field. When other fields are addressed, the differences in disposition (the commitments and specific actions that make the other discourses of a completely different field) come to the fore. This is precisely what happens in the following cases of medical authors addressing the law in order to gain some form of hegemony over the object of same-sex practices.

This chapter, then, is a study in how authority is constructed and given public validity, including the role of the print media in that construction. This authority was part of the process of debate central to the management of social panics, largely expressed through the rhetoric of the associated moral outrage in the public domain. Part of its aim was to keep the citizens at ease by suggesting that the object of their panic—be it a rapist, a poisoner, or a cross-dressing homosexual—was understandable, identifiable, and thus manageable (though Taylor, for example, has touched on the increasing tensions in this perspective). Some fields, particularly sexology, posited the idea that there was no need for a panic because the problem (male homosexuality in this chapter) was merely misunderstood, and so a witch hunt was not required after all. The claims of forensic medicine, on the other hand, meant that a credible identification could be put into place, and that doctors could facilitate the law in their management of the problem. They might even leave the British public safe in the knowledge that sodomy was a particularly Continental vice that had not affected the shores of Britain, as most expertise was either French or German. In this sense, British medical ignorance about homosexuality was actually celebrated as proof that it was not a major problem on these shores (a point that emerged in the summing up of *R v Boulton and Park,* 1871[10]). Without the law, we might ask whether there would have been a social panic over homosexuality at all, by doctors or by the public at large.

The Medicalization of Sodomy: Forensic Medicine

Medical discussions of same-sex acts, particularly sodomy, initially developed within forensic medicine. This was not because of a wide knowledge of sodomy held by physicians. In fact there is a relative absence of detailed discussion of same-sex practices. Rather, forensic medicine had good ties within the legal framework that the other fields of medicine concerned with sodomy did not have. The main position occupied by those within the field of forensic medicine was a supportive role to the passage of the law. The defense and the prosecution enrolled forensic arguments into their narratives to secure the freedom or punishment for the defendant.

The most prominent contributions to jurisprudential medicine came from Alfred Taylor, whose *Manual of Medical Jurisprudence* was continually updated from the 1840s until well into the twentieth century. Taylor specified that a case of sodomy could be brought before the courts only when anal penetration had taken place; "if it is done elsewhere it is not sodomy."[11] He also noted that sodomy was "commonly sufficiently proved without medical evidence."[12] Further, Taylor added that unless the individual "be in a state of insensibility, it is not possible to conceive that this offence should be perpetrated in an adult of either sex against the will of the party. . . . [The] slightest resistance will suffice to prevent its perpetration."[13]

To the medical historian, the most interesting aspect of the 1871 case of Boulton and Park is that all of the medical evidence tendered was purely physical in nature. Seven different doctors were called to give evidence, from Dr. Paul, a police surgeon who made the initial examinations, to Alfred Taylor and other doyens of the world of English forensic medicine. Of this physical evidence, the general conclusion was that the physician could not tell with any degree of accuracy if sodomy had been committed, although some doctors came down on both sides, believing that there were definite signs of penetration in some cases, and that the anuses of Boulton and Park had never been penetrated at all in others. It could be said that knowledge about sodomy in medical circles was scant indeed, and the national press confined itself to reporting regularly that the full details of the case were both disgusting and confused.[14] This is hardly surprising in late Victorian times. Even in Germany, where the most important developments in sexology were beginning to take place, Carl Westphal's important article, "Die Conträre Sexualempfindung," had been written only two years prior to the trial.[15] Sexology had not developed to the point where it could advance the concept of "homosexuality," although it was soon to do so on the Continent.[16] But in England things remained much the same for the time being. Other, lower-key examples could be chosen, and further attention to the rape sections of forensic medical textbooks could be examined to show that the knowledge in the high-profile case of Boulton and Park was not unique. In other examples, forensic medical knowledge still maintained a position of serving the interests of the law: this was, after all, the main aim of the field. It did not have a powerful position; its own views were by and large ignored in favor of nonmedical issues. This becomes particularly apparent when we consider venereology.

Other Ways of Medicalizing Sodomy: Venereology

Venereology was an important branch of medicine in the nineteenth century. The panics about prostitution and syphilis were in some cases justified, as the dire venereal condition of the armed forces demonstrate in the Victorian period.[17] In the preantibiotic age, syphilis was a serious issue, so a series of complicated measures involving mercury were required. Death came to those infected in the long run. Syphilis could also be an important forensic point. Medical jurisprudence texts abound with descriptions of syphilitic chancres and gonorrheal oozes as proof of sexual intercourse. It is important to realize, however, that there were other more specialist medical fields that addressed these venereal complaints: particularly venereology. Nevertheless, venereology was hardly a great specialty in terms of medical prestige. It was associated with prostitution, police work, and treating anonymous upper-class gentlemen. It was also a particularly French profession. I will exemplify some of the issues of English venereology in the Victorian period by focusing on one of the premier players, who also wrote about sodomy and its detection.

William Acton (1813–75) was an important venereologist, though he has been much maligned by recent historians. His writings have been characterized by some as "the official views of sexuality held by Victorian society," although this view is not particularly sophisticated.[18] Acton was interested in some the medicolegal aspects of sodomitic crime, and attended to cases "in which no doubt can arrive that contagion has had its source in unnatural intercourse, as the parties were taken *in flagrante delicto,* or the patients have acknowledged that such had been the origin of the complaint." From these cases, Acton argued that one could derive a "true interpretation of the symptoms" that "is very necessary to medico-legal inquiries."[19] He suggested that diagnoses of nonspecific venereal infections of the rectum (rectal discharges caused by neither gonorrhea nor syphilis) are difficult, especially considering the jurisprudential ramifications of such a diagnosis. Acton preferred to address definite cases with knowable causes. In this case, he addressed the signs left by sodomy rather in the manner that Taylor had, above, although it is significant to note that Acton did not ally himself with British forensic experts, but rather with the work of French venereologists (he had studied venereology in France after his time at Barts, and was one of the most significant importers of French venereological knowledge to England). Acton noted that "previous writers have stated that there are certain appearances of the rectum which betoken the fact that unnatural crimes have been committed." For instance, the French surgeon Auguste Cullerier advocated the opinion concerning "the funnel-shaped appearance of the rectum," although Acton emphasized that in a case which he had examined, "it was satisfactorily proven that this funnel-shaped appearance of the anus does not necessarily follow the commission of an unnatural crime; no such appearance was there present." Additionally, Acton described how dissection of a phthisical patient demonstrates that "this infundibuliform appearance will often be found, as it depends on the absorption of fat; an inflammatory affection may cause a swelling of the parts around the anus, and give the opening a funnel-shaped appearance." Acton therefore inferred that sodomy could take place "without this sign being present;" he also noted that "if it does exist there is no reason to suppose that the crime has been perpetrated."[20]

Acton elaborated on some of the methods of ascertaining if sodomy had taken place. Simple rectal discharge afforded no assistance. However, if syphilitic chancres were present, "and inoculation produces the characteristic pustule," the case could assume a different aspect especially if the chancre does not exist on any other part of the sexual organs.[21] There were exceptions to this rule: "if chancres exist on the external organs of the female, there is nothing to prevent the belief that the virus may have dribbled back and provided the affection of the rectum."[22] He emphasized caution when considering the "habits of the patient, or the history of the complaint," as these "seldom aid the diagnosis, as in judicial inquiries an acknowledgment of the cause of the disease is not likely to be made." Thus Acton suggested that medical evidence given in cases of alleged unnatural offenses was a difficult subject, for "when no chancre exists, there is no one unequivocal sign that the complaint which the surgeon is called to pronounce upon, depends on a disease contracted in unnatural connexion." However, Acton did note that there is a particular sign upon which his teacher, the Parisian venereologist, Phillipe Ricord, laid great stress: "a rent or tearing of the margin opposite the *coccyx* and *perinaeum,* which [Ricord] never found in persons unaccustomed to the crime."[23]

Venereology, as the example of Acton demonstrates, was involved with the law only insofar as to provide more efficacious methodologies for the detection of sodomy, and more detailed descriptions of the results of anal penetration, for forensic medicine. It did not try to challenge the ideas being promulgated by forensic medicine or by the law. Instead, it maintained the basic beliefs of same-sex behavior while adding descriptions of sodomy to its expanding group of sexual objects that could be medicalized. It is important to realize that boundaries between venereology and both forensic medicine and the law were drawn by venereologists. The descriptions of the sodomized anus were much more detailed and speculative in venereology than in forensic medicine, where hypothetical knowledge was not considered admissible evidence, and the facts of the case only were to be reported. These practical constraints are one of the reasons that different dispositions were maintained between fields.

The Medicalization of Homosexuality: Sexology and Psychology

The psychologization of same-sex activity was concerned neither with venereological description of the consequences of anal penetration, nor with forensic medicine. Rather, psychology and sexology emerged in order to explain same-sex behavior. Sexology often actively attempted to alter the law as a part of the "proto-gay liberation" movement.[24] Psychology was content to describe clinical cases. In the mid-1880s, George Savage contributed a homosexual case to the *Journal of Mental Science*. Savage described a twenty-eight-year-old single man who "felt so ashamed of his unnatural state that he wished he were dead, to prevent scandal to his family."[25] The man, who was very religious, was also hard working and led a solitary life. He had no desire for women, and doubted that he ever did have. But "The sight of a fine man causes him to have an erection, and if he is forced to be in his society he has an emission."[26] Germane to this paper, Savage questioned whether this "perversion is as rare as it appears," for he found that it was often met with in the courts, thus again emphasizing the role of the law in making medical practitioners justify their discourses on homosexuality in terms of the law, while also highlighting that the law was not totally effective for eradicating the problem, as the case he was examining was not a legal one.[27] Savage was implicitly suggesting that medical practitioners had more to offer in certain circumstances: he was redressing the boundaries around the object of homosexuality by introducing the homosexual as a type rather than a series of signs on an anus. This new strategy is one of the things that set the fields of psychology apart from venereology and forensic medicine. It should be seen as a challenge to the law over the nature of the object, rather than supporting the detection of crime.

To turn to sexology proper, the man-of-letters, John Addington Symonds, addressed the legal situation in a number of anonymously authored, privately printed, early sexological texts. Like Savage, he drew attention to the fact that although homosexual activity was punished, it still persisted. Symonds demanded treatment of homosexuality in medical and legal literature because he considered it to be hereditary: "every family runs the risk of producing a boy or girl whose life will be embittered by inverted sexuality, but who in all other respects will be no worse or better than the normal members of the home." He considered it society's duty "to learn what we can about its nature, and to arrive through comprehension at some rational method of dealing with it."[28] In *A Problem in Modern Ethics,* Symonds argued that England should adopt the same stance on homosexuality as other European states that held the Napoleonic Code, under which male homosexual behavior was only illegal if performed in public, or if it abused minors.[29]

Writing against many medical approaches to homosexuality, Symonds presented his own categories:

> (1) Forced abstinence from intercourse with females; (2) wantonness and curious seeking after novel pleasure; (3) pronounced morbidity; (4) inborn instinctive preference for the male and indifference to the female sex; (5) epochs of history when the habit has become established and endemic in whole nations.[30]

Symonds emphasized that those with an instinctive inborn desire for their own sex "behave precisely like persons of normal sexual proclivities, display no signs of insanity, and have no morbid constitutional diatheses to account for their peculiarity."[31] This was in distinction to social feeling, which "moulded by religion, by legislation, by civility, and by the persistent antipathies of the majority, regards sexual inversion with immitigable abhorrence."[32] For the first time in English writing, homosexuality was being conceived of as a "type," and not as a series of either physical signs or behavioral symptoms. Furthermore, Symonds noted that scientific investigation had proved that

> a very large proportion of persons in whom abnormal sexual inclinations are manifested, possess them from their earliest childhood, that they cannot divert them into normal channels, and that they are powerless to get rid of

them. In these cases then, legislation is interfering with the liberty of individuals, under a certain misconception regarding the nature of their offence.[33]

In other words, homosexuality should be considered natural and should not be illegal.

Symonds died before any of the legal reforms for which he had argued materialized. So did the prominent English sexologist, Havelock Ellis, with whom Symonds collaborated on the first English medical textbook published on homosexuality, *Sexual Inversion* (1897). *Sexual Inversion* was written in order to reclassify homosexuality. Ellis and Symonds mooted that "It can scarcely be said that the attitude of society is favourable to the invert's attainment of a fairly sane and well-balanced attitude." This, they thought, was "indeed, one of the great difficulties in his way and causes [the homosexual] to waver between extremes of melancholia and egoistic exaltation."[34]

Ellis and Symonds's *Sexual Inversion* followed in the style of Continental sexologists, describing homosexuality in both men and women, and demonstrating that it was but another manifestation of the sexual instinct: itself a natural process. The major difference between homosexuality and "normal" sexuality was that the homosexual had the same sex as the object of their sexual desire. This was supported with many case studies that, like Savage's case above, illustrated how desire was manifest in an individual. Homosexuality was, in Ellis and Symonds's eyes, either congenital or acquired. They actively addressed English law; the ramifications of the Criminal Law Amendment Act 1885 made "'gross indecency' between males, however privately committed, a penal offence." Ellis and Symonds were "of the opinion that neither 'sodomy' . . . nor 'gross indecency' ought to be penal offences, except under special circumstances." In other words, "if two persons of either or both sexes, having reached the years of discretion, privately consent to practise some perverted mode of sexual relationship, the law cannot be called on to interfere." Ellis and Symonds considered the law's function was "to prevent violence, to protect the young, and to preserve public order and decency."[35] They did not think it necessary to persecute homosexuals in order to achieve these aims. The liberating approach to homosexuality advocated by Ellis and Symonds was not heeded by the legal profession. When Ellis died in 1939 *R v Boulton and Park* was still referred to in cases of unnatural acts; physical signs were still looked for when other evidence was not forthcoming. Psychological "justifications" for homosexual desire were not sought.[36] It was only after an important sexological inquiry, tabulated in the Wolfenden Report, that sex acts between men became decriminalized in private. This was in 1967.

Chapter 8

Conclusion

Medical writing about homosexuality in nineteenth-century England developed in relation to the law in a number of ways. First, forensic medicine was used in court in some instances (but far from all, as usually medicine was not relied upon to prove a crime had been committed). Forensic medicine did not challenge the legal definition of sodomy, but rather supplied further evidence necessary to the passage of law. Second, venereology added to the corpus of medical knowledge about sodomy by providing detailed descriptions of the physical signs and symptoms of sodomy that could be utilized in medical jurisprudence. Venereology did not attempt to alter the legal situation of those who had been charged with committing sodomy, but acted very much in the line of forensic medicine in its provision of support for the available medical evidence by which homosexuals could be convicted, even though it provided much more detailed knowledge that would not be admissible to English courts of the day. Lastly, psychology and sexology can also be seen to have developed in relation to the law in England in the latter part of the nineteenth century. Unlike those disciplines that relied upon physical evidence, sexology rested upon psychological theories of sexual development that were, by and large, imported from the Continent by Ellis and his colleagues. Ellis's sexology primarily challenged the legal status of those who indulged in same-sex activity by suggesting that homosexuality was not an unnatural state, and therefore should not be a criminal offense. Much of the impetus behind the development of sexology came from the liberal political views of its English proponents, particularly of Ellis and Edward Carpenter.[37] In this sense, the medical challenge to the law, which encapsulated the aims of medical specialization in that it attempted to gain hegemony over a specific area of knowledge, was a part of a political movement as much as it was a medical phenomenon.

It would be a truism to say that medicine and the law were both fields that maintained their power in society by their ability to isolate and define members of that society. In the case of medical theories of same-sex activity we see the challenge to move from the dominance of one discipline (law), which had the support of certain varieties of medicine (venereology and forensic medicine), to a position where a new branch of medicine, sexology, became the orthodox medical position on same-sex activity by the mid-twentieth century.[38] This move can be identified by the invention of new categories (psychological and congenital reasons for homosexual behavior, rather than the purely deviant behavior with which the sodomite was accused), which undermined the efficacy of the traditional legal position (that is, once sexology's natural model for the homosexual was accepted, it would render legal models of "unnatural" behavior irrelevant). The fact that sexology's attempt to challenge the law as the dominant discourse in the control of same-sex behavior was primarily unsuccessful does not alter the fact that the law acted as a motor for changes in medical knowledge because of the antagonistic role it played in relation to the growth of medicine in the nineteenth century. These developments were either in support of or in opposition to the law, depending on the field being considered.

Notes

1. This chapter is derived from a previous publication: Ivan Crozier, "The Medical Construction of Homosexuality and Its Relation to the Law in Nineteenth-Century England," *Medical History* 45 (2001): 61–82.

2. Harold Perkin, *The Rise of Professional Society: England since 1880* (London: Routledge, 1990).

3. See, for a representative sample, Rictor Norton, *The Myth of the Modern Homosexual* (London: Cassell, 1997); Randolph Trumbach, "Sex, Gender, and Sexual Identity: Male Sodomy and Female Prostitution in Enlightenment London," *Journal of the History of Sexuality* (1991): 186–2003; Jeffrey Weeks, *Coming Out: Homosexual Politics in Britain from the Nineteenth Century to the Present* (London: Quartet, 1977); Matt Houlbrook, "The Private World of Public Urinals: London, 1918–1957," *The London Journal* 25 (2000): 52–71.

4. See, for example, the attention which has been paid to the most famous nineteenth-century sodomy trial, *Regina v Boulton and Others (Park),* Queen's Bench, May 1871. William Roughead, *Bad Companions* (London: Green and Co., 1930), 149–83, seems to have been the first historical account of Boulton and Park and has been used to frame most of the later accounts. The best account of the trial is William Cohen, *Sex Scandal: The Private Parts of Victorian Culture* (London: Duke University Press, 1996), 73–129. For a recent contribution addressing some of the medical literature, but in a way removed from other contemporary medical writing, see Charles Upchurch, "Forgetting the Unthinkable: Cross-Dressers and British Society in the Case of the Queen vs. Boulton and Others," *Gender and History* 12 (2000): 127–57.

5. See Nell Bartlett, *Who Was That Man? A Present for Mr. Oscar Wilde* (London: Serpents Tail, 1988), 93–163; Jeffrey Weeks, "Inverts, Perverts, and Mary-Annes: Male Prostitution and the Regulation of Homosexuality in England in the Nineteenth and Twentieth Centuries," in *Against Nature: Essays on History, Sexuality, and Identity,* ed. Jeffrey Weeks, 63–68 (London: Rivers Oram, 1991). A. Sinfield, *The Wilde Century: Effeminacy, Oscar Wilde, and the Queer Moment* (London: Cassell, 1994), addresses the differences between Weeks and Bartlett on Boulton and Park.

6. See, for example, Lesleuy Hall, "Heroes or Villains? Reconsidering British Sexology of the *Fin de Siècle,*" in *New Sexual Agendas,* ed. Lynn Segal, 1–16 (Basingstoke: Macmillan, 1997).

7. Much attention has been directed toward Continental sexology: see Jorg Hutter, "The Social Construction of Homosexuals in the Nineteenth Century: The Shift from Sin to the Influence of the Medicine in Criminalizing Sodomy in Germany," *Journal of Homosexuality* 24 (1993): 73–93; Gert Hekma, "A History of Sexology: Social and Historical

Aspects of Sexuality," in *From Sappho to De Sade: Moments in the History of Sexuality*, ed. Jon Bremmer, 173–93 (Routledge, 1989); Harry Oosterhuis, "Medical Science and the Modernization of Sexuality," in *Sexual Cultures in Europe: National Histories*, ed. Franz Eder et al., 221–41 (Manchester: Manchester University Press, 1999).

    8. For more on fields, see Pierre Bourdieu, "The Peculiar History of Scientific Reason," *Sociological Forum* 6 (1991): 3–26. For more on boundary working, see Thomas Gieryn, "Boundary-Work and the Demarcation of Science from Non-science: Strains and Interests in Professional Ideologies of Scientists," *American Sociological Review* 48 (1983): 781–95.

    9. See R. Smith, "Legal Frameworks for British Psychiatry," in *150 Years of British Psychiatry*, ed. Hugh Freeman and German Berrios (London: Athlone, 1991); R. Smith, "Expertise and Causal Attribution in Deciding between Crime and Mental Disorder," *Social Studies of Science* 15 (1985): 67–98.

    10. *R v Boulton and others* (1871) 7 Cox CC 87.

    11. Alfred Swaine Taylor, *A Manual of Medical Jurisprudence*, 2nd ed. (London: J. Churchill, 1846), 560–61. Specifically, this meant that same-sex fellatio was not illegal, something which would change in 1885, under the Criminal Law Amendment Act. See F. B. Smith, "Labouchère's Amendment to the Criminal Law Amendment Act," *Historical Studies* 17 (1976): 165–75. A case of fellatio could lead to a charge of conspiracy to commit sodomy, but this charge amounted to proving whether or not sodomy had been committed. Cohen, *Sex Scandal*, 87–89.

    12. Taylor, *Medical Jurisprudence*, 561.

    13. Alfred Swaine Taylor, *Principles and Practice of Medical Jurisprudence* (London, 1865), 2: 1018.

    14. For example, *Daily Telegraph*, 31 May 1870; 12 July 1870.

    15. Carl Westphal, "Die Conträre Sexualempfindung: Symptom eines neuropathischen (psychopathischen) Zustandes," *Archive für Psychiatrie und Nervenkrankenheit*, 1869. This text was noticed after the trial in an anonymous report on *Archive für Psychiatrie*, 1869, in *Journal of Mental Science* (October 1871): 422. Westphal's article has been hailed by Foucault as the beginning of a science of sexuality; see Michel Foucault, *Introduction*, vol. 1, *The History of Sexuality* (Harmondsworth: Penguin, 1990), 43.

    16. V. M. Tarnovsky, *The Sexual Instinct and Its Morbid Manifestations Considered from the Double Standpoint of Jurisprudence and Medicine* (Paris: Charles Carrington, 1898); Richard von Krafft-Ebing, *Psychopathia Sexualis* (London: F. A. Davis, 1892); Albert Moll, *Perversions of the Sexual Instinct: A Study of Sexual Inversion Based on Clinical Data and Official Documents* (1891; New York: Julian Press, 1976), were the most important psychological texts addressing homosexuality and the law. S. Vern Bullough, "The Physician and Research into Human Sexual Behaviour in Nineteenth-Century Germany," *Bulletin for the History of Medicine* 66 (1992): 21–48.

    17. Kenneth Ballhatchet, *Race, Sex, and Class under the Raj* (London: Weidenfield & Nicholson, 1980).

    18. Stephen Marcus, *The Other Victorians: A Study of Sexuality and Pornography in Mid-Nineteenth Century England* (New York: Meridian, 1974), xix; Ivan Crozier, "William Acton and the History of Sexuality: The Medical and Professional Contexts," *Journal of Victorian Culture* 5 (2000): 1–27.

    19. William Acton, *A Practical Treatise on Diseases of the Urinary and Generative Organs (in Both Sexes)*, 2nd ed. (London: John Churchill, 1851), 330.

    20. Acton, *Practical Treatise*, 331–32. This material was also dealt with by Ambrose

Tardieu, *Etude médico-légale sur les attentants aux mœurs* (Paris, 1857); Johann L. Casper, *Handbook for the Practice of Forensic Medicine,* 4 vols. (London: The New Sydenham Society, 1861–65), vol. 3. Both were given considerable importance in the trial of Boulton and Park.

21. Inoculation was the practice of extracting some of the pus from a suspect ulcer and infecting a clean site on the patient's body. If a characteristic syphilitic ulcer appeared in the newly contaminated site, then one concluded the original sore was syphilitic. If not, then the original sore was concluded to be nonspecific, caused by gonorrhea or another such nonspecific disease (theory developed by Phillipe Ricord, pregerm theory). See William Acton, "On the Advantages to Be Derived from the Study of Inoculation, in the Investigation of the Treatment of Disease," *Lancet* 1 (1839–40): 351–54; W. Acton, "Advantages of Inoculation in Venereal Disease," *Lancet* 1 (1839–40): 533–35.

22. Acton, *Practical Treatise,* 332. The law in England specified against unnatural acts, which did not necessarily mean male-male sodomy. Theoretically, one could be hanged for consensual sodomizing of one's wife before 1861.

23. Acton, *Practical Treatise,* 332.

24. See pioneering works: John Lauritsen and D. Thorstad, *The Early Homosexual Rights Movement, 1866–1935* (New York: Times Change Press, 1974); and James Steakley, *The Homosexual Emancipation Movement in Germany* (New York: Arno Press, 1975).

25. George Savage, "Case of Sexual Perversion in a Man," *Journal of Mental Science* 30 (1884), 390–91.

26. Ibid.

27. Ibid., 391.

28. J. A. Symonds, *Studies in Sexual Inversion,* privately printed, 1928, 6–7.

29. J. A. Symonds, *A Problem in Modern Ethics: Being an Inquiry into the Phenomenon of Sexual Inversion, Addressed Especially to Medical Psychiatrists and Jurists,* privately printed, 1891, 18.

30. Ibid., 123.

31. Ibid., 124.

32. Ibid., 125.

33. Ibid., 129.

34. Havelock Ellis and J. A. Symonds, *Sexual Inversion* (London: Addington Symonds, 1897), 147.

35. Ibid., 155–56.

36. Chris Waters, "Havelock Ellis, Sigmund Freud, and the State: Discourses of Homosexuality in Interwar Britain," in *Sexology in Culture,* ed. Lucy Bland and Laura Doan, 165–79 (London: Polity, 1998).

37. Sheila Rowbotham and Jeffrey Weeks, *Socialism and the New Life: The Personal and Sexual Politics of Edward Carpenter and Havelock Ellis* (London: Pluto Press, 1977); C. Nottingham, *The Pursuit of Serenity: Havelock Ellis and the New Politics* (Amsterdam University Press, 1999).

38. See Waters, "Havelock Ellis."

9

A Mania for Suspicion: Poisoning, Science, and the Law

TONY WARD

Introduction

In Wilkie Collins's *Armadale* (1865–66), the cynical private detective Jemmy Bashwood recounted what happened after the villainess of the tale, Lydia Gwilt, was convicted of poisoning her wealthy husband:

> On the evening of the Trial, two or three of the young Buccaneers of Literature went down to two or three newspaper officers, and wrote two or three heartrending leading articles.... The next morning the public caught light like tinder; and the prisoner was tried over again, before an amateur court of justice, in the columns of the newspapers.[1]

What Bashwood described was something very like a social panic with its accompanying moral outrage, but not one inspired by the many alarming stories the public could read about the supposed new menace of domestic poisoning.[2] On the contrary: "Here was the Law that they all paid to protect them, actually doing its duty in dreadful earnest! Shocking! shocking!"[3]

Collins modelled this episode on the events that followed the trial of Thomas Smethurst in 1859.[4] In contrast to the alluring Lydia Gwilt, Smethurst, a retired hydropathic doctor convicted of poisoning the woman with whom he had gone through a bigamous ceremony of marriage, appeared an unlikely object of chivalry.[5] Nevertheless, as the Home Secretary wryly observed,

> There has been great excitement about the case, and I was told that there were some people—some male Jeanie Deans—who wished to go to Balmoral and seek an interview with the Queen—thinking that they were more

likely to obtain mercy from Her Majesty than from the flinty heart of a male Secretary of State.[6]

In much the same vein as Jemmy Bashwood, the jurist James Fitzjames Stephen complained that "one or two papers constituted themselves amateur champions of the convict, claiming openly the right of what they called popular instinct to override the verdict of the jury" prompting a flood of letters to the Home Secretary "founded upon no real study of the case."[7] The *Daily Telegraph* proclaimed that "a greater jury has spoken"—the public—"and it pronounces his guilt Not Proven."[8] In both the real and the fictitious case, the Home Secretary referred the case to a medical adviser, in the light of whose report the prisoner was pardoned, but then tried and convicted for a lesser offense (Smethurst for bigamy, Lydia for theft).

Despite his character's skepticism, Collins returned several times to the evidential ambiguities surrounding poisoning.[9] Stephen knew about such ambiguities at first hand from his defense two years earlier of Thomas Fuller Bacon, who in a story worthy of Collins was first acquitted of murdering his two children, with his wife being found not guilty by reason of insanity, and then convicted of having previously poisoned his mother.[10] Bacon's conviction might have become as great a *cause célèbre* as Smethurst's had the prosecution not conceded that the cause of death was uncertain and reduced the charge to administering poison with intent to murder.[11] In the wake of Smethurst's case Stephen read to the Juridical Society a closely argued paper on the issues raised by scientifically contentious poisoning trials.[12] He later incorporated this paper into his *General View of the Criminal Law* (1863). All the English cases which Stephen discussed in detail in an appendix to the *General View* (and again in his *History of the Criminal Law*) were poisoning trials: Donellan (1781), Palmer (1856), Dove (1856), and Smethurst.

Stephen's paper was a sophisticated (but not entirely successful) attempt to allay two conflicting anxieties by resolving a high-profile Victorian conundrum that is at least equally pressing in today's debates: how can a lay tribunal decide a question on which experts disagree?

> Is the fear of a charge of secret poisoning, more horrible than the fear of being secretly poisoned, to be infused into the tenderest relations of life? ... If there be a mania for the commission of crime, there is also a mania for the suspicion of it; and both affections are strikingly epidemic in their nature.[13]

Smethurst's was one of a series of highly controversial poisoning trials in the

1850s. This chapter will discuss these and Stephen's response to them, as well as touching briefly on Stephen's much later role as the judge in one of the most controversial of all poisoning trials, that of Mrs. Maybrick in 1889.

Ann Merritt

When James Merritt, a turncock at a London waterworks, died in 1850, arsenic was found in his stomach and his widow was charged with murder. She admitted buying arsenic but said she had intended to take it herself if her husband's drunken behavior did not improve. She had put the arsenic in a cupboard and her husband must have mistaken it for an indigestion remedy. Dr. Letheby, Professor of Chemistry at the London Hospital, who found the arsenic in Merritt's stomach, expressed the opinion that, as it was dissolved in undigested gruel, it must have been taken within two to three hours of death. Both the judge and Mrs. Merritt's own counsel pointed out that, if accepted by the jury, this was fatal to the defense case that Merritt died in the evening from a dose taken accidentally in the morning. Mrs. Merritt was convicted. The jury recommended her to mercy on account of her previous good character, but the judge warned her that in view of "the strange and horrible frequency of the crime" which she had committed "against the man whom at the altar of God you solemnly swore to love and cherish," she should not expect that recommendation to be acted on.[14]

The *Daily News* took up Ann Merritt's case, questioning the "positive dogmatism" of Letheby's evidence and claiming to have found new evidence that Mr. Merritt had taken doses of powder throughout the day.[15] The columns of the *Daily News* hosted a spirited "conversation" between Dr. Letheby and a number of anonymous correspondents. Mrs. Merritt's supporters used "primitive" religious practices as a metaphor for modern faith in science: "Shall a destitute female be sacrificed at the shrine of chemical speculation?"[16] "Shall we, like a set of savages, upon a mere dogmatical opinion, drag . . . this helpless woman from her dungeon and lead her on the public scaffold?"[17] Letheby, on the other hand, pointed out that "the lives and liberties of the people of England are dependent on a medical opinion every day, some of them every hour of the day, and yet no man hesitates to put all his trust therein." Portraying himself as the victim of unjustified "insults" by defense counsel, he asked: "Shall public safety be sacrificed at the shrine of legal subtlety?"[18]

The Under-Sheriffs (court officials at the Old Bailey) supplied the Home Secretary with three further medical opinions (including one from Sir Benjamin Brodie, who was to play a similar role in the Smethurst case) which apparently cast doubt on this aspect of Letheby's evidence.[19] Letheby conceded that it was "within the range of possibility," albeit improbable, that Ann Merritt's story was true.[20] Merritt was reprieved, but transported to Van Diemen's Land for life, a sentence apparently justified by defense counsel's concession that the prisoner's "culpable negligence" in leaving the arsenic in the cupboard in an unmarked wrapper might have amounted to manslaughter.[21]

Speaking shortly afterward in the House of Commons in support of a motion to abolish the death penalty, the Liberal MP John Bright pointed to Merritt's conviction on the basis of Letheby's "rash if not unscientific" testimony as evidence of the "uncertainty" inherent in poisoning cases.[22] In response to an angry letter to *The Times* from Letheby, Bright insisted that he was not attacking Letheby personally, but "arguing against the infliction of an irrevocable punishment" on the basis of testimony "liable to dispute and to much and unavoidable uncertainty."[23]

Joseph Wooler

In June 1855, "Mrs. Wooler, wife of a retired mercantile gentleman, residing a few miles from Darlington, died of a tedious illness."[24] The eminent toxicologist Alfred Swayne Taylor testified that he had found small quantities of arsenic in Mrs. Wooler's organs, in a condition indicating that it had been taken in small doses during life, but he could not say from the postmortem findings alone whether arsenic was the cause of death.[25] The equally distinguished Dr. Robert Christison was, however, prepared to say from his knowledge of Mrs. Wooler's symptoms that repeated doses of arsenic were the cause of death. There was little more to the prosecution case than the scientific evidence and the fact that Joseph Wooler, who took an active part in nursing his wife, had ample opportunities to poison her.

The censures of counsel and the judge were not directed primarily at the toxicologists but rather at the medical men who had attended Mrs. Wooler in her last illness, and whose roles were equivocal in several respects. First, although they denied giving any arsenic to Mrs. Wooler, contained in the "vast farrago of medicaments" were prussic acid, henbane, and strychnine, which one commentator suggested might have induced the "tetanic spasms" that raised the suspicion of arsenical poisoning.[26] It was also suggested that Dr. Jackson (or his assistant Mr. Henzell) who also attended Mrs. Wooler, had accidentally poisoned another patient with arsenic. Second, though Jackson, Henzell, and Dr. Haslewood all claimed to have suspected that Mrs. Wooler was being poisoned long before she died, they kept their suspicions to themselves for more than a week. But for this "infamous conduct," averred defense counsel, Mrs. Wooler might have survived.[27] Third, another local surgeon claimed at the committal proceedings to have detected arsenic in a syringe which Mr. Wooler had borrowed from him to give injections to his wife.[28] He later discovered that the acid he used to carry out the test was itself contaminated with arsenic (the great Dr. Taylor was to make a similar blunder in the Smethurst case). The judge, in a summing-up critical of the medical men and strongly favoring the prisoner, remarked that "there is a person on whom my fancy would rest, rather than upon the prisoner, if I had to give an opinion"— a phrase which Dr. Jackson took to refer to him.[29] Jackson's indignant letter to the judge, and the judge's reply assuring him that no such imputation was intended, were published in *The Times*.[30] Jackson had his supporters among the citizens of Doncaster: after he successfully sued Wooler for his fees, "he was drawn in triumph to his house by the populace."[31]

It was Wooler's case that prompted the *Dublin University Magazine's* warning against the "mania for the suspicion" of poisoning. In a similar vein, *The Spectator* argued that the "horrible fear that poisoning may be much more extensive than we had supposed," with English villainy rivaling "dissipated Paris or degenerate Rome," gave rise to the "much more horrible" prospect that suspicion "must in many cases light upon the innocent."[32] Wooler's trial raised these conflicting fears acutely because of its "all or nothing" character. When poisoning was suspected in a Victorian bourgeois household, it usually turned out to be part of a pattern of deviant conduct which showed "what may be going on in the inmost core of all that is apparently pure and respectable."[33] Madeleine Smith may or may not have poisoned Emile L'Angelier in 1857 (a Scottish jury returned the verdict "not proven"), but she certainly had an illicit affair with him.[34] John Tawell, apparently "a benevolent and hospitable Quaker, noted for his charities," turned out not only to have poisoned his mistress in 1845 but also to be a returned convict, transported to Australia for possession of a forged bill.[35] William Palmer, whose case followed hot on the heels of Wooler's, was certainly a forger even if he was not a serial killer; and Smethurst was a bigamist even if he was not a murderer (unless, as the defense suggested at his trial for bigamy, the real bigamist was his first wife).[36] Nothing of this sort emerged at Wooler's trial. A succession of witnesses testified to the seemingly kind and affectionate relationship between Wooler and his invalid wife, and the prosecution could suggest no motive for the crime. The only sinister thing about Wooler was that, like the doctors, he seemed to know more than most people about poisons. Either he was innocent, or he exemplified "the pitch of refinement" in what *The Times* called the "high art" of murder:

> The darkest deed of blindest passion must be accomplished with the patience and clearsightedness of a cold intellect; the final stroke of enmity,

the unkindest cut of all, must be dealt as IZAAK WALTON recommends the angler to impale a frog on his hook—"tenderly, as though you loved him."[37]

William Palmer

For one leader writer in *The Times,* the epitome of this new style of murder (though he had yet to be tried) was William Palmer, surgeon, of Rugeley, Staffordshire. Although Palmer was to be the first in a line of notorious Victorian medical murderers (followed by Smethurst and Drs. Pritchard, Lamson, and Cream)[38] his resemblance to the recent serial killer Harold Shipman is hardly so uncanny as Matthew Sweet's recent comparison of the two cases makes out.[39] Palmer barely practiced as a doctor (his life centered on the racetrack) and his suspected victims were relatives and acquaintances whose deaths were financially convenient to him for one reason or another, including his wife, brother, mother-in-law, and as many as seven legitimate and illegitimate children.[40] Serial murder of unwanted spouses and relatives was nothing new, but most early practitioners (with the possible exception of Thomas Griffiths Wainewright)[41] were female and poor.[42] Like Shipman's case, however, Palmer's crimes aroused concern at weaknesses in the system for the registration and investigation of sudden deaths, and became a reference point in debates over reform of the inquest system.[43]

Palmer was tried only for one murder, that of his friend and racing associate John Parsons Cook. The most famous "poison hunter" of the day, Alfred Swayne Taylor, found small traces of antimony in Cook's body, which he initially reported "may" have caused the death.[44] After hearing Cook's symptoms described at his inquest, Taylor decided that Cook must have been poisoned with strychnine, which Palmer was shown to have purchased. Taylor had to admit that he could he find no strychnine in the body, and had observed the effects of the poison only in rabbits.[45] He nevertheless considered it a matter of farreaching importance that the jury should accept his evidence. In a letter to the *Lancet,* read out at the trial, Taylor had "no hesitation in saying that the future security of life in this country will mainly depend on the judge, the jury and the counsel who may have to dispose of the charges of murder which have arisen out of these investigations."[46]

Palmer's defense counsel condemned this as an inappropriate attempt to "influence the public mind."[47] He portrayed the threat to public security very differently:

> But, merciful Heaven! In what position are we placed for the safety of our own lives and those of our families, if, on evidence such as this, men are to

> be put on trial for foul murder as soon as a sudden death occurs in any household! If science is to be allowed to come and dogmatise in our courts—and not science that is secure in its operations and exact in its nature, but science that is baffled by its own tests, and bears upon its forehead the motto "a little knowledge is a dangerous thing" ... life is no longer secure, and there is thrown upon judges and jurymen a weight of responsibility too grievous for human nature to endure.[48]

In the event, the evidence of Taylor and his colleagues, along with much circumstantial evidence of Palmer's devious dealings, carried the day, despite the evidence of expert witnesses for the defense that Cook's symptoms could have been due to natural causes and that had Cook been poisoned with strychnine, Taylor ought to have been able to find it. Lord Chief Justice Campbell's summing up defended Taylor's impartiality, while suggesting that some of the defense witnesses had come to act as advocates for the prisoner.[49] A pamphlet in defense of Palmer commented on the one-sided nature of these remarks: "The competition of these medical men is quite natural, laudable and valuable.... Now, why are one half of these gentlemen to be held up to indignation for doing just what they all came to do?"[50]

As Ian Burney notes in his excellent study, historians have given very different assessments of the Palmer trial, labeling it either a triumph or severe setback for Taylor's reputation and for public confidence in science.[51] Taylor's own assessment, however, was far from triumphal:

> It cannot be denied ... that the conflict of scientific testimony ... at the trial of this great criminal, has thrown disgrace upon the medical profession, and has created in the public mind a feeling of insecurity in relying upon scientific opinions in any circumstances. It will, I fear, take many years to remove this feeling.[52]

Naturally, Taylor blamed this sorry state of affairs entirely on the witnesses and counsel for the defense.

Thomas Smethurst

Taylor could not so easily escape responsibility for his blunder in the case of Thomas Smethurst and his alleged victim Isabella Bankes, the woman he had bigamously married. At the committal proceedings, Taylor gave dramatic testimony about a bottle of chlorate of potass found in the prisoner's possession. Chlorate of potass was "by itself, an innocent sort of medicine," but Taylor had become convinced that there was "something very peculiar" about this bottle. He tested for arsenic using Reinsch's process, boiling the suspect substance and hydrochloric acid and inserting copper gauze: but the gauze, instead of becoming coated with arsenic, dissolved. So Taylor went on putting in copper gauze until his solution was saturated with it, whereupon he was able to obtain the deposit he was looking for. Chlorate of potass possessed another remarkable property, according to Taylor: once it had deposited its poison in the stomach, "the surplus would be carried off rapidly," thus accounting for the fact that no arsenic was detected in Isabella Bankes's body, though some was found in one sample of her feces.[53] In short, Taylor attributed to the poison and the poisoner alike a diabolical ability to evade detection, thwarted only by his own even greater acuity.

Fortunately for Smethurst, however, his trial was postponed. Taylor became worried by his inability to repeat his successful test for arsenic and, after consulting another chemist, realized that the arsenic had been present in the copper gauze that he had dissolved in the medicine. Taylor promptly informed prosecuting counsel of his discovery, but as the *Lancet* remarked, it had created "an enormous prejudice" against the prisoner.[54] The defense produced medical evidence that Miss Bankes's symptoms could be ascribed to dysentery, and the traces of antimony in her body and (if any reliance could be placed on the chemical tests in this instance) of arsenic in her feces could have been innocently present in medicines she had taken. Baron Pollock's summing-up was clearly hostile to the prisoner. He invited the jury, "supposing [they found] the medical evidence was evenly balanced," to consider whether, having induced the erstwhile respectable Isabella Bankes, by going through what she probably knew was a bigamous marriage, to become "a felon and a strumpet . . . the scorn of one sex and the horror of the other," Smethurst "had not a motive to get rid of her."[55]

The jury took forty minutes to find Smethurst guilty. To the *Daily Telegraph,* that seemed

> an appallingly brief period for twelve middle-class men, of average intellect, to have cut the gordian knot of a problem, whose solution has puzzled, and is even now the subject of bitter dispute and disagreement among Doctors and Professors the most learned and eminent in the present era of medical science.

Any verdict based on science "of which they were ignorant" must be "essentially fallacious," the *Telegraph* argued: "it is not, it should not, it must not, be a subject for the consideration of a common Middlesex jury to decide upon "conflicting medical testimony" when a man's life hangs in the balance."[56] The

Telegraph's objection was not to the principle of trial by jury, but to the way in which a biased judge, who was a personal friend of Alfred Taylor, was able to "cajole and bully" the jury into deciding a question that was simply undecidable.[57]

> The profession tells us that DR. SMETHURST administered [arsenic]. The profession tells us that he *did not* administer it. Science indicates that he mixed it with his victim's medicine; Science also tells us that the lady might have taken it innocently. How shall we decide—we who are neither Lord Chief Barons, petty jurymen, nor analytical chemists? We must leave the problem where it is; the mysteries of creation cross our path, and all is darkness.[58]

Both the *Lancet* and the *British Medical Journal* supported the campaign for Smethurst's reprieve, though not out of any personal sympathy for the accused, who was not only "a liar, a cheat, a scoundrel of the blackest die," but a practitioner of "hydropathic quackery."[59] The *British Medical Journal* went further than the *Telegraph* in its criticism of the jury system, arguing that it was because they were mere "tradesmen" that jurors were "but too apt to give fatal weight to the summing up of the judge." Their task required "persons of a higher stamp, accustomed to think for themselves."[60] Turning from poisoning to insanity, of which Dove's trial had been the most controversial recent case, the *British Medical Journal* argued that to decide such questions a jury should "contain a large share of the scientific element," rather than comprising "twelve untrained John Bulls led by a crafty barrister."[61]

Witches and Juries

Newspapers and periodicals used similar metaphors to express the fear the conviction aroused. If Smethurst were executed, declared the *Lancet*, "an infinitesimal toxicology might, in the present day, become almost as dangerous as the accusations of witchcraft in the fifteenth century."[62] The *British Medical Journal* prophesied that "the horrors which flourished in the days of witchcraft, when human life hung upon the lips of any old crone, will be but too faithfully represented by the horrors which will flow from the pseudo-scientific evidence of the present day."[63] The *Telegraph* and its letter writers expressed similar fears of "middle-age witchcraft."[64] They complained of Taylor being "set up as the Pope in scientific discovery" when he was "considered in intelligent circles no better than a Titus Oates or a witchfinder."[65] They resolved "to make a stand against the medical magicians, with their copper wands, who are deep in the confidence of Chief Barons."[66]

The metaphor of the witchfinder inverted what Robb claims was the dominant image of toxicology as science's "heroic, masculine response to the dark, irrational ways of criminal women."[67] According to Robb, "the popular image of the poisoner remained overwhelmingly female.... The hidden nature of poisonings created an image of women as witches, practicing their arcana on guileless men."[68] Robb's imagery rings true for the succession of women in the 1840s suspected of multiple murders of their husbands, children, and other relatives.[69] The women's impoverished backgrounds, the unflattering descriptions of their appearance, the rumors surrounding some of them, and the supposed existence of a "secret society" of poisoners in the Essex village of Clavering, recall seventeenth-century witchcraft trials so strikingly that even one modern historian of murder has speculated that the poisoners were somehow carrying on where the witches left off.[70]

The trial of one male poisoner had explicit overtones of witchcraft or sorcery. William Dove claimed to have been influenced by the prophecies of one Henry Harrison, known as the Wizard, or Witchman, of Leeds. Harrison was one of several "cunning men" and astrologers practicing in Leeds, but Dove believed he could "rule devils."[71] The defense unsuccessfully argued that this was evidence of insanity, and despite attempting to make a pact with Devil, written in blood, Dove was hanged. The toxicological evidence on his use of strychnine was, in this case, not controversial, but the evidence of insanity aroused much debate.[72]

Although the witch trials served the Victorians as "standard comparative metaphors for credulity,"[73] the analogy between witch finding and toxicology had an additional significance. As readers of *Blackwood's Magazine* for May 1859 were reminded, a belief in witchcraft was one that no "educated" person could any longer hold, but that many educated persons *had* entertained in the relatively recent past.[74] Today's "science," the witchcraft analogy implied, might turn out to be tomorrow's superstition.[75] Stephen's jurisprudence of expert evidence addressed this concern directly. For Stephen, critics of the jury system such as the *British Medical Journal* misunderstood the role of the jury, which was to establish not whether the defendant was guilty, but whether "twelve men, who represent the average intelligence of the country . . . have any reasonable doubt that he is guilty."[76] If a conscientious jury had no reasonable doubt of the guilt of a man who was, in fact, innocent, that would be a "true verdict," though it was not the truth:

> How, then, can an honest man be free from all reasonable doubt of the truth of a false proposition which has been discussed before him with all the case which practised skill can supply? Because every man brings to the investigation of every question a vast number of data which rest on mere authority,

> and several of which are false; but which he must of necessity accept as true, in the transaction of the common affairs of life, however momentous may be the conclusions which rest upon them; and because the only alternative is to shrink from framing any important decisions at all.[77]

Stephen's argument seems to overlook the fact that, for a jury, the alternative is not to shrink from a decision but to decide to acquit. But it was a tenet of his political philosophy that those in authority must be prepared to act decisively on the basis of established opinions.[78] For example, given the established opinions of the seventeenth century, "upright judges and honest jurors" had been right to convict defendants of witchcraft.[79] Stephen may well have had in mind the famous witchcraft trial over which Chief Justice Hale presided in 1662.[80] "At the present day" Lord Campbell wrote in 1849, "we regard the trial as a most lamentable example of credulity and inhumanity," an "enormous violation of justice."[81] Stephen argued, however, that it would have been unreasonable for a seventeenth-century judge or jury to enter into "fanciful speculation" as to the reality of witchcraft.[82] It "would be a *reductio ad absurdum* of any system to show that no conviction for witchcraft could ever have taken place under it."[83] The "common business of life," as opposed to the advancement of learning, was done not by questioning established opinions but by acting on them; "and the province of juries is not speculative, but active."[84]

The Palmer case showed, in Stephen's view, that a jury was competent to judge even the most difficult conflicts of scientific evidence. The combination of the prosecution's scientific evidence, the concessions extracted from the defense experts by skilled cross-examination, plus circumstantial evidence of Palmer's motive, opportunity, and possession of poison "was evidence upon which any man would have acted in weighty affairs of his own, and greater evidence than that it would be absurd to require."[85] If evidence of death by strychnine had "rested on grounds which were a matter of *bona fide* dispute amongst scientific men," a jury should and probably would have acquitted; but that "such disputes are not *bona fide*, but are got up for the occasion is an inference which a sensible jury is thoroughly competent to draw."[86]

Stephen's insistence that existing scientific knowledge must be accepted, for the purposes of lay decision making, on the basis of "mere authority" did not sit easily with his celebration of the power of cross-examination. The natural tendency of the adversarial system was to promote a skeptical questioning of *all* forms of scientific authority, as Taylor, in his account of the Palmer trial, bitterly complained.[87] The only way that Stephen, or the courts in general (or indeed Taylor) could find to resolve this tension was to draw a contrast between *"bona fide"* science to which juries rightly deferred, and deviant scientists, whose false science the adversarial process would expose.[88] Yet it was the adversarial process itself that arguably *created* the appearance of partisanship.[89]

As a judge, thirty years later, Stephen had recourse to the same dichotomy between science and advocacy in the trial of Florence Maybrick. A small quantity of arsenic was found in Maybrick's body, but the defense denied that it was the cause of his fatal illness, producing evidence to suggest that Maybrick habitually took "poisonous medicines." Stephen instructed the jury that having observed the medical witnesses and formed a judgment on their "impartiality" or "partisanship," it could, by "an act of high moral and civil courage," decide whether or not the deceased's symptoms were those of arsenical poisoning. This even though the scientific dispute on the subject raised questions "too difficult for us. At all events, they are too difficult for me."[90] It might have been acceptable had he not also suggested, almost exactly as Baron Pollock had in the Smethurst case, that the jury could resolve the medical deadlock by focusing on the prisoner's admitted adultery, and considering "how a horrible woman, in so terrible a position, might be assailed by some fearful and terrible temptation."[91] These remarks aroused enormous public indignation in a wide variety of print outlets, not just because they were logically flawed.[92] Stephen appeared to confuse the question whether Mrs. Maybrick had a motive to give her husband arsenic with the question whether arsenic had killed him. The criminal conversation turned on perceptions of Mrs. Maybrick's adultery, promoted "as a trifle light as air," compared to the "debauchery" of her husband, of which the jury was not told.[93] As in Ann Merritt's case, the outcry won Mrs. Maybrick a reprieve but not her liberty.[94] Rather than being evidence of mental decay as Mrs. Maybrick's supporters have maintained, Stephen's summing-up was essentially consistent with his earlier theory.[95] The jury should not "shrink from making any decision at all" but must decide which (if any) of the expert witnesses spoke with the authority of science and whether their findings formed part of a larger pattern of evidence that would justify "a true verdict." Nor would the Stephen of 1863 have criticized his future self for partisanship: "Impartiality and indecision are totally different things. A judge summing up is an advocate who chooses his side impartially."[96] But he prudently dropped this comment on the 1871 Donellan case from the second edition of the *General View*, published after the Maybrick trial.[97]

Conclusion

William Dove's defense counsel was no doubt justified in complaining that "there prevailed a sort of public panic about poisoning; as if the ties of wedlock were only an opportunity to perpetrate the offence."[98] Domestic poisonings not only struck at the institution of matrimony; they seemed, as Burney has suggested, to show how market forces (particularly the market in insurance) could reduce the most intimate of relationships to matters of cold calculation.[99] But if poisoning itself was a threat to one cherished social institution, the alleged errors and excesses of toxicology threatened another. As Ericson and colleagues point out:

> conceptions of justice are crucial to the co-ordination of activities through mutual trust and respect. Trust and respect are attributed to people in authority who seem knowledgeable (they know what they are doing and offer instruction to others) certain (they are predictable in their actions and offer predictability or reduced equivocality to others), and moral (in acting morally themselves they offer morality to others).[100]

When, therefore, scientists, judges, and juries appear to be neither knowledgeable, certain nor moral, they manifest a deeply threatening kind of social deviance. Professionals who stir up "moral panics" can themselves become the object of a "counterpanic," as has happened in recent years especially in cases of child abuse. The 1987 Cleveland affair, when 197 children were taken into care following medical diagnoses of sexual abuse, was even compared by the local MP to the Salem witchcraft trails.[101] What is perhaps most remarkable about the Victorian cases, however, was the ability of the press to mobilize public outrage *on behalf* of acknowledged deviants: particularly Thomas Smethurst, whom even his greatest champion, the *Telegraph*'s leader writer, "stigmatised . . . as a mean and immoral adventurer,"[102] "a bad and a dangerous man."[103] To the *Lancet*, the campaign to save a man who "excited so little personal sympathy" bore witness to the English public's "pure love of justice."[104]

Notes

1. Wilkie Collins, *Armadale* (1866; Oxford: Oxford University Press, 1989), 644.
2. George Robb, "Circe in Crinoline: Domestic Poisonings in Victorian England," *Journal of Family History* 22 (1997): 176–90; Judith Knelman, *Twisting in the Wind: The Murderess and the English Press* (Toronto: University of Toronto Press, 1998).
3. Collins, *Armadale*, 645.
4. T. Boyle, *Black Swine in the Sewers of Hampstead* (London: Viking, 1989), 166–67.
5. L. A. Parry, ed., *Trial of Dr. Smethurst* (London: Hodge, 1931).
6. PRO30/22/25, Letter, Sir George Cornewall Lewis to Lord John Russell, 4 September 1859. Jeanie Deans, heroine of Sir Walter Scott's *The Heart of Midlothian* (1818), traveled *from* Scotland to London to seek a royal pardon for her sister.

7. James Fitzjames Stephen, *A General View of the Criminal Law of England* (London: Macmillan, 1863), 425.

8. *Daily Telegraph*, 25 August 1859.

9. Wilkie Collins, *The Law and the Lady* (1875; Harmondsworth: Penguin, 1998), revolved around a false accusation of poisoning, as did the purportedly true story "The Poisoned Meal" from W. Collins, *My Miscellanies* (1875), available online at http://www.mtroyal.ab.ca/programs/arts/english/gaslight/posnmeal.htm. W. Collins, *The Legacy of Cain* (1888), available at http://www.blackmask.com/jrusk/wcollins/cain/cain1.htm, ends with another female poisoner posing as the victim of a miscarriage of justice.

10. Leslie Stephen, *The Life of Sir James Fitzjames Stephen* (London: Smith, Elder, 1895), 146–48.

11. *The Times*, 27 July 1857.

12. *Papers Read before the Juridical Society*, 1863, 2, 236–49.

13. Anon., "The Doctor in the Witness-Box," *Dublin University Magazine* 47 (1856): 178–195, at 195.

14. *The Times*, 9 March 1850.

15. *Daily News*, 11 March 1850.

16. "Alpha," Letter, *Daily News*, 14 March 1850.

17. "A Constant Reader," Letter, *Daily News*, 20 March 1850.

18. *Daily News*, 18 March 1859.

19. G. L. Browne and C. G. Stewart, *Reports of Trials for Murder by Poisoning* (London: Stevens, 1883), 372; John Bright, Letter, *The Times*, 17 July 1850.

20. H. Letheby, "The Convict Ann Merritt," *Medical Times*, 23 March 1850.

21. *The Times*, 25 March; 9 May 1850; Browne and Stewart, *Reports*, 272. By contrast, Thomas Puttick, whose wife's and son's deaths were attributed to his carelessness in leaving arsenic in a cupboard, was merely censured by the coroner's jury: *The Times*, 5, 11, and 12 January 1858.

22. *The Times*, 12 July 1850.

23. *The Times*, 15 July; 17 July 1850.

24. Robert Christison, "Account of a Late Remarkable Trial for Poisoning with Arsenic," *Edinburgh Medical Journal* 1, 7 (1855): 625.

25. *The Times*, 10 December 1855.

26. "Doctor in the Witness-Box," 191. *The Times*, 25 July 1860; Browne and Stewart, *Reports*, 49; George Robinson, *Observations on Some Recent Cases of Poisoning* (Graveshead: D. Dunglison, 1856), 5.

27. *The Times*, 12 December 1855.

28. Christison, "Account," 627, remarked this was an unusual service for "a nonprofessional husband" to perform.

29. *The Times*, 17 December 1855. See Christison, "Account," for a robust defense of the doctors.

30. *The Times*, 22 December 1855.

31. "Finale of the Burdon Poisoning Case," *Lancet* 1 (1856): 470.

32. "The Poison Cases," *Spectator*, 12 January 1856, 49.

33. "Madeleine Smith," *Saturday Review*, 11 July 1857, 27. This theme is explored by, among others, Mary S. Hartmann, *Victorian Murderesses* (London: Robson, 1977); and Boyle, *Black Swine*.

34. See Douglas MacGowan, *Murder in Victorian Scotland* (Westport, CT: Praeger, 1999).

35. Browne and Stewart, *Reports*, 16.
36. Parry, *Trial*, 235–40.
37. *The Times*, 24 December 1855. The chilling word "tenderly" does not in fact appear in Walton's *The Compleat Angler* (1653).
38. Glasgow doctor who poisoned his wife and mother-in-law in 1865: Browne and Stewart, *Reports*, 397 ff; William Roughead, *Trial of Dr. Pritchard* (Edinburgh: Hodge, 1906); William Roughead, *Classic Crimes* (1951; New York: New York Review Books, 2000). Lamson poisoned his brother-in-law in 1882: Hargrave L. Adam, *Trial of Dr. George Henry Lamson* (Edinburgh: Hodge, 1922); Giles St. Aubyn, *Infamous Victorians* (London: Constable, 1971). Cream murdered his wife, four patients, and four prostitutes: Angus McLaren, *A Prescription for Murder: The Victorian Serial Killings of Dr. Thomas Neil Cream* (Chicago: University of Chicago Press, 1993).
39. Matthew Sweet, *Inventing the Victorians* (London: Faber and Faber, 2001), chap. 7.
40. St. Aubyn, *Infamous Victorians*. Robert Graves, *They Hanged My Saintly Billy* (London: Cassell, 1957), argues ingeniously for Palmer's innocence.
41. Wainewright, critic and artist, supposedly murdered three people with strychnine, 1828–30, though he was convicted only of forgery. Andrew Motion's *Wainewright the Poisoner* (London: Faber and Faber, 2000) argues that his guilt is uncertain.
42. Knelman, *Twisting*.
43. See Joan Sim and Tony Ward, "The Magistrate of the Poor? Coroners and Deaths in Custody in Nineteenth Century England," in *Legal Medicine in History*, ed. Michael Clarke and Catherine Crawford, 249–67 (Cambridge: Cambridge University Press, 1994).
44. *The Times Report*, 70.
45. Ibid.
46. *Lancet* 1 (1856): 134; *The Times Report*, 71.
47. Ibid.
48. Ibid., 98.
49. *The Times Report*, 175; 179.
50. Henry Coningsby, *In Favorem Vitæ* (London: John Russell Smith, 1856), 15–16.
51. Burney, "Poisoning"; Carol A. G. Jones, *Expert Witnesses* (Oxford: Clarendon Press, 1994), 84–85; Boyle, *Black Swine*, 74.
52. Alfred Swaine Taylor, *On Poisoning by Strychnia, with Comments on the Evidence Given at the Trial of William Palmer for the Murder of John Parsons Cook* (London: Longman, Brown, Green, Longmans and Roberts, 1856), 6.
53. Parry, *Trial*, 156.
54. Ibid., 86–87; *Lancet* 2 (1859): 219.
55. Parry, *Trial*, 132–33.
56. Leader, *Daily Telegraph*, 20 August 1856.
57. E. T., Letter, *Daily Telegraph*, 24 August 1859.
58. Leader, *Daily Telegraph*, 23 August 1859.
59. "The Trial of Thomas Smethurst," *British Medical Journal* (1859): 702; *Lancet* 2 (1859): 219. Smethurst (who like the majority of hydropaths was medically qualified) observed in his petition for mercy that "between the hydropathic professors and many of the ordinary practitioners of physic there is no friendly feeling." Cited, Parry, *Trial*, 166.
60. Leader, *British Medical Journal* (1859): 725–26.
61. "Law and Physic," *British Medical Journal* (1859): 743.

62. Ibid., 220.
63. Leader, *British Medical Journal* (1859): 703.
64. Leader, *Daily Telegraph,* 22 August 1859.
65. Letters, *Daily Telegraph,* 24 August 1859. For Titus Oates see Sir John Pollock, *The Popish Plot: A Study in the History of the Reign of Charles II* (London: Duckworth, 1903), 347–51.
66. Leader, *Daily Telegraph,* 24 August 1859.
67. Robb, "Circe," 181.
68. Ibid., 177.
69. Ibid.; Knelman, *Twisting;* P. Wilson, *Murderess* (London: Michael Joseph, 1971).
70. Wilson, *Murderess,* 53–54.
71. Owen Davies, *Witchcraft, Magic and Culture, 1736–1951* (Manchester: Manchester University Press, 1999), 234.
72. *The Times,* 19 July 1856; C. Williams, *Observations on the Criminal Responsibility of the Insane, Founded on the Trials of James Hill and William Dove* (London: Churchill, 1856); Browne and Stewart, *Trials,* 235; Roger Smith, *Trial by Medicine* (Edinburgh: Edinburgh University Press, 1981), 134–37.
73. Davies, *Witchcraft,* 70.
74. "The Witch of Walkerne," *Blackwood's Edinburgh Magazine* 85 (1859): 567.
75. A point made explicitly in "Doctor in the Witness-Box."
76. Stephen, *General View,* 210.
77. Ibid.
78. See Sir James Fitzjames Stephen, *Liberty, Equality, and Fraternity,* 2nd ed. (London: Smith, Elder, 1874).
79. Stephen, *General View,* 211.
80. See Gilbert Geis and Ivan Bunn, *A Trial of Witches* (London: Routledge, 1997).
81. John, Lord Campbell, *The Lives of the Chief Justices* (John Murray, 1849), 1: 566–67.
82. Stephen, *General View,* 211.
83. Ibid., 213.
84. Ibid., 211.
85. Ibid., 389; 214.
86. Ibid., 217.
87. Taylor, *On Poisoning by Strychnia,* 2: 133.
88. See Jones, *Expert Witnesses;* Roger Smith and Brian Wynne, eds., *Expert Evidence* (London: Routledge, 1989); Sheila Jasanoff, *Science at the Bar* (Cambridge, MA: Harvard University Press, 1995).
89. Robinson, *Observations,* 3.
90. H. B. Irving, ed., *Trial of Mrs. Maybrick* (Hodge, 1912), 301–2, 309.
91. Ibid., 352.
92. See PRO/HO/144/1639 A 50678 for various pamphlets and petitions. Also Joseph Levy, *The Necessity of Criminal Appeal, As Illustrated by the Maybrick Case and the Jurisprudence of Various Countries* (London: King and Son, 1899).
93. W. T. Stead, "Ought Mrs. Maybrick to Be Tortured to Death?" *Review of Reviews* (1892): 392.
94. Stephen, *General View,* 312. See also T. Christie, *Etched in Arsenic* (London: Harrap, 1968).

95. See, for example, Levy, *Appeal* 465; PRO/HO/144/1639 A 50678D/99, Petition, Baroness de Roques (Maybrick's mother). Stephen's mental powers were declining less than two years after the trial. He was persuaded to resign in March 1891. K. J. M. Smith, *James Fitzjames Stephen: Portrait of a Victorian Rationalist* (Cambridge: Cambridge University Press, 1988), 250–52.

96. Ibid., 354.

97. Stephen, *General View*, 229.

98. *The Times*, 19 July 1858.

99. Burney, "A Poisoning."

100. Richard V. Ericson et al., *Representing Order: Crime, Law and Justice in the News Media* (Milton Keynes: Open University Press, 1991), 109.

101. Stuart Bell, *When Salem Came to the Boro: The True Story of the Cleveland Child Abuse Crisis* (London: Pan, 1988).

102. *Daily Telegraph*, 14 November 1859.

103. Leader, *Daily Telegraph*, 25 August 1859.

104. *Lancet* 2 (1859): 268.

10

A Little of What You Fancy Does You . . . Harm!! (with Apologies to Marie Lloyd)

SANDRA MORTON

Introduction

Realization of the extent of the adulteration of innumerable items of everyday food and drink in the mid-nineteenth century was spread through the print medium, leading to the evolution of new food safety legislation. According to Burnett: "Adulteration of food prevailed in the first half of the nineteenth century to an unprecedented and unsupposed extent," with farreaching consequences.[1] The sense of panic and outrage engendered by print revelations related both to the sense of being cheated and to fears about actual physical harm done by adulteration. A *Cornhill Magazine* article emphasized that adulteration "not only lowers the money value of an article" but also "lessens its dietetical qualities," so that it could become "positively unwholesome." Worse, "it has of late years become a complete science," being carried out "with consummate art and skill," so making detection difficult.[2] This is a particularly interesting "criminal conversation" because of the links promoted between medical experts and the print media when both were striving for professional status. Medical experts were responsible for the alarmist attitudes reported in print, using their own journal, the *Lancet,* as an initial location for airing views that later found their way into nonspecialist organs like *The Times.*

Food adulteration was not new.[3] However, there was a valid belief not only that it had more prevalent and threatening since 1800, under the pressure of widespread industrialization and urbanization, but also that existing legislation was ineffective.[4] Urban dwellers had neither resources nor time to produce their own food and daily commodities were purchased from expanding numbers of retail outlets.[5] Contemporary comment underlines the perception that this was a new phenomenon: "Now bread is almost universally bought from a baker, and the baker universally purchases his flour from a wholesale miller; . . . vinegar, sauces, confectionary [*sic*], pickles etc. are bought from shopkeepers."[6] This chapter locates the conversation about food adulteration in this new context, so emphasizing the wider cultural reasons for panic and uncertainty about this area of consumption.

The Emergence of Consumerism

Along with social and demographic change came new attitudes toward consumerism sponsored by the dominant political and economic philosophies of the day, which took the concept of *caveat emptor* (buyer beware) to new dimensions. For "the capitalist class and the early classical economists" these *laissez-faire* philosophies "had achieved the status of laws of nature as inexorable as the law of gravity."[7] Crudely, it amounted to: "if I am allowed to make my own fortune without State interference, then both I and the State benefit. We will both become prosperous and rich, the British Empire will expand and flourish, and that is all very patriotic and Good For The Whole Nation."[8] However, in the arena of food production, *laissez-faire* was an encouragement to fraudulent adulteration practices, making it positively detrimental to public health.[9] The extent of human involvement in adulteration was enormous and complex. At one obvious level there were the traders and retailers. But honest traders could be deceived into selling adulterated goods: "[Flour] mills work day and night, alum is sometimes ground at night and added when nobody observed them."[10]

The defense of current practice used in aspects of the print conversation was the *supply and demand* principle.[11] If the customer kept coming back, it was because (s)he willingly chose to do so, being equally free to buy goods elsewhere, so ensuring the business of the "bad" retailer/supplier would fail through the (cheap) operation of market forces. Reportage in *The Times* demonstrates the extent of support at the highest levels:

> Great efforts were made by some members of the [1856] Committee to get this whole question of adulteration regarded strictly according to the rules of political economy, and treated simply as a question of supply and demand. It was assumed that the public could tell a genuine article from a mixed one, and that they preferred a mixed one because it was cheaper, and upon that assumption, the inference was made that, after all, the seller of mixed or adulterated articles only met with the wishes of the public in the kind of article he sold. The public had rather have a cheap article mixed,

than a dear one genuine, and that they got what they wanted. There was no pecuniary fraud in such a transaction.[12]

Editorial comment, though, begged leave "to doubt the truth of that assumption." It was a flawed argument for very cogent practical reasons. Poor customers would only be able to afford prices at local (second-rate) shops, and also, might well not be clean or well dressed enough to shop at reputable outlets: "There are extensive neighbourhoods in which the poor, without going to some distance, have not the power of buying to advantage" as "only a low class of tradesmen" operated locally.[13] Economic realities also meant that poorer customers were likely to be in debt to local shopkeepers. Thus "Customers were forced to go, by the system of credit, back to butchers convicted of selling slinked meat," for instance.[14] Further pressures could arise through the network of connections between employers. When the 1856 Select Committee asked a witness why artisans and operatives refrained from prosecuting adulterating retailers, it was informed that it was "very likely the working man's master's brother or cousin might be connected with the shop and it might have the tendency of sacrificing his means of subsistence."[15] Moreover, "the working people . . . know if they take any prominent part in a conviction of that description, that they may be picked out by their employers and thrown out of employment and they will have difficulty in getting employment. . . . They will be marked men."[16]

The legal principle of *caveat emptor* was another control acting in favor of retailers rather than customers, laying the onus on the purchaser not the supplier. The 1856 Select Committee identified problems with this: "It has been objected that the best course will be to leave the buyer to take care of himself. But there are many adulterations which it is impossible for the buyer to detect."[17] However, the legal position was that if a customer could not detect adulterations, there should be neither complaint nor recompense, since (regardless of practicalities) it was the purchaser's *own* fault for not identifying the flaw prior to purchase. Only the challenge posed by the fact that previously undetectable adulteration was now being revealed by scientific analysis forced the admission that this principle needed modification in the area of food adulteration at least:

> it must be remembered too how absolutely the public are at the mercy of shopkeepers in these matters. The rule of *caveat emptor* would be a very unfair one to apply rigidly in such cases. How is a man, when he goes into a shop, to know a spurious article from a genuine one?[18]

Publicly expressed fears about the extent of the threat of adulteration was also a factor in actions taken from 1850 to ameliorate the negative impacts of free market principles: "Death is not only in the pot, it is everywhere; not only in our food and in our drink, but in the very medicines which should cure our diseases."[19]

The Extent of the Problem

The problem of food and drink adulteration reached a peak in the 1850s. Contemporaries claimed that "almost every article of food that can be adulterated is so . . . very often . . . with highly poisonous ingredients, the consequences being an immense amount of imposition, and what is still worse, of disease."[20] A brief (though certainly not exhaustive) survey follows, covering some of the key everyday items and their common forms of adulteration.

Drinking Water

Of the state of drinking water, especially that flowing through London, it was commented:

> the water which is supplied to this Metropolis is hardly anything else but diluted mud and sewer refuse . . . it contains the excreta of two and a half millions of inhabitants, their daily ablutions, the washings of their foul linen, the filth and refuse of hundreds of factories; the offal of markets, the foul matter of slaughter houses and the purulent abominations of hospitals. . . . I think it is astonishing that we are not much worse off in point of public health than we really are.[21]

London's experience, if extreme, differed only in degree from other industrialized urban centers. Drinking water was also used for fraudulent dilution purposes.

Flour

Millers added sulfate of lime, chalk, china clay, and powdered flints as whiteners and a cheap addition to bulk.[22] Large amounts of alum (sulfuric acid, potash, and alumina) were also commonly added.[23] Apart from being a powerful astringent, repeated and continuous doses of alum also lowered the capacity for nutritional intake of food.[24] Further down the production chain, bakers bulked out flour with damaged foreign wheat and other cereals. They also added alum to inferior grades of flour, as well as (less harmfully) beans, peas, and boiled potatoes, enabling them to add more water to the bread, boosting profits.[25] To save yeast while making adulterated dough rise, carbonates of magnesium, ammonia, and gypsum (i.e., lime and sulfuric acid) were added. The good looking but inferior bread could then be passed off as a more expensive "first" loaf. With bread a crucial element in the diet of the poor, its adulteration was a key concern: "If bread was once the 'staff of life,' it is now certainly very often the crutch of destruction."[26]

Milk

Commonly watered down by between 10 and 50 percent to increase profit, this not only lowered nutritional value but use of polluted water introduced further damaging elements to the food production chain.[27]

Beer

Water pollution ensured beer was a staple drink. However, the liberalizing provisions of the Beerhouse Act 1830 had meant that beer sold in beer shops, mainly to the poorest sections of the population, was of notoriously bad quality. Since strength was not a standard requisite, it was diluted with polluted water. Salt in varying amounts was added to give the drinker a thirst, witness the habits of Sarah Page, described by the magistrate as the "worst case" to have come to his notice. Analysis showed that two quarts of adulterated ale from her Wednesbury beerhouse contained nearly 169 grains per gallon, about 119 more than allowed.[28] To replace the alcohol (ie: intoxication potential) lost through dilution, *Cocculus Indicus* (a dangerous poison containing picrotoxin) was commonly added as a substitute for malt in the brewing process.[29] Provided by brewers' druggists under the name of "multum" or "hard mixture," its only use was beer adulteration.[30] Grains of paradise and tobacco could also be added (both containing drugs), along with quassia, gentian, chiretta, cayenne pepper, and coriander.[31] To replace the head lost through dilution, copperas or sulfate of iron was added.[32] Public expressions of concern advertised both the physical effects of adulteration and wider social anxieties about the effects of drink on the working population:

> The adulteration of drinks deserves also special notice because Your Committee cannot but conclude that the intoxication so deplorably prevalent, is in many cases less due to the natural properties of the drinks themselves, than to the admixture of narcotics or other noxious substances intended to supply the properties lost by dilution. [33]

Tea

As with flour, there was a positive chain of adulteration in this heavily adulterated item. Damaged green tea was treated in Canton factories by coloring and mixing it with mineral dyes. At one stage it was calculated approximately five million pounds of adulterated tea was imported annually, amounting to half of all imported green China teas.[34] Even originally good quality green tea was commonly adulterated in China, with "lie tea," so named because it was "an article expressly manufactured for the adulteration of tea."[35] "Lie tea" included not just tea dust, but also china clay, gum, sand, sulfate of iron, and Prussian blue (to give it a green bloom). Bought extensively for mixing with genuine tea, dealers sold the resulting mixture at inflated prices as the real article.[36] This so distorted the market that "We could hardly sell true Green tea before the exposures by the *Lancet* in 1850 and 1851."[37] It was not the only adulteration. "Spurious" tea was produced by English retailers, large and small, from (among other things) hedgerow leaves (beech, elm, ash, sloe, hawthorn, and elder). The leaves were curled and colored in copper plates, and, along with gum and dust, were added to reused, dried tea leaves (there was a flourishing black market trade with hotels, etc.). The result was colored and "faced" with verdigris or sulfate of lime, to give a green bloom.[38]

Coffee

This was commonly heavily adulterated with chicory, the best of which, according to one Board of Inland Revenue analytical chemist, came from beetroot. Chicory was itself commonly grossly adulterated with ground roasted wheat, mustard husks, ground acorns, mangel-wurzel, sawdust, and burnt sugar. Other favored adulterations included roasted corn, roots of various vegetables, baked horse's liver and coloring matter such as red iodine.[39]

Baking Powder

Alum was a cheap substitute for tartaric acid. Its deleterious effects meant that the potential combination of contaminated baking powder and flour in bakery goods, and in home-baked articles was a real concern.

Bottled Pickles, Preserves, Fruits, and Vegetables

Poisonous copper sulfate was used to provide the green coloring that was characteristic of these products. While "Sometimes apparently [the copper is] obtained from the copper vessel in which they are prepared" it was also added more deliberately.[40]

Sugar Confectionery

Sugar was often adulterated with hydrated sulfate of lime, but confectionery also featured a wide range of adulterations, including flour, starch, clay, plaster-of-Paris, chalk, arsenic, chromate of lead, red lead, arsenite of copper, and bisulfate of mercury, plus poisonous pigments such as Prussian or Antwerp blue or vermillion. Many samples contained at least seven different colors and four poisons. In some cases, colors had been painted on with white lead.[41] The combinations could be disastrous, especially since "The effect of such adulteration [upon children] is likely to be much greater than upon a grown person."[42]

The Victims and the Perpetrators

All levels of society were victims, though contemporaries recognized the poor were most affected: "Though adulterations prevail more or less in all districts, it may be assumed as a rule, that the poorer the district, the greater is the amount of adulteration."[43] From the millers to the bakers; the dairy farmers to the milk sellers; the tea and coffee importers to the wholesalers and retailers; and the brewers to the publicans, all were implicated. If retailers had less chance for individual enterprise in some areas such as confectionery making and production of bottled fruit, vegetables, and sauces, the unpackaged (loose) sale of so many items ensured that many, if not most, were involved in some adulterating practices. All levels of production and retail were involved because "A man feels he cannot maintain his position in trade unless he does what his neighbour does; consequently, if his neighbour adulterates, he does so too to agree with him in his prices."[44] Consequently it was not always done out of motivations of pure individual greed:

> Though happily very many refuse under every temptation to falsify the quality of their wares, there are unfortunately, large numbers who, though reluctantly practicing deception, yield to the pernicious contagion of example, or to the hard pressure of competition forced upon them by their less scrupulous neighbours.[45]

The pressures placed on those involved in food production and retail were recognized as being considerable:

> I believe there are a great many people who adulterate in self-defence and who would be glad if something could be done to prevent it.... I believe many honest traders would be glad to have done with adulteration but in self-defence they must do it.[46]

However, the reality was that from the raw ingredients to the finished items of food adulteration was a "normal" part of production practice by the 1850s. The more steps were involved in the food production chain the worse adulteration got with every step carrying out their own form of tampering. This was the first era of mass retailing of cheap food and drink, and that cheapness was achieved through adulteration, not low profit margins.[47]

Knowledge of likely adulteration did not mean that purchasers and consumers could identify specific adulteration.[48] Buying in ignorance, they did not intend to buy staple items of their daily diet consenting to adulteration. Yet retailers and others involved in the production chain claimed that they were as much driven by consumer demand as greed. *The Times* commented on the consequent problems:

> Wherever you go, people talk about bread. It stands next to the weather as a topic.... There can be no doubt that the bakers could give us pure wheat bread if they would... but they are carried away by the spirit of rivalry and competition.... They use a deceitful expedient for this purpose in the shape of alum, and they say "Oh there is no harm in it because every baker can do the same; so there is not really any unfair advantage taken by one baker over another." The public indeed, it is known, want pure white bread; but then the bakers agree that the public is prejudiced and that alum will do them no harm and they give themselves the licence of ... a superior acquaintance with the subject.[49]

By midcentury, virtually every item of diet had the potential to hurt both the pockets and the stomachs of customers, cheating them of good honest purchases in the short term, and cumulatively of their physical health in the long term. But generally, customers could only identify adulteration if, and when, a particular item had a violent consequence, such as an outbreak of food poisoning clearly related to a certain event.[50]

The effects, of course, told most harshly on those on the economic margins, especially those (in workhouses or prisons, say) unable to take any role in the purchase. Take the prosecution of Messrs. John Collier and Co., found guilty of supplying a workhouse with adulterated butter, consisting of 70 percent foreign fat. On the grounds that the butter was not of the quality agreed, the firm was fined £10 plus costs, and the expenses attending the analyst's certificate, hardly enough to deter future adulterations.[51] Economic pressures on such institutions ensured that such incidents did not put suppliers out of business, regardless of the taint from past incidents.[52] Equally, these adulterative practices had been going on for such a long time, that as a general rule, poor urban-based consumers did not know that food and drink could taste or look better. An honest retailer could discover that "[The public] did not believe that my genuine article was genuine; there are many things in this country of which the true flavour is lost."[53]

Revelations and Denouements

Apart from suspecting something was wrong in individual cases, general public awareness only developed slowly. Campaigns against adulteration began in earnest about 1820, instigated by philanthropic businessmen, medical practitioners, surgeons, coroners, journalists, and "whistle-blowing" food adulterators (like journeymen bakers).[54] These campaigns only slowly gathered momentum from the 1840s on.[55] While informative and/or denunciatory books were published from time to time, "the writings of these gentlemen . . . made little public impression." One important reason was that "the existing state of our knowledge at the time did not in all cases enable them to make their statements sufficiently exact and precise," so it was taken as self-interested scaremongering.[56] The catalyst for change leading to actual legal reforms was the campaign led by Dr. T. Wakely, proprietor of the *Lancet*. He and his medical colleagues undertook an antiadulteration crusade from 1851 onward as part of their wider campaign to heighten the public profile of medicine, and to establish medical practitioners as professionals. Their method was random purchase from London retailers of basic food items, and their careful analysis under microscope.

Only chemical analysis had previously been available, and it had been "seldom possible to distinguish one vegetable powder from another" and "until the microscope was brought to bear upon the subject . . . no means existed whereby the great majority of adulterations could be discovered." Initially, "the parties practising [adulterations] little dreamt that an instrument existed capable of bringing to light even these secret and guilty proceedings."[57] Soon consciousness spread that

> [in] the microscope . . . the scientific observer is provided with the most powerful and searching means of discovering adulteration. The application of

this instrument created no little surprise and alarm amongst the perpetrators of such frauds. Hundreds of sophistications were brought to light which had for years escaped delivery, and thus a blow [was dealt] to adulteration from which it can never wholly recover.[58]

These medical men set up the Analytical Sanitary Commission, including Dr. A. H. Hassall and Dr. H. Letheby as leading lights. The results of their analyses were published weekly in the *Lancet* from 1851–1854, together with the names and addresses of the fraudulent traders. It was a gift to the nonspecialist media, who published key extracts. In so doing, they ensured for the first time that the issue of food adulteration became a matter of genuine public concern, leading to the kinds of newspaper rhetoric that encouraged the growth of social panic: "The results disclosed by the labours of the Analytical Sanatory [*sic*] Commission of the *Lancet* were of so serious and alarming a character that they excited almost universal attention."[59] Hassall's revelations of "The amount of adulteration in almost every article of food and drink" was "very appalling," and undermined "a great deal of our conventional and almost stereotyped boasting of our commercial integrity."[60]

The massive publicity resulting from this reprinting in leading national newspapers of the *Lancet*'s carefully orchestrated campaign delighted Dr. Hassall and boosted medical pretensions.[61] It also ensured that any incidents of death, poisoning, paralysis, or illness caused, or suspected to be caused, by food adulteration attracted real publicity, as when over 200 people were poisoned in Bradford in 1858 as a result of the accidental adulteration of a batch of sweets. The intention had been to "extend" the mix by adding plaster-of-Paris as "normal," but arsenic was used instead and seventeen died![62] The resulting moral outrage, expressed in newspapers and periodicals, soon affected the legislature.

A House of Commons Select Committee was established in July 1855 to inquire into the adulteration of food, drink, and drugs. Volunteer witnesses came from all over the country to give evidence, including "converted" food adulterators such as journeymen bakers and Messrs. Crosse and Blackwell, plus representatives from the medical profession and the newly formed Co-operative Societies. It is moving, 150 years later, to read their evidence. Their honest altruism and the horrific experiences recounted make impressive reading:

> I was 30 years a mustard, chicory, drug and spice grinder . . . I have done as much in the way of adulteration as any man in the trade and I have done more than almost any man to expose it. I have done it in defiance of my employers, with a view to crush it and I have felt exceedingly glad to have

an opportunity of giving it a severe blow. I believe many honest men will thank anyone who will put an end to it.[63]

Many representatives of the alleged fraudsters (large and small concerns) also attended to give their accounts and the evenhandedness of the Committee's members in receiving their testimonies is noteworthy. Of the explanations and excuses, *The Times* pointed out "The defence of the adulterators is the old one '*populus vult decipi et decipiatur.*'"[64]

Excuses ranged from generic claims that accused individuals were not responsible for adulteration, to particular claims, such as "High price bakers around London do not add alum."[65] Mr. Jackson claimed: "In all parts of Lancashire and Yorkshire they have used [alum] steadily for the last, say, a dozen years. But not me."[66] Mr. Wickham claimed that "Brewers are not adulterators of beer . . . where adulteration takes place, it is generally in the publicans' cellars."[67] Retailers claimed either not to know products were adulterated, or that the reason for cheapness of a particular source of, say, flour, was that it was not "pure" but that this was not the same as being "adulterated": "we were providing cheap versions for poor people who could not afford better quality." Arguing that they were "providing a public service," giving "what our customers wanted," such retailers would even argue that adulteration improved the original article: "There is a vague impression upon the public mind that a little admixture of chicory improves the beverage we call coffee."[68]

Such retailers had some supporting evidence to call on, as in the case of that key staple, bread. Knowing no better, poor customers not only wanted unnaturally white bread but also, equally unnaturally, loaves "with no holes in it." According to one miller:

> the reason why there should be no large holes[in bread] is, that the industrious classes are very particular when they spread their butter it should not slip into holes and consume a large quantity of butter; they like an even surface. It may perhaps appear trivial to the gentlemen present, but the lower classes consider it to be of great importance. To give the above qualities to my flour, I add one part of bean flour to 60 parts of wheatmeal. Never more than one part in 40. [69]

The Times commented severely on such deceptions practiced on the ignorant:

> when they have . . . for a long time mixed all the bread in England with alum; when they have familiarised the public with this false colour of bread,

then they take advantage of the mistake which they themselves have caused to claim the public on their side and say that people will not buy any bread but what is mixed with alum. . . . Such is the ground of the conspiracy which is now depriving the whole country of good bread; and it is only an instance of how very easily people can justify to themselves any mode of action to which they are accustomed and with which their interests agree. [70]

Others gave more honest justifications for the enduring profit motive, as in the 1875 prosecution in Salford Police Court, reported in the *Manchester Guardian*, of the farmer who admitted adulterating his milk with 29 percent of water, because he "could not be expected to supply pure milk at the contract price of 1s per gallon" (the "average" price was ninepence). He was fined £20 in what was headlined the "worst" example to come under that magistrate's notice.[71] In 1856, Mr. Wickham, representing the brewing industry, claimed that because it was "customary for publicans to sell beer at the price which they pay to brewers," adulteration "forms their actual profit." A change would mean that the public would "pay a higher price for their beer."[72] There was also always the implicit claim that an adulteration was really harmless: as the Chairman of the Leamington Board of Health, commented, "'What the eye never sees the heart never grieves for' is the rule which I should adopt in reference to that."[73]

There were wide-ranging implications. As *The Times* pointed out, "It may be said that the poor want cheap articles, and that cheap articles must be adulterated; and the defender of 'innocuous' adulteration may use this argument for the conclusion he arrives at." But "how can you check adulteration when it begins; and when it has outgrown the harmless limit and becomes poisonous, who are so absolutely the victims of this worst and most fatal kind of adulteration as the poor?" when this vulnerable social category was "in the hands of that class of tradesmen who are least under the influence of public opinion and who are most tempted to make their way by the low arts and tricks of trade."[74]

Despite the pressures on it to endorse the *status quo*, the Committee's Report was unequivocal in its conclusions: "Not only is the public health thus exposed to danger and pecuniary fraud committed on the whole country, but the public morality is tainted and the high commercial character of this country seriously lowered both at home and in the eyes of foreign countries."[75] *The Times* headlined a meeting of the citizens of Manchester which concluded that the

> adulteration of food having been proved to exist to a very large extent and the consequences resulting thereof being most injurious to the public, both

in sanitary and commercial points of view . . . it is the opinion of this meeting that the corporate and other local authorities ought to possess the power of inspecting all food offered for sale and that the vendors of food injuriously adulterated should be subject to a penalty. [76]

As in other places, such comments from "concerned" citizens were followed up by petitions to Parliament.

Responses to the Need for Consumer Protection

Faced with such pressures, there seemed little option but to enact new legislation. Legislation dealing with food and drink standards already existed, but in practice had either been repealed or had no practical effect. Earlier Bread Acts for London were practically obsolete: "so far as I know, there is not a single baker in London who makes bread without alum."[77] The legislation arising out of the 1856 Report was the Adulteration of Food or Drink Act 1860, the first to deal generally with the sale of food and drugs in a pure state by promoting analysis of goods.[78] The Recital to the Act stated that the practices of adulteration "were a fraud on Her Majesty's subjects and a great hurt to their health," and also acknowledged that "more effectual laws than before were required to repress the practice of adulterating articles of food and drink." At one level, it is simply one example of the many pieces of public health legislation "seen as one long campaign orchestrated by (though not confined to) the professional class against the vested interests of the propertied classes," which enjoyed limited success.[79] Its provisions were a compromise, too limited in scope and resources for enforcement, given the vested interests involved. As the subsequent 1874 Select Committee Report commented, it did not think that Parliament desired "needlessly to hamper" trade, and "still less to interfere between buyer and seller with the view of regulating prices," or to attempt to help consumers assess the "real money value of any marketable commodity."[80] However, it was the first acknowledgement of the principle that consumer protection measures were the general responsibility of the state.[81]

Ultimately it was ineffectual, and the hints that it would not achieve its advertised aim were contained in the evidence to the Select Committee, as when Dr. Postgate commented that he "had been sent messages by millers and bakers that they would not be interfered with in their business; they had introduced alum and potatoes and would continue to do it."[82] Its practical limitations soon became apparent. Dr. H. Letheby (recently appointed Public Analyst of Food) reported that the poor would be "unable to pay the fee named" for analysis, and therefore, "unless something is done to assist them ... they will be shut out most completely from the benefits of the Act."[83] He suggested giving analysts discretionary powers to conduct inquiries without charge, and that Inspectors of Meats and Markets make their own purchases of samples of food and drink.[84] This was not done, but the legislation did facilitate changes in attitudes and ensured continued public debate about the need to improve standards both through legislation and promotion of changes in consumer attitudes, because the "most beneficial" strategies were those "to prevent adulteration, rather than punish it."[85]

The 1860 Act was amended by the Adulteration of Food, Drink, and Drugs Act 1872.[86] A Select Committee followed in 1874. Its Report resulted in the introduction of the more effective Sale of Food and Drugs Act 1875, the basis of modern equivalent legislation, such as the Food Safety Act 1990.[87] Space does not permit detailed examination of its provisions but it established as a criminal offense "knowingly selling adulterated food which was injurious to health" and a strict liability offense of selling to the prejudice of a purchaser any article of food not of the nature, substance, and quality of the article demanded.[88] "Bulking up" items with other articles (unless the purchaser's notice was drawn to it by labels), was also prohibited.[89] More Public Analysts were appointed and greater powers to procure samples given to local authority-appointed Inspectors of Nuisance or Weights and Measures or Markets, leading to prosecution of offenders.[90]

Under the 1875 Act all imported teas became subject to Customs' analysis for purity, and any unfit for consumption were destroyed, an action recommended by the 1874 Select Committee Report.[91] The same tea could be further scrutinized by a Public Analyst to check on possible later adulteration.[92] Tea also now began to be sold in sealed packets under proprietary names, such as Lyons, Liptons, and Hornimans, to guarantee their purity.[93] After the 1856 Report, many retail organizations began to clean up their acts voluntarily because "There is such a desire on the part of tradesmen to get rid of these dishonest practices, that they would submit to almost any inconvenience ... for the purpose," though the effects of public disapproval or prosecution cannot be discounted![94] Local and national press reported on bodies such as the Birmingham and Midland Counties Association, established to detect and prevent adulteration of flour. In 1858, when its committee reported its activities, they stated that when inspections had started, "they had found many instances" of adulteration with alum, but cautions, backed up by hint of prosecution, had produced a "salutary effect." Consequently, the committee had "reason to believe" that that evil was "nearly suppressed" in their locality.[95] Crosse and Blackwell, for example, changed their practices, no longer pickling products in copper vessels or coloring sauces with demonstrated poisons.⁹⁶ The 1875 Act provided for guarantees of purity to be printed on the packet wrappers used by shops, along with certificates from reputable analysts to guarantee the purity of articles.⁹⁷ Another impetus for purity came with the development, from 1844, of the Co-operative Retail Societies aiming to provide their mainly working-class members with pure items of food.⁹⁸

There were hiccoughs along the way, though, in terms of consumer attitudes. Crosse and Blackwell, for instance, had been obliged to advertise the reasons for the changes in color of their pickles, and so forth, before the public would accept the pure articles.⁹⁹ Co-operative Societies found that their members were not happy with the different taste and appearance of unadulterated items, facing complaints that "this [adulterated] bread is nicer than the bread made from the flour you turn out and we buy it at 2d a score cheaper."¹⁰⁰ The Societies had to resort to adulterating their own items, to "wean them off" and gain public acceptance of the pure articles," being "compelled to adulterate with alum to gain the customers and bring back the . . . lost profits over nine months."¹⁰¹ Such bodies resorted to the use of traveling lecturers to "explain matters to the working classes."¹⁰² As Birmingham surgeon John Postgate commented: "They had to explain to people that bread was not naturally of white appearance, but of a yellowish colour."¹⁰³ Despite difficulties, efforts were rewarded:

> We are working and turning out now a pure article. The people seem to be more convinced than they were at first that an impure article is not good for the constitution, and now we are doing three times the business that we were doing after we began to adulterate.¹⁰⁴

Shifts in public taste also helped, as with the development of preference for Indian and Ceylon teas, rather than the commonly adulterated green teas.¹⁰⁵

Conclusion

The role played by the media in publishing, on a national and local scale, the details of the extent and nature of such practices, was crucial to the outcome, as contemporaries readily acknowledged:

> I consider I am greatly within the mark when I say that there is not one-twentieth part of the adulteration prevailing at the present moment that did prevail four or five years from this time. I attribute that to the frequent and repeated exposures which have taken place of adulteration and to the fact

that adulteration has been brought home to the persons practising it; their names have been more known to the public.[106]

Mr. Farrand of the Corn Mill Society also accepted that "There was such a noise in the newspapers of the injury that was being done to the constitution by the use of alum that people began to be convinced that it was injurious."[107] Indeed, while the 1856 Select Committee was receiving evidence, there were almost daily media reports of its witnesses' statements.[108] Hand-in-hand with the preventative advice, publicity was also given to prosecutions undertaken throughout the country, as in the case of the prosecution of the Newcastle dealer convicted of selling pepper adulterated with mustard husks and given the maximum fine of £100.[109] Even less severely punished cases were included in the national newspaper debate on a daily basis, as the typical examples of the Birkenhead tea dealers fined five shillings and costs by the magistrates for selling tea laced with Prussian blue, and of the butter seller fined £5 and twelve shillings costs for selling butter "containing no butter whatever."[110] Such publicity had a clear preventive effect, but it was not all positive. The media also circulated advice for the avoidance of criminal actions, and newspapers regularly published letters of complaint and declarations of innocence from traders.[111] Given the breadth of contrary evidence also available in the press, it may be doubted whether these complaints were believed widely by the public, but they cannot have helped efforts to eradicate adulteration.

An 1872 report in *The Times* referring to a recent article in the *Food Journal* provides a fitting conclusion:

> Mr. Muntz's Adulteration Bill has by its third clause given great offence to the manufacturers of some articles of daily consumption which have hitherto deceived the public with impunity. . . . Some of the wholesale warehouses have very properly refused to deal in many cocoas, mustards, and spices unless they receive a guarantee from the manufacturers that the article is genuine or that the outer wrapper or tin containing adulterated articles bears a label stating the composition of the mixture. It may be assumed that this course of conduct on the part of the wholesale warehouses will considerably benefit the public, while the manufacturers themselves will not be overanxious to enlighten the community as to the composition of the articles they have hitherto supplied. . . . Doubtless much evasion will be practised, but the public must be on the alert; and now that the adulteration question is to the front, it should not be allowed to slumber until the present unhealthy state of trade is remedied. . . . We now have the delightful spectacle of witnessing manufacturers preparing to tell the people the composition of what they are eating and drinking. . . . It is consolatory to those

who have long known the secrets of the trade and who being well aware of the rubbish sold under popular names, have done all in their power to put a stop to such a barefaced deception, to observe the consternation among certain manufacturers caused by the Adulteration Act of last Session.[112]

Sadly, the optimism was ill founded. More than a hundred years later, it was deemed necessary, essential even, that a Food Standards Agency be established to carry out certain prescribed functions, including protecting public health from risks connected to production or supply of food, developing food policy, and providing advice for public authorities, as well as monitoring the performance of the enforcement authorities in enforcing the relevant legislation.[113] All these are up-to-date variations on the debates and themes considered above—*plus ça change, plus c'est la même chose!*

Notes

1. John Burnett, *Plenty and Want: A Social History of Diet in England from 1815 to the Present Day* (London: Methuen, 1985), 99.

2. T. Arthur, "Adulteration, and Its Remedy," *Cornhill Magazine* 2 (July 1860): 86–96.

3. S. J. Fallows, *Food Legislative System of the UK* (London: Butterworths, 1988), 29; Burnett, *Plenty and Want*, 99.

4. PP, House of Commons Select Committee 1856, Evidence, Dr. A. H. Hassall, 13 July 1855; Dr. A. H. Hassall, *Food and Its Adulterations, Comprising the Reports of the Analytical Sanitary Commission of the Lancet* (London: Longman, Brown, Green and Longman, 1855); Burnett, *Plenty and Want*, 100, 109; Fallows, *Food*, 30. Examples of ineffectual earlier legislation covering other foodstuffs include the Adulteration of Tea and Coffee Act 1724, and the Adulteration of Tea Acts 1730 and 1776.

5. T. L. Kemp, "Review," *Dublin Review* 39 (1855): 60.

6. Ibid., 61.

7. Harold Perkin, *The Rise of Professional Society in England since 1880* (London: Routledge, 1990), 121.

8. Fallows, *Food*, 31.

9. PP, House of Commons Select Committee 1856, Evidence, Dr. W. B. Carpenter, M.D., March 1856.

10. Ibid., Evidence, J. Woodin, grocer and tea dealer for the Co-operative Central Agency, March 1856; Evidence, J. Jackson, miller, Wakefield, 25 April 1856. Woodin was author of *The System of Adulteration and Fraud Now Prevailing in Trade* (London, 1852).

11. Burnett, *Plenty and Want*, 110.

12. Leader, *The Times*, 20 August 1856.

13. PP, House of Commons Select Committee, Evidence, Dr. T. Wakely, March 1856. Wakely was coroner for Middlesex and owner/editor of *The Lancet*.

14. Ibid., Evidence, Prof. F. C. Calvert, March 1856. "Slinked meat" was from naturally aborted calves.

15. Ibid., W. Emerson, manager of the People's Flour Mill, Leeds, March 1856.
16. Ibid., Response, E. Farrand, Corn Mill Society, Rochdale, March 1856.
17. Select Committee Report, 1856.
18. Leader, *The Times,* 20 August 1856.
19. Leader, *The Times,* 24 July 1855.
20. Kemp, Review, 62.
21. PP, House of Commons Select Committee, Evidence, Dr. A. Normandy, 25 July 1855. A professional chemist, Normandy was author of *The Commercial Handbook of Chemical Analysis* (London, 1850).
22. Ibid., Evidence, J. Jackson, 25 April 1856.
23. Ibid., Evidence, Dr. J. Postgate, August 1855; Dr. A Normandy, 25 July 1855.
24. Ibid., Evidence, Dr. J. Postgate, August 1855.
25. Ibid., Evidence, J. Mitchell, 25 July 1855. Mitchell, an analytical chemist, was author of *A Treatise on the Falsification of Food and the Chemical Means Employed to Detect Them* (London, 1848).
26. Kemp, Review, 65. See also Burnett, *Plenty and Want,* 118.
27. Burnett, *Plenty and Want,* 242; Kemp, Review, 72. See also *Daily Telegraph,* 10 April 1874.
28. *Manchester Guardian,* 5 May 1875.
29. Burnett, *Plenty and Want,* 102.
30. PP, House of Commons Select Committee, Evidence, J. Rodgers, April 1856.
31. Ibid., Evidence, E. Wickham, April 1856; G. Phillips, 1 August 1855.
32. Ibid., Evidence, J. Mitchell, 25 July 1855.
33. Select Committee Report, 1856.
34. Burnett, *Plenty and Want,* 245.
35. Hassall, *Food,* xv–xvi.
36. Ibid.
37. PP, House of Commons Select Committee, Evidence, J. Woodin, March 1856.
38. Burnett, *Plenty and Want,* 103; Kemp, Review, 71.
39. PP, House of Commons Select Committee, Evidence, G. Phillips, 1 August 1855; Burnett, *Plenty and Want,* 107.
40. Kemp, Review, 68.
41. PP, House of Commons Select Committee, Evidence, Dr. Lethaby, August 1855.
42. Ibid., Evidence, Dr. A. Hassall, 13 July 1855.
43. Ibid., Evidence, Dr. W. B. Carpenter, March 1856.
44. Ibid., Evidence, Dr. T. Wakely, March 1856.
45. Select Committee Report 1856.
46. PP, House of Commons Select Committee, Evidence, R. Gay, March 1856. Gay was superintendent of the Mustard Department at HM Victualling Yard, Dartford.
47. Ibid., Evidence, P. Mackenzie, 30 April 1856. Mackenzie was editor of the Glasgow *Reformers' Gazette.*
48. Burnett, *Plenty and Want,* 115.
49. Leader, *The Times,* 21 August 1856.
50. See Burnett, *Plenty and Want,* 119, 256, for examples of food poisoning causing deaths and illness.
51. PP, House of Commons Select Committee, Evidence, Prof. F. C. Calvert, March 1856; *Daily Telegraph,* 10 April 1885.

52. PP, House of Commons Select Committee, Evidence, Dr. A. H. Hassall, 2, May 7 1856.
53. Ibid., Evidence, R. Gay, March 1856.
54. Fallows, *Food*, 125; Burnett, *Plenty and Want*, 101; Kemp, Review, 62 refers to F. Accum, *A Treatise on Adulterations of Food and Culinary Poisons* (London, 1820).
55. See Mitchell, *Treatise*; Fallows, *Food*, 30.
56. Kemp, Review, 62.
57. PP, House of Commons Select Committee, Evidence, Dr. A. H. Hassall, 13 July 1855.
58. Arthur, "Adulteration," 90.
59. Ibid., 88.
60. Kemp, Review, 75.
61. Letter, Dr. A. H. Hassall, *The Times*, 31 July 1855.
62. *Daily Telegraph*, 4 May 1858.
63. PP, House of Commons Select Committee, Evidence, R. Gay, March 1856.
64. Leader, *The Times*, 3 January 1856.
65. PP, House of Commons Select Committee, Evidence, T. K. Callard, baker, 16 April 1856.
66. Ibid., J. Jackson, 25 April 1856.
67. Ibid., E. Wickham, April 1856.
68. Kemp, Review, 74.
69. PP, House of Commons Select Committee, Evidence, P. Brown, miller, 16 April 1856.
70. Leader, *The Times*, 21 August 1856.
71. *Manchester Guardian*, 5 February 1875. See also PP, House of Commons Select Committee, Evidence, T. K. Callard, baker, 16 April 1856.
72. Ibid., Evidence, E. Wickham, 16 April 1856.
73. Ibid., Evidence, R. A Wallington, August 1855.
74. Leader, *The Times*, 20 August 1856.
75. Select Committee Report 1856.
76. "Meeting of the Citizens of Manchester at the Town Hall on 1 January," *The Times*, 18 January 1859.
77. PP, House of Commons Select Committee, Evidence, P. Brown, miller, 16 April 1856; J. Rodgers, April 1856; Dr. A. Normandy 18 July 1855. See also S.2 Bread Act 1822 for list of permissible ingredients in bread.
78. Burnett, *Plenty and Want*, 258.
79. Perkin, *Professional Society*, 121.
80. Select Committee Report on the Adulteration of Food Act 1872, f 1874.
81. Fallows, *Food*, 31.
82. PP, House of Commons Select Committee, Evidence, Dr. J. Postgate, August 1855.
83. 1860 Act S.4; *The Times*, 1 December 1860.
84. *The Times*, 1 December 1860.
85. Ss. 6, 7, 8.
86. See, for example, *Fitzpatrick v Kelley* (1873) LR 8 QB 337, cited in K. J. M. Smith, *Developments in English Criminal Jurisprudence, 1800–1957* (Oxford: Clarendon, 1998), 214.
87. See Report of the Select Committee on the Adulteration of Food Act 1872, dated 3 July 1874; Fallows, *Food*, 32; Burnett, *Plenty and Want*, 260.

88. S.3; s. 6. See, for example, *Parker v Alder* [1899] 1 QB 20; *Andrews v Luckin* (1917) 117 LT 726.
89. Ss. 6, 7, 8.
90. S.13. Compare with 1872 Act, ss. 6, 8, 10, 13, 18, 21.
91. S.30. Report of the Select Committee on the Adulteration of Food Act 1872, 1874.
92. Burnett, *Plenty and Want*, 265.
93. Ibid., 252.
94. PP, House of Commons Select Committee, Evidence, Dr. T. Wakely, March 1856.
95. *Manchester Guardian*, 6 December 1858.
96. PP, House of Commons Select Committee, Evidence, T. Blackwell, 18 July 1855.
97. S.12.
98. PP, House of Commons Select Committee, Evidence, W. Emerson, March 1856; E. Farrand, March 1856. Emerson was manager of The People's Flour Mill, Leeds, established in 1847 to provide pure genuine flour and bake bread in their own ovens.
99. Burnett, *Plenty and Want*, 252.
100. PP, House of Commons Select Committee, Evidence, E. Farrand, March 1856.
101. Ibid.
102. Ibid., Evidence, J. Woodin, March 1856.
103. Ibid., Evidence, Dr. J. Postgate, August 1855.
104. Ibid., Evidence, Mr. E. Farrand, March 1856.
105. House of Commons Select Committee Report on the Adulteration of Food Act 1872.
106. PP, House of Commons Select Committee, Evidence, Dr. Hassall, 2 May 1856.
107. Ibid., Mr. E. Farrand, March 1856.
108. "Proceedings of the Select Committee," *The Times*, 3 April 1856.
109. *Manchester Guardian*, 24 May 1858.
110. *Illustrated London News*, 28 June 1873; *Daily Telegraph*, 10 April 1884.
111. "Money Market and City Intelligence," *The Times*, 11 September 1860.
112. *The Times*, 30 September 1872.
113. Food Standards Act 1999.

Figure 4. *Illustrated Police News*, 11 October 1870. This page is largely taken up with depictions of episodes in the career of baby-farmer Mrs. Waters, but also shows aspects of assaults upon women, and the results of the escape of a mad cow.

SECTION THREE

The Threat from Within

This section features the chapters examining the threats from within the boundaries of respectable society, threats from sources which were not expected to disturb the tranquility and stability of the Victorian domestic sphere because of the "normality" of their social position or expected instincts. Thus the strong emphasis here is on the conversations which highlighted how the law struggled to deal with challenges to conventionality from within and, consequently, has a strong focus on the feminine element within Victorian society, that domestic element seen as underpinning national greatness. What thus becomes apparent is the Victorian consciousness of the extent of contradictions and discontinuities between daily practice and the gender stereotypes invoked by the law, because of its inclination to view things in absolutes of positives and negatives, and their unhappiness with the consequent tensions. D'Cruze sets the scene for this section through her examination of the bewildered unhappiness caused by signs which were ambiguous and so threatening to social conventionalities, one which was eventually disposed of by identifying a form of external threat (providing a link with the previous section). This was a case which acquired national importance through the public debates over what actually took place, making it a quintessential newspaper-driven conversation. In essence, a small, even rather sordid, family tragedy, the Novelli case was poured over by readers across the nation and given a symbolic significance for wider issues of class, gender, and race. It only calmed down as it became "proved" that Mrs. Novelli's "goodness" remained unassailed through the "eloquence" of her virtuous corpse, while her murderer was shown to be "other" in both his mental instability and his foreignness. There was therefore no "scandal."

The remaining chapters, however, focus on issues less easily disposed of as threats coming from outside the British culture, as being the source of alien natures. Bentley examines the high profile surrounding baby-farming, when society's expectations of maternal instincts were outraged, while the chapters from Gleeson and Stevenson highlight the problems caused by women's vocalization within the legal system of sexual issues affecting them: rape and husbandly duty. Edwards's continues the discussion of the hollowness of the conventionality that a woman's submission and her protection by the legal system were correlative, and despite some Irish involvement, the uncomfortable fact for most Victorians was that the "crimes" at the heart of these conversations were unequivocally homegrown.

II

The Eloquent Corpse: Gender, Probity, and Bodily Integrity in Victorian Domestic Murder

SHANI D'CRUZE

Introduction

The bourgeois family was a crucial site of formation of the Victorian middle classes, and the gendered, raced, and classed identities that were produced as much in the home as out of it are increasingly being recognized as partaking in the constitution of national identity, particularly following the passage of the Reform Act 1832. The family provided one of the key underpinnings of nineteenth-century perceptions of social stability and a growing scholarly interest in spousal and domestic homicide in the nineteenth century is demonstrating that the law took a partial and gender-biased view of such killings.[1] Victorian public opinion was both shocked and fascinated by such abrupt breaches in domestic felicity. Lethal violence within the middle-class home provided an opportunity through court hearings and their publication in the newspapers for both local and national public reflection on the proper conduct of domestic relations between male and female family members, between adults and children and indeed between masters, mistresses, and servants, in ways that were comparable to (but rather more thrilling than) the publication of Divorce Court proceedings from 1857.[2] The disruption of the classed and gendered order of the respectable household by the violent eruption of "fearfully excited passions" enabled the cultural production of moral melodramas which reinforced but at the same time drew attention to the fragility of normative domestic ideals.

A Melancholy Tragedy

The particular melodrama of domestic homicide discussed here is a case of murder and suicide in an affluent suburb of Manchester. There was a coroner's hearing, but since the murderer had committed suicide, this was the limit of the legal proceedings. The accounts I am dealing with here are principally those of the local Manchester and Lancaster press. The localized and immediate preoccupations of the coroner's hearing emerge more clearly as the tale was retailed for local and regional consumption. Harriet Novelli, thirty, devout and (we are told) of "considerable personal attractions" was a recent widow. Her husband, a prosperous Manchester merchant had died aged thirty-five in October 1848 at Scarborough, leaving her with two young children, Louisa Harriet, not yet four years old and Lewis William, just over two.[3] The Novellis had lived at Prestwich House, a considerable mansion opposite the church.[4] Louis Novelli and his father Phillip before him had maintained business premises in Manchester. His father had retired around 1844 and lived in London. Late in 1849, Harriet and her children had moved to a house bought for her by her father-in-law at Broughton Mount, Higher Broughton, a pleasant, recently built villa overlooking the new race course. Harriet Novelli had furnished the house with "taste and elegance" augmented by many of her late husband's collection of paintings.[5] He had named his brother, Alexander Novelli, one of the executors of his will. Since Lewis's death Alexander had been living with Harriet and her children in order to settle the estate and had accompanied them to Broughton. Alexander wanted to marry his sister-in-law, but she refused him. He was a couple of years younger than she. They had visited a phrenologist in Manchester who, from the form of her skull, had reassured Novelli that she would make a good wife. The Novelli household seems to have incorporated itself successfully into Broughton society and on the Sunday of her death Harriet had attended religious services in Prestwich and in Broughton and had taken tea with her neighbors, the Costans. Mr. Edmund Costan, a Manchester merchant in his early forties, was another executor of the Novelli will, and thus business, social, and family connections overlapped. Alexander Novelli was due to travel home to London the following morning.

Harriet and Alexander Novelli returned home from the Costans's around 9:30 P.M. After family prayers, they ate a supper of "oatmeal porridge and milk and treacle" and sat together, anticipating a glass of brandy and hot water before retiring.[6] The servant who delivered the hot water unlaced her mistress's boots, but otherwise left them seated on either side of the fireplace, in attitudes of complete domestic probity. The two were not seen alive again, and so the story of what happened next necessarily had to be deduced by excited journalists, juries, and newspaper readers from constructions and interpretations of the material and corporeal signs that were discovered the next morning. The detective process of course names rather than finds "clues"—evidence is always already in the process of interpretation. And what first the servants and then the across-the-road neighbor, Mr. Grundy, Mr. Costan, and the doctor found early the following morning, were two bodies.[7] The cold corpse of Harriet Novelli was lying on the thickly carpeted floor of the dining room and the still warm body of Alexander Novelli was in his bedroom, hung from the bedpost by his dressing gown cord. And thus the "melancholy tragedy," the "terrible catastrophe" unfolded.

Reading the Body

There is a difference in tone between the national and the provincial press. The national *Times* sketched a picture of the widow's corpse lying awry with an empty gin glass on the table beside it.[8] The implication of immorality was explicit, signed most clearly in the substitution of the glass of gin for brandy and water. The semiotics of gin as a marker for working-class depravity, was well known to Victorian readers. Gin was the tipple of the prostitute. Victorian Manchester temperance reformers particularly despaired of the women drinkers in the city's "low spirit vaults."[9] The more sympathetic and extensive reporting in the Manchester press nevertheless still allowed for an examination of the more pejorative view on Mrs. Novelli's demise, bringing the shocking possibilities of female depravity to mind even as they were refuted.

The inquest convened first in the Novelli's house, in a drawing room adjoining the dining room where the murder (and later the postmortem) had taken place and the jurors viewed both the bodies, lying as they had been found. It then adjourned to the Griffin Inn in Lower Broughton. So first, the law appropriated the (violated) domestic space of Harriet Novelli's home and then shifted the disclosure of domestic and emotional life to the public space of the Inn. By that time the bodies had been buried; Mrs. Novelli's in a grave shared with her husband in Prestwich Church and Alexander Novelli's (as befitted a suicide) in a common grave at Stand.[10] Materially disposed of, the corpses nevertheless retained a potent discursive reality, through the operation of the law and the publication of its proceedings. As the newspaper accounts layered the evidence of the two coroner's court hearings over the initial details gleaned by journalists in the neighborhood, the reader came to know a fair amount about Harriet Novelli's body. It was found lying on its left side, with its feet toward the fireplace and its head toward the door, in an "easy posture" with its legs slightly apart and its arm stretched out. Beside it was a table on which the cloth had been displaced and with an antimacassar from the chair beneath it. She was wearing the dress she had worn earlier in the day, but her handkerchief had been removed and the dress was unfastened at the back.

The pin of a broach had been bent out of shape. Despite all this "the countenance was placid" and early examinations did not disclose the bruising on her throat.[11] At first poison was suspected (a glass of brandy and water had been consumed by someone) and the authority of medical examination was required to disperse this supposition, and in so doing brought a great deal more of Mrs. Novelli's corpse into imaginary and discursive view. There were no "marks of violence" elsewhere than on her neck, testified Dr. Ainsworth—evidence which of course required the removal of clothing. Thumbprints on the windpipe and the state of the blood vessels of the lungs, neck, and heart indicated death by strangulation. This conclusion required the opening of the chest cavity and skull. There was no trace of poison in the contents of her stomach, which resembled pea soup and had a sour smell. In response to direct questioning (from Edmund Costan), surgeon Mr. Harris gave "in the strongest terms his opinion as a medical man" that she had not had sexual intercourse on the evening of her murder, nor was she pregnant. We must therefore assume that his opinion as a medical man was based on physical examination.

If the corpse is eloquent here, exactly what is it saying? Thomas Laqueur argues that by this period, specific corpses were scrutinized in the medicolegal record, not as signifiers inscribed with religiously derived markers of grace or sin, but in their detail, particularity, and materiality, as *human* bodies in their own right. Such medicolegal discourses were productive of a gesture of humanitarian empathy in the reader and at the same time a movement toward some possibility of improvement of the human condition.[12] The gaze was directed to a specific, known body, sickening or dead, saturated with recognizably human suffering, which required progressive, rational even political activity to decipher and address the causes. The Victorian middle classes, of course, had very firm (if debated) ideas about the causes of bodily suffering and (particularly in regard to the bodies of the poor) deployed extensive energies to address them through philanthropy, remoralization, local government, and the political lobbying of central government.

The newspaper took care to detail the evidence of the physical cause of Harriet Novelli's suffering (strangulation by hands around her windpipe, which bruised her neck and "engorged" the vessels of her brain, neck, and lungs with dark venous blood). But it also used her body—externally, in its disposition and appearance and internally through the postmortem examination evidence—as a text to decipher her mental and emotional condition and question her chastity and probity. Her eventual vindication as a tragic figure was secured only once her potential culpability and fragile sexual and moral reputation had been extensively canvassed. One must surely assume that the allegedly "placid" countenance is a fictional signifier of respectability; the physical processes of strangulation are not conducive to calm facial expression. Victorian ideals of genteel femininity required the careful regulation of facial and bodily comportment. For this reason, the "easy posture," the outflung arm and the slightly open legs, produced suspicions—signified the possibility of a compromised woman—which with the discovery of the unfastened dress, unlaced boots and discarded handkerchief grew into questions, only eventually settled at the reconvened inquest, after several days of rumor and speculation. It was all very well for the *Manchester Courier* to assert that "we cannot account for the unfastening of the dress except upon a supposition which makes the affair still more hideous; we shall not further allude to it."[13] That remark by itself necessarily did all kinds of imaginary work in the minds of its readers.

Thus, largely following the work of Mary Poovey, this corpse (I would argue) was enabled to recuperate Harriet Novelli's reputation, but only after a process whereby the medicolegal gaze first scrutinized and then formulated judgments on the evidence yielded by her body.[14] Harriet Novelli had been a woman from a "wealthy family" in "affluent circumstances." Her class position and the tropes of bourgeois femininity which attached to it nevertheless did not excuse her body from this kind of imaginary and actual display, though they may have contributed to the vigor with which her male defenders, principally Edmund Costan, questioned the doctor to secure her vindication. The Manchester commercial and manufacturing elite was a self-conscious and cohesive if not undifferentiated "social formation," for whom business and public probity were not divorced from domestic concerns.[15] So foundational was home and family to middle-class *mores* that the Novelli "tragedy" had a wider significance than its implications for one family. That such extensive violence could occur so suddenly and easily within the sanctified precincts of the middle-class home questioned the social and cultural underpinnings of Manchester middle-class respectability, not to mention the reputation of Higher Broughton as a developing suburb. And this in itself I think is important in defining the composite nature of the gaze fixed upon the corpse of Harriet Novelli. She was looked at not only by the doctors but also by the coroner's jury, and imaginatively by the readership of the newspaper (male and female) that consumed these melodramatic revelations. The comparative informality and immediacy of the structure and proceedings of the coroners' court facilitated this level of participation. The newspaper reporter's investigations and the retailing of "our own impression after carefully considering the facts we have collected" shaped the publicly presented narrative.[16] But more than this, the selection of jury members in the comparatively small neighborhood of Broughton meant that witnesses and interested parties were also called upon to serve on the jury. In particular, Edward Costan, key witness, discoverer of the body and cross-examiner of the medical witness, was also a family friend and coexecutor of Harriet's husband's will. The position of her body on discovery is given on his evidence. Note the mixture of observation, recollection, and hearsay in his testimony:

> She had the same dress on as when at my house, with the exception of the cuffs. Her dress was unfastened at the back, as though she had been preparing for bed.... I should say Mrs. Novelli had taken some brandy and water as she usually did before going to bed.[17]

The Domestic Sphere and Local Society

Of course, other interested and knowledgeable observers had no voice in the journalistic account. The women of the respectable social networks of church and visiting and taking tea must have been close observers of the relationship between brother and sister-in-law and doubtless constituted part of the readership of the newspaper articles. Elizabeth Gaskell, the novelist, wrote to a friend in London (who would of course have only seen the less sympathetic London papers): "such a tragedy here yesterday, which you will see in the papers. We knew Mrs. Novelli! She was a Madonna-like person with a face (and character I believe) full of thought and gentle love."[18] Thus Mrs. Gaskell, too, was ready to read character from physical appearance. The Novellis seemed the ideal middle-class family, underpinned by gender differentiation in familial roles. Mrs. Novelli's beauty was the counterpart to her husband's money, apparent business success and cultivated taste. Harriet Novelli came from a Lancashire textile family. It is likely that she was an only child, born some nine years after her parent's marriage. Her father, Richard Hall, was a calico printer from Tottington, near Bury.[19] He could style himself as a "gent[leman]" on his daughter's marriage certificate, but at her birth, he is recorded as a mere shopkeeper. Although occupational attributions are not always reliable indicators of material substance, the Halls, though affluent, were perhaps less well heeled than the Novellis.[20] The marriage, apparently an advantageous match from the point of view of the Halls, nevertheless conforms to the common pattern in textile families; where immigrants tended to ground themselves in regional association, and where marriages were endogamous, both by class and by region.[21]

The Novellis had been fully part of Manchester middle-class society. Despite their apparent Italian ancestry there is no discoverable indication of Catholicism in the available sources. In Prestwich, they took part in charitable and philanthropic activity in Prestwich parish. Along with other major householders they contributed to the Infants' School (£2 in 1847–48), Lewis Novelli added his two guineas to the all-male subscription list for the church choir and Mrs. Novelli subscribed ten shillings to the Girls' Clothing Club and a guinea to the Ladies Charity (apparently a lying-in charity). Lewis Novelli served as parish overseer in 1845.[22] Most notably, he had left £1,000 in his will to establish an educational charity in Prestwich, to be administered by trustees drawn from among the major ratepayers and the parish clergy.[23] The Novellis were resolutely attached to the Established church. The house to which Mrs. Novelli moved in Higher Broughton was also very close to the parish church. Religious subjects by Renaissance Italian artists featured predominately among those in Lewis Novelli's will, and legatees included Manchester friends and colleagues including the Prestwich curate and his wife. A copy of a Raphael "Madonna" was left in trust to hang in the Prestwich Rectory.

Novelli's collection also included English painters of the period. There was a landscape by Sir Peter Francis Bourgeois, an "Orphelia" and a "Juliet" by the water-colorist, John Bostock, and Novelli left two pictures by Manchester artist William Knight Keeling. One of these, a "Gil Blas" left to his brother Alexander, had been exhibited at the Royal Academy. Keeling had been leading figure in the 1823 foundation of the Royal Manchester Institution for the Promotion of Literature, Science and Art, and was later its President (1864–77). Lewis Novelli had paid the £42 subscription to become a hereditary governor of the Manchester Institution.[24] Thus Lewis Novelli was not only a businessman, but also a member of the Manchester bourgeois elite in a wider sense and, judging by what can be gleaned of his home surroundings, was an exemplar of the domestic middle-class masculinity that John Tosh has defined as characteristic of the period.[25]

Both Prestwich and Higher Broughton were by the 1830s established as middle-class suburbs, providing the Manchester men with a pleasant living environment a carriage ride away from the polluted, overcrowded city center populated by the poor bloody infantry of early industrialization.[26] These neighboring parishes northwest of Salford were a few miles out of town via the Bury New Road (opened in 1827). Prestwich had a population of over four thousand in 1851, but working and manufacturing households concentrated in the central settlement, leaving many airy, semirural locations for the houses of the middle class. In 1780 Broughton had been almost entirely rural; its population in 1801 had numbered 866. It had acquired its church only in 1836 and by 1851 it had a population of 7,126. Higher Broughton in particular comprised new developments of large villas along and near to the Bury New Road.[27] The marked spatial residential segregation of early-Victorian Manchester was highly class based. In 1842 it could be said that "Ardwick

... (or indeed Broughton) ... knows less about Ancoats than it does about China."[28] But if Ancoats was out of the sight of the leafy environs of Broughton it was hardly out of mind. The Manchester middle classes at midcentury were still vulnerable to the vagaries of a turbulent early industrial economy and of course much exercised about the subversive and seditious potential as well as the moral and sanitary condition of the multiplying numbers of the laboring poor. In January 1850 the "Hungry 40s" were barely past. In 1847–48 the Manchester Guardians had to assist an additional 17,000 souls, some 56,000 in total, and the slump "was not finally overcome until 1853."[29] If family was of both practical importance to the middle classes as well as of symbolic and cultural value, the disruption of idealized family norms by the Novelli deaths surely resonated with wider social anxieties in respectable Broughton and Manchester society. The *Manchester Guardian* was careful to mention that Alexander Novelli was "not in business" and "in no way connected" with the family firm: its financial credit and business probity were jeopardized by the scandal as doubtless were those of all its creditors.

The Novellis and the Manchester Business Community

Lewis Novelli had made his will in 1844, when he was in his early thirties. This was probably the year that his father retired to London, so the will was a gesture made by a man not contemplating early death, but the possibility of a growing family and his own future as the head of the firm of Messrs. Novelli and Albanelli, merchants of Bond St and later Tib Street.[30] As well as Alexander Novelli and Edmund Costan, his executors were his partner, Charles Albanelli, and two other Manchester businessmen.

There had been a handful of Italian bankers, merchants, and woolworkers in Manchester in the sixteenth century, and by the 1820s there were a number of Italian craftsmen established in city-center workshops. By the mid-1830s poorer Italian immigrants, particularly the street musicians and hurdy-gurdy men "who infest the streets with box organs," were a recognized (and policed) feature of Manchester street life.[31] Thus, to be "Italian" in mid-nineteenth-century Manchester could have meant a number of things, not all of them positive. Through their business, social, and domestic life, their control and ownership of material possessions, and their patterns of consumption, the Novellis systematically adopted the social and cultural characteristics of the city's commercial and manufacturing elite. The firm of Novelli was well established in Manchester by 1850. Lewis Novelli's father, Philip, had lived at Clarendon House in Cheetham Hill, with business premises at 23–5 York

Street, Manchester in 1834. Alexander Novelli had gone to school in Manchester, remembered as a nervous and withdrawn boy by his schoolfellow, John Hampson, later the Novelli family solicitor.[32] Philip Novelli sat as one of the directors of the Manchester Chamber of Commerce from at least 1839 until 1844, where he was a fairly regular attender (though less assiduous than key figures such as Richard Cobden).[33] Both Lewis and Philip Novelli attended the Special General Meeting in 1840 that petitioned for the repeal of the Corn Laws.[34] Unsurprisingly the Novellis were free traders. The Manchester Chamber of Commerce, though smaller than the Exchange and counting more merchants than manufacturers among its members, was a vital and recognized voice for Manchester trading and commercial interests.[35]

The Manchester middle class is now being shown to have been more diverse than was once assumed. Although around 80 percent of Manchester mill owners were from Lancashire, the wider commercial middle class including merchants and the professions had a somewhat different profile, containing a minority of immigrants including Germans, Italians, and Jews.[36] Export markets were crucial to the growth of Manchester textiles. By the late-eighteenth century several Manchester textile firms had representatives abroad and by that period some fifteen foreign merchants were living and working in Manchester. The increasing complexity of trade after the Napoleonic wars led to greater specialization as between merchants, manufacturers, and those who, as acceptance houses, concentrated on finance rather than dealing in goods. The comparatively slow and late development of banking in Lancashire meant that merchant houses with their frequent London and Liverpool connections and good knowledge of particular foreign markets were important to trade where long and extensive credit terms and seismic market fluctuations rapidly undermined capital and undid reputations.[37] The majority were German or German Jewish, and the largest had trading offices around the world. By 1840 Manchester had eighty-four German merchants, nine Greeks (i.e., from the Ottoman empire), and seventeen others. There were several Greek merchants and one Spanish living in Higher Broughton in 1851. A medium-sized merchant firm commanded capital of over £100,000 around midcentury, much more than most manufacturing establishments.[38] Lewis Novelli's executors paid trade debts of over £60,000 in settling his estate and his will created trusts to the capital value of £6,400 as well as disposing of what must have been a pretty extensive residual personal estate. His father Philip, whose will was proved in 1852, left a considerable amount, including an absolute bequest of £50,000 to his surviving son, Augustus Novelli.

The Novellis had business interests in Italy and the Middle East. Charles Albanelli, Lewis's partner and executor, came from Milan. In 1840, Philip's expertise on Italian markets was called upon by the Manchester Chamber of

Commerce to draft a memorial to the Board of Trade putting forward the Manchester interest in the debate over new import duties into the "Kingdom of the Two Sicilies," which particularly disadvantaged Manchester handkerchief pieces compared to German-made items.[39] Lewis had acted as banker to Ibrahim Pasha, of Egypt, the son of Muhammad Ali who had detached Egypt from the Ottoman empire, establishing its own Middle Eastern empire and inaugurating programs of selective reform, industrialization (including cotton textile production), and military and naval expansion.[40] Western Europe had viewed these developments with some anxiety in the 1820s.[41] In the longer term, these fears proved to be unfounded. Egyptian textile production never turned an effective profit and Muhammad Ali's finances were heavily overstrained by the late 1830s. Egyptian production of raw cotton never dominated the English market.[42] During the boom of 1835–36 plenty of Manchester men made a killing on Egyptian cotton, though losing out in the subsequent slump was also a real possibility.[43] Consequently, Egypt and the Middle East was a live issue for the Manchester men in the 1830s and 1840s. So the possibilities of anything but reliability and creditworthiness in a leading merchant house with Egyptian interests would certainly have been of concern to the Manchester commercial public.

The Middle-Class Family

Gender historians have demonstrated that the "social imaginary" of the nineteenth-century family provided templates through which people organized and conceptualized their relationships of "blood, contract and intimacy."[44] This imaginary depended on "boundaries and binaries of gender, class and indeed separations between the English and other races."[45] The notion of a move to a far more "privatized" "nuclear" bourgeois family centered on the heterosexual couple by midcentury is being revised and the role of kin outside the "nuclear" model of parents and children is being rethought.[46] There was heavy romantic cultural investment in sibling relationships as being both an emotionally intimate but also an asexual realization of the "almost compulsive focus on contrasting masculine and feminine categories, at a time when these attributes were integral to bourgeois identity."[47] Notwithstanding, adult sibling or in-law relationships remained potentially vulnerable to sexual attraction. Hence the decades-long controversy from 1835 over marriage between a widower and his deceased wife's sister. Elisabeth Gruner emphasizes that in both the parliamentary debates and political pamphlets and literary use of the device, the core debate was less about the suitability of a widower's marriage to his sister-in-law but more about the possibility of sexual attraction between these parties during the wife's lifetime.[48]

"Deceased wife's sister" also had implications for the key role of family as a welfare system for dependent kin and children; as remarrying widowers argued, what better replacement mother and housekeeper for a mourned wife was there, than her own unmarried sister? Middle-class family property ownership was socially embedded and gendered and involved a web of obligations as well as rights, made ever more complex by systems of partible inheritance. Philip Novelli's will made provision not only for his grandchildren (Lewis and Harriet's children) but also provided annuities for several other more distant relations by marriage. Siblings and in-laws were part of the social and property holding network of the middle-class family, but their claims threatened to divide family property. As Eleanor Gordon and others have pointed out, middle-class women were not excluded from holding significant and potentially substantial amounts of property.[49] Nevertheless, their role was essentially as custodians or caretakers of that property. They were denied absolute ownership, in the interests of the family. Neither Philip nor Lewis Novelli left property absolutely to female relations. Harriet Novelli was left household goods and the interest on an investment of £5,000, but only during her life or widowhood. However, neither were men entirely autonomous agents. The third Novelli brother, Augustus, eventually inherited absolutely the bulk of the Novelli fortune from his father, but took on the obligation of bringing up his orphaned niece and nephew. Men had gendered obligations as protectors and providers to look to the welfare needs of family, particularly wives and children.[50] In some ways a match between Harriet and Alexander Novelli would have appropriately secured the Novelli family property, some of which might otherwise reenter the circulations of wealth in the middle-class Manchester marriage market. Harriet was an affluent and attractive young widow. Although the direct legacy left to her was due to cease with her widowhood, her possible remarriage may well have been something that the Novellis would have wished to broker. Although we do not know the terms of the settlement, the house in Higher Broughton had been bought for her by her father-in-law, rather than being paid for from her husband's estate. Although "deceased wife's sister" is not the same thing as marriage to a deceased husband's brother (a relationship about which the Victorians were far less exercised), the controversy still "interrogates masculine desire" and was in part about the ways that the Victorian family required restraint of desire from men.[51] There were particular ways in which a widow/brother-in-law relationship could tap into recurrent Victorian fears of "frenzied passions," and the Novelli case articulates these in an acute form because they are allied to madness and, perhaps, to miscegenation.

Chapter 11

Madness and the Masculine Corpse

There were, of course two corpses in this case and Alexander Novelli's also had the potential for revelation. However, what we know about his body is more limited than that of his sister-in-law, practically because no postmortem was carried out and also because the aspect of Alexander Novelli that the court and newspapers were keen to probe was his mind. The body was suspended, but with its feet on the ground, the dressing gown cord having stretched. It was still warm. We know that he died in his trousers and shirt, that he had received a scratch on his nose, that he had left the marks of his boots on the sofa in the dining room and that he had vomited on the dining room carpet and over his clothes. But we don't know his facial expression, his corpse is never unclothed, and we have no information about the condition of his internal organs. The evidence as to the state of his mind is surmised by the fact of the murder and from peripheral evidence. His lawyer described his odd behavior on a recent visit about his brother's estate. The carpenter who did some work on the Broughton house had found him agitated. A correspondent had recounted information derived from a third party that Alexander had once tried to hang himself when on a visit to Augsburg. His family history was also introduced. His mother was insane and had been confined. Two of his brothers had committed suicide and his sister was not in a fit state of mind; her "unfortunate condition" was mentioned in both her brother's and her father's wills. Although it remained a crime, by this period insanity rather than sin was increasingly seen as the cause of suicide.[52] Insanity "was lurking in the blood—a fatal inheritance of the family" and when, the journalist surmised, a renewed proposal of marriage was rejected, suddenly "reason had forsaken its throne [and] the act was perpetrated in the height of the paroxysm." In the decades before Freud, individuals who did not comply with normative family roles could be the more easily adjudged mad and confined, and asylums laid their claims to cure on their "family-like" regimes.[53] In this case, of course, there was arguably role confusion between that of brother-in-law and potential husband as well as an inability on Alexander Novelli's part to act out the tropes of respectable bourgeois masculinity. At the age where Alexander Novelli could be expected to have the kind of business and family life of his brother, he could achieve neither; arguably the kind of lifecycle crisis that Victor Bailey sees as a frequent precipitant of suicide.[54]

Victorian middle-class masculinity depended on autonomy and the ability to govern both other individuals and material possessions. Madness feminized male subjects because it fractured their autonomy; the implication seems to be (given the apparent sanity of Philip, Lewis, and Augustus Novelli) that madness has stolen into the Novelli family through the maternal line. The initial suspicion was that Harriet had been poisoned and poison was a woman's weapon deployed within the domestic sphere.[55] Contemporary cultural representations repeatedly depicted suicide as a feminine act, despite the higher number of successful male suicides.[56] Alexander Novelli was a subject whose masculinity was compromised by overlapping inadequacies. He was subject to occasional odd behavior. The way was open for him to take an active role in the family business, but he declined and a man, after all, "must act." He was unable to cope with the demands of acting as his brother's executor, becoming agitated and distressed at the administration involved. His fascination with phrenology associated him with a practice that by this date had lost its radical and progressive currency in middle-class circles.[57] He was unable to achieve his objective of marriage and (we assume) sexual relations with Harriet. Incestuous sexual advances and excess of passion were unmanly and un-English. Insanity tainted the blood of the Novellis, blood that was already "other" through its foreign connections and associations. Despite their integration into the Manchester commercial elite, the disintegration of Novelli family probity and discretion through the circumstances of the murder and suicide was (once Harriet Novelli had been vindicated) visited upon Alexander (or rather upon the madness within him) as the threatening "other"; a category repeatedly racialized as well as gendered in nineteenth-century discourse. Thus "family" among the Novellis became pernicious and destabilizing, rather than affective, ordered, and stable. Connections of blood of course articulated both family and nation; miscegenation was an anxiety around the simultaneous rupturing of both these boundaries. Conventional assumptions of feminine beauty may allow us to read Harriet Novelli's "considerable personal attractions" as signifying whiteness. We know nothing about Alexander Novelli's appearance, perhaps a speaking silence. We know through the postmortem examination of Harriet Novelli's corpse that she was not carrying her brother-in-law's child. However, she was already twice a mother. If insanity was the "fatal inheritance" of the Novellis, remaining dormant until moments of (certainly in this case) heightened passion caused by sexual and emotional desire, in January 1850 a question mark surely remained over the futures of Harriet's two children.[58]

Insane passions had produced the disordered and distressing corpses that defaced the Novelli home, clashing with the elegance and comfort of its decoration and furnishings. Women's responsibilities at whatever level for the ordering and maintenance of the domestic environment of family life was about the regulation of boundaries expressed through the control of disorder and pollution. As Davidoff argues, "Women's 'physical, intellectual, even emotional work' in maintaining such boundaries 'enabled the public and intellectual self-realization of higher status men.'"[59] To the contemporary local readership, did Harriet Novelli's rejection of her brother-in-law's proposal of marriage constitute an inappropriate refusal of legitimate male protection, preferring the independence of wealthy widowhood and provoking his latent insanity to the surface? Or was it an entirely proper and feminine assertion of the asexual relationship between brother and sister-in-law? Were the seeds of the "tragedy" sown long before that Sunday, in fact on 27 February 1841 at Saint Mary's Church, Bury, Lancashire, England when twenty-one-year-old Miss Harriet Hall first married into the tainted blood of the Novellis?[60]

Conclusion

Through one particular and well-publicized murder, this essay has taken up the concerns of current research in gender and crime history to review how the murdered body of a young, highly respectable, middle-class widow was used, both in the comparatively informal and local context of the coroners' court hearing and before a local and a national newspaper readership, as a surface on which to inscribe a romantic and speculative narrative of compromised respectability and fractured domesticity. The evidence of friends and servants, couched in discourses of neighborliness and sociability, was juxtaposed with the forensic assessment of medical witnesses, but both groups fixed their gaze upon a detailed examination of Harriet Novelli's corpse, scrutinizing it both externally and (through the postmortem) internally, seeking for it to yield up its own narratives about pregnancy, illicit and almost incestuous sexual activity, excessive alcohol consumption, or, indeed, poison. The body of her brother-in-law and murderer, however, was less at issue than the state of his mind. His foreign ancestry and personal and family history of mental instability combined with hearsay evidence of his (illicit) sexual attraction to his recently widowed sister-in-law called into question both his sanity and his manliness, but thereby also his criminal responsibility. If the closure and chastity of middle-class femininity could be rendered precarious by the medicolegal scrutiny of a woman's body, then masculine probity could be undermined by the feminizing influences of an un-British mental instability.

Notes

1. Judith Knelman, *Twisting in the Wind: The Murderess and the English Press* (Toronto: University of Toronto Press, 1998); Martin J. Wiener, "Alice Arden to Bill Sikes: Changing Nightmares of Intimate Violence in England, 1558–1869," *Journal of British Studies* 40, 2 (2001): 184–212; Martin J. Wiener, "The Sad Story of George Hall: Adultery, Murder, and the Politics of Mercy in Mid-Victorian England," *Social History*

24, 2 (1999): 174–95; George Robb, "Circe in Crinoline: Domestic Poisonings in Victorian England," *Journal of Family History* 22, 2 (1999): 176–90.

2. A. James Hammerton, *Cruelty and Companionship: Conflict in Nineteenth-Century Married Life* (London: Routledge, 1992), chap. 4; J. M. Robson, *Marriage or Celibacy? The Daily Telegraph on a Victorian Dilemma* (Toronto: University of Toronto Press, 1995).

3. *Manchester Courier*, 26 January 1850; Lancashire Record Office (LRO), Prestwich, Parish Registers: Baptisms, 13.8.1846, Louisa Harriet, daughter Lewis Novelli, Prestwich, merchant, and wife Harriet Novelli, and 13.10.1847, Lewis William; Burial Registers, Lewis Novelli buried 11 October 1848, aet. [aged] 35.

4. G. Middleton, *The Annals of Prestwich: A Chronological Record* (Manchester, 1902), 68; Manchester Central Library (MCL), *Manchester & Salford Directory* (Manchester, 1841).

5. *Lancaster Guardian*, 26 January 1850; *Manchester Courier*, 26 January 1850.

6. *Manchester Courier*, 26 January 1850.

7. LRO, Broughton Census, Cliff House, Broughton, John C. Grundy, printer, publisher, and guilder, aet. 44.

8. *The Times*, 22 January 1850; 23 January 1850; 25 January 1850.

9. Select Committee on Drunkenness, 1834, V11, Evidence of N. Card; W. Howarth; T. Wright, ff.102–24; Brian Harrison, *Drink and the Victorians: The Temperance Question in England, 1815–1872*, 2nd ed. (Keele: Keele University Press, 1994).

10. George Middleton, *The Annals*, 90; LRO, Prestwich Burial Register, 25 January 1850, Harriet, widow of Lewis Novelli, Broughton late Prestwich, aged thirty-two years, "murdered by her brother-in-law Alexander Novelli."

11. *Manchester Courier*, 26 January 1850.

12. Thomas Laqueur, "Bodies, Details, and the Humanitarian Narrative," in *The New Cultural History*, ed. Lynn Hunt, 1–23 (Berkeley: University of California Press, 1989).

13. *Manchester Courier*, 26 January 1850.

14. Mary Poovey, *Uneven Developments: The Ideological Work of Gender in Mid-Victorian England* (London: Virago, 1989).

15. Anthony Howe, *The Cotton Masters, 1830–1860* (Oxford: Clarendon, 1984), chap. 2.

16. *Lancaster Guardian*, 26 January 1850.

17. *Manchester Courier*, 26 January 1850.

18. J. A. V. Chapple and A. Pollard, eds., *The Letters of Mrs. Gaskell* (Manchester: Manchester University Press, 1966), 101 (Letter to Elisa Fox, Tuesday 22 January 1850).

19. *International Genealogical Index (IGI)*; Baptism Harriet Hall, Tottington St. Ann's Chapel, 22 June 1817, Marriage, Richard Hall and Dolly Lomax, 25 August 1808, Bury, Tottington St. Ann.

20. There is no Prerogative Court of Canterbury will for Richard Hall, where wills of the wealthier were generally proved, nor at the Archdeaconry of Chester. Possibly it was proved at the Archdiocese of York.

21. Howe, *Cotton Masters*, 76.

22. MCL, M6/59/5, Archdeacon's Visitations for Prestwich, 15–17; Middleton, *Annals*, 68.

23. Will, Lewis Novelli; Middleton, *Annals*, 68–69.

24. *Dictionary of National Biography*; A. Graves, *A Dictionary of Artists Who Have*

Exhibited Works for the Principal London Exhibitions from 1760–1893, 3rd ed. (Kingsmead Reprints, 1969); M. Rose, "Culture and Philanthropy and the Manchester Middle Class," in *City, Class, and Culture,* ed. Alan Kidd and K. W. Roberts, 101–18 (Manchester: Manchester University Press, 1988); S. D. Cleveland, *The Royal Manchester Institution* (Manchester, 1931).

25. MCL, M6/1/49/5, Royal Manchester Institution, 51; John Tosh, *A Man's Place: Masculinity and the Middle Class Home in Victorian England* (New Haven: Yale University Press, 1997).

26. Martin Hewitt, *The Emergence of Stability in the Industrial City: Manchester, 1832–67* (Aldershot: Scolar Press, 1996), 54; A. J. Kidd, *Manchester* (Keele: Ryburn Publishing, 1993).

27. R. L. Greenall, *The Making of Victorian Salford* (Lancaster: Carnegie, 2000), 2; 55; I. S. Pratt, *Prestwich, the Priest's Retreat* (Manchester, 1973), 62.

28. Cooke Taylor, "Notes of a Tour of the Manufacturing Districts of Lancashire," 1842, quoted in Hewitt, *Emergence,* 26.

29. Hewitt, *Emergence,* 52–53.

30. MCL, M6/59/5, Archdeacon's Visitations for Prestwich, 18, 19, 108, for a reproduction of the Raphael, correspondence over its transfer and a clipping of the *Manchester Courier* coverage of the murder. See *Manchester and Salford Directory,* 1841; *Slater's Directory,* 1848; *Manchester and Salford Directory,* 1851.

31. A. Rea, *Manchester's Little Italy: Memories of the Italian Colony in Ancoats* (Manchester: Manchester University Press, 1988), 3–4; B. Ronchetti, "The Earliest Italian Immigrants in Manchester," in *Italians in Manchester,* ed. A. Ria (Musumeci Editore, 1990), 51–55; *Manchester Guardian,* 22 December 1827.

32. *Piggot's Directory,* 1834; *The Times,* 25 January 1850.

33. MCL, M/8/2/4, Manchester Chamber of Commerce Proceedings, 1, 13, 17, 39, 62–64, 166, 318.

34. Ibid., 39.

35. Anthony Howe, "The Business Community," in *The Lancashire Cotton Industry: A History since 1700,* ed. Mary B. Rose, 36–58 (Preston: Lancashire County Books, 1996),

36. Howe, "Business Community," 97.

37. Stanley Chapman, "The Commercial Sector," in *Lancashire Cotton,* ed. Mary B. Rose, 70, 72–73, 77.

38. Howe, "Business Community," 80–81.

39. MCL, M/8/2/4, Manchester Chamber of Commerce Proceedings, 62 (19 August 1840); 63 (25 August 1840); 64.

40. K. Fahmy, "The Era of Muhammad Ali Pasha, 1805–1848," in *Modern Egypt from 1517 to the End of the Twentieth Century, The Cambridge History of Egypt,* ed. M. W. Daley (Cambridge: Cambridge University Press, 1998), 2: 139–79; R. Owen, *The Middle East in the World Economy, 1800–1914* (London: Methuen, 1981), 64–76, 83–91.

41. A. Redford, *Manchester Merchants and Foreign Trade, 1794–1859* (Manchester: Manchester University Press, 1934), 218; W. H. Chaloner, introduction to *The History of the Cotton Manufacture of Great Britain,* 2nd ed., by F. Baines (Frank Cass, 1966), 306–8; Afaf Lutfi Al-Sayyid Marsot, *A Short History of Modern Egypt* (Cambridge: Cambridge University Press, 1985), 63; D. A. Farnie, *The English Cotton Industry and the World Market, 1815–96* (Oxford: Clarendon, 1979), 90.

42. N. Longmate, *The Hungry Mills,* 214, 224.

43. B. W. Clapp, *John Owens, Manchester Merchant* (Manchester University Press, 1965), 129.

44. Leonore Davidoff, *Worlds Between: Historical Perspectives on Gender and Class* (Cambridge: Polity, 1995); Leonore Davidoff and Catherine Hall, *Family Fortunes: Men and Women of the English Middle Class, 1780–1850* (London: Hutchinson, 1997); John Gillis, *A World of Their Own Making: Myth Ritual and the Quest for Family Values* (Basic Books, 1996); Leonore Davidoff et al., *The Family Story: Blood, Contract, and Intimacy, 1830–1960* (London: Longman, 1999).

45. Davidoff, *Worlds Between,* 5.

46. E. R. Gruner, "Born and Made: Sisters, Brothers, and the Deceased Wife's Sister Bill," *Signs* 24, 2 (1999): 423–47.

47. Davidoff, *Worlds Between,* 213, 215.

48. Gruner, "Born and Made"; B. S. Bennett, "Banister versus Thompson and Afterwards: The Church of England and the Deceased Wife's Sister's Marriage Act," *Journal of Ecclesiastical History* 49, 4 (1998): 668–82, at 669.

49. Eleanor Gordon and Gwyneth Nair, "Middle Class Family Structure in Nineteenth Century Glasgow," *Journal of Family History* 24, 4 (1999): 468–77.

50. Alastair Owens, "Property, Gender, and the Life Course: Inheritance and Family Welfare Provision in Early Nineteenth-Century England," *Social History* 26, 3 (2001): 299–317.

51. Gruner, "Born and Made," 425.

52. Olive Anderson, *Suicide in Victorian and Edwardian England* (Oxford: Clarendon, 1987); Victor Bailey, *This Rash Act: Suicide across the Life Cycle in the Victorian City* (Stanford: Stanford University Press, 1998).

53. Roy Porter, "Madness and the Family before Freud: The View of the Mad Doctors," *Journal of Family History* 23, 2 (1998): 159–72.

54. Bailey, *Rash Act.*

55. Robb, "Circe in Crinoline."

56. L. J. Nicoletti, "Women and Suicide in Victorian London," paper presented to the Berkshire Conference on the History of Women, University of Connecticut, June 2002.

57. R. Cooter, *The Cultural Meaning of Popular Science: Phrenology and the Organisation of Consent in Nineteenth-Century Britain* (Cambridge: Cambridge University Press, 1985).

58. The future of the boy is unclear. Louise was bought up by her uncle Augustus in London, marrying H. C. Grove in 1869.

59. Davidoff, *Worlds Between,* 6–7.

60. LRO, Bury St. Mary Marriage Registers, 27 February 1841, Harriet Hall, dtr Richard Hall and Lewis Novelli, gent, of Kersall Hall, Manchester, witnessed by Anne Walmsley, John Hall, Jn. [*sic*] Hall, P. Novelli, C. Albanelli.

12

She-Butchers: Baby-Droppers, Baby-Sweaters, and Baby-Farmers[1]

DAVID BENTLEY

Preamble

The Editors, to maintain the spirit of "conversation" in this volume, refelect as follows on the wider context of this chapter: Issues of child-care have always substantial potential for creating moral panic. For Victorian's, women having children outside marriage was a major problem, as they stood to lose their respectability. True, in an age when many single working women were in domestic service, recent work has shown that many mistresses could be sympathetic to girls seduced after promises of marriage.[2] But their help to arrange child-care could touch only a small percentage of those "in trouble." The resources of such concerned individuals or supportive philanthropic societies were too slender to permit them to help more than a fraction of those in need. Serious and difficult decisions, therefore, had to be made by the rest. Such predicaments were not new, but what was new for those not taking the road of infanticide was an increased potential for anonymity of action to hide "inconvenient" children, especially through the resources of the burgeoning print media. "Baby-farming" became a widespread child-care practice as a result of the implicit promise of anonymity in the "conversation" arranging the contract. But it also became notorious (despite genuine establishments) for disposing of children. The first important "criminal conversation" on baby-farming was that covering the case of Charlotte Winsor, executed in 1865 for killing children committed to her care.[3] If today the need for anonymity has gone, conversations about child-care and criminality continue through high-profile media reportage of cases like Louise Woodward, tried in 1997 for the death of her charge, Matthew Eappen. Child-care for working mothers thus remains a key issue, with fears focused on the parental eyes, indicating an enduring social inability to resolve this dilemma.

Introduction

Baby-farming was one of the great unresolved scandals of the Victorian period. Its roots lay in the powerful economic pressure upon working-class women to work, especially if single, and in the difficulties which those considered not respectable faced in getting and keeping employment. This chapter examines the practice of baby-farming, how it was represented in the press and dealt with in the criminal justice process, and the consequences to those involved in such operations as well as the implications for women and unplanned motherhood generally. The dialogue surrounding official responses and measures to control the practice and implement monitoring and registration schemes constituted one of the major media debates of the last half of the nineteenth century.

A Widespread and Notorious Practice

In Victorian England, one way in which poor women could supplement their income was by taking in children to nurse. There was never a shortage of nurse-children. Each year thousands of women, many young girls in domestic service, were forced by harsh economic reality to give their illegitimate offspring for adoption or board them out. To a single woman, pregnancy was generally a disaster. As news of her condition got out she would, if a domestic, be likely to be dismissed, thus at a stroke losing both accommodation and income. To stave off dismissal, girls commonly concealed their condition as long as they were able. Most, however, were found out and, if turned out of work or family, their options were few. From the father little could be expected: the Poor Law Amendment Act 1834 had made bastardy orders hard both to obtain and enforce.[4] If a man had money he might be prepared to pay for an abortion or to provide the cash premium demanded by a would-be adopter, but not all would do this. A girl with no support from her employer or her family (if she had one) faced stark choices: to have the child secretly and kill it at birth, or to give birth in the workhouse or whatever lodgings she could find, and then get back to work as soon as possible. Getting back to work (a necessity with not only herself but also a child to support) meant that some arrangement for the child's care had to be made, since working women, whether domestics or factory workers, could not take their offspring to work.[5] Yet many scarcely earned enough to support themselves, let alone a child.

To some, infanticide (often easily concealed in a city the size of London by dumping the body in an area remote from that in which the mother lived or by obtaining a false certificate of stillbirth from a compliant midwife) seemed the only answer. "I determined . . . to kill it, poor thing," explained seventeen-year-old Mary Morgan, hanged in 1805 for cutting the throat of her newborn child, "being perfectly sure that I could not provide for it myself."[6] A less desperate solution was to part with the child, either temporarily or for good. Servants were not the only class of women who had children they wished to be rid of; others included prostitutes, married women carrying children conceived in adultery, and single women of good family whose reputations and marriage prospects would be seriously harmed if it became known that they were pregnant.

In the second half of the century the easiest way of funding a person to adopt or board a child was through newpaper advertisements. The abolition of stamp duty on newspapers in 1855 had led to the appearance of popular national and local sheets, retailing for as little as a penny, most of which by the late 1860s carried daily advertisements from persons offering to take children for a weekly payment or a lump sum. Where a lump sum was sought it was usually on the basis that there should be no further contact between parent and child. Some of those placing advertisements were childless couples genuinely anxious to adopt a baby. Many, however, were repeat advertisers taking babies for the money to be made from them. Such persons usually took great pains to conceal their identity, using false names, representing themselves to be married, childless, and in comfortable circumstances and using letter-drops at post offices to communicate with those answering their advertisements. In London the handover of the child in such cases often took place at railway stations. In law, transactions such as these were ineffective to divest the mother of parental rights (until 1926 adoption was a concept unknown in English law).[7] But where the mother wished to have no more to do with the child, these arrangements worked as a *de facto* transfer of custody which, because of the defective state of the law as to registration of births, it would often prove impossible later to upset.

Not all those who put their children out to adoption dealt with the adopter direct. In some cases, the placing would be done by a midwife. Alongside advertisements for adoption could often be found ones offering private lying-in facilities for pregnant women. These were expensive but, for a single woman of means or a married woman pregnant by a man other than her husband, they offered a means of disposing of her unwanted child without scandal. Leaving home on the pretext of a trip to London or to see friends, she would visit the lying-in house and deliver her child, which would then be put out for adoption or to nurse by the proprietor of the house, it being understood on all sides that there should be no further contact between mother and child.

In the 1860s, a group of London doctors decided to carry out an investigation into "baby-farming," as it had been dubbed.[8] In 1866 a committee appointed by the Harveian Society, after correspondence with doctors and charitable institutions, reported that baby-farming was carried on to a great extent in towns and manufacturing districts and that mortality among nurse-children was very high.[9] It recommended, *inter alia,* that persons taking in children to nurse be subject to supervision.[10] In 1868 Ernest Hart, editor of the *British Medical Journal,* commissioned Dr. Alfred Wiltshire to conduct an enquiry into abortion and baby-farming. Wiltshire placed two advertisements in the *Clerkenwell News* offering two children for adoption. He received no less than 330 replies which he proceeded to follow up.[11] His findings were summarized by the Earl of Shaftesbury:

> The system [may] be divided into two parts. One . . . was the baby nursing, where infants were placed out to nurse by persons who really looked after them to some extent; the other part was the baby-farming, where infants were put out for the sole purpose of being got rid of altogether, or of never being heard of again by the parents. To this class . . . belonged Mrs. Winsor.[12]

In 1869 James Greenwood took up the subject, asking:

> Was there no remedy for [the modern and murderous institution known as baby-farming]? Would it not be possible, at least, to issue licences to baby-keepers as they are at present issued to cow-keepers? It may appear a brutal way of putting the matter, but it becomes less so when one considers how much at present the brutes have the best of it.[13]

The practice of baby-farmers deliberately murdering, by starvation or worse, children entrusted to their care was, in fact, not new. In 1724 Defoe had written of the "unfortunate mother" of an illegitimate child having the "dreadful affliction" of either losing her job and starving, or "seeing the poor infant packed off with a piece of money to some of those she-butchers who take children off their hands," who then "starve 'em and murder 'em."[14]

Potentially disturbing cases featuring baby-farming had been regularly mentioned throughout the 1860s but (despite a small panic surrounding the Charlotte Winsor case) had not caused sustained concern. Equally, while the results of the investigations by Wiltshire, Greenwood, and the Harveian Society did not pass unnoticed, neither did they provoke widespread clamor for reform. What served to bring baby-farming to the notice of the general public was the trial of Margaret Waters.

Chapter 12

The Case of Margaret Waters

Waters, fifty-four at the time of her execution, had once been in comfortable circumstances. She and her husband had settled in Newfoundland, where they had prospered. In 1864, they came to Britain on a visit. In Glasgow her husband died. After winding up his estate in Newfoundland, she returned to England with £300 capital, took premises in Clerkenwell, and started a collar-making business. This quickly failed, swallowing up most of her capital. She resorted to taking in lodgers, particularly women about to be confined. Very soon the premises were being operated as a lying-in house, Waters taking the babies off their mothers' hands for payment. Her financial situation deteriorated further and she began to advertise for, and take in, children. In 1868 she opened up a new line of the business. Knowing from the string of adoption advertisements regularly found in the *Clerkenwell News* that there were plenty of local women willing to take in nurse-children, she contacted these advertisers and placed with them children whom she had herself obtained by advertisement. Such placements usually cost her no more than two weeks' payments in advance, far less than the premium she had herself been paid for taking the child. Having no intention of making any further payments, she took care to ensure she could not be traced. This fraud could not of course be perpetrated on the same baby-farmer twice, and eventually she began to resort to even more desperate and despicable ways of turning adoption premiums into profit. She would take a child got by advertisement into the streets, and when she saw a group of youngsters at play, she would call one over and say, "Oh, I am so tired! Here, hold my baby and here is sixpence [to get yourself something from] the sweet-stuff shop." Then while the boy or girl was in the shop, she would make off.[15] How many children passed through Waters's hands during her career as a baby-farmer can only be guessed but, on her arrest, she was prepared to admit to forty in four years.

The events which led to her apprehension smack of carelessness, bad luck, or both—and realization of the implications of this was responsible for much of the resultant panic.[16] By late May 1870 the Metropolitan Police were becoming concerned at the number of dead children's bodies turning up on the streets of Brixton, and Sergeant Relf was given the task of tracing the persons responsible. "Baby-dropping" was common enough in Victorian England: mothers of stillborn or dead children commonly left the bodies in the streets and places such as parks, sometimes to conceal crime but, as often as not, to save the cost of burial. In 1870, 276 children were found dead in the streets of the capital. But the number of bodies turning up in Brixton that May was abnormally high: sixteen in a matter of weeks. On Sunday 12 June two more were discovered. Around midday, two children found a parcel under some logs of timber; when it was opened it was found to contain the badly decomposed body of a child, wrapped in a piece of blue cloth and tied up in brown paper. On the paper, in a female hand, was written "Mrs. Waters." Later that day, the body of a seven-week-old child was found by a lamplighter underneath a railway arch in Peckham. It too was wrapped in brown paper.

By the time these bodies were found, Waters and her sister Sarah Ellis were already in custody. Suspecting that a lying-in house was the source of the crop of corpses, Relf had begun, in late May, to keep watch upon an establishment in Camberwell Road run by a Mrs. Castle. One young woman seen leaving this address was seventeen-year-old Janet Cowen. Having discovered where she lived, Relf called and spoke to her father, who explained that his daughter, seventeen, had become pregnant following a rape, that he had arranged for her to have her child at Mrs. Castle's premises, that the child had been born on 14 May, and that on 7 June he had handed it over at Walworth railway station to a woman giving the name of Willis. Being anxious to find a home for the child, he had answered an adoption advertisement which he had seen in *Lloyds' Newspaper*. After an exchange of letters he had met the woman, who claimed to be married and in respectable circumstances, at Brixton station. She had declined to disclose her address, saying that she and her husband desired to avoid any risk of the child being taken back in the future.

Relf had meanwhile himself replied to a similarly worded advertisement in *Lloyds' Newspaper* and had arranged to meet the advertiser at Camberwell station.[17] The meeting took place on 8 June, with Cowen waiting close by. Cowen did not recognize the woman who turned up (who was in fact Ellis) but noticed that she was wearing the same dress as Willis had been wearing the day before. Relf agreed terms with Ellis and arranged to meet her the following night to hand over a child. When she left, he followed and traced her to an address at Gordon Grove, Brixton. On 9 June, Relf went there with Mr. Cowen and his housekeeper and demanded to see Cowen's grandchild. After some prevarication, Ellis let them in and the child was produced. Plump and healthy when handed over, John Walter Cowen was now little more than skin and bone. In another downstairs room, Relf found five more children. All were dirty, emaciated, and like the Cowen child appeared to be drugged. In the yard were another five children. These were in a much better physical condition. Asked why they were so much healthier than the others, Waters replied, "We have so much a week for them."

The Parish Medical Officer was sent for. He seized a bottle smelling of laudanum and arranged for Cowen's grandchild to be placed immediately with a wet nurse. The following day Waters and Ellis were arrested for neglect and the remaining children taken to the Lambeth workhouse. On 24 June, the

Cowen child died. A postmortem examination established that death was due to want of sufficient food and the administration of narcotics. An inquest jury returned a verdict of manslaughter against Waters who was committed for trial at the Old Bailey. Reporting the verdict, *The Times* observed, "Manslaughter appears a mild expression for a woman . . . proved to have traded for some miserable gain in the lives of unprotected infants," predicting that Waters would probably have to meet "not only this charge but others of equal enormity."[18] Given that by 4 July four of the children taken from Gordon Grove had died and two more would die within the week, this was an accurate prophecy.

The case was by now attracting huge press interest, with every inquest hearing and every appearance of the two accused before the Lambeth magistrates fully reported, along with any other cases relating to possible baby-farming.[19] In mid-July Waters and Ellis were committed for trial at the Old Bailey, but their trial was postponed until the September Session. It was not open to the Crown to try all the murder charges at the same time. The indictment they elected to proceed with first was that charging both with the murder of John Walter Cowen. That five other children had died was by then notorious, making it a matter which the jury was likely to have difficulty putting out of their minds, however much they might be enjoined to do so by counsel and judge.

The trial took three days. At the end of the prosecution case, the judge, Lord Chief Baron Kelly, ruled that there was no evidence upon which the jury could convict Ellis of murder and directed her acquittal. The jury were urged by counsel for Waters to find that she had never intended that John Cowen should die; true he had been found in a weakly condition, but this was due to his having contracted diarrhea and thrush. Evidence was produced on the amount she spent weekly on milk and to show that she had called in a doctor. Some of the most difficult evidence for the defense to rebut concerned the drugging of the boy. Waters had denied that she had administered any sleeping medication to the children, but a bottle of laudanum had been recovered, and the doctors were adamant that, when found, Cowen and his five small companions were all exhibiting signs of being under the influence of narcotics. The *coup de grâce* was administered by a doctor, called on behalf of the defense, who conceded readily that opium killed children "like a shot." The all-male jury retired on the third day. They were back forty-five minutes later with a verdict of guilty. Waters having been sentenced to death, Ellis was brought back up, pleaded guilty to the conspiracy indictment, and was sentenced to eighteen months' hard labor.[20]

Waters's conviction was greeted in the press with almost universal rejoicing.[21] Yet there were some who felt uneasy.[22] Waters continued to protest her innocence, claiming that the Cowen child had been intended for a couple in affluent circumstances who wanted a male child and that his death, which she had never desired, had been a pecuniary loss to her, not gain. She had done her best but he had simply failed to thrive. Particularly difficult to reconcile with the thesis of murder for gain was the fact that she had, when the boy was handed over, initially refused to take any money from Mr. Cowen and, in the end, would only accept two guineas, half the agreed premium. From a medical point of view the evidence was not strong. Babies deprived of mother's milk often failed to thrive and then contracted disease. As for the administration of narcotics, soothing syrups for children containing opiates could be bought over the counter and were sold in huge quantities in working-class districts.[23] The *Daily Telegraph* reported the claim that it had been Ellis who had administered the laudanum, not Waters.[24] Certainly Dr. Edmunds, who saw Waters in the death cell, came away convinced she had no intention of murdering any of the children. The reality, however, was that she never had the slightest hope of acquittal: the pretrial press publicity had been too damaging for that.[25] Nor were her prospects of reprieve any better; she was hanged at Horsemonger Lane Gaol on 11 October, her death intended as a warning to other baby-farmers.

The Public Response

In 1872 Mr. Charley, the MP for Salford, had claimed that Waters's execution "had had the effect of breaking up many criminal establishments in the metropolis."[26] Certainly for a time there was a dropping off of adoption advertisements, with some newspapers refusing to accept them. But the impact was short-lived. Although the conviction in August 1871 of a Manchester baby-farmer called Rodgers for attempting to murder a child which she had been paid £8 to take off its mother's hands kept the subject before the public eye, the public was losing interest.[27] As Greenwood put it: "the fierce indignation . . . quickly settled down. . . . [I]t is hardly too much to say that our overwrought sympathies as regards baby neglect and murder fell so . . . flat that little short of a second edition of Herod's massacre might be required to raise them again."[28] Adoption advertisements were soon as common as ever. The wider social realities were simply too pressing to permit this panic and its associated moral outrage to produce an enduring change in attitudes toward single mothers and their unfortunate offspring.

The only organization displaying any desire to tackle the problem was the newly founded Infant Life Preservation Society. In November 1870, a month after its inaugural meeting, its chairman, Charley, led a widely reported deputation to the Home Office to press for legislation.[29] He was given a courteous hearing, assured that government would not seek to obstruct a private member's bill on the subject, and urged to include in such a bill a clause for the suppression of clandestine lying-in houses. In February 1871, Charley introduced his Bill.[30] Based upon proposals which Curvegen, Secretary of the Harveian Society, had placed before the Social Science Association Congress in 1869, it provided that all persons taking in children to nurse, including day-nurses, must be licensed by a justice of the peace and regularly inspected by the Poor Law Medical Officer. Licensees were to be restricted as to the number of children they could take and under a legal obligation to notify the coroner of death of any nurse-child in their care. There were to be exemptions for persons taking in children for less than twenty-four hours, for boarding schools, public orphanages, and for persons looking after children whose parents were resident abroad. Far from being welcomed, the Bill drew a torrent of criticism down upon the heads of its promoters. Becker, editor of the *Women's Suffrage Journal,* suggested that they would do better addressing the root causes of infanticide: the iniquitous bastardy laws, prejudice against employing unwed mothers, and basic maternal ignorance. Particularly objected to was the inclusion of day-nurses. Child minding represented an indispensable source of income to many honest poor women and provided a vital service for single women.[31] Others were scandalized by the burden which registration and inspection would place on public funds. Realizing that the Bill had little chance of becoming law, Charley agreed to withdraw it in return for a Select Committee inquiry into the subject.

The Select Committee first met in July 1871. With Charley as Chairman, it sat for thirteen days, taking evidence from twenty witnesses' conclusions. It mirrored those of the 1866 Harveian Society report.[32] It found that the vast majority of cases where children were put out to nurse were to enable the mother to work. In manufacturing towns in Lancashire and Yorkshire, the usual practice was placing children with day-nurses, but in other areas the child was left with the nurse full-time. Most children placed out to nurse were illegitimate. Their mothers had generally no wish that they should be harmed, the high mortality amongst children under one year being due in most cases to such causes as lack of a mother's care, ignorance, dirt, improper feeding, use of opiates to make children sleep, and sleeping a large number under one roof, not to criminal neglect. However, there were also criminal establishments (principally in London but also in Edinburgh, Glasgow, and Greenock) which took children with whom the mother desired no further connection, usually for a lump sum or at a weekly rate wholly inadequate for their support. These turned a profit by making sure that the child did not survive long, acquiring their babies either from lying-in houses or through newspaper or circular advertisement. Much of the difficulty which the police experienced in bringing criminal baby-farmers to book was due to the great secrecy in which the trade was conducted (women who gave birth in lying-in houses generally refused information to the police) and their lack of a right of entry. The Committee's recommendations had a familiar ring to them: lying-in houses should be licensed and women taking in two or more nurse-children under one year of age should be required to register; all illegitimate children should be under the supervision of the Poor Law Medical Officer for the district and registration of births and deaths should be made compulsory.

Press reaction to the report was generally favorable, but with the government showing no inclination to act, it was left to Charley to take the matter up again. In 1872 he introduced the Infant Life Protection Bill.[33] In order to get it through he found himself obliged to make concession after concession. Because of alleged difficulties in drafting, lying-in houses were left untouched. So that the Bill should not impose any burden on public funds, it contained no provision for the inspection of baby-farms. The 1872 Act made it a criminal offense to receive for hire or reward more than one child under a year for more than twenty-four hours, unless the house in which it was received had been registered with the local authority. Local authorities were given power to refuse and to cancel registration. Exempted from the Act's provisions were relatives, guardians, and persons with whom children were boarded out by Poor Law authorities.

The Act's Shortcomings

Even before the Act reached the statute book there were press predictions that it would be easy to evade and would turn out to be a dead letter.[34] And so it proved. In its first two months, just five houses had been registered in London, and the number still stood at five in 1877. Outside London, no houses were registered at all. These pitifully low figures were taken by some as confirmation of the Act's effectiveness. In March 1876 it was stated, in the course of a hearing at Greenwich police court, that the Act had virtually abolished baby-farming.[35] In the same month the *British Medical Journal* announced that this was also the view of the Ladies' Committee of the Infant Life Preservation Society: "Nearly all the baby-farms have been broken up . . . the Act has been the means of protecting infants from systematic violence."[36] What the low registration figures in fact showed was that the Act was having little or no impact.

There were two problems. The first was the lack of enforcement machinery. In 1878, the Metropolitan Board of Works, the registration authority for

London, which had, up until then, taken no steps to implement the Act other than maintaining a register, was persuaded by the Home Office to introduce a system of inspection. A retired police sergeant, the aptly named Samuel Babey, was appointed. By replying to adoption advertisements and acting on tip-offs from the police and others, he busied himself trying to track down unregistered houses. But the Board was the only authority prepared to act with such vigor. Outside London the Act went almost wholly unenforced, neither police nor local authorities being prepared to devote resources to seeking out unregistered baby-farms. Five years after the Act had come into force, the local authority in Newton Abbott, Devon, had not even troubled to set up a register.[37] In 1896, the Reverend Benjamin Waugh, director of the National Society for the Prevention of Cruelty to Children (NSPCC), summed the position up: "The Act is not carried out [outside London] because local authorities do not appoint an inspector to do it. . . . In seven years . . . we have met with one and I think that was at Bristol."[38]

Second, the Act had no application where all, or all but one, of the children were aged one or over. Even before Babey's appointment, it had been the belief of the Metropolitan Board that most baby-farmers would be found to be outside the provisions of the Act. Babey's work simply confirmed this. Between 1878 and 1894 only 205 of 9,573 unregistered houses inspected by Babey and his fellow inspector were found to be within the Act. One of the most glaring deficiencies of the Act was that it did not apply at all to baby-sweaters, women who adopted children one at a time and then, once the premium had been paid, immediately passed the child on to another baby-farmer for a smaller premium or simply abandoned it: the ill-treatment of children "in single file" as the *British Medical Journal* called it.[39]

How little the Act had done to deter the criminal baby-farmer was demonstrated by a clutch of horrific cases, which hit the headlines in the years 1877–79. In 1877, Sophie Todd, twenty-nine, was convicted of strangling a three-week-old child she had obtained by an adoption advertisement, the third who had died in her care.[40] Two years later a Birkenhead couple called Barnes stood trial for the murder of a little girl who was but one of many they had obtained as a result of advertising for children.[41] In the same year, Annie Took was convicted of murdering a handicapped child she had taken in return for payments. In poverty herself and with four children of her own to support, she had murdered the infant when the mother stopped making the weekly payments.[42] Of the four accused, only Took went to the gallows. Although sentenced to death, Todd was later reprieved, while in the Barnes's case the jury convicted only of manslaughter. But there were immediate calls for the Act to be amended and extended.

In February 1880, a deputation from the *British Medical Journal* urged the introduction of stringent regulations for enforcement of the Act because, as the *Pall Mall Gazette* commented acidly, "A case tried at Chester this week shows that the arm of the law is not long enough or strong enough to deal effectually with the 'baby-farmers.'"[43] In March, the Home Office wrote to the Metropolitan Board of Works asking for its recommendations. Its reply urged extension of the Act to cover single-child cases, raising of the age limit from one to five years, and outlawing "lump sum" adoptions. However, the General Election turned the Conservatives out of office and the incoming Liberal administration showed no interest in the question. The steady trickle of reporting of cases, and criticism of the legislation, continued.

In 1888 baby-farming was again in the news. A coroner's inquest exposed to public gaze the activities of Arnold, a baby-sweater who had been dealing in children on a huge scale (twenty-four children were proved to have passed through her hands in short order; police suspicion was that these represented merely the tip of the iceberg).[44] Later that year boys playing football on waste ground in Edinburgh were horrified when the bundle of rags they were using as a ball spilled open to reveal a body of a dead boy. The child was traced to Jessie King who lived nearby. She had adopted it days previously in return for a small premium. The lad was in fact the third nurse-child she had murdered. Expecting but a small sentence, she was hanged for murder.[45]

Reaction to the two cases was immediate. In early December, the Home Office sent out a circular letter to local authorities requesting their opinion on the need for new legislation. In 1890 two Bills were introduced, one by the Home Office and a more farreaching measure sponsored by the NSPCC.[46] Both proposed to extend the 1872 Act to all cases where a child under five was taken in for hire or reward for more than twenty-four hours. On its second reading, the government Bill met with a storm of opposition. It was, declared one MP, a Bill for the persecution of honest poor families.[47] "As the Bill stands," declared another, "if a widower moves in search of work and leaves his child with his mother, married sister or some other relative [she] must have her house registered as a baby-farm."[48] Again, the Bill was referred to a Select Committee. Evidence was called to the effect that, unless there was an exemption for those to whom children were boarded out by charitable organizations like the Foundling Hospital, such bodies would find it difficult to find suitable families to take children, since respectable people had a great antipathy to, and would not submit to having to register as though they were, baby-farmers.[49] In the face of the objections, both Bills were withdrawn.

Baby-farming cases, however, continued to catch the headlines in the press. In 1891 a woman named Reeves was convicted of the manslaughter of a child (the evidence revealed that out of twelve children placed in her care eight had died).[50] Also tried at the Old Bailey that year were Joseph and Annie Roadhouse, a pair of baby-sweaters. They had obtained children by advertising in the press and, like the Barneses, had induced parents to pay the premiums asked by misrepresenting their status and making false claims as to the kind of home they would provide; no less than thirty-five children had been obtained in this way and immediately farmed out. Convicted of obtaining by deception, they were sentenced respectively to eighteen and twelve months' imprisonment.[51]

In 1895, a Bill drawn in similar terms to the government Bill of 1890, was introduced by Lord Onslow, but again a general election intervened to prevent its further progress. After the election the matter was taken up by the Earl of Denbigh who, in 1896, introduced a Safety of Nurse Children Bill. Drawn in particularly stringent terms, it was referred to a Select Committee, where the evidence given was a rehash of that in 1871 and 1890.[52] It was asserted by Babey and other witnesses that, if baby-sweaters and others presently outside the Act were to be subjected to control, it would be essential for it to be amended to require registration in any case in which a child under five was received for more than twenty-four hours for hire or reward, and for registered houses to be inspected regularly. As in 1890, however, there was no shortage of witnesses willing and anxious to spell out the harm which a blanket extension would do to the work of charitable bodies. The need to regulate lying-in houses, described by Benjamin Waugh as "a great source of infanticide and the [places] from which baby farmers got the material for their trade," was also stressed by a number of witnesses.[53] The evil of adoptions for lump sums was returned to, although it was emphasized that a child taken in return for weekly payments was often in as much danger. If the payments stopped the child would be at great risk of being either starved or abandoned. It was also pointed out that baby-dropping was as prevalent as ever. Essentially the message was the same as before. The present Act was a dead letter.

While the Committee was sitting, Amelia Dyer stood trial for murder at the Old Bailey.[54] Aged fifty-seven, with a history of mental illness, she had been taking in babies for years. She first came to the notice of the authorities in 1879 when she was prosecuted for failing to register her house and jailed for six months. On discharge, she quickly returned to her old trade. She took one child at a time and few survived long. In April 1896 the bodies of two children were found in the Thames; both had been strangled and both were traced to her. While in custody she made a confession telling the police they would be able to tell which were hers by the ribbons around their necks. Tried by Mr. Justice Hawkins, with his customary unfairness, she was convicted and executed. The press, the country, and the Queen all rejoiced at the hanging.⁵⁵ It was the highest profile baby-farming case since that of Margaret Waters, and this time legislation quickly followed, taking immediate advantage of the furor. In 1897 Lord Denbigh's Infant Life Preservation Bill reached the statute book although only after being much cut about in Committee.

Yet like the 1872 Act which it replaced, it was unfortunately a poor thing.⁵⁶ It imposed on all persons receiving two or more children under five for hire or reward, for longer than twenty-four hours, a duty to notify the local authority within forty-eight hours, and also to notify the local authority if any such child was removed and the coroner if it died. Local authorities were required to provide for the execution of the Act and given power to appoint inspectors to enforce it. Inspectors were given the right to apply for a justice's warrant if refused entry or inspection, and local authorities had the power to remove to the workhouse or a place of safety any child kept in unfit premises or by a person unfit to have its care and maintenance. Exempted from the obligation to notify were relatives and guardians, hospitals, convalescent homes of institutions established for the protection and care of infants, and persons with whom infants were boarded out by the Poor Law authorities. The most glaring shortcoming of the Act was its failure to deal with baby-sweaters, a defect which would attract future press criticism on an annual basis.⁵⁷ Once again lying-in houses had been ignored, presumably because of the alleged difficulties of definition, while the provision concerning lump sum payments was next to worthless.

In Australia, as the 1896 Select Committee had been made aware, the problem was, by contrast, being tackled with far greater vigor. In 1890 the State of Victoria had enacted its own Infant Life Protection Act. This, like its English counterpart, imposed upon any person receiving a child under two for nursing or maintenance, a duty to register with the police and likewise to register the premises where the child was to be kept; registration was to be for one year and could be refused or revoked for good cause. The Act also required any person adopting or taking in a child under three to give notice of the fact. The police were given power to inspect any premises or child registered under the Act, accompanied, if necessary, by a doctor. Significantly, lying-in houses were required to be registered as private hospitals and the occupier of any premises where an illegitimate child was born was required to give notice of its birth to the Registrar of Births, Deaths, and Marriages or the police within three days of the birth. The death of a child in a registered house was likewise to be notified within three days as was the death of any illegitimate child under five. Also, no child who died within a registered house was to be buried without a burial certificate. In England it would take another quarter of a century to put in place a similarly rigorous regime.⁵⁸

Conclusion

While the 1897 Act was an improvement upon that of 1872, few can have expected that it would mean the end of criminal baby-farming, nor did it. In the first decade of the twentieth century four baby-farmers were hanged for murder.[59] It is impossible to estimate how many infants were deliberately done away with by such women during the nineteenth century. Few baby-farmers resorted to strangulation or violence. Neglecting a baby was just as effective a method of killing and far safer, such a death commonly wearing the appearance of, and being treated as, due to natural causes. Cases such as those of Margaret Waters and Amelia Dyer caused huge anger at the time, but they were seen as atypical and once the perpetrators had been hanged, the public forgot about baby-farming until the next case hit the headlines.

By the start of the Second World War the evil of baby-farming was no more. Had Parliament in Victoria's day shown the same determination to grapple with the problem as it did during the years 1910–1939, many young innocents could have been saved, but the political will was never there. The crimes of Waters, King, and Dyer shocked Victorian society, but once they had been convicted and executed, the public, press, and politicians quickly lost interest because the moral outrage was not sustained, due to the realities of the need for easy and cheap solutions to providing for bastard children and getting working-class mothers back to work. But as recent child-minding cases have shown, a society with large numbers of working mothers is always vulnerable to such abuses, and to panics made short-lived by the practical pressures of requirements for child care.

The passing of the Acts of 1872 and 1897 created the illusion that action was being taken to deal with the evil. But, as those interested in the subject knew, they were little more than window-dressing. Rooting out the evil would have required a comprehensive scheme or registration and the creation of an army of public officials armed with wide ranging powers of inspection and entry, and for that politicians and public alike had little enthusiasm. As Prime Minister Lord Salisbury put it in 1896, "People do not like being registered or to have their homes inspected by a government official by day or by night and he desired to see [measures] framed in conformity with the liberty of the subject and the rights of persons who are acting in perfect innocence."[60]

Notes

1. Valuable material is found in Lionel Rose, *The Murder of the Innocents* (London: Routledge and Keegan Paul, 1986); George K. Behlmer, *Child Abuse and Moral Reform in England, 1870–1908* (Stanford: Stanford University Press, 1982).

2. Françoise Banet Ducroq, *Love in the Time of Victoria* (London: Penguin, 1992). Pressure of work prevented the author responding to renewed comments which are reflected in this preamble.

3. It was not a straightforward case, as reportage made plain. See *Pall Mall Gazette*, 2 August 1865; R. S. Lambert, *When Justice Faltered* (London: Methuen, 1935), 92ff.

4. After 1834 such an order could only be made where there was evidence to corroborate the allegation of paternity.

5. Even home workers could not easily have a child with them, if single.

6. Letter, George Hardinge, cited J. Green, *The Morning of Her Day* (London: Darf Publishers, 1990), 106. See also: *The Times*, 14 April 1837: "In nine cases out of ten . . . infanticide [is] perpetrated . . . rather from . . . despondency and destitution than from vice."

7. Adoption of Children Act 1926.

8. First used in the 1840s to describe Drouett's so-called Infant Pauper Asylum in Tooting, where children were boarded out by Poor Law authorities in large numbers, the term "baby-farm" had come to mean a house where nurse-children were taken in for money.

9. The Herveian Society was a London-based medical society with an interest in social matters.

10. In 1867 their recommendations were endorsed by the Social Science Association Congress.

11. See *British Medical Journal*, 25 January, 75; 8 February, 127; 22 March, 175; 28 March 1868, 301.

12. *British Medical Journal*, 1 February 1868, 121; Lambert, *When Justice Faltered*, 92.

13. J. Greenwood, *The Seven Curses of London* (London: Stanley Rivers, 1896), 38.

14. Daniel Defoe, *Roxanna, or The Fortunate Mistress* (1724; Oxford: Oxford University Press, 1964), 79–80. *Select Committee on the Preservation of Infant Life*, 1871, Evidence, Curvengen.

15. *The Times*, 7 October 1870.

16. See OBSP 72 (1870), 539 ff.

17. *Lloyds Newspaper*, 5 June 1870.

18. Leader, *The Times*, 4 July 1870.

19. See, for example, *Daily Telegraph*, 15 June; 23 June; 9 July; 6 August; 15 August 1870.

20. Sergeant Relf was awarded £20 out of public funds. *The Times*, 24 September 1870; *Daily Telegraph*, 24 September 1870.

21. Leader, *The Times*, 24 September 1870: "A heavy blow has ben struck at one of the greatest iniquities of our day . . . society may be thankful that such a crime has been brought home to one of its perpetrators."

22. *Daily Telegraph*, 5 October 1870.

23. *Select Committee on the Preservation of Infant Life* 1871, Evidence, Curvengen; Evidence, Herford.

24. *Daily Telegraph*, 5 October 1870.

25. See for example *The Times*, 23 June 1870, which saw fit to opine, "The evidence conclusively proves foul play."

26. *Hansard*, 209, 1872, col. 1489.

27. *The Times*, 2 August 1871.

28. Greenwood, *Seven Curses*, 22.

29. *The Times*, 10 November 1870; *Daily Telegraph*, 10 November 1870.
30. PP II, 1871 (49), 483.
31. *Infant Mortality, Its Causes and Remedies* (London, 1870).
32. PP VII, 1871 (372), 607.
33. PP II, 1872 (6), 269.
34. *Pall Mall Gazette*, 30 October 1872.
35. *Daily Telegraph*, 20 March 1876.
36. *British Medical Journal*, 25 March 1876, 388.
37. See Lush J's observations in *R v Binmore*, *The Times*, 22 March 1875.
38. PP X, 1896, *Select Committee on the Infant Life Preservation Bill and the Safety of Nurse Children Bill, 1896*, Evidence, Waugh, 225.
39. *British Medical Journal*, 30 August 1879, 345.
40. *The Times*, 30 July 1877.
41. *The Times*, 29 October 1879; 30 October 1879.
42. *The Times*, 23 July 1879.
43. *Pall Mall Gazette*, 6 February 1880.
44. *The Times*, 5 October 1888.
45. W. Roughead, *Twelve Scottish Trials* (Edinburgh: William Green, 1913).
46. PP V, 1890 (142), 523.
47. *Hansard*, 342, 1890 col. 1083.
48. Ibid., col. 1084.
49. For its proceedings, see PP XIII, 1890 (346), 623.
50. OBSP, 1890–91, 113, 643.
51. *The Times*, 8 May 1891; 9 May 1891.
52. PP X 1896 (343), 225.
53. PP X (1896), *Select Committee, Infant Life Preservation Bill*, Evidence, Waugh, 225.
54. *The Times*, 22 May 1896; 23 May 1896; OBSP 1896, 124, 725.
55. F. W. Ashley, *My Seventy Years in the Law* (London: Bodley Head, 1936), 128: "[Mrs. Dyer's] execution was said to have afforded Queen Victoria more than ordinary satisfaction."
56. Benjamin Waugh, "Baby-Farming," *Contemporary Review* (1890): 700. "A poor little Bill" was the comment on the 1872 Act in *The Saturday Review*, 3 September 1872.
57. See, for example, Letter, Francis Zanetti, *The Times*, 20 January 1903.
58. Five years after the coming into force of the Victoria Act, in the case of *Makin v AG for New South Wales*, Judge Stephen, an Australian judge and cousin of Sir James Fitzjames Stephen, had taken a bold stance when confronted with an issue as to the admissibility of similar fact evidence in a baby-farming murder case. In *Waters* Kelly LCB had refused to admit such evidence but, in *Makin*, Stephen J held it admissible, a decision upheld on appeal by the Supreme Court of New South Wales and finally by the Judicial Committee of the Privy Council ([1894] AC 57), thereby becoming one of the leading authorities on the law of similar fact evidence.
59. They were Ada Chard Williams (hanged 8 March 1900), Amelia Sach, Annie Walters (hanged 3 February 1903), and Rhoda Willis (hanged 14 August 1907).
60. *Hansard* 38, 1896, col. 418.

13

Sex, Wives, and Prostitutes: Debating *Clarence*

KATE GLEESON

Introduction

Eighteen eighty-eight was a dangerous year for women. The contemporary social and legal climate was fuelled by contradictory sexual phobias and paranoia, to the point of sexual hatred. Women's sexuality was viewed with particular suspicion, as newspaper crime reporting underlines. Any suggestion of female immorality reflected negatively upon any case. Yet where women were victims, a commonplace was that the Victorian media regarded the details as "unfit for publication." Notoriously, 1888 was the year of the Whitechapel serial murders of women, famed as the work of Jack the Ripper.[1] It was an age in which women's independence was under scrutiny, both social and legal, and in which a legal backlash of a magnitude worthy of the Ripper's era was forthcoming in response to increased female sexual agency, and was hotly debated in the media. This chapter examines the criminal case of *R v Clarence*, the trials of which appeared before the Court of Queen's Bench from June to November 1888.[2] It was a significant case, yet its content meant that the press coverage was mixed. *The Times* effectively ignored it, presumably because of its unpleasant subject matter; more sensationally inclined organs, including nationals such as the *Daily Telegraph,* and local press such as the *East London Observer,* gave it attention, but even then shied away from the "disgusting" details. *Clarence* concerned charges of Assault and Grievous Bodily Harm (GBH), yet the judgment was notorious for its confirmation of the marital rape exemption, and the breadth of its influence extends today far beyond marital rape. The case involved Selina Clarence in her bold attempt to seek redress for the assault she identified in her husband's deceitful transmission to her of gonorrhea. A woman's claim of sexual harm, particularly in the context of marriage, was a novel move met with considerable judicial suspicion.

This chapter provides a detailed analysis of the Queen's Bench appeal decision. The discussions of the Bench and nature of their reporting provide a perfect example by which to illuminate the peculiar sexual paranoia and fears of the Victorian establishment of the day. Although the charges of this trial concerned assault, the judges of the Bench quickly seized the opportunity to digress to a discussion *obiter dicta* of the damning obligations of the "marital contract" for women. And they did not stop here. The *Clarence* decision provides judgment on many facets of sex beyond that of the marital obligation, clearly illustrating the underlying motivations and sentiments of the Bench. In particular, the righteous debates of the court provide great insight into the prevailing moral fear of prostitutes and sexually visible women, enabling a greater insight into wider media representations of women's sexuality. A consistent theme of panic over the sexual agency of women can be identified in the frequently rambling discussions, most notably concerning the fear of sexually "aggressive" and potentially litigious women. This panic, together with a contemporary association of women with disease and therefore danger, combined to produce the long-standing, damning decision of *Clarence:* a denial of women's capacity to experience sexual harm and a declaration of the inherently dishonest nature of the sexual contract.

Clarence is not mere historical curio. It is a tenacious case that somehow is still cited, even since its overruling in England in 1991, when Justice Owens described the marital rape exemption as "as offensive a fiction as it is senseless."[3] Indeed *Clarence* continues to be cited in a variety of cases, with little surrounding controversy, not least of all to define the boundaries of consent.[4] To appreciate fully the logic of these modern legal interpretations of sex, harm, and consent which descend from the *Clarence* decision, one must understand first the social and legal climate of the day, and the prevailing moral fears fuelling the majority judgment. Somehow, in the midst of a mass social fear of prostitutes, arose a legal decision that confirmed men's position as normally the primary victims of sexual harm. In an era where women were viewed metaphysically as sexual disease, to make allegations of men's sexual culpability was indeed a brave move on Selina Clarence's part.[5]

The Prostitute and Social Panic

Certain new sexual freedoms and rights of social movement had been experienced by women in the wake of the repeal of the repressive Contagious Diseases legislation in 1886, ending the degrading and intrusive ritualized detainment and inspection of so-called "common prostitutes." Also, the Criminal Law Amendment Act 1885 had raised the age of female heterosexual consent from twelve to sixteen, a move viewed variously as benevolently paternalistic, repressive, and misguided, or now viewed as primarily in *men's* cynical interest.[6] Nonetheless, the massive public campaigns and agitation surrounding its inception were indicative of a novel, yet growing, discourse of female sexual rights, albeit tinged with a paternalism fuelled by the large-scale hysteria promoted in the press about the supposed white-slave traffic.[7] While the discourse may be understood as misguided in its paternalism and as ultimately sexually oppressive, particularly in its legislative association with hostility to male homosexuality and antibrothel provisions, its symbolic attachment to women's sexual agency should not be overlooked. The mass and organized sectarian campaigns visible in the press for legislation against (trafficked) prostitution and for the raising of the age of female consent involved a public pronouncement of female sexual choice (admittedly this involved primarily the choice not to participate in prostitution).[8] The media dimension ensured these were *very* public debates which, at their core, concerned female sexual rights and must be located in reaction also to the Married Women's Property Act 1882, which advanced both female economic independence and popular fears about female morality.[9] Female sexuality, its incumbent rights, and regulation, were on the public agenda and this agenda was pressing the legislature for response. Women's sexuality was demanding independent recognition and attention in the form of protection from both civil exploitation and state-based harassment.

This discourse combined with the prevailing morbid fear of prostitution (actually, *prostitutes themselves*) to provide a peculiar social climate of *panic* over female sexuality and more specifically, female sexual independence. Years of public association of prostitutes with disease and the notion of the "great social evil" had produced grave social suspicions over the moral nature and character of prostitutes, and consequently of women generally. Strengthened by the newly developed *medical model* of analysis that focused on recently identified (though often confused) venereal disease, the fear of prostitutes proved strangely contradictory.[10] In the ultimate sense of the "necessary evil" paradigm, prostitutes were posited as the "potential source of both physical and moral contagion" for men.[11] The underlying premise of this concern, of course, was the unquestioned acceptance of men's large-scale commercial use of women:

> Women . . . were the targets of surveillance, harassment and incarceration. For at no time could medical practitioners and politicians, despite their misgivings about the ineffectiveness of a partial system of identification and compulsory treatment, challenge the collective privileges of men for unencumbered heterosexual indulgence.[12]

Davidoff's sewer metaphor captures it best: "defenders of prostitution saw it as a necessary institution which acted as a giant sewer, draining away the distasteful but inevitable waste products of male lustfulness, leaving the middle class household and middle class ladies pure and unsullied."[13] Mary Spongberg also uses this metaphor, claiming that "The task of public hygienists was to sanitise these sewers so as to promote their cleanliness and efficiency."[14] In the Victorian period,

> Fear of venereal disease had become the way in which men articulated the anxieties caused by prostitution. It opened the debate on prostitution, making it a health problem. It allowed an expression of the idea that prostitutes were a necessity. On one level it left the notion of women as innately pure and untainted by making the prostitute pathological. But on another level it meant that all women were tainted because of the connection between venereal disease and femininity.[15]

All women were, after all, potential prostitutes.

For Davidoff, Victorian sexuality (particularly male) became the "focus of a more generalised fear of disorder and of a continuing battle to tame natural forces."[16] The social panic over prostitutes' independence and its accompanying phobias are best comprehended as linked to wider social fears. Early "social investigators" had identified prostitution as an "intolerable evil that threatened the sanctity of the family as well as the social order."[17] Yet oddly, regulation and free access to "clean" prostitutes was deemed the appropriate remedy for this evil. The greater fear, of men's unnaturally constrained lust, was preeminent. Ironically, in this analysis, prostitutes may be viewed as the unreliable, immoral guardians of social stability where any increase in agency, or their inclusion in the modern discourse of individual rights, was terrifying. These were dangerous, if necessary, women.

Indicative of this complicated "love-hate-need relationship" with prostitution, Parliamentary debates over the raising of the age of consent were influenced explicitly by concern for men's sustained access to prostitutes, and especially the fear of women's increased sexual agency in the face of disputed consent. The 1885 Act was exhaustively entitled "An Act to make further provisions for the Protection of Women and Girls, the suppression of brothels, and other purposes." However Stevenson identifies the driving motivation behind it as "the perceived need to protect men from immoral girls and women, rather than any primary desire to protect vulnerable females from male sexual violence," noting the influence of a fear of "wholesale extortion by 'girls of bad character.'"[18] As Weeks comments,

Most of the men who wished to keep the age of consent at twelve and thirteen accepted as a matter of course an outlook in which young girls from the working class were perceived to be easy sexual targets. For many upper class men, prostitution appeared both necessary and inevitable; and their objections to raising the age of consent often arose from fear that either they or their sons might be threatened by the new legislation.[19]

Indeed, "a casual acceptance of male sexual licence was traditional among the British upper classes and continued to be upheld by aristocratic 'reprobates' in parliamentary debates."[20]

Into this climate (sustained by regular newspaper comment) of medically "justified" female phobia, of unquestioned acceptance of men's inalienable right to use prostitutes, and widespread paranoia over sexually aggressive, litigious women, Selina Clarence marched with her accusations of sexual harm. It is beyond irony that Selina's claim of assault concerned gonorrhea. Walkowitz points out that the denial of her harm was too concertedly deliberate to be considered ironic:

> complications due to untreated gonorrhoea can in fact be very serious, but doctors barely recognised it as a serious disease for women, mistaking its asymptomatic early stages as a sign of a condition that women passed on to men but did not suffer from themselves, [that is], women as carriers of gonorrhoea, as producers of disease in men, but not sufferers.[21]

This prevailing medical and social prejudice both informed the judiciary and thrived on its blind sight regarding women's capacity to experience sexual harm. Selina's allegations were manipulated to extend this denial beyond the case of disease, to the broader context of sexual harm in general.

Creating the Marital Rape Exemption

On 20 December 1887 Charles Clarence had sex with his wife, Selina. It appears that Charles knew he was infected with gonorrhea, but declined to inform his wife of his condition. Clarence was convicted of assault and GBH contrary to the Offences Against the Person Act 1861. *The Times* had felt compelled to report the matter in as demure a tone as possible, obscuring the precise content by explaining that the case was one that raised "questions as to the law affecting the domestic relations."[22] Both convictions were quashed by the Queen's Bench Division with the apparent aid of the logic of the marital rape exemption. Newspaper reporting either failed to report this development, like *The Times*, or, like the *Daily Telegraph*, did its best to obscure the sordid details behind the decision.[23] It simply did not appear to be understood by the majority of the Victorian Bench that a wife could be assaulted sexually by her husband (except perhaps in the most physically violent of circumstances). As she was akin to his legally contracted property, for her to charge this would be as inane as a man bringing charges against himself. This is unsurprising, given that in Victorian England the marital contract was considered so binding that a wife's rights to personal freedoms were contingent on her husband's discretion, as the words of Chief Baron Pollock underline: "Such a [marital] connection may be accompanied with conduct which amounts to cruelty, as where the condition of the wife is such that she will or may suffer from such connection."[24]

The apparent misogyny of such archaic legal conventions as the marital rape exemption is well documented, as is the judicial system's historic disregard for female complaints of sexual harm.[25] However, even such "well-documented" history is complicated, and far from straightforward. For example, in *Clarence*, "despite the overwhelming decision that no crime had been committed at common-law, the judgments were in no means similarly in support of the idea that a wife could never withdraw consent to intercourse."[26] Thus even in 1888 there was far from judicial unanimity surrounding the legal understanding of "rape" in marriage. This makes the apparent uncontroversial manner in which the logic of the *Clarence* ruling has been cited and upheld recently seem all the more surprising, especially in light of the official judicial and parliamentary discrediting of such outdated conventions as the marital rape exemption.

Although the Crown in *Clarence* had charged specifically nonsexual assaults, the case was introduced, ruled, and publicized as one of sexual propriety and morality. Some discussion was given to the nature of criminal assault and the crime of inflicting GBH. Fitzjames Stephen (for the majority) thought that "the word 'inflict' implied an assault and battery of which GBH was the manifest, immediate and obvious result. As this was not the manifest, immediate and obvious result of Clarence's act he did not 'inflict' harm onto this wife."[27] Yet the judiciary's analysis swiftly deferred to that of the nature of the marital contract of consent to sex, a deferral that "was clearly not incumbent on them."[28] The cleverly chosen charges of assault and GBH were dismissed as misguided in a case involving not only sex but also marriage.[29]

The defense immediately set the tone for the decision, revealing what was to surface in much of the judicial discourse as the wider agenda: "if the conviction is right, it appears to follow that any man who is accused by a prostitute of having defrauded or infected her may be prosecuted for an indecent assault, if not for rape."[30] The physical harm to Selina was summarily dismissed as the primary concern, and the case was transformed into a lengthy discussion of the damning wider repercussions of allowing a wife to charge her husband with nonconsensual sex. Although Selina had not claimed rape, she did state that she would not have had sex with Charles had she known of his disease. And the prosecution did argue, "irrelevantly" according to Gilbert Geis, that had she resisted her husband's advances, that had he persisted with force he would then be guilty of rape.[31] The case was hastily rephrased by the defense and the court in terms of *consent,* rather than *assault,* and almost as if by magic there appears the first instance of an English appellate court discussion of the rape-in-marriage doctrine that was to be authoritatively upheld in Britain, in some form, until 1991:

> The comments in *Clarence* upon rape-in-marriage amounted to little more than stray, unfocused observations. But later, these inconclusive musings would come to serve as a major basis for more fixed judicial views upholding Lord Hale's statement on the inviolability of the husband's right of sexual access to his spouse.[32]

The logic employed in this conceptual leap of faith from GBH to marital rape appears bizarre. How was it able to occur?

The Logic of Marital Rape

Charles Clarence was charged under sections 20 and 47 of the Offences Against the Person Act 1861. Both sections relate to physical assault and are explicitly and clearly separate from those dealing with matters of sexual assault. Selina argued that she had been assaulted in the harm inflicted by her husband's informed and deceitful transmission of gonorrhea. Clarence was convicted on both counts with reference to two previous judgments of a similar nature, neither of which involved a married couple.[33] On appeal, defense counsel argued that according to Lord Hale's Pleas of the Crown a husband "cannot be guilty of rape upon his wife," and that as "consent to coition on the part of the wife is a matrimonial obligation . . . coition cannot as between them constitute assault."[34] Therefore, her allegations were both misguided and unfounded. Defense logic was accepted as sound and uncontroversial by the majority of judges and even the four dissenting judges declined to contest the logic or sense of this conceptual leap from GBH to rape. Their dissent was based mainly on a more subtle reading of Hale's marital rape opinion. Surely, they reasoned, a wife need not consent to every act of marital intercourse, under every circumstance, particularly if it will leave her injured. Hawkins argued that

> by the marriage contract a wife no doubt confers upon her husband an irrevocable privilege to have sexual intercourse with her during such time as the ordinary relations created by such contract subsist between them.... [T]his marital privilege does not justify a husband in endangering his wife's health and causing her grievous bodily harm.[35]

In fact, many of those of the majority were also hesitant to hold Hale's proposition as sound in all circumstances. Mr. Justice Wills was "not prepared to assent to the proposition" that marital rape was "impossible," and both Mr. Justice Field and Mr. Justice Charles thought "there might be cases in which a wife might lawfully refuse intercourse and in which, if the husband imposed it by violence, he might be held guilty of a crime." In other words, they suggested, there were certain exceptional circumstances that might allow a wife to revoke consent. This ambiguity surrounding the limits of Hale's opinion adds further curiosity to the tenacity of *Clarence* and the motivation behind its consistent use in modern law. The authority of *Clarence* is perhaps "not the bulwark of the irrevocable consent argument it may have been considered."[36] Unfortunately for Selina, hers was not the situation to warrant exception.

Despite momentary misgivings over the extent of Hale's pronouncement, the logic that Selina's complaint amounted to rape was uncontested. It was most uncontroversially accepted that as the assault (gonorrhea) was sexually based, that therefore if any criminal assault was committed, it had to be rape. As Wills asserted, "If an assault—a rape also."[37] And, as stated, marital rape was a crime the allegations of which could not be upheld against a husband (except apparently in certain circumstances, the details of which were not illuminated). As such, no basis for Clarence's conviction prevailed. The marital rape exemption exonerated the defendant of any culpability, thus precluding the convictions, despite the fact that Selina had not charged rape.

The creative invocation of the marital rape exemption against charges of assault and GBH is indicative of a profound disinterest in, or perhaps even an incapacity to conceive of, the harm of sex, particularly within marriage. To speak of assault in relation to sex is to immediately invoke the notion of rape, even today. The nature, therefore harm, of rape is typically understood as the lack or abuse of consent. Thus in instances where consent may be "proven" or taken for granted, there exists no crime and legally no harm. Selina's marital contractual "consent" to sex meant that she had not been raped, or indeed assaulted. And as the only harm of sex is rape (nonconsent), no crime (or harm) was legally recognized. As Hawkins (who was actually more sympathetic to a wife's rights, than, say Baron Pollock, and who urged the conviction of Clarence) explained:

> A wife submits to her husband's embraces because at the time of marriage she gave him an irrevocable right to her person. The intercourse which takes place between a husband and wife after marriage is not by virtue of any special consent on her part, but mere submission to an obligation imposed upon her by law. Consent is immaterial.[38]

Quite simply, the harm of sex is nonconsent and consent in marriage is immaterial. Therefore, what harm of sex may prevail in marriage? It is unclear where this logic leaves a wife deceitfully infected with a serious illness by a knowing husband, except for the obvious; that it leaves her beyond the protection of the law, apparently simply because the vehicle for her assault was sex. Selina Clarence remains unvindicated.

The Other "Harm" of Sex

Aside from "rape" or contested consent to the sex that infected her, the other common theme in the discussion of Selina's fate was the panic over prostitution, or more tellingly, fear of prostitutes themselves. Remember, the defense for Clarence's appeal introduced the case with this fear as explicit priority. The ramifications from acknowledging Selina's assault at the hands (or penis) of her husband were deemed considerable by both the defense and the court. The fear of the application of the principle to women in general, beyond the wife, prompted a lengthy digression from the charges at hand to discuss the varied "dangers" of allowing women legal recourse for the harm of sex. The notion that a man could be held legally responsible for sexual activities was patently unthinkable, if it were not so implicit a threat. Indeed Wills's analysis extended beyond commercial prostitution to that of private seduction, exhibiting a grave antipathy toward regulating or in any way interfering with the "contract" of sex. The indignation and cynicism with which he framed this "problem" of assessing harm and sex suggests that Selina probably never stood a chance with her bold allegations.

In his judgment, Wills was obsessed with prostitution. More specifically, he was preoccupied with the potential harm to men at the hands of unscrupulous prostitutes and other dishonorable women. So charges of GBH against a husband led to not only a discussion of the illogicality of marital rape, but also involved a disorderly parade of all number of hypothetical situations surrounding sex and the inherent extortive dangers for men therein. Far from providing mere obscure historical insight into the curious personal fears of the Victorian establishment, *Clarence* is still with us today. When the full bench seized the opportunity in 1888 to muse at length, providing "random, cryptic comments" over the perils of sex for men, it furnished explicit precedents for contemporary understandings of the legal conceptions of rape, fraud, consent, and not least of all, the harm of sex.[39] The obsession with potential harm to men at the hands of women in this context could only arise from a presupposed disinterest in or dismissal of the actual harm of sex in and of itself. It exhibits instead, a particular interest in the sexual availability of women to men, beyond the limits of the law. Rather than concerns for the regulation of the harm of sex, the *Clarence* judgment presents almost hysterical fears for the harm of men around the *contract* of sex. And top of this list was the fear of the most obvious contractual participant, the defamed manipulative prostitute.

The Sexual Contract—The Fear of Fraud

Defense counsel introduced *Clarence* as of great importance, arguing that the upholding of Charles's convictions could pave the way for the liability of sexual activity as such. It opened the door to future extortions and false accusations. Men across the nation, it would appear, were already at grave risk of harm from prostitutes, and Clarence's conviction would provide even more avenues for their malevolent ways. Wills, who introduced the verdict, was in agreement with the defense's paranoid logic. He focused particularly on the suggestion that perhaps Selina's consent was vitiated by the fact that it was induced fraudulently. Apparently the idea of extending legal protection against fraud from the legitimate commercial world to the intimate one of sex was dangerous, and plainly misguided. Wills concurred with the rather contradictory Stephen: "The act of intercourse between a man and a woman cannot in any case be regarded as the performance of a contract. In the case of married people that act is part of the greater relation based on the greatest of all contracts but standing on a footing peculiar to itself."[40] Apparently the greatest contract of all was beyond the greatest reach of the law.

Wills conceded that Clarence's actions were both "wicked and cruel enough."[41] But this acknowledgment did not outweigh his greater concern, the protection of the subtle nuances of the contracting of sex:

> If the first [prosecution] view be correct, every man, as has been pointed out, who knowingly gives a piece of bad money to a prostitute to procure

her consent to intercourse or who seduces a woman to by representing himself to be what he is not, is guilty of assault, and it seems to me therefore, of rape.[42]

Despite the apparent logic of the proposition, it was simply not a palatable consideration for the court. Wills and his "brothers" presented many such hypothetical scenarios to display the absurdity they identified in attempting to regulate the "mysteries of sex."[43] He ardently pandered to the hysterical fears raised by the defense, warning that the logic of the conviction proved not only distasteful but, quite frankly, too difficult:

> Surely these considerations point to the conclusion that a wide door will be opened to inquiries not of a wholesome kind in which the difficulties in the way of arriving at the truth are often enormous, and in which the danger of going wrong is as great as it is by people in general inadequately appreciated.[44]

So, a wife's charge of GBH against her husband was opportunistically seized upon to determine the legal protection of fraud within sex, primarily aimed at the protection of men from false accusation, and most profoundly the protection of sex from the rigors of the law.

Selina claimed she would not have consented to sex with Charles had she been aware of his disease. As such, the prosecution argued optimistically that had she expressed nonconsent, and Charles had "proceeded with force," he would have then been guilty of rape.[45] Given that Hale's marital rape opinion had not yet been discussed in court, perhaps this optimism was not as misplaced as it now seems. The prosecution were apparently unaware that, as Hawkins came to explain, within marriage a wife does not *consent* but merely *submits*. Indeed the argument for the prosecution indicates just how profoundly the nine judges of the majority were actively making law, in their often vague and unfocused discussions. Hale's seventeenth-century opinion that a man cannot be guilty of raping his wife had not been judicially confirmed prior to the frequently contradictory, opinionated departures of the court in *Clarence*. The hypothetical proposition of Selina's nonconsent suggested that as such, her consent was not "real." Given that she would have resisted sex if she had known the facts, and given that such resistance ought to be upheld in court, it would follow that her consent should not be accepted as "real." That is, it should be recognized as vitiated by the fraudulent representation by Clarence as to the nature of the sex act (although it should be noted that this too is a digression from the straightforward charges of assault and GBH which do not involve a constituent component of consent). While this was a discrete aside from the charges laid, the court again took the opportunity to muse prolifically, this time over the nature of that fraud (if any) which may vitiate consent to sex.

The Deceit of Seduction

James Fitzjames Stephen in particular was concerned with the consequences of acknowledging through this debate that fraud may vitiate consent to sex. For him, "the proposition that fraud vitiates consent in criminal matters is not true if taken to apply in the fullest sense of the word."[46] In particular, sexual matters proved well beyond the "maxim that fraud vitiates consent."[47] Stephen concluded that consent may only be vitiated where the fraud related to the nature of the act itself, or as to the identity of the person who does the act. His attempt to narrow the scope of that fraud which may be recognized legally in sex was still ambiguous, however, but may be found cited today as authority to uphold the most narrow interpretation of fraud in rape.[48] His concerns lay also with the dangers of extending rights of recourse to those engaging in acts of "immoral" (nonmarital) sex. Like Wills, Stephen was particularly concerned that perhaps "seduction" may be captured as criminal should the contract of sex come to be regulated by law: "Many seductions would be rapes, and so might acts of prostitution procured by fraud, as for instances by promises not intended to be fulfilled."[49]

The fear of extending criminal fraud provisions more broadly to the contract of sex was quite simply the fear of female reaction in the face of disputed consent. For Wills this specifically implicated the prostitute and the contract of commercial sex. What had the most worrying long-term implications was his assessment of seduction, or noncommercial sex, as primarily a deceitful pursuit:

> If the conviction be upheld on the grounds of the difference between the thing consented to and the thing done, the principle will extend to many, perhaps most cases of seduction, and to other forms of illicit intercourse, including at least theoretically, the case of prostitution.[50]

Thus although seduction or the negotiation of sex was identified as almost entirely dishonest, it did not warrant legal intervention. In fact, *because* seduction was identified as almost entirely dishonest it *could not* warrant intervention. The *Clarence* judgment explicitly identified the dishonest, manipulative nature of the contracting of sex and used this "fact" as reason for legal immunity. Clarence's behavior was acknowledged as immoral, "wicked and cruel," but the court could not legally acknowledge harm, for almost all seduction (apparently) is similarly immoral. Wills explained, "a great many rapes must be constantly taking place without either of the parties having the least idea of the fact."[51] Or, put more crudely: "we simply cannot convict Clarence, because then we'd have to convict all those other men too."[52]

Thus, the *Clarence* judgment of 1888 was a culmination to a debate over women and their rights in the sexual contract taking place against the background of increasing panic over women's independence. This panic has never entirely disappeared, and partly explains why *Clarence* has been so enduring. In its vague and disjointed offerings, *Clarence* has set as precedent for over one hundred years that the sexual contract is normally dishonest, yet still beyond the interests of the law. It cemented the onus on "consent" as determining the presence or absence or harm in sex, despite the rather contradictory acknowledgment that seduction at least is inherently dishonest. The wisdom of *Clarence* holds that the presence of consent acquits, or prevents, harm in sex. Yet at the same time, sexual consent in marriage is considered largely immaterial, if not nonexistent. And "consent" in seduction is deemed almost entirely deceitfully induced. It is difficult to avoid the conclusion that the *Clarence* judgment exhibits primarily a fundamental disinterest or disbelief in the harm of sex, and in contrast, a most concerted offensive against the legal regulation of the sexual contract, something which is interestingly contradictory of sociocultural stereotypes about feminine sexuality. With the understanding of sexual negotiations as inherently dishonest, and with marital consent deemed little more than contractual submission, it is not surprising that the court displayed scant interest in legally intruding into the "mysterious" sexual realm. With such a normalized understanding of hurt and manipulation and dishonesty in sex, it was probably quite a surprise to the court that anyone would complain.

The deceit of seduction and the duplicity of the sexual transmission of gonorrhea were deemed in *Clarence* problems of morality, rather than problems of criminal harm. The only harm that could be legally identified to arise from sex was that of the potential extortion of men (in particular those who used prostitutes), and that connected to the rather narrowly defined construct of "consent." Consent obtained by lies (seduction) or fraud (as to say, the health risk) was not so problematic as to warrant legal intervention. Both may be "immoral" perhaps, but for Wills, such immorality was not the business of the law. Indeed, he identified in the original *Clarence* conviction "a fresh illustration afforded of the futility of trying to teach morals by the application of the criminal law to cases occupying the doubtful ground between immorality and crime, and of the dangers which beset such attempts."[53]

Chapter 13

Conclusion

The conversation leading to the *Clarence* judgment both constructed and confirmed certain understandings of sex which underlay so much newspaper reporting of women and sexuality, especially in the courtroom. Most notoriously, this ratified Hale's seventeenth-century opinion that the marital contract implies (all but) irrevocable consent on the part of the wife. Aside from marital sex, it also established legally a particular view of sexual negotiations and the nature of sex itself. First, it held that sex is by typical nature of no legally recognized harm (to women), that sex is rather an issue of morality beyond the practicable interests of the law. Second, it confirmed that the civil or commercial contract of sex is both relevant and irrelevant to the law. It was relevant in establishing consent (to ensure lack of "force" and violence, outside of marriage at least). Yet oddly the nature of this contract was primarily of little interest to the law. Fraud in the sexual contract was acknowledged only in extreme, narrowly defined circumstances. The day-to-day fraud of deception involved in seduction is of no business to the law, because sex itself was seen as of little, if any harm. The contracting of sex, either commercial or social, was not to be limited by law. That is, the liberty of men's *access* to sex was not to be limited by law.

Third, it declared sex, especially extramarital, a routinely dishonest activity. The *Clarence* judgment not only pronounced disinterest in the regulation of sex. It actually defined sexual negotiations as typically dishonest. The Court's disinterest in the deceit of seduction flowed from an understanding of sex as fundamentally harmless to women and, most importantly, merely an issue of morality. Sexual dishonesty might well be immoral, but it did not constitute a harm relevant to law. If sex was harmless, then what was the "real" harm in being fraudulently induced to participate? Where was the "real" harm in lying to encourage someone to participate in an essentially harmless act? The morally righteous sex of marriage was beyond the reach of the law. And the immoral sex of seduction was quite simply just that: immoral. Indeed, only with a committed understanding of sex as fundamentally harmless could one make the spectacular conceptual leap necessary to overlook the obvious physical harm of gonorrhea.

With women posited typically *as* sex and indeed the very essence of sexual danger in their "contagion" and manipulative ways, the motivation of the Bench was skewed ferociously toward the discrediting of female testimonies of sexual harm and, therefore, toward the denial of the actual capacity of women to experience sexual harm inflicted by men. *Clarence* was decided amidst social paranoia and panic regarding the danger of prostitutes. These distracted motivations of the Bench ensured that sex was declared an issue of morality beyond the interests of the criminal law. The ambiguities or "mysteries" of seduction were used to justify the presumption that sex was essentially dishonest and difficult to regulate, that therefore the law was best kept at bay, particularly if "consent" were apparent. *Clarence* explicitly denied the capacity of sex for assault, indeed asking rhetorically if the legal construct of assault "could really have been intended to apply to circumstances so completely removed from those which are usually understood when an assault is spoken of, or to deal with matters of any kind involving the sexual relation or act."[54] Yet the panic of 1888 has maintained its influence to this very day.

(Editors' postscript: A 2004 Court of Appeal opinion has finally settled the Clarence controversy—apparently?[55])

Notes

1. L. S. Barbee, Introduction in S. P. Ryder and J. A. Piper, "Casebook: Jack the Ripper," http://www.casebook.org/intro.html.

2. *R v Clarence* (1888) 22 QBD 23.

3. *R v R* [1991] 1 All ER 749.

4. For example *Clarence* has been cited in *R v Miller* [1954] All ER 529, *Papadimitropoulos v The Queen* [1956] 98 CLR 249; *Sidaway v Bethlem Royal Hospital Governors and Others* [1984] 1 All ER 1018; *R v Petrozzi* [1987] 35 CCC (3d) 528; *R v Mobilio* [1991] I VR 339; *R v Brown* [1993] 2 All ER 102; *R v Linekar* [1995] 3 All ER 68; *R v Burstow* [1996] EWHC Admin 49; *R v Cuerrier* [1997] 111 CCC (3d) 261 (CACB); *R v Richardson* [1998] EWCA Crim 1086.

5. M. Spongberg, *Feminising Venereal Disease: The Body of the Prostitute in Nineteenth Century Medical Discourse* (Bastingstoke: Macmillan, 1997), 45.

6. Nickie Roberts, *Whores in History: Prostitution in Western Society* (London: HarperCollins, 1992), 257; Kim Stevenson, "Observations on the Law Relating to Sexual Offences: The Historic Scandal of Women's Silence," *Web Journal of Current Legal Issues* 4 (1999).

7. W. T. Stead's use of the *Pall Mall Gazette* in his "Maiden Tribute to Modern Babylon" is the best known example of this. *Pall Mall Gazette*, 1885.

8. *Pall Mall Gazette*, 15 December 1880, for example.

9. *Illustrated Police News*, 29 August 1885, for example.

10. The Contagious Diseases Acts 1864 aimed at control of both gonorrhea and syphilis. There was no effective scientific diagnosis for gonorrhea before 1879; the development of a blood test for syphilis came as late as 1906. P. McHugh, *Prostitution and Victorian Social Reform* (London: Croom Helm, 1980), 259.

11. Leonore Davidoff, "Class and Gender in Victorian Britain," in *Sex and Class in Women's History*, ed. J. L. Newton, M. P. Ryan, and J. Walkowitz, 17–71, at 19 (London: Routledge and Keegan Paul, 1983).

12. Kay Saunders, "Controlling (Hetero) Sexuality: The Implementation and Operation of Contagious Diseases Legislation in Australia, 1868–1945," in *Sex, Power, and Justice: Historical Perspectives on Law in Australia*, ed. D. Kirkby, 2–18, at 18 (Oxford University Press, 1995).

13. Davidoff, *Class and Gender*, 19.
14. Spongberg, *Venereal Disease*, 37.
15. Ibid., 47.
16. Davidoff, *Class and Gender*, 20.
17. Judith Walkowitz, *Prostitution and Victorian Society: Women, Class, and the State* (Cambridge: Cambridge University Press, 1980), 33.
18. Stevenson, "Women's Silence," 1, 9
19. Jeffrey Weeks, *Sex, Politics, and Society: The Regulation of Sexuality since 1800* (London: Longman, 1981), 88.
20. Walkowitz, *Prostitution*, 3.
21. Judith Walkowitz, private email correspondence with author, April 2002.
22. *The Times*, 11 June 1888.
23. *Daily Telegraph*, June 1888.
24. *R v Clarence* (1888), 64, per Baron Pollock. See also Edward's chapter in this volume.
25. J. A. Scutt, "Consent in Rape: The Problem of the Marriage Contract," *Monash University Law Review* 3 (1977): 255–88; G. Geis, "Rape-in-Marriage: Law and Law Reform in England, the United States, and Sweden," *The Adelaide Law Review* 6, 2 (1978): 284–303; M. D. A. Freeman, "'But if You Can't Rape Your Wife, Who[m] Can You Rape?': The Marital Rape Exemption Re-examined," *Family Law Quarterly* 15, 1 (1981): 1–29; Stevenson, "Women's Silence."
26. Scutt, "Consent in Rape," 257.
27. C. Strickland, "Why Parliament Should Create HIV Specific Offences," *Web Journal of Current Legal Issues* 2 (2001).
28. Freeman, "Marital Rape Exemption," 11.
29. Ormerod and Gunn argue the charges were actually not so cleverly chosen: "The judges do not appear to have realised that Parliament had chosen to make criminal the administration of poisons, destructive and other noxious things, so that the persons passing on smallpox to a friend or a child would be guilty of a crime which did not require improper extension of the concept of assault." Realization would have enabled those judges of the view Clarence *should* have been guilty of an offense to point out he was "prosecuted for the wrong offence." See sections 23 and 24, Offences Against the Person Act 1861. D. C. Ormerod and M. J. Gunn, "Criminal Liability for the Transmission of HIV," *Web Journal of Current Legal Issues* 1 (1996).
30. *R v Clarence* (1888), 23, per Fulton.
31. Geis, "Rape in Marriage," 287.
32. Ibid., 288.
33. *R v Bennett* (1866) 4 F & F 1105; *R v Sinclair* (1867) 13 Cox CC 28. In 1866, in *Bennett*, a syphilitic uncle had been convicted of assault on the basis of "consensual" sexual intercourse with his niece. The following year, in *Sinclair*, a man affected with gonorrhea had been similarly convicted after sexual congress with a "consenting" female of twelve. Ibid., 287.
34. *R v Clarence* (1888) at 25, per Fulton.
35. Ibid., at 51, per Hawkins J.
36. Scutt, "Consent in Rape," 260; *R v R* [1991], 4 All ER, at 485, per Lord Keith.
37. *R v Clarence* (1888) at 34, per Wills J.
38. Ibid., at 54, per Hawkins J. Original emphasis. Freeman, "Martial Rape Exemption," 11, urges that Hawkins's judgment "was thoroughly confused, contains gross

inconsistencies, and is best ignored." Unfortunately the similarly confused majority sentiments have yet to be ignored.

39. Geis, "Rape in Marriage," 288.
40. *R v Clarence* (1888) at 44, per Stephen J.
41. Ibid., at 34, per Wills J.
42. Ibid., at 28, per Wills J.
43. Ibid.
44. Ibid. at 32, per Wills J.
45. Geis, *Rape in Marriage,* 287.
46. *R v Clarence* (1888) at 44, per Stephen J.
47. Ibid.
48. *R v Linekar* [1995] at 68.
49. *R v Clarence* (1888) at 44, per Stephen J.
50. *R v Clarence* (1888) at 32, per Wills J. Emphasis added.
51. Ibid. at 34–35, per Wills J.
52. Ormerod and Gunn, "Criminal Liability," 16, argue "this is an irrelevant argument if there is an offence covering the activity in question. If the activity is criminal . . . there is nothing necessarily wrong in there being hundreds of convictions."
53. *R v Clarence* (1888) at 34–35, per Wills J. The lack of medical interest in this aspect of the moral dimension of sex stands in interesting contrast to that explored in Crozier's chapter in this volume.
54. Ibid.
55. *R v Dica* (2004) *EWCA* Crim 1103.

14

"Crimes of Moral Outrage": Victorian Encryptions of Sexual Violence

KIM STEVENSON

Introduction

Sexual attacks perpetrated on women in public places, particularly rape and indecent assault, were regularly reported in the Victorian press, often accompanied with dramatic headlines such as "Moral Outrage," "Shocking Outrage," or "Abominable Case." At first glance, and at least to modern eyes, it is not clear whether such representations were intended as "public service messages" designed to attract the public's attention and warn of the dangers and incidence of such attacks, or as sensationalist attention-grabbing headlines feeding the public thirst for real life crime stories. However, on closer examination it is evident that these reports conveyed more complex messages and the issue of *whose* interests were being served is not always apparent. The language and rhetoric used in these reports and more generally in the public, and especially legal, presentation and representation of female sexual violence was often ambiguous and desexualized. Social codes and metaphors avoiding the use of graphic and sexually explicit detail were deployed at all levels and inexorably encroached into the legal discourse.

    The utilization of such anodyne and neutralized language gave the appearance of respectability and sexual purity, but at the same time it underlined and reinforced the prevailing sexual hypocrisy and masculine values. This chapter explores the sexualized, or rather, it is argued, desexualized, nature of the public discourse surrounding the crime of rape and sexual violence in the mid-Victorian period. Newspaper commentary and press reports of court cases of sexual assault are used to demonstrate the type of "conversations" that were taking place both within the legal discourse and more widely in the public domain. Generally, feminine participation in these public conversations was somewhat muted, but in individual cases the voices of women victims who had been attacked could sometimes make themselves be heard in other ways. Conduct and behavior were often just as powerful a communicator as oral expression and where, for example, women demonstrated absolute conformity to society's stereotypical expectations then such communications could not be ignored. However, if women expressed themselves in ways that suggested nonconformity or independence, then this could be perceived as a threat by certain masculine elements signaling the likelihood of false allegations and potential risks to male repute. The amorphous nature of the law relating to rape, ambiguity of language employed and confused sexual diaspora therefore created a climate in which, from time to time, it is argued, apparent moral (or rather sexual) panics about the dangers of female sexuality were able to thrive.

Desexualizing the Discourse

Both official and popular representations and reports of sexual assault and violence published in the mid-Victorian period appear to be somewhat ambiguous and cryptic. The anodyne language used, particularly in newspaper reports of trials of rape and indecent assault, serves to disguise the precise nature of the assault committed, making it difficult for today's researchers to recover and interpret the factuality of events. The Victorians, in both written and oral expression, employed a coded language for describing sexual acts and sexually explicit detail. Such discourse was often asexual, cryptic, and nebulous, avoiding graphic terms and etymology. However, it is evident that whosoever the recipient audience, such linguistics were clearly understood and decoded at the time. The use of double-entendres, contradictions, and metaphors formed the basis of this ambiguous sexual language, presenting a number of issues and difficulties in relation to any modern examination of the prosecution, presentation, and reception of cases involving sexual violence, as well as raising issues about the discourse used today. The cultural context within which this linguistic coding evolved is therefore of considerable significance, especially since work on pre-Victorian cases reveals a much greater explicitness of expression.[1]

As the respectability imperative permeated throughout Victorian society, the subject of sex, and any explicit expression of sexual matters, submerged into the public ether.[2] Today, the English language formally identifies some 1,232 words for sexual intercourse, 997 words for penis, and 856 for vagina.[3] Many of these expressions existed by the eighteenth century, forming part of the everyday discourse, but came to be regarded as unacceptable (or *unrespectable*) language by the Victorians. Though such terms have survived, most are largely forgotten. Where used, these words are often regarded as slang, or as inappropriate language, thus demonstrating the enduring effects of Victorian social norms. Apparently much more robust in our attitudes and language today, there remains a coyness surrounding the way in which explicit sexual language is used by those in established positions, especially within the formal confines of the legal world. Up to the 1950s, even in the popular press, the word "rape" was relatively rarely used in newspaper reports.[4] And the Victorian age was very conscious of what it identified as the negative effects of language, particularly where women and children were concerned. "Inappropriate" language in some of the great literary texts had already been expurgated in the 1820s and 1830s making them more suitable for such "vulnerable" audiences.[5] As Walkowitz has commented, the result of such attitudes on daily life included the desexualization of intimate words and descriptors, a constant element in Victorian respectable discourse: "Where Victorians talked sex, they mostly focused on sexual danger, or the proliferation of sexual practises outside the sanctity of the home, disengaged from the procreation act."[6]

This raises the question of how far there was an overlap between written and spoken language. Arguably, the change came first in written texts, which over succeeding generations, had a profound effect on Victorian speech patterns, reflecting back, in turn, on Victorian textual products.[7] Within this dynamic, the public representation of crime and violence played an important role. Its absorption into the legal arena is not surprising. In an age of sensitivity to the effects on vulnerable elements of the public of unrestrained language, the reality that more and more information was available to this increasingly literate population through national and local publications was worrying to many.[8] Concern was expressed about the "mischief to the young of both sexes caused by cheap periodicals" as such literature was thought to inspire youths to commit criminal acts.[9]

In the area of sexual violence, euphemistic metaphors were commonly adopted and interposed into the public lexicon to *express linguistically without actually stating* the reality of occurrences such as the act of penetration and intercourse. Even where sexual issues were respectably encountered in the public domain, there was an interest in glossing this over. Thus even lawful, that is, "normal"/heterosexual intercourse was referred to as "the act," "connection, or "carnal knowledge," reflecting Old Testament influences on the evangelical inspiration that influenced many publishers and newspaper proprietors and editors at the time. Male dominance, operating through masculine language, was also apparent. The penis was the "male member" or the "person," the coded language emphasizing the sexualized nature of popular understandings of what constituted manhood or masculinity.[10] But metaphors for the female sexual equivalent, the "female person," were less specific, less powerful, and often not invoked at all. In the legal discourse "male person" was intentionally used to designate expressly the male sex, whereas "man" could on occasion be interpreted to include women.[11]

The Legal Lexicon

Naturally and inevitably the desexualization of the public discourse fed into the legal discourse. In the popular and legal lexicon, sexual offenses were not separately categorized as "sex crimes" or segregated from other physical assaults, so sexual descriptors and definitions were arguably of less importance. Sex offenses might be included under general statistical returns as "offences against the person," "crimes of violence" or "crimes of morals."[12] This emasculation of language is evident both in terms of the substantive law itself and in the practical operation of the law in the courtroom and trial process. With respect to the former one need look no further than the Offences Against the Person Act 1861, which, despite its intention to consolidate the law relating to offenses that caused physical harm, is heavily biased toward the protection of the male rather than female person. The omission in the Act, and failure through the Parliamentary debates, expressly to define the crime of rape underlines public ignorance of the importance of female sexuality.[13] No statutory definition for rape was articulated in the 1861 Act, section 48 simply provides that it is a felony for a man to rape a woman on penalty of life imprisonment. It was left to the judges to develop the common law principles as regards what could vitiate consent. As a result criminal process for dealing with sexual crimes became confused and arbitrary. Newspaper reports of sex crimes confirm that actual rape might be charged as either "attempted rape," "unlawful carnal knowledge," "assault with intent to commit a felony" or even more problematically indecent assault. To add further complexity, indecent assault might also be charged as "attempted rape," "felonious assault," "gross indecency," or "criminal assault," especially where the victim was a young girl. Yet "felonious assault" was also used where nonconsensual penetration had occurred, that is, rape or attempted rape. Many police court assault cases of physical harm turn out, on closer examination, to be failed charges of sexual assault with the lesser conviction for common assault, or the slightly more serious aggravated assault, being substituted. A reference in *The Justice's Notebook* confirms that this practice continued throughout the period. In a case "suspiciously like an attempted rape" but with less than overwhelming evidence, justices took the safer option and the defendant was convicted of aggravated assault. He then appealed on the grounds that they had erred in fact and should have charged him with rape (of which he would probably have been acquitted). The Divisional Court of the Exchequer held that the justices had acted correctly as there was substantive evidence to support a charge of aggravated assault.[14] Many complainants, including servants and those without family, were unable (financially and practically) even to instigate proceedings for rape without the support of employer or benevolent institution such as the Association for the Protection of Women and Children, making the police court an accessible alternative.

A further twist in the desexualization of the legal discourse in terms of both law and procedure arrived with the advent of the railways. New opportunities presented themselves to those predisposed toward sexual predation and violation, and (especially during the 1860s) a number of sexual assaults on women in railway carriages occurred. Often these were not prosecuted by the female victim but by the railway company concerned, under byelaws concerning the "comfort and non-interference of passengers" which could encompass anything from rape to the theft of a purse, again neutralizing both the severity and sexuality of such attacks. This meant that no custodial sentence was possible: perpetrators would be merely subjected to a fine for breaking company bylaws, regardless of the seriousness of any attack involved. While such penalties failed to reflect the seriousness of the assault, newspaper headlines regularly described such attacks with vigor, indicating the serious nature of the transgression, and precipitating thereby public moral concern.

Typical newspaper bylines, such as "Abominable Outrage in a Railway Carriage," appeared regularly. The *News of the World*, for example, reported the assault by Robert Agar on two respectable ladies, Mrs. Blackburn and Miss Robinson, traveling one evening in separate (unlit) carriages on the North Eastern Railway. Mrs. Blackburn told a magisterial investigation at the East Riding sessions that he "expressed his intention and conducted himself in a most brutal manner, hurting her so much she was ill for a week," thus indicating at least the likelihood of penetration. Another passenger managed to lock Agar out of their carriage but he entered another compartment and attacked Miss Robinson, using "the most disgusting language." Both were so traumatized that they refused to reenter the train while Agar was still aboard, as given the lack of light in the carriage, other passengers had difficulty in restraining him. Despite the seriousness of the incidents, Agar was prosecuted only by the railway company for breach of its bylaws concerning the interference with other passengers. The magistrates declared the case to be one of the most brutal they had heard, expressing concern at their inability to impose a higher fine than allowed under the bylaw: 40 shillings and £3.18 costs. What remained an unspoken part of the debate in such cases was recognition that while theoretically the women could have initiated their own criminal proceedings for indecent assault or even rape, this could have placed them in a vulnerable position as regards their reputations, especially if a defendant was ultimately acquitted through the use of clever defense tactics to destroy the credibility of their evidence (here the darkened nature of the carriage was an obvious factor). Agar offered no defense, merely stating he felt "rather fresh." The *News of the World* recorded that he left the court laughing.[15]

Seduction or Violation?

The utilization of sanitized language purportedly protected feminine morals in an age where the dominant ideologies attributed moral status to the idealized and sexually chaste woman cocooned and denied it to her symbolic opposite, the "fallen woman," too readily exposed in her actions and person to the public gaze. But equally such language worked to deny active female sexuality, promoting female passivity and asexuality. Further, it reinforced masculine attitudes and myths, blurring the distinction between seduction and violation, and between violation and violence. A good example is the ambiguity of the verb "to ravish." In literature it was a positive descriptor, if used adjectivally of a woman: a "ravishing creature." In court reports it described an act (or attempted act) of sexual violation, as in the case of Matilda Atlee, indecently assaulted by three young men in fields near Hounslow.

The Times reported she was seized by the youths "with intent to ravish." The use of the word "*intent*" indicates that the evidence was that the defendants had rape in mind, but that this did not necessarily support the actual *fact* of the crime being fully committed. It also suggests that Matilda herself, apparently virginal and true to stereotypical expectation, did not know the difference between rape and attempted rape and probably thought that any assault short of penetration was in fact the full act. This case highlights the difficulties facing the courts in their determination of exactly what offense had been committed. With no direct evidence or clear testimony the judge advised the jury to find the defendants guilty of common assault and sentenced them to twelve months imprisonment each, indicating at least an implicit acknowledgment that something more serious than a common assault had taken place.[16]

Another example of the confusion that such cases caused to judge and jury alike was reported in detail in the *News of the World*.[17] Stephen Rudland, twenty-one years, was indicted at Chelmsford Assizes for burglary and "feloniously ravishing" the woman of the house, Jane Marrott. He "made his appearance in the bedroom . . . and at once threw her down and effected his object." A broken window confirmed forcible entry into the building, but the allegation of forced entry into the person of the complainant was less certain. For one thing, they had met before, when Rudland had taken "liberties," albeit in the presence of the widow's son, aged nine (though as the learned judge concluded, "they must have been very quiet about it" as he was not awakened!). Jane Marrott immediately reported the burglary, but not the violation, to a policeman, who confirmed her distress and the broken window. The doctor "found her in her usual health," with no serious physical injury, and Jane also failed to mention the violation to him. She had not made any noises during the alleged violation or done anything else to raise the alarm. As *The News of the World* opined, "A woman surely ought to struggle against being ravished; and if a woman and a man really were struggling, surely there would have been marks of violence." The court's sympathies clearly lay with the victim, however, perhaps because she was a widow and because Rudland had clearly been an intruder. The jury found him guilty but recommended mercy.

Justice Crompton, unhappy with this verdict, asked, "Why do you recommend mercy if you think he forced her? Is it that you have any doubt?" The foreman's response that there should "have been more resistance" indicates the impossible position of many women, confirming the stereotype that "genuine" victims must bear marks of fighting back. But this case is genuinely ambiguous, now as then. Perhaps it was a case of sexual violation without consent, but it could also have been that, lonely and flattered by a younger man's attention, Jane allowed herself to be compromised. Rudland may have been a brutish rapist, or a young risk taker who misread and misunderstood the signals on a previous encounter and foolishly took advantage. The judge in recognition of the jury's dilemma sentenced him to the lightest possible penalty: five years imprisonment.

Thus the ambiguity of the phraseology, and any distinction between seduction and violation, was often neither clearly articulated nor apparent, being clouded by underlying social codes and behavioral expectations which silenced not only those personally affected but the wider public discourse. And the *Modern Oxford Dictionary* still cites two conflicting alternatives for the meaning of "ravish," the romanticized "to enrapture, charm, entrance, or fill with delight," and more brutally, "to carry off by force, rape or violate." The distinction between seduction and violation has remained blurred, underlining how dominant Victorian social attitudes concerning appearance, respectability, conduct, and behavior could generate linguistic descriptors embodying specific connotations, labeling women for legal consumption and the reporting of court proceedings in a stereotypical gendered way as wanton, licentious, depraved, or corrupt, silencing them almost completely.

At an everyday level, then, women (and indeed men) became increasingly ignorant, and no doubt confused about the language of sex and sexuality. Ambiguity and anodyne language removed the necessary tools of available communication and expression to describe sexual acts. If women were not expected to experience sexual passion or sexual danger then neither were they expected to be able to articulate it. For women subjected to violence, this discretion of language could shroud the realities of the actual violence perpetrated, thereby limiting public offense, a necessity given the high profile taken by court cases in local and national publications. It also limited or removed women's capacity to comprehend, let alone articulate, accurate descriptions of the sexual acts perpetrated against them. Plainly many "seduced" girls had no idea of the unlawful nature of the act often forced upon them, or in fact what was actually happening at all. As Clark suggests, what society referred to as seduction might often have been forcible sex but the victim knew of no language to define it as such.[18] The difficulties this raised for victims is illustrated in the case of William Bailey, reported in the *News of the World*, accused of attempted rape at Gloucester Assizes.[19] Emma Reeves, his servant, plainly believed the magistrates would understand what lay behind her statement that Bailey had "pulled her about in an indecent and brutish manner": nonconsensual sexual violation. The magistrates, however, did not seem to (or want to seem to?) comprehend the significance of her testimony, as they ordered both parties to settle the matter informally rather than hear the case, suggesting that they believed Bailey's actions were less in fact than Emma alleged. Emma, now in an untenable situation, having made a serious allegation against her master, asked to be released from his employ but Bailey threatened that he would send a policeman after her if she left. Devastated, she attempted suicide. Bailey subsequently offered her half a sovereign and a new dress if she retracted her complaint. She refused, finally forcing the magistrates to hear the case. Bailey was sent for trial at the assizes on a lesser charge than that originally alleged: the newspaper reporter confirmed he was committed *only* for assault *with intent* to commit rape. He was eventually convicted of attempted rape and sentenced to eighteen months' hard labor. If convicted of the full offense, he would probably have received six years plus penal servitude.

Were a woman to seek to depict her complaint graphically, especially in the context of a prosecution and so subject to public scrutiny, her very willingness to use graphic language would stamp her as immodest, probably untruthful, and tell against her case with judge and jury. As Conley found, women who brought rape charges were themselves suspect because they were female, had been at least temporarily outside the supervision of their male guardian, and were publicly announcing their loss of sexual innocence.[20] The *News of the*

World reporting illustrates the point: Mrs. Merrick, rapidly dying of consumption, accused her former physician of indecent assault and rape after he allegedly drugged her with chloroform. The newspaper gloated over the unusually full descriptions of how helpless she felt after what she claimed was the administration of a drug and how the defendant kissed her and forced himself upon her. But it rejoiced even more in the jury's refusal to convict, endorsing the defense's claim that her accusations were the result of a mixture of fevered illness causing a diseased mind, combined with an equally unhealthy, and unfeminine, downright lie.[21]

There were also difficulties in distinguishing between acquiescence and consent. After all, the courtroom and its participants were overwhelmingly male. These difficulties were amplified by the nature of the legal discourse and trial practice, which objectified women, downplaying their individuality and sexual identity. The *Pall Mall Gazette* cautioned that female complainants were becoming such "a common phenomena in our law courts" that they could seriously affect the public's interest: "it will be observed that there is a peculiar tortuousness and intricacy about female cases, arising either from a hopeless confusion of facts, or from an absence of facts."[22] Women could not be relied upon to present their case plainly and objectively. Faced with this pressure, testimonies were littered with anodyne euphemisms encrypting the precise nature of the assaults committed. Offenders were alleged to have taken "indecent liberties," to have committed an "outrage," to have "effected their purpose," or to have "violated the person." The women who made these allegations claimed to have suffered "ill-health," were in a "distressed" state, or their "person was bruised." Such euphemistic language rarely presented a clear statement of the facts, enabling a sound conviction. As the cases cited underline, women were unable linguistically to express themselves through lack of knowledge and lack of vocabulary. Consequently, cases often turned on medical opinion, in itself rarely determinate as the medical discourse was as much confused as the legal one, as Ivan Crozier discusses. Thus it was often left to judge and jury to interpret and amplify the intended meaning of such vague statements and testimonies, forcing them to second-guess or augment oral evidence with other signifiers, including the appearance and demeanor of those involved, and character witnesses. Testimonies might be misconstrued, their content minimized by defense counsel, the magistrates, or judge, suggesting to jurymen or spectators another possible explanatory factor for public indifference and equivocation. But, as D'Cruze confirms, "The social practices which could secure a woman's reputation with her neighbours did not necessarily do so with a circuit judge at the assizes or a man she encountered while crossing a lonely patch of ground on her way home from work."[23]

Theoretically, provided a woman did not step beyond society's defined boundaries of behavior, she could rely on the reciprocal protection of the law. As Stephen affirmed in relation to the legal status of women, "submission and protection are correlative . . . withdraw the one and the other is lost and force will assert itself a hundred times more harshly through the law of contract than ever it did through the law of status."[24] So if a female complainant crossed that boundary by jeopardizing her respectability—by speaking frankly or demonstrating her sexuality—then she was more likely to be ostracized by the prevailing social forces than by any legal rules. But this correlation was less mutual than Stephen supposed. Experience demonstrated women could *not* always rely on the singular protection of the law. The experiences of victims like Emma Reeves suggest that legal professionals could not comprehend and so could not accept, that the practical pressures imposed by societal concepts of respectability and the desexualization of the sexual discourse, made such an interpretation of gender relations and law deeply unfair in practice.

A Shameful and Shocking Outrage? Press Encryptions

However, not all the blame for the difficulties experienced by violated women can be laid on the legal discourse, even though it is the traditional scapegoat. There was practical collusion between the law and the public reporting of legal events in the press.[25] Newspapers regularly reported cases providing representations of sexual violence and the associated behavior not just of the protagonists, but also of other members of the cast, including the jury. The language was increasingly sanitized, especially in the "respectable" national press, though toward the end of the century, a more robust, even "sensationalist," coverage could be found in some provincial papers, especially northern ones. The Sunday newspapers, targeting a working-class readership with a more radical political edge, were also likely to be more robust in reporting the details of certain types of case, such as breach of promise cases where a degree of comic innuendo was commonplace. But even here, both provincial and Sunday papers became affected by a spirit of self-censorship in cases of sexual violence, making it plain this was in the interests of public decency, and so contributing to the social education of potential jurymen.

Certainly, in making judgments in these cases, much depended on the expectations of magistrates and juries of the "good" behavior of the protagonists. Thus the role played by the language of newspaper reportage in establishing such expectations should not be downplayed. Respectable society increasingly depended on printed texts to educate and inform it about good behavior in various situations, and newspapers provided regular and detailed commentary on what constituted this. An apparent increase in the allegations of sexual offenses prompted *The Spectator* to advise that:

> The great number of unfound charges of indecent assault seems to have produced something like a panic, and the magistrates are displaying extra caution in their investigations. They are hampered by two difficulties, the lack of direct evidence usual in such cases, and the freedom of manners still existing among certain classes. It is of course, impossible to refuse convictions on the evidence of the prosecutrix alone, yet to accept that as sufficient places every man at the mercy of every woman who happens to be five minutes alone with him. The temptation to turn mere broad joke into a criminal charge needs to be very carefully watched. For a man to put his arms around a woman's waist without her consent may be an assault, even an indelicate assault, but it is not exactly what the law means to be the technical phrase. The social penalty in such cases so enormously aggravates the penalty fixed by law that there is a risk, a crime becomes common because its punishment is too severe for the common instinct of ordinary man.[26]

The unique difficulties in prosecuting sex crimes where there are often no other witnesses present or independent corroborating evidence available is acknowledged. But the caution expressed in this extract also demonstrates a lack of understanding about the nature of such offenses and the potentially impossible position in which women attacked found themselves. If newspaper reportage and crime statistics both sustained contemporary belief in an increase in sexual assaults, this spoke to "mounting public and police concern about these offences."[27] But contemporary perceptions were that a major factor in such increase must be the greater freedom of movement and independence enjoyed by the women and the opportunities this presented for sexual offenders.

As examples from newspapers show, the increasingly ambiguous and coded nature of the language used to give the details of cases involving sexual violence did not avoid making implicit judgments on the correct behavior of the various participants, comment being made generally in terms of their respectability or disrespectability through the rhetoric of outrage or concern. For instance, why did only certain incidents attract descriptors such as "shocking or shameful outrage," "moral outrage" or "abominable crime"? What, if any, was the contemporary distinction between these categories? It would appear that such labeling had less to do with the severity of the actual crime perpetrated and much with the respective social positions of the parties involved. Consider two cases reported in *The News of the World* in 1861. An attack on Mary Strother, "a very respectable looking woman," involving three men, was described by the paper as a "Shameful Outrage."[28] Pulled to the ground with "great violence," Mary struggled violently while Joseph Waller, twenty-seven, "tore away from her person her crinoline and petticoat, and in other ways most grossly and infamously assaulted her." Mary, left with only her chemise, was still suffering from the violence, the court was told. While Waller's offense was not specifically outlined in the press, these facts suggest the probability of at least attempted rape, but though convicted, the sentence was only twelve months' hard labor, suggesting the charge was for the lesser offense of indecent assault. So what aspect of the assault made it a "Shameful Outrage"? That her reputation was of a respectable woman while he was only a carman? That he had two accomplices? Or the linguistic ambiguity over the question of penetration?

In July, the paper reported a "Shocking Outrage on a Young Woman."[29] James Smith, twenty-five, described as a gypsy, was convicted at Hertford Assizes for "feloniously assaulting" Anne Hearn, also a respectable young woman. She too was thrown to the ground, resisted with all her might as "a desperate struggle took place during which her clothes were literally torn from her back," leaving her with only her chemise. The prisoner successfully forced her to the ground "and accomplishing his object," suggesting full penetration. Anne tried to escape, but her attacker's two accomplices dragged her back and the prisoner "repeated the offence." She eventually ran free, informed her father of the "outrage," and Smith was later arrested. He apparently believed his actions did not amount to rape, intimating to the arresting constable that he expected a twelve-months' sentence and would consider himself lucky if he "got off" with three. However, Mr. Justice Blackburn described it as "one of the most atrocious outrages that he ever remembered" and, sentencing him to fifteen years penal servitude, reportedly debated making the sentence more.[30] As far as the newspaper representation was concerned, was this case "shocking" because it was clearly rape, because accomplices were involved, or because Smith was a gypsy? Or was it more "shocking" than "shameful" because it was more obviously a repeated rape?

While it is very difficult to draw any clear conclusions, it is suggested that these linguistic descriptors tend to relate more to the relational status of the parties than the severity of the offense committed as another case illustrates, that of an "Outrage on a Lady's Maid," on the Midland Railway.[31] The complainant, "a good-looking young lady," was alone in a third-class compartment when Hiram Smith entered the carriage. As the train moved off he seized her and demanded her purse. She tried to attract attention by waving her handkerchief out the window, but Smith put his hand over her mouth to silence her. At the next station she managed to inform the stationmaster, who apprehended the prisoner. She "was nearly exhausted, and there were marks on the side of her face as if a hand had been placed there" but no suggestion in the report of any sexual interference. Smith was sentenced to six months' hard labor as he had a previous conviction for theft, but the actual crime was not specified in the report, again suggesting that the descriptor "outrage" is less sexualized than might be expected and implying violations of social status and vulnerability instead.[32]

Where briefer reports are concerned, it is particularly problematic to compare cases and understand what lay behind the convictions and sentencing rationales used, as three further examples published in sequence on the same page of *The Leeds Express* illustrate.[33] The paper briefly noted the trials of three young men at the Leeds Summer Assizes, all charged with criminal assault suggesting carnal knowledge of girls under fourteen. Patrick Jennings, twenty-five, a laborer, was sentenced to eighteen months for criminal assault upon Maria Ward, twelve. Miner Matthias Hunt, twenty-three, was sentenced to twelve months' imprisonment for criminal assault on Mary Jane Goldthorpe. Her age was not given but his conviction was for the lesser offense of attempting the assault. William Needham, twenty-three, a collier, was indicted for criminal assault upon Elizabeth Beevers. Needham was found guilty and sentenced to seven years' penal servitude, indicating the probability that Needham was actually found guilty by the jury, and punished by the judge, for rape even though that term was not used in the reportage. Thus the use of press reports to recover the actuality of cases of sexual violence requires careful interpretation, because at first glance the true nature of the crime reported is not always apparent. A range of contextual issues, particularly in relation to Victorian gendered expectations, must be taken into account when attempting to "read" and comprehend the "truth" behind such reports.[34]

Conclusion

It is clear that the Victorians embraced and developed their own coded desexualized discourse and vocabulary to deal with a range of issues relating to sexual violence and assault and applied it to both the official and popular dialogue. The language used in the public, that is, masculine, domain was encrypted and ambiguous; while within the private domain, at least where engaged in "unrespectable behavior" (seeking sexual favors from prostitutes) it was no doubt more explicit. The Victorians' desire to preserve innocence and reinforce female morality produced a complex and contradictory discourse full of linguistic reticence and innuendo. The endemic use of such encrypted language in the legal process meant that only those "in the know" (men) could interpret this "alien" language. Women, especially those alleging sexual violations, were expected to portray their innocence not only through their conduct but through their courtroom testimonies. Denied both the knowledge of sex and the language to articulate it, they were disengaged from the trial process and must have found it immeasurably frustrating, if not impossible, to communicate with, and testify in front of, their masculine audience. But despite the silences and neutralized discourse many cases were ultimately successful and both judges and jurors alike must have had to demonstrate a degree of effort and sensitivity to interpret and apply the social codes and nuances of the day to the cases presented before them if justice was not only to be done, but seen to be done.

Notes

1. Anna Clark, *Women's Silence, Men's Violence: Sexual Assault in England, 1770–1845* (London: Pandora, 1987), chap. 3.

2. Kim Stevenson, "The Respectability Imperative: A Golden Rule in Cases of Sexual Assault?" in *The Golden Age: Essays in British Social and Economic History, 1850–1870,* ed. Ian Inkster et al., 237–48 (Aldershot: Ashgate, 2000).

3. J. Green, ed., *The Cassell Dictionary of Slang* (London: Cassell, 1998).

4. Keith Soothill et al., "Judges, the Media, and Rape," *Journal of Law and Society* 17 (1990): 211–33, at 229.

5. The concept of "Bowdlerization" originated from Dr. Bowdler's sanitization of "great" literature. In his Family Edition of Shakespeare's works (1818), Bowdler eliminated explicit words "to protect the purity of British womanhood from indecent language." The Victorians themselves expurgated many more texts on similar lines. N. Perrin, *Dr. Bowdler's Legacy* (London: Nonpareil Books, 1992).

6. Judith Walkowitz, "Dangerous Sexualities," in *A History of Women in the West,* ed. Geneviève Fraisse and Michelle Perrot (Cambridge, MA: Harvard University Press, 1993), 4: 370.

7. Dickens provided glossaries for readers to interpret the "criminal cant" of Bill Sikes since respectable readers of his novel *Oliver Twist* (1839) would not understand the language of the criminal underworld!

8. Unwholesome publications, including Chartist newspapers, were blamed by many for pre-Victorian disorder and diaffection. Violence, pure and simple, was still depicted in some graphic detail, but usually with some moral aspect attached. See Judith Rowbotham, "All Our Past Proclaims Our Future," in *The Golden Age,* ed. Ian Inkster et al., 225–36; Judith Rowbotham, "'Only When Drunk': The Stereotyping of Violence in Britain, 1850–1900," in *Everyday Violence in Britain, c. 1850–1950: Gender and Class,* ed. Shani D'Cruze, 155–69 (Harlow: Longman, 2000).

9. *The Times,* 5 January 1870; G. Sutter, "Penny Dreadfuls and Perverse Domains: Victorian and Modern Moral Panics," in *Behaving Badly: Visible Crime, Social Panics, and Legal Responses—Victorian and Modern Parallels,* ed. J. Rowbotham and K. Stevenson, 159–76 (Aldershot: Ashgate, 2003).

10. Unsurprisingly, the Court of Criminal Pleas was not prepared to hold as a general principle that "man" extended to include "woman." See *Chorlton v Lings* (1868–69) LR 4 CP 374 per Bovill, CJ., at 387.

11. See Kim Stevenson, "Observations on the Law Relating to Sexual Offences: The Historic Scandal of Women's Silence," *Web Journal Current Legal Issues* 4 (1999).

12. See J. Holt Schooling, "Crime," *Pall Mall Magazine,* vol. 2, 1898.

13. Kim Stevenson, "Observations on the Law Relating to Sexual Offences"; and "Unequivocal Victims: The Historical Mystification of the Female Complainant in Rape Cases," *Feminist Legal Studies* 8 (2000): 343–66.

14. W. Know Wigram, *The Justice's Notebook Containing the Jurisdiction and Duties of Justices and an Epitome of Criminal Law* (London: Stevens, 1892), 106.

15. *News of the World,* 12 November 1865.

16. *The Times,* 24 October 1850.

17. *News of the World,* 23 July 1861.

18. Clarke, *Women's Silence,* 8.

19. *News of the World,* 18 August 1861.

20. Carolyn A. Conley, *The Unwritten Law, Criminal Justice in Victorian Kent* (Oxford: Oxford University Press, 1991), 93–95.

21. *News of the World,* 12 November 1865.

22. *Pall Mall Gazette,* 7 February 1865.

23. Shani D'Cruze, *Crimes of Outrage, Sex, Violence, and Victorian Working Women* (London: UCL Press, 1998), 62.

24. James Fitzjames Stephen, *Liberty, Equality, Fraternity* (1873), ed. R. J. White (Cambridge: Cambridge University Press, 1967), 209. Also see Millicent Garrett Fawcett, *Mr. Fitzjames Stephen on the Position of Women* (London: Macmillan, 1873), 11.

25. Judith Rowbotham and Kim Stevenson, "Causing a Sensation: Media and Legal Representations of Bad Behaviour," in *Behaving Badly,* ed. Rowbotham and Stevenson, 31–46.

26. *The Spectator,* 22 October 1864.

27. V. A. C. Gatrell et al., eds., *Crime and the Law: The Social History of Crime in Western Europe since 1500* (London: Europa, 1980), 289.

28. *News of the World,* 26 March 1861.

29. *News of the World,* 21 July 1861; *The Times,* 15 July 1861.

30. *The Times,* 15 July 1861.

31. *The Leeds Express,* 19 September 1878.

32. Ibid.

33. Ibid.

34. Ibid.

15

"Kicked, Beaten, Jumped On until They Are Crushed," All under Man's Wing and Protection: The Victorian Dilemma with Domestic Violence

SUSAN EDWARDS

Introduction

Nineteenth-century men extolled themselves as the protectors of women, reflecting Blackstone's presumption of male protectiveness in his much-quoted words:

> By marriage, the husband and wife are one person in the law; that is, the very being or legal existence of the woman is suspended during the marriage, or at least incorporated and consolidated into that of the husband. . . . Even the disabilities which the wife lies under are for the most part intended for her protection and benefit. So great a favourite of the female sex are the laws of England.[1]

The popularist conversation encapsulated in this was challenged, interrogated, and contested by an equally compelling "conversation" about women's protection under the law.[2] Matilda Blake chose a somewhat excoriatingly satirical title *The Lady and the Law* in her 1892 contribution to this ongoing "conversation" in which she showed that under common law, women were denied rights to property, custody of their children, and protection from male domestic violence:

> the sentences given for violent assaults by husbands on their wives at police and sessional courts are evidently guided by such a theory of the marriage relationship. Cases might be quoted by scores in which the killing of wives is brought as manslaughter, and punished by a few years' (or even months') imprisonment.[3]

Lord Chief Justice Coleridge commented:

> I can scarcely believe that if the House of Commons was as much aware as every lawyer is aware of the state of the law of England as regards women, even still, after the very recent humane improvements in it, it would hesitate to say it was more worthy of a barbarian than of a civilised State.[4]

Or, as Fitzjames Stephen remarked, "common instances of brutality seldom find their way into the papers" because they were seen as part of a daily normality.[5]

Blake devoted a further article specifically to the treatment of victims of domestic violence by men and by the courts:

> Their so-called protectors daily beat, torture and violently assault them, often with such violence that death results; while the male judges, appointed by a Government chosen by an exclusively male electorate, punish the offenders in a most inadequate manner, holding a woman's life at a lesser value than a purse containing a few shillings.[6]

This alternative "criminal conversation" challenged the portrayal of women as "protected by the law," exposing this version as masculinist hegemony inherent in the common law wherein the male point of view was taken as objective.[7] This chapter explores the reality behind the hypocrisy underpinning debates based on assumptions of male protectiveness, examining the treatment of violence against women in the substantive law, issues around the trial process itself, and media reporting of such matters. There are powerful modern echoes: the most pressing issue with regard to contemporary legal treatment of violence against women remains the fact that so few perpetrators are formally prosecuted.[8] The same was also an urgent concern for Victorian jurisprudence.[9]

Women under the Rod of the Common Law

The first major obstacle to Victorian women's protection was long-standing enshrinement of male violence. Common law effectively allowed women to be beaten at men's will, if it could be shown that the assault was committed in the name of moderate chastisement, as the old authority's stated *moderate castigone*. If her behavior was considered deserving of masculine resentment, then violent conduct was regarded as justifiable, because the common law provided that a husband could subject his wife to physical punishment or "chastisement" so long as he did not inflict permanent injury. That legacy ensured that women lived *sub virga*, under the rod. By the Victorian period, debates on the topic had a long pedigree, with comment from earlier periods being still regularly invoked.[10]

Whately argued that beating a wife was only justified where she was of "unwifelike carriage":

> But for blows . . . nothing should drive a husband to them, except the utmost extremities of unwifelike carriage, unless she be peremptory and wilful in cursing, swearing, drunkenness etc . . . unless she outface him with bold maintaining, that she will do as she doth, in despite of him, unless she begin the quarrel and strike or offer to strike.[11]

Nicolas Brady stated that "A man may beat an outlaw, a traitor, a pagan his villain or his wife because by the Law Common, these persons can have no action."[12] Essentially, "unwifelike carriage," the common law justification for violence, provided the dominant justificatory rationale where so long as "correction was confined within reasonable bounds," the "law thought it reasonable to intrust him with this power" because a man was legally bound to "answer for her misbehaviour."[13] Nineteenth-century interpretations proclaimed that "A man can beat a wife with a whip or a stick but he cannot knock her down with a cudgel or an iron bar."[14] Often referred to as "the rule of thumb," subsequent debates have raged over whether in fact it ever existed in law.[15] However, it was certainly the case in practice in England, and cannot be dismissed as a fiction.

Male Violence against Women in the Nineteenth Century

Cobbe famously detailed the problem of domestic violence:

> Wife-beating exists in the upper and middle classes rather more, I fear, than is generally recognised; but it rarely extends to anything beyond an occasional blow or two of a not dangerous kind. In his apparently most ungovernable rage, the gentleman or tradesman somehow manages to bear in mind the disgrace he will incur if his outbreak be betrayed by his wife's black eye. . . . The dangerous wife-beater belongs almost exclusively to the artisan and labouring classes. . . . In the worst districts of London as I have been informed by one of the most experienced magistrates, four-fifths of the wife-beating cases are among the lowest class of Irish labourers a fact worthy of

more than passing notice ... seeing that in their own country Irishmen of all classes are proverbially kind and even chivalrous towards women.[16]

Victorian women inherited not only a tradition of male brutality but also the legacy of the violence of the common law which sanctioned commission of that violence against them with relative impunity. The regular newspaper reports of domestic violence cases corroborate Cobbe's thesis that unwifely behavior could amount to "a bell not answered with the required promptitude—a dinner somewhat late or badly cooked—a pair of slippers not to be found when wanted—a book carried off—a set of papers disarranged."[17] In a further echo of the press reporting, Cobbe added "Should she be guilty of nagging or scolding, or of being slattern, or of getting intoxicated, she finds usually a short shrift and no favour—and even humane persons talk of her offence as constituting, if not a justification for her murder, yet an explanation of it."[18]

Mrs. Fenwick Miller wrote a letter to the *Daily News* (picked up and commented on by the *Pall Mall Gazette* in an interesting interpress dialogue):

> Week by week and month by month, women are kicked, beaten, jumped on until they are crushed, chopped, stabbed, seamed with vitriol, bitten, eviscerated with red-hot pokers and deliberately set on fire—and this sort of outrage, if the woman dies, is called "manslaughter": if she lives it is a common assault.[19]

"Unwifelike carriage" has obvious parallels with modern justificatory narratives attempting to exculpate masculine violence. Such narratives are not only embedded in cultural explanations of legitimate reasons for assaults against women but also within legal discourse, becoming embodied in legal method itself.[20] When men kill wives, then the narrative of the provoked "reasonable" man is in effect the anthropomorphization of masculinist rhymes and reasons, which justify male violence by an appeal to the fiction of an objective authority of "reasonableness."

Modern feminists have exposed these narratives as privileging male violence in much the same way as their Victorian counterparts took issue with the masculinism of the law and the media.[21] The evolution of mass feminine (and feminist) journalism has roots in this discontent, as feminist activists used newspapers and periodicals to argue for the preeminent necessity of protecting women from men, commenting that to do so, it was first necessary to protect women from the law's violence.[22] Recognition of this, quite as much as of the issue of male violence, prompted Robert Kerr to take issue with Blackstone's eulogy: "With the exception of the protection afforded to the separate property of the wife by the courts of Equity, it is difficult to find any substantial ground upon which to support this conclusion; in other respects, the law always favoured, and in many respects still favours, the husband."[23] Other Victorian male legal commentators concurred: "Blackstone, we know, wrote his famous book with a bottle of port by his side; and we would wager a dozen that (describing women as the sex singularly favoured by English law) he sipped his glass and chuckled."[24]

The Substantive Law

Nineteenth-century feminists turned to reform of the substantive law in efforts to defend themselves and to challenge the law's collusion with male violence, developing a lively print conversation to forward their campaigns. The scale of the task they undertook in tackling the legal system was enormous. If today, British women can call on a wide range of remedies, their mid-Victorian sisters had little formal redress.[25] After years of strenuous print campaigning, during which the feminist protagonists regularly encountered fierce and vociferous opposition in the dominant print productions of the day, criminal remedies began to appear, starting with the Aggravated Assaults Act 1853. Its full title read "An Act to provide better legal protection for women and children and for preventing delay and expense in the administration of certain parts of the criminal law." Upon conviction, an offender could be imprisoned for a period of not more than six months or receive a fine of up to £20.

That Act was later consolidated into section 43 of the Offences Against the Person Act of 1861:

> When any person shall be charged before Two Justices of the Peace with an Assault or Battery . . . upon a male child . . . or upon any female, whether upon the Complaint of the Party aggrieved or otherwise, the said Justices, if the Assault or Battery is of such aggravated Nature that it cannot in their Opinion be sufficiently punished under the Provisions herein—before contained as to Common Assaults and Batteries [see section 42 of the said Act], may proceed to hear and determine in a summary way.

"Aggravated assault" embraced both domestic violence and sexual assault against women and physical assaults against children within and outside the domestic context.[26] In fact many indecent assault cases were proceeded against as aggravated assault.[27] Despite the regular newspaper reporting of cases which invoked the conditions of the Act, its success could be held to be limited, witness the fact that further efforts to provide better protection for women and children against violence failed.

The Aggravated Assaults Bills of 1860 and 1882, introduced to provide what was intended by their advocates as a more effective system of sentencing (to include whipping perpetrators), were defeated by the same mentality that marginalized any serious consideration of the reality of domestic violence by reasoning that the battered wife brought violence upon herself. In debates brought to public consciousness via reportage in *The Times,* for instance, one of the 1860 Bill's main opponents asserted:

> But though there are many cases in which delicate women came forward and claimed protection against brutal husbands, it must be remembered, on the other hand, that a mischievous and ill-tempered woman could very easily impose on a magistrates, and by aggravating her husband until he struck her, might continue to bring him into a police court, rid herself of his society, and disgrace him by the punishment which this Bill proposed in to inflict.[28]

Another MP spoke out in similarly vehement opposition to such measures, warning the House to be wary of "the venom of an angry woman's tongue."[29] Indeed, how far either the Aggravated Assaults Act 1853 or its successor, the Offences Against the Person Act 1861, section 43, actually improved the protection of women has been the subject of considerable academic debate by feminist historians in an interesting echo of the Victorian conversation.

For instance, Nancy Tomes, in a diligent study of the statistics of cases of aggravated assaults proceeded with, argues that a decline in such can be taken without question as an indicator of the deterrent impact of the new law.[30] Yet one might reasonably expect any improvement in the substantive law to be reflected in a greater confidence of women to report abuse, with the resultant effect of an increase in prosecutions. Tomes examined aggravated assaults in the London police courts, finding that between 1853 and 1889 "aggravated assaults" fell markedly from 800 cases in 1853 to 200 cases in 1889.[31] I do not dispute this evidence. Indeed my own examination of Judicial Statistics[32] and later Criminal Statistics demonstrates this decline as a continual one into the twentieth century (see Table 1).

The question is, how is this decline in aggravated assault cases to be interpreted? The first point is that summary courts provided only one of several court forums for hearing criminal cases. Summary courts supposedly dealt with minor criminal cases, referring more serious criminal cases to the Petty Sessions, Quarter Sessions and Assizes. These included assault charges laid in accordance with the Offences Against the Person Act 1861, including those

Table 1. Aggravated Assaults on Women and Children in Courts of Summary Jurisdiction, 1863–1983

Year	Number
1863	3,043
1866	3,047
1879	2,229
1883	2,102
1886	1,721
1889	1,774
1893	1,879
1896	1,743
1898	1,637
1904	1,212
1910	798
1950	115
1983	12

Source: Judicial Statistics, and later, Criminal Statistics for the respective years

brought under section 47 (assault occasioning actual bodily harm), section 20 (grievous bodily harm) or section 18 (grievous bodily harm with intent). Essentially, analysis of aggravated assault figures provides only one part of a wider picture.

The decline in the use of section 43 observed by Tomes in the London police courts was, I suggest, the result not of any deterrent effect of the new legal measures but instead a disenchantment with the use of the new aggravated assault provision. As the widespread reporting of the working of the new law emphasized, section 43 seemed not to enhance the focus on violence against women but quite the reverse. Its effect was to downgrade the seriousness of violence against them by driving the prosecution of such assault almost exclusively into the summary courts which, by definition, only concluded "less serious" matters. The creation of a specific offense of aggravated assault against women and children to be dealt with at summary level meant that whenever a crime of violence was committed against a woman, whatever its features, however serious or life threatening, it was unlikely to be referred higher.

By contrast, other violence involving men was legally constituted according to its severity, as a section 18, section 20, or section 47 offense under the 1861 Act. Qualitative evidence, using newspaper reporting among other sources, indicates that while magistrates did have a power, under section 46 of the 1861 Act, to commit serious domestic violence cases to the Assizes, it was rarely invoked, if only because of fears that the time lapse between committal and trial, plus the cost of taking such cases to the higher courts, would induce women to drop charges.[33] The reluctance of many women to initiate serious proceedings against brutal husbands was widely recognized, and formed a consistent thread in the reporting of magistrates' comments. It was not long after the introduction of the 1861 Act that magistrates, after presiding over many section 43 aggravated assault cases, began to express their collective disquiet about the use and implications of the new legislation in a number of print outlets.

They expressed reservations to the Home Secretary in 1874 about its use to deal with violence against women, claiming that such cases were effectively relegated to the lower courts regardless of the actual seriousness of the offense.[34] The case against William Babbington was typical of the kind causing them such anxiety. Babbington was charged before Warrington Police Court with brutally assaulting his wife, kicking her with his mining boots in the face, body, and ribs. Four women testified against him, including to his repeated kicking of her even after she was on the ground. Press reporting commented: "The Bench, as it is only an occasional court, could not inflict a heavy penalty, so gave the heaviest sentence they could—viz, fourteen days' hard labour and ordered the payment of seventeen shillings costs."[35]

Of course, violence against women might still be treated as a common assault under section 42, but "the statistics needed for a good study of male-female violence were not kept consistently in the London police courts. Thus any conclusions about the incidence of such crimes must be advanced tentatively."[36] In those cases where the accused was committed for trial "the classification adopted in the Parliamentary return does not permit of identifying the cases which concerned women only."[37] This means that it is difficult to provide an accurate comprehensive review of the prosecution of domestic violence in all courts.[38] Cobbe noted that more accurate information was to be found in the abstracts of the Reports of Chief Constables presented to the Home Secretary for 1870–74. Here, the total number of convictions for violent assault on women for that period was 6,029, although such figures for convictions were an underestimate as many Chief Constables failed to provide a return or simply stated that there was no brutal assault in the counties for which they were responsible. As Table 2 suggests, crime statistics (then as now) are notoriously difficult to interpret. Taking one magistrates' court in London, Bow Street, between 1860 and 1864, it can be observed that whereas "aggravated assaults" declined overall, the proportion of husbands charged with "aggravated assault" actually increased. This might indicate a greater commitment by the women to prefer charges against violent husbands than hitherto.

Notwithstanding admirable efforts to interpret nineteenth-century figures

Table 2. Aggravated Assaults at Bow Magistrates Court, 1860–1864

Charges	690	199
Remitted to sessions	16	-
Disposed		
Discharged	424	137
Convicted	250	62
Total	674	199
Husband total	97	58
Convicted	23	41
Discharged	74	17

Source: Judicial Statistics for the respective years

on cases of violence against women proceeded against, the general warning not to read too much into crime statistics must be remembered. The statistics of cases recorded by police, of cases proceeded against and the number of convictions is no more (then as now) than an artifact of the process of the social construction of crime figures. Cobbe noted that one report to the Home Secretary recorded a figure of 351 such assaults on women in the London area alone, adding it was unlikely to be a full picture.[39] Modern print analyses of the production of crime figures can greatly assist in interrogation of nineteenth-century material. Research in 1984 found that 384 cases of domestic violence were recorded by police in the London area; but also that the Metropolitan Police were only presenting the Home Office with those cases of recorded violence which were proceeded with (ie: resulting in a prosecution) for entry into the official Crime Statistics.[40] Thus, cases where violence had been reported and investigated but where charges had been withdrawn by the complainant or dropped by police prior to a court hearing were later systematically removed for the purpose of the final classification. It was little different in Victorian times, with police recording always prone to systematic manipulation for political ends. Cobbe reported that in 1874, 2,841 cases were proceeded with; in 1875 it was 3,106; and in 1876 it was 2,737 cases.[41] But she also stated that it was impossible to ascertain how many of these assaults were on women and children by husbands/partners and fathers, as these were not elements that the police wished to add to the conversation.

Underreporting—Motives for Silence

What was the reality behind the statistics indicating a decline in violence against women on the basis of cases dealt with under summary jurisdiction?

Victorian women, even more so than modern women, underreported such offenses for a variety of reasons. A fundamental reality, though, was that domestic violence was habituated and common practice: "The working class response to . . . assaults cannot be separated from working class culture, employment, social aspects of their lives and the societal reaction to such women." Additionally, working-class women generally "did not regard police as protectors."[42] Pearsall has noted that domestic assaults rarely came to the attention of police unless the assault was very brutal or resulted in death.[43] When women did report violence to the police, the police rarely took independent action to press charges unless (as Victorian newspaper reporting underlines) the violence was such an open scandal that local authorities endorsed such an expense. Commonly therefore, unless a woman had herself the financial and temperamental will to prosecute, individual incidents (no matter how brutal) would have a short life in the public debate, rarely reaching the wider criminal conversation on this vexed issue.

In my view, therefore, the Aggravated Assaults Act of 1853 did little to alter or change the public and legal perception of such violence. Motives for women's relative silence in the face of male violence reflected very similar motives to those that still silence women. Economic dependency, family pressures, fear, and shame provided powerful constraints. Implicit in the reporting of many cases which did come to court was the pressure of economic dependency. There was, outside the dreaded workhouse, no guaranteed maintenance provision for wives or for children if a husband was imprisoned. Alternatively, if a woman decided to escape domestic violence by leaving the matrimonial home, she remained vulnerable to husbandly depredations on any income she generated until the Married Women's Property Act 1882, and until 1895 she could, theoretically, be dragged back for desertion.[44] Harriet Taylor asserted in 1851 that underreporting of violence by women was related among other factors to women's economic dependency on men.[45]

The Matrimonial Causes Act 1878 was primarily concerned to address this problem by offering improved support to a wife forced to leave a husband because of his violence toward her. Under section 4, the Act allowed for a separation order on the grounds of cruelty with provision of a maintenance order to the wife and the legal custody by her of children under ten, so long as no immoral conduct could be proved against her. If the magistrate was satisfied that her future safety was in peril, he could invoke the provision that "the husband shall pay to his wife such weekly sum as the court or magistrate may consider being in accordance with his means." A consideration of the case law suggests that it was a section only relatively rarely properly implemented and reveals the difficulties which confronted women who applied for such orders. Elizabeth Hetherington was granted a judicial separation from her husband and an order for maintenance. After it was granted, she gave birth to a child, and the payment order was therefore discharged.[46] In an 1888 case, both parties were guilty of adultery, so that even though the husband was also found guilty of cruelty, all relief to the wife was refused.[47] Proving cruelty at a level sufficient to invoke maintenance payments could be difficult. James Broad appealed against an order to pay seven shillings weekly. His counsel argued successfully that the Act demanded more than a single act of cruelty.[48] Mabel Sharman Crawford asserted "the 1878 Act required the wife to be beaten and assaulted to the point of near death before an order was ever granted."[49]

Often, women were frightened to report violence against them. Tomes noted one case where a wife took out a warrant for the arrest of her husband, and he proceeded to stab her fatally, with the words "You———, you want to swear my life away." In another case the wife had acid thrown over her by the husband.[50] It is interesting to contrast the case cited by Tomes with another in the *Daily Telegraph,* when Edward Kelly was charged with throwing vitriol at his partner, Catherine Moiran. He was discharged because she claimed the incident was her fault, and their son endorsed this.[51] As other chapters in this volume underline, sexual assault against women was especially shrouded in silence and underreported.[52]

Charging Practices

Decisions about the bringing of any charges, including the definition of the offense involved, was complex, providing a real dilemma for contemporaries, as the debate surrounding the question "what is an aggravated assault upon a woman?" indicates. An example came before the Middlesex Sessions on 19 July 1879, referred on an appeal from a stipendiary magistrate's decision. George Coppleston had been convicted of an aggravated assault upon his wife and sentenced by Mr. Woolrych to three months' imprisonment with hard labor. The question was whether this was a proper punishment for the violence involved. Mr. Edlin held that the true reading of the statute required the assault to be of an aggravated nature. Since the assault in question "merely" involved striking his wife's breast and knocking her down, resulting in bruising, the Bench quashed the conviction.[53] Women were also frequently deterred from reporting cases by members of the public. *The Times* reported that a wife who had brought and supported a prosecution for assault against her husband was herself, upon his conviction and sentence to six months' hard labor, assailed by "several scoundrels with the foulest abuse—a course not frequently adopted to deter wives from prosecuting."[54]

The Recanting Victim

The recanting victim who withdrew her case before a conclusion, or who refused to bring charges against an abusive man, was an all-too-familiar feature in the Victorian landscape of prosecution of male violence, to the frustration of many magistrates. Cases tried under section 43 were brought at the expense of the prosecutor, generally supposed to be the female victim, and finding the necessary guinea fee provided one clear problem for many poor women. Some cases might be supported by philanthropic societies, such as the Society for the Protection of Women and Children, but societies had limited funds and more demands upon their resources than they could meet.[55] On occasions, the police would act to bring prosecutions themselves, often without the support of the injured wife but using instead the evidence of neighbors scandalized by a level of violence perceived by them as unreasonable. However, pressures on police costs meant that local policies of support for such initiatives were patchy, and varied over time from place to place. The unwillingness of wives to prosecute husbands (or children, fathers) was behind one suggestion from the stipendiary magistrate of Marlborough Street Police Court that "the deposition of the wife or child, taken before the magistrate, should be received in evidence in event of the non-appearance of the witness at the trial; otherwise there might be a failure of justice."[56] Edward Cox noted that in the witness box the wife "denies all that she has stated to the magistrate," and if wounded, would claim that "the wound was caused not by any blow from him, but she fell by accident against the knife; the black eye was caused by the bed-post."[57] Comprehending this reluctance to prosecute ensured that legal authorities were eager for domestic violence cases to be heard speedily and was one factor prompting the Aggravated Assaults Act 1853.

The example provided by Henry Bennett further reflects the predicament of magistrates dealing with cases which depended on the willingness and financial ability of women to undertake a prosecution. Bennett, who no longer lived with his wife, was charged at Bow Street police court with assaulting her. On 4 December 1852 she was walking in Drury Lane when she met the defendant, who asked her how she was getting on. She replied "pretty well," but he then called her "a w——— and without provocation struck her as hard as he could," knocking her down and injuring her back severely. With the "assistance of others she got away from him and went home"; he followed and "struck her repeatedly with all his force on various parts of her body." The following morning he again went to her room, seized her by the hair, drew a knife from his pocket, and attempted to cut her throat. In trying to defend herself she was badly injured. The magistrate suspected that (motivated by fear) she would not appear at the sessions if Bennett were committed for trial on a charge of attempted murder, and instead, concluded the case by fining him five shillings for assault.[58] It was a commonplace occurrence that once women were in the witness box, they recanted their earlier complaints or remained silent. Cox commented:

> When in the witness box the wife refuses to convict her husband. She denies all she had stated to the Magistrate while under the influence of her anger. . . . What can be done in such a case? Her deposition tells quite another story. She was beaten, bruised, stabbed, without provocation, without resistance.[59]

Furthermore, men frequently frightened and intimidated female witnesses in court. As the *Illustrated Police News* demonstrated through a series of front-page court sketches, husbands routinely threatened wives in court.[60]

Domestic Violence in the Courtroom— Mitigatory Accounts and Sentencing

The higher courts in particular often condoned male violence as a reasonable response to a woman's unreasonable provocation.[61] More, even on conviction, sentence and sentencing practice in summary and higher courts was very much influenced by mitigating pleas accusing women of being aggravators, naggers, and provokers. One defendant convicted before Warrington County Police Court in 1880 of brutally assaulting his wife (repeatedly kicking her in the head and ribs as she lay barely conscious) was reported as claiming "he was aggravated." His sentence was fourteen days' hard labor.[62] Such "aggravation" of husbandly feelings regularly formed the attempted justification for male violence, as in the case headlined "An Aggravating Wife." William Miller was charged with assaulting his wife, a "delicate young woman" who had irritated him by suggesting that, when he returned home drunk on Saturday night, he go to bed and she bring him his supper there. But this was one case where even the neighbors "complained of his general conduct to her," and so the mitigation did not exonerate him totally. Mr. D'Eyncourt insisted on punishing him for his brutality—by three months' imprisonment.[63]

Defense counsel regularly relied on narratives of provocation/aggravation, invoking stereotypes of nagging or drunken wives to provide the necessary exoneration for their clients. Even wives could show themselves complicit in this defense, especially in the lower courts and where the police, not the wife, brought the prosecution. John Green, charged with wounding with intent to do his wife grievous bodily harm, was aided by his wife's evidence that "they were singing a song and I joined in the chorus, which aggravated him." This echoed his admission upon arrest that he had done it, was "very sorry" but had had "great provocation." He was found not guilty.[64] At the Old Bailey in 1885, Mr. Justice Grove held that one offender who had killed his wife had been "grievously provoked" and should be pitied.[65] When William Norman killed his wife in 1879, Mr. Justice Manisty at the Old Bailey said one should pity the prisoner on account of the wife's conduct in passing a sentence of three years' imprisonment.[66] In 1885 the *Illustrated Police News* reported a wife as addicted to drink and frequently misbehaving, while portraying the husband as a sober and hard-working man who, on the "fatal" night, had been provoked to the point of frenzy, upon which he had an epileptic seizure and killed her.[67] The jury found the prisoner guilty, but the judge sentenced him to five years rather than pronouncing the capital sentence. Thomas Quigly, thirty-five, who killed his wife by drunkenly beating her with a poker, had the capital sentence commuted when further evidence about her behavior was provided: "She was drunk and unchaste and had given him provocation."[68] As this underlines, all-male juries were reluctant to convict fellow men in domestic violence cases, though if perpetrators appeared in the higher courts in the character of repeat offenders, this reticence was partially overcome. For instance, John Thomas was found not guilty of feloniously wounding his wife by causing a broken leg (he said she fell and broke it), but on being again indicted for unlawfully assaulting her, he was found guilty and received fifteen months' imprisonment.[69] Similarly, Louis Droz, a habitual wife abuser, was acquitted of throwing corrosive fluid on his wife but was convicted for a subsequent assault upon her.[70] However the sentences meted out were hardly deterrent, despite press reporting of pious hopes that they would be, which helped to keep up the illusion of legal protection for women.[71]

Examples of executions of wife murderers can be found, but generally speaking men were rarely convicted of murder in cases involving fatal assaults on women. Manslaughter was commonly substituted with perceived feminine provocation being used in mitigation.[72] Dr. Thomas Smethurst was sentenced to death in 1859 for poisoning his wife, but her bigamy facilitated his later reprieve.[73] Martin Doyle, who tried to batter a woman companion to death, was executed, but Radzinowicz notes he was "the first to suffer death for attempted murder in twenty-one years and also the last."[74] The *Woman's Suffrage Journal* satirically noted:

"Kicked, Beaten, Jumped On until They Are Crushed" 261

> From a Plymouth paper we learn that a man named THOMAS ELLIOT, who had been drinking, found his wife in a public house. THOMAS ELLIOT struck and pushed his wife; she fell, and received a FATAL BLOW. The judge, though he appeared to sympathise with the injured husband in his domestic troubles, said violence was not the way to remedy them, and that he would "make a serious example" of the prisoner, which he did by awarding him six months' imprisonment. . . . At the Lincolnshire summer assizes MARTIN PINCHBECK, chimney sweeper, was indicted for attempting to kill and slay CATHERINE PINCHBECK by throwing her out of a railway carriage on the Hull-Grimsby line. The woman remained for weeks insensible, and is now a confirmed idiot. The jury found the prisoner guilty of common assault, and he was sentenced by Mr. Justice MELLOR to twelve months' hard labour.[75]

Newspapers headlined a regular litany of cases such as these which fuelled understandable feminist indignation. Typical examples include reports of Michael O'Donnell's trial at the Central Criminal Court. During a supposed epileptic fit he had seized his wife by the throat and stabbed her in the thigh, being consequently convicted of manslaughter and sentenced to five years' penal servitude. In 1867 John Daley was charged with attempted murder by throwing his wife out of a first floor window. He was discharged, and the court said if the wife wished to pursue the case by summons she could![76]

Emphasizing the negative influence on Victorian sentencing practice of the stereotypes of good and bad womanhood, barrister and influential penologist Edward Cox argued:

> In the vast majority of these cases, the suffering angel of the sensational "leader" is found to be rather an angel of the fallen class, who has made her husband's home an earthly hell, who spends his earnings in drink, pawns his furniture, starves his children, provides for him no meals, lashes him with her tongue when sober and with her fists when drunk, and if he tries to restrain her fits of passion, resists with a fierceness and a strength for which he is no match. He is labouring all day to feed and clothe her and his children and when he returns home at night, this is his greeting.[77]

In 1889 Walter McLaren, MP, presented an official return to Parliament on the question of assaults against females. The return showed assaults, murders, and manslaughters committed upon females and sheds some important light on sentencing practice.

Table 3. McClaren Return of Sentencing in Violence against Women for 1889

Offenses determined summarily	Over six months and under 1 year	3–6 months	2–3 months	1–2 months	14–28 days	1–14 days	Total
England / Wales							
Common assault	-	4	2	244	425	249	
Aggravated assault	-	109	117	34	31	68	
Subtotal	-	113	119	278	456	317	1,183
Scotland							
Common assault	-	-	-	106	430	934	
Aggravated assault	-	-	-	101	112	184	
Subtotal	-	-	-	207	542	1,118	1,867
Ireland							
Common assault	-	1	1	12	29	62	
Aggravated assault	1	32	49	90	167	57	
Subtotal	1	33	50	102	196	119	501
Total	1	146	169	587	1,194	1,554	3,551

Source: McClaren Return 1889, Parliamentary Papers

In 293 cases where charges of murder were involved, the sentences were of two years and above in 43 cases; 25 men were sentenced for between one and two years; 158 men were imprisoned for between 3 months and one year; 67 were imprisoned for less than three months. Of aggravated and common assaults on women, 7,782 men were convicted; with 4,079 defendants being fined; 2,800 being sentenced to up to one month's imprisonment; 756 for between one and three months; and 146 for between three and six months.

Challenging the Violence of the Law

Mid-Victorian legislative reform did little to prevent the "Wife Torture" so meticulously documented by Cobbe.[78] By the end of the century the wheels of reform had begun to grind, albeit slowly. The so-called lady of the law was to receive some protection and freedom from her domestic slavery and servitude as when Jackson tried forcibly to repossess his wife, under the terms of *habeas corpus*. In a widely reported judgment it was established as a principle that a husband had no right to use violence of any kind on his wife's person, nor to imprison her, and that such rights had never existed. Lord Esher, Master of the Rolls, declared in his judgment:

> In this case it is really admitted that this lady is confined by the husband physically so as to take away her liberty. The only question for us to determine is whether in this case we can allow that to continue. The husband declares his intention to continue it. He justifies such detention; and the proposition laid down on his behalf is that a husband has a right to take the person of his wife by force and keep her in confinement, in order to prevent her from absenting herself from him so as to deprive him of her society. A series of propositions have been quoted which, if true, make an English wife the slave, the abject slave, of her husband. . . . I should say that confining a person to one house was imprisonment. . . . I do not believe that this contention is the law or ever was. It was said that by the law of England the husband has the custody of his wife. What must be meant by "custody" in that proposition so used to us? It must mean the same sort of custody as a gaoler has of a prisoner. I protest that there is no such law in England.[79]

That wholly indefensible law dubbed by Coleridge as more worthy of barbarism than a civilized country (an interesting echo of Rowbotham and of recent work by Martin Wiener) seemed in retreat.

But it was a false dawn: the criminal conversation on the reality of violence against women, the purveying of rhymes and reasons, exculpations and mitigations defining and articulating such violence, have continued to inform the public and legal minds of the twentieth century and beyond, though the challenges have become more vociferous and the excuse of provocation and aggravation is now being challenged.[80]

Notes

1. *Blackstone's Commentaries of the Laws of England* (1765; Oxford: Clarendon Press, 1857 edition), 1: 468, 471.

2. Frances Power Cobbe, "Wife-Torture in England" (1869), in *The Sexuality Debates,* ed. S. Jeffreys, 219–53 (London: Routledge, 1987).

3. Matilda M. Blake, "The Lady and the Law," *Westminster Review* 133 (1892): 367.

4. Ibid., 364.
5. *Pall Mall Gazette,* 11 May 1865.
6. Matilda M. Blake, "Are Women Protected?" *Westminster Review* 137 (1892): 44.
7. J. E. Gorbich, "The Body in Legal Theory," in *At the Boundaries of Law,* ed. M. A. Fineman and N. S. Thomadsen, 60–76 (London: Routledge, 1991).
8. Crown Prosecution Service, "Policy Document on Domestic Violence," November 2001; Metropolitan Police, "Enough Is Enough," December 2001; Lord Justice Auld, "Review of the Criminal Courts of England and Wales," October 2001, see www.criminal-courts-review.org.uk; John Halliday's Report "Making Punishment Work," July 2001, www.homeoffice.gov.uk/cpg/halliday.htm.
9. Elizabeth Pleck, *Domestic Tyranny* (Oxford: Oxford University Press, 1987), 110.
10. A. Fitzherbert, *La Graunde Abridgment, c1514* (Richardi Tottelli, 1577).
11. Whately, *A Bride-Bush: or, A Direction for Married Persons* (Felix Kyngston for Thomas Man, 1619), 123–24.
12. Nicholas Brady, *The Law's Resolution of Women's Rights* (1632). It was rare for men to be legally identified as exceeding their lawful prerogative; for example see *Bradley v Wife* (1663) 1 Keble 637; 83 English Reports 1152.
13. Blackstone, *Commentaries,* 1: 36.
14. J. C. Jeaffreson, *Brides and Bridals* (Hurst and Blackett, 1872), cited in G. Rattray Taylor, *Sex in History,* 66 (London: Thames and Hudson, 1953).
15. See www.fathers.ca/rule_of_thumb.
16. Cobbe, "Wife-Torture," 222. This provides an interesting echo with Swift's chapter in this volume.
17. Anon., "Outrages on Women," *North British Review* (1856), 133. See also SOLON database, http://solon.law.mmu.ac.uk for a range of newspaper entries on this topic.
18. Cobbe, "Wife-Torture," 227.
19. *Pall Mall Gazette,* 2 October 1888.
20 See J. Horder *Provocation and Responsibility* (Oxford: Oxford University Press, 1992).
21. See, for example, Sue Lees, "Naggers, Whores, and Libbers," in *Femicide: The Politics of Woman Killing,* ed. J. Radford and D. Russell, 132–56 (Milton Keynes: Open University Press, 1992).
22. Bessie Parkes, cited in Susan Hamilton, "Making History with Frances Power Cobbe: Victorian Feminism, Domestic Violence, and the Language of Imperialism," *Victorian Studies* (Spring 2001): 437–60.
23. Blackstone, *Commentaries,* 1: 47. Kerr was editor of the 1857 edition.
24. Augustine Birrell, "Women under the English Law," *Edinburgh Review* 184 (1896).:324, cited in Carol Bauer and Lawrence Ritt, eds., *Free and Ennobled,* 169 (Oxford: Pergamon, 1979). Direct modern parallels with common and statutory law are still apparent, with English courts still showing reluctance to prosecute male domestic violence. Masculinist reasons for male anger remain potentially anthropomorphized into the objective test of provocation, making anger an excuse for murder, yet feminine despair is not. The injection of a human rights dimension, however, may lead to a new agenda for this criminal conversation and be of critical importance to the policing of male violence. See *Osman v United Kingdom* (2000) 29 EHRR.
25. See J. Taylor-Browne, *What Works in Reducing Domestic Violence* (London: Whiting and Birch, 2001).

26. Nancy Tomes, "A 'Torrent of Abuse': Crimes of Violence between Working Class Men and Women in London, 1840–1875," *Journal of Social History* (1978): 328–45, describes an "aggravated assault" as one attended with circumstances of peculiar outrage or atrocity. This, with respect, can hardly be the case if the act designed to prosecute such assaults confined such cases to the courts of summary jurisdiction where the maximum sentence was a fine or six months' imprisonment.

27. Susan M. Edwards, "Sex Crimes in the Nineteenth Century," *New Society,* 13 September 1979, 562–63.

28. *Hansard,* 158, 1860, col. 524.

29. Ibid., col. 519.

30. Tomes, *Torrent of Abuse.*

31. Ibid., 330.

32. The first continuous series of criminal statistics for the whole of England and Wales dates from 1835. From that year to 1856, the Criminal Statistics published each year gathered together figures about those tried on indictment in the higher courts. From 1857 the enlarged series known as the Judicial Statistics included information about those dealt with summarily in the magistrates' courts as well. J. J. Tobias, *Nineteenth Century Crime and Punishment: Prevention and Punishment* (Newman Abbot: David and Charles, 1972), 82.

33. See cases on the SOLON database.

34. PP, Report to the Secretary of State for the Home Department, on the State of Law relating to *Brutal Assaults,* 1874.

35. *Illustrated Police News,* 22 May 1880.

36. Tomes, *Torrent of Abuse,* 329.

37. Cobbe, "Wife-Torture," 234.

38. See Leon Radzinowicz, *A History of English Criminal Law* (London: Stevens, 1968), 4: 68.

39. Cobbe, "Wife-Torture," 223.

40. Susan S. M. Edwards, *Policing Domestic Violence* (London: Sage, 1989), chap. 4.

41. Cobbe, "Wife-Torture," 234.

42. Susan S. M. Edwards, "Female Sexuality, the Law, and Society: Changing Socio-Legal Conceptions of the Rape Victim in Britain since 1800" (Ph.D. diss., University of Manchester, 1979), 246.

43. Ronald Pearsall, *The Worm in the Bud* (Harmondsworth: Penguin, 1969).

44. *R v Jackson* [1891] 1 QBD 671.

45. *Morning Chronicle,* 28 August 1851.

46. *R v Hetherington* (1887) PD XX.

47. *Otway v Otway* (1888) PD 13.

48. *Broad v Broad* (1889) LT 687.

49. Mabel Sharman Crawford, "Maltreatment of Wives," *The Westminster Review* 139, 3 (1894): 297.

50. Tomes, *Torrent of Abuse,* 333.

51. *Daily Telegraph,* 1 October 1870.

52. Anna Clark, "Rape or Seduction? A Controversy over Sexual Violence in the Nineteenth Century," in *The Sexual Dynamics of History: Men's Power, Women's Resistance,* 13–27 (London: Pluto Press, 1983); Edwards, *Female Sexuality.*

53. *Women's Suffrage Journal,* 1 August 1879, 132.

54. Cited in "Outrages on Women," *Women's Suffrage Journal,* 1 August 1879, 234.

55. Kim Stevenson, "Helping the Vulnerable or Helping Themselves?" *Crime Law and Societies/Crime, Histoire et Société* 18 (2004): 93–110.

56. Tomes, *Torrent of Abuse,* 333.

57. Edward Cox, *Principles of Punishment* (London, 1877), 103.

58. *Women's Suffrage Journal,* 1882.

59. Cox, *Principles of Punishment,* 108.

60. *The Illustrated Police News,* 9 April 1898.

61. Cobbe, "Wife-Torture," 237.

62. *Illustrated Police News,* 22 May 1880.

63. *Daily Telegraph,* 14 May 1856. Mrs. Miller was not grateful, having requested only a separation order.

64. PP, XI Session 1879–80 611.

65. *Illustrated Police News,* 8 August 1885.

66. *Women's Suffrage Journal,* 1 October 1879, 166.

67. *Illustrated Police News,* 8 August 1885. Lawyers might care to examine the parallel of this case with contemporary law on automatism and epilepsy.

68. *Judicial Statistics,* xxvii (London, 1868).

69. PP, X Session 1879–80, 535.

70. Ibid., XII Session 1869–70, 649.

71. For example, *Daily Telegraph,* 14 May 1856.

72. Those convicted of wife murder and executed usually had wives who fulfilled the expected Victorian stereotypes of good womanhood. See, for example, the case of William Corrigan, *Daily Telegraph,* 18 February 1856.

73. PP IV, 341.

74. Ibid., 342.

75. *Women's Suffrage Journal,* 1 August 1876, 112.

76. *Illustrated Police News,* 19 October 1867, 3.

77. Cox, *Principles of Punishment.*

78. C 1138, 1875 8, Report, State of the Law relating to Brutal Assaults in Wife-Beating, 1874.

79. *R v Jackson* [1891] 1 QB 671. See also Martin Wiener, *Men of Blood, Violence, Manliness and Criminal Justice in Victorian England* (Cambridge: Cambridge University Press, 2004).

80. Ibid., 308h.

Epilogue

JUDITH ROWBOTHAM
AND KIM STEVENSON

The modern news media is a different phenomenon from the Victorian media. Technological advance means that newspapers are no longer the main source of immediate news. Instead, they are for most people, the means which amplify and fix information already in the public domain. Victorian newspapers also looked rather different. Few, apart from the *Illustrated Police News,* used banner headlines in the ways which are familiar to consumers of modern newsprint. They did, increasingly, make use of headlines (banner and cross-headlines), often marked out not by differences in font size, but by use of capitals. Developments from the 1880s saw the cheaper papers in particular, such as *Lloyds News,* become more eye-catching in their layout—a development associated with the so-called New Journalism.[1]

But there was less need for such devices, because Victorian newspapers were much more clearly demarcated in terms of where they located their news content within their pages. Readers of *The Times,* for example, who wanted to read law and crime reports would turn to the pages after the leading articles, usually around page ten or eleven. In the *Daily Telegraph,* pages four and/or five were so occupied. News of breaking crime might indeed appear earlier in the papers, when such news was defined by headlines to alert the reader, but that was relatively unusual. Today, crime news is scattered throughout the papers, and headlines are useful as identifying the nature of the report as well as catching the eye and appealing to the reader.[2] But despite these differences, there remain powerful echoes between the criminal conversations which interested the Victorians, and those which resonate today. This volume has concentrated on issues given prominence by public debate, conducted through the media but invoking both popular opinion and the pronouncements of experts. While Victorian experts are not ready replicas of those of today, an unease about the trustworthiness and validity of expert testimony is discernible in both periods, arguably because expert testimony sought (and seeks) to replace the judgment of peers, especially in the higher courts.

The print dialogue promoted contemporary understandings of how the legal system worked to define the boundaries between acceptable and unacceptable behavior by relating incidents and transgressions to society as a whole. What has been demonstrated is the essentially fluid nature of much of what is considered "criminal" at any point in time, something underlined by the media's continuing focus on scandals and their ready metamorphosis into a larger scale panic, sustained and disseminated by the ensuing rhetoric of moral outrage produced by often self-appointed social commentators. As such, these chapters have important lessons for a consideration of the (un)-certainties of the modern age.

The reality is that the topics covered in this volume are not, despite Victorian perceptions to the contrary, new or original in terms of the offensive conduct covered; it is the discourse context of the perceived threats they presented to society and the degree of outcry caused that provides a new academic perspective. Competing pressures tended to ensure that the results of popular outcry (in terms of legislation and practice) were at best mixed, and often virtually ineffective, something which modern society is relearning. The public persona of the Victorian age was that it was a moral age. Many later scholars identify it as an age of moral certainties. The evidence of these chapters reveals it to be rather different, certainly in its own perception of itself at times of crisis. Equally, then, how different is the present confusion? If our morality is more secular and our confidence in its "rightness" when compared to other ages is apparently no less, when uncertainties creep in as a result of events which shake social self-confidence, such as major political or commercial scandals, media endorsement of that state of uncertainty only reinforces that perspective.[3]

What this volume, with its echoes from the past, reveals is the enduring nature of types both of offensive conduct and offenders and the importance of the media in providing a platform where discourse can be mediated between various interest groups and the mass of public reaction. Then there was the question of appropriate and effective "punishment" for transgressors, including the vexed question of deterrence. After all, one important reason why these various types of crime and bad behavior received a high public profile was the fear that, left uncontrolled, they would threaten the prosperity and stability of the community and the nation. An important dilemma thus arose—how to deter and to punish without destroying that spirit of initiative which also underpinned the wealth and health of the country and its individuals. Social and cultural controls were portrayed in the news media as having failed. Sometimes, this encouraged calls for new legislation, or improvements to the existing workings of the legal system, in order to give the legal world the opportunity to intervene and control these expressions of bad behavior and crime—yet, as these chapters show, new legislation was regularly resisted once the peak of a panic had passed.

Graham Ferris shows us how a simultaneous analysis of both newspaper and official law reports can shed even more light on the complexities of interpreting crime and bad behavior. Linked to this, many chapters also emphasize the regular failure of legislation to eradicate bad behavior from society, despite clamor for such tools at times of perceived crisis. Each crisis, equally, evolves new terminology for what is generally an old problem. For example, David Bentley asserts that baby-farming as such no longer exists; yet the underlying problems of child care and working mothers remains current, as does the potential for associated social panic as recent high-profile cases of child minding and supposed delinquent practitioners like Louise Woodward underline. Further, in the present age of corporate scandals, where "initiatives" to produce the best possible gloss fuelled recent economic booms, the current prospects of fraud and deception are an eerie reflection of the upsets and uncertainties which beset Victorians, as Paul Barnes so powerfully points out.

The vexed issue of expert testimony and its widespread ramifications was explored in many chapters, but particularly those by Ward, Morton, and Crozier. Again, they raise disquieting modern echoes, especially where events have served to modify the expected certainties of scientifically based experts as in the recent widely reported trials and appeals of mothers such as Trupti Patel and Sally Carter, accused of murdering their babies and "disguising" this as cot-deaths. Their return to the community as innocent of wrongdoing has prompted the media to find new scapegoats in the shape of medical experts who played leading roles in the prosecution. As Simon Jenkins commented of the trial of Trupti Patel, which he described as a trial resembling the Salem witch hunt trials, "This mother was acquitted with little thanks to science."[4] There was and is an underlying tendency for expert testimony to be regarded with hostility by a wider public less educated in the niceties of intellectual disagreement, arguably because it is seen as superseding the role of wider society to make the necessary judgments about where the boundaries lie at any one time between guilt and innocence. This, certainly, is suggested by the far from flattering comments on expert testimony and intellectual disagreement which, then as now, characterize media coverage of these. Linked to this, the impact of gender on the "believability" of testimony in court, and on the interpretation of the behavior of defendants and accusers, remains significant, as chapters from Edwards, Stevenson, and Gleeson unhappily remind us, removing the temptation to complacency about how much society has "improved" in its attitude towards vulnerable groups.

Equally, Taylor's examination of the presentation of the Victorian versions of the modern underclasses has interesting echoes for present-day attempts to classify criminality on the one hand, and on the other, to provide some reassurance through the contribution of the forces of law and order in guarding the lives and property of respectable citizens. Sergeant Field is no longer a reassuring image for many, again possibly because the police force has in some way become professionalized and so more distant (even alienated) from everyday society.[5] Indeed, the issue of alienation of supposedly identifiable groups of "others" is another theme with powerful resonances for modern society. The Victorian popular villains who were never out of the news for long were the Irish, and the media reinforcement of popular stereotypes hampered realistic assessments of this group and the threat it posed—something to consider when exploring current dimensions for similarly stereotyped groups at the start of the twenty-first century. As D'Cruze, Swift, and Rowbotham reveal, certainties and complacency about the moral validity of our own society can be shaken by conduct which does not match expectations and ideologies, and the media plays a key role in evolving strategies to reconcile these—strategies which may not be "just" in any dispassionate sense, but which restore a balance of consent.

—◄○►—

It is easy to blame the modern media for the faults and prejudices of the society it serves. A high moral tone is often taken by members of the public (as Moses's chapter exemplifies) and even members of the media in condemning the press for falsely creating panics, and serving the cause of injustice, as in the case of the furor over the treatment meted out to the killers of James Bulger.[6] That debate existed in Victorian times as Abbott highlights, but interestingly, modern scholars do not blame the Victorian media for creating the prejudices and hypocrisies of that age. What these chapters indicate is the extent to which the media of an age is complicit in the discourse it produces for popular consumption, but does not bear sole responsibility for the ideas and ideologies it purveys. The press did not create the incidents highlighted in this collection, or the genuine alarm they aroused, but it undoubtedly magnified what were often (though by no means always) quite small-scale problems into issues of national significance. Just as the Victorians, we read and watch consciously, making choices about the nature of our consumption. Victorian newspapers did not create a social appetite for "bad" news—nor do their modern counterparts. That appetite exists because society wishes to acquire information about the extent of disorder afflicting it, and a forum for exchange of ideas about strategies to deal with disorder. The texts in the Appendix which follow this Epilogue reveal this reality very powerfully.

Notes

1. Joel H. Wiener, ed., *Papers for the Millions: The New Journalism in Britain, 1850s to 1914* (Westport, CT: Greenwood Press, 1988).

2. For more details on the layout of Victorian newspapers, see Laurel Brake, Alex Jones, and Lionel Madden, eds., *Investigating Victorian Journalism* (Basingstoke: Macmillan, 1990); Wiener, ed., *Papers for the Millions*.

3. This epilogue is written at such a time in British history, where the Hutton Enquiry into the death of Iraq weapons expert Dr. David Kelly has thrown an unflattering light on Prime Minister Tony Blair and on the current political establishment, according to the majority of media comment. See, for example, *Sunday Telegraph*, 31 August 2003; *The Independent on Sunday*, 31 August 2003; *Mail on Sunday*, 31 August 2003.

4. Simon Jenkins, "Trupti Patel and the Rotten Courts of Salem," *The Times*, 13 June 2003.

5. Charles Dickens, "On Duty with Inspector Fields," *London Crimes*, ed. N. Aisenberg (Boston: Rowan Tree Press, 1982).

6. Judith Rowbotham, Kim Stevenson, and Samantha Pegg, "Children of Misfortune: Parallels in the Cases of Child Murderers Thompson and Venables, Barrett and Bradley, *Howard Journal of Criminal Justice* 42, 2 (2003): 107–22.

Appendix

This contains typescript extracts from a number of Victorian newspapers, focusing on those which are less readily available to those without access to the British Newspaper Library at Colindale. It also contains further reproductions of pages of the original newspapers. Since, globally, *The Times* is the most readily available of newspapers, in various libraries and repositories, followed by the *News of the World* and the *Manchester Guardian* (some years of which are internet-available through access to the Newspaper Library's website), the choice has largely been taken from less readily accessible papers. The extracts include the full text of some reports referred to in various footnotes in the chapters. The object is to give a fuller flavor of the rich source that Victorian newspapers provide, not just for the history of crime and policing, but also for wider social and cultural histories. The spellings and punctuations of the original sources have been retained, and any original headlines are provided. Footnotes and parentheses are added only where necessary to add clarity, but we have not tried to annotate to give geographical locations, and so forth. Interested readers are directed towards the various historical maps of London and Manchester, for example, which are available on the internet.

It should be noted, also, that the choice of reproductions of original pages has been driven as much by the practicalities of choosing those years and volumes of the bound originals held at Colindale which were in a fit state to be photographed. This meant that many first choices had to be dismissed, especially from the *Illustrated Police News,* as the originals are in particularly poor condition. Equally, a choice had to be made of showing a whole page of text, where none of the print (even the headlines) would be distinguishable, in an effort to show the layout of pages reporting crime news, or selecting typical extracts from a page, and creating a montage. In the end, we decided that the former was the more fruitful path. Illustrations from the *Cassell's Saturday Journal,* and those forming most of the frontispiece montage, are from volumes in Judith Rowbotham's personal possession.

Illustrated Police News

Starting in 1864, this was a penny weekly, appearing on Saturdays, and the epitome of sensational newsprint. The front page of this highly popular precursor to the modern tabloid newspaper was lavishly illustrated. Over the years, illustrations became increasingly sophisticated. The usual style was for the front page to contain illustrations supporting stories reported on the inner pages (more illustrations were added there, increasingly from the 1880s on). The stories could range from the bizarre (the rampage of an infuriated cow) to the high-profile murders of the day. It was not a "respectable" paper, but its graphic style of reporting and visual depictions of real-life horrors ensured its sales.

Cassell's Saturday Journal

Starting in 1883, as a weekly complement to the monthly *Cassell's Family Magazine,* but with a slightly "racier" character (while avoiding unrespectable sensationalism), it not only reported the news, but also concentrated on articles and interviews, many illustrated, on topical issues. This ensured that issues relating to crime and bad behavior had a high profile in its pages, and its cartoons were frequently concerned with the idiosyncrasies and vagaries of the legal process in operation.

Figure 5. *Illustrated Police News,* July 1871. This page provides visual depictions of a range of crimes, revealing a range of stereotypical assumptions linked to the preoccupations of the day, including class, gender, and race. The scenes include the fatal attack on the dairy keeper by the provision keeper at St. Luke's workhouse; the murder of Chief Constable Talbot in Dublin; the murder of Mr. Manwaring by a woman claiming to be his wife; and deaths in Stratford of a drunken husband, wife, and child.

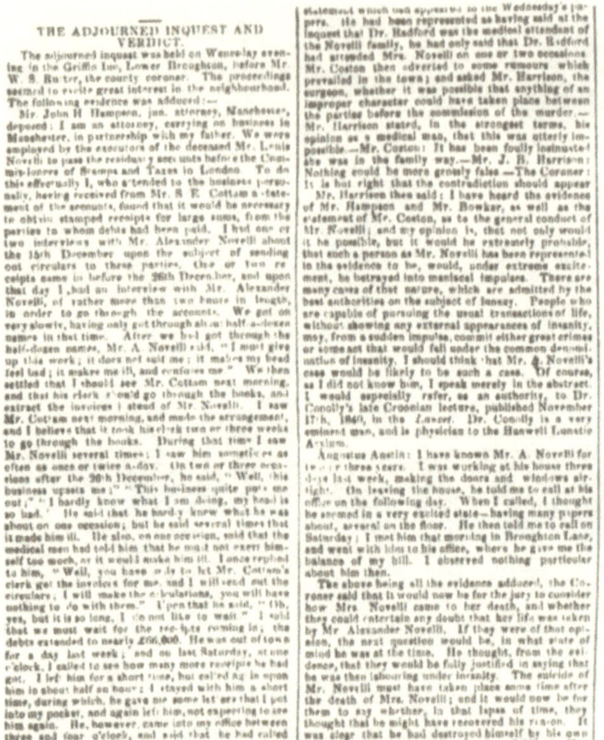

THE ADJOURNED INQUEST AND VERDICT.

The adjourned inquest was held on Wednesday evening in the Griffin Inn, Lower Broughton, before Mr. W. S. Rutter, the county coroner. The proceedings seemed to excite great interest in the neighbourhood. The following evidence was adduced:—

Mr. John H. Hampson, jun. attorney, Manchester, deposed: I am an attorney, carrying on business in Manchester, in partnership with my father. We were employed by the executors of the deceased Mr. Louis Novelli to pass the residuary accounts before the Commissioners of Stamps and Taxes in London. To do this effectually I, who attended to the business personally, having received from Mr. S. E. Cottam a statement of the accounts, found that it would be necessary to obtain stamped receipts for large sums, from the parties to whom debts had been paid. I had one or two interviews with Mr. Alexander Novelli about the 15th December upon the subject of sending out circulars to these parties. One or two receipts came in before the 26th December, and upon that day I had an interview with Mr. Alexander Novelli, of rather more than two hours in length, in order to go through the accounts. We got on very slowly, having only got through about half-a-dozen names in that time. After we had got through the half-dozen names, Mr. A. Novelli said, "I must give up this work; it does not suit me; it makes my head feel bad; it makes me ill, and confuses me." We then settled that I should see Mr. Cottam next morning, and that his clerk should go through the books, and extract the invoices instead of Mr. Novelli. I saw Mr. Cottam next morning, and made the arrangement, and I believe that it took his clerk two or three weeks to go through the books. During that time I saw Mr. Novelli several times; I saw him sometimes as often as once or twice a-day. On two or three occasions after the 26th December, he said, "Well, this business upsets me;" "This business quite puts me out;" "I hardly know what I am doing, my head is so bad." He said that he hardly knew what he was about on one occasion; but he said several times that it made him ill. He also, on one occasion, said that the medical men had told him that he must not exert himself too much, or it would make him ill. I once replied to him, "Well, you have only to let Mr. Cottam's clerk get the invoices for me, and I will send out the circulars; I will make the calculations, you will have nothing to do with them." Upon that he said, "Oh, yes, but it is so long, I do not like to wait." I said that we must wait for the receipts coming in; the debts extended to nearly £66,000. He was out of town for a day last week; and on last Saturday, at one o'clock, I called to see how many more receipts he had got. I left him for a short time, but called again upon him in about half an hour; I stayed with him a short time, during which, he gave me some letters that I put into my pocket, and again left him, not expecting to see him again. He, however, came into my office between three and four o'clock, and said that he had called about the papers, and that he wanted to know about these accounts, as he wanted to go to London. I said that I had previously told him that he could go to London, as the business could be settled there, through our agents there. He replied that he must have something settled decisively; to which I returned, that nothing could be done until the accounts were got in. To satisfy him, however, I directed a clerk to make some calculations relative to the probate duty, which, when finished, I submitted to him. We had some further conversation as to the transaction of the business with the stamp office, in the course of which he became cross and irritable; more so than I had ever seen him before. While I was adding up some accounts, he made a remark which I did not catch, and after I had finished I asked him what he said. He did not reply, but continued staring at the fire, and did not look at me. He continued staring at the fire, and there was a singular look about him which I did not like and had not seen before. The peculiarity of his appearance might arise from the fire. He never spoke again, but jumped up from the chair, slipped on his coat and hat in a minute, much quicker than I could have done, even had I been in a hurry, and bounced out of the room and took no notice of me, while I was adding up another column of accounts. I called to him, saying that I supposed I should see him again on Monday evening, but he did not reply to me. I never saw him again. I thought his conduct more peculiar that afternoon than I had ever seen it before, and I felt relieved when he was gone. He was more excited and irritable than I had seen him before, and did not calm down as he had done before when he had been irritated. If contradicted, he was excitable. I remember him at school nineteen or twenty years ago, and he was always looked upon as a weak, light, soft-headed lad. He seemed passionate at times, and appeared to have no control over himself. He never could sit down to two or three hours' work like another man, but always gave up again after doing two or three things. It did not appear to be anger, but sudden impulse. When I last saw him at school, he would be about nine or ten years of age. . . . .

statement which was apparent in the Wednesday's papers. He had been represented as having said at the inquest that Dr. Radford was the medical attendant of the Novelli family, he had only said that Dr. Radford had attended Mrs. Novelli on one or two occasions. Mr. Coston then adverted to some rumours which prevailed in the town; and asked Mr. Harrison, the surgeon, whether it was possible that anything of an improper character could have taken place between the parties before the commission of the murder.—Mr. Harrison stated, in the strongest terms, his opinion as a medical man, that this was utterly impossible.—Mr. Coston: It has been foully insinuated she was in the family way.—Mr. J. B. Harrison: Nothing could be more grossly false.—The Coroner: It is but right that the contradiction should appear.

Mr. Harrison then said: I have heard the evidence of Mr. Hampson and Mr. Bowker, as well as the statement of Mr. Coston, as to the general conduct of Mr. Novelli; and my opinion is, that not only would it be possible, but it would be extremely probable, that such a person as Mr. Novelli has been represented in the evidence to be, would, under extreme excitement, be betrayed into maniacal impulses. There are many cases of that nature, which are admitted by the best authorities on the subject of lunacy. People who are capable of pursuing the usual transactions of life, without showing any external appearances of insanity, may, from a sudden impulse, commit either great crimes or some act that would fall under the common denomination of insanity. I should think that Mr. A. Novelli's case would be likely to be such a case. Of course, as I did not know him, I speak merely in the abstract. I would especially refer, as an authority, to Dr. Conolly's late Croonian lecture, published November 17th, 1849, in the *Lancet*. Dr. Conolly is a very eminent man, and is physician to the Hanwell Lunatic Asylum.

Augustus Austin: I have known Mr. A. Novelli for two or three years. I was working at his house three days last week, making the doors and windows air-tight. On leaving the house, he told me to call at his office on the following day. When I called, I thought he seemed in a very excited state—having many papers about, several on the floor. He then told me to call on Saturday; I met him that morning in Broughton Lane, and went with him to his office, where he gave me the balance of my bill. I observed nothing particular about him then.

The above being all the evidence adduced, the Coroner said that it would now be for the jury to consider how Mrs. Novelli came to her death, and whether they could entertain any doubt that her life was taken by Mr. Alexander Novelli. If they were of that opinion, the next question would be, in what state of mind he was at the time. He thought, from the evidence, that they would be fully justified in saying that he was then labouring under insanity. The suicide of Mr. Novelli must have taken place some time after the death of Mrs. Novelli; and it would now be for them to say whether, in that lapse of time, they thought that he might have recovered his reason. It was clear that he had destroyed himself by his own hand. With regard to the question of Mr. A. Novelli's insanity, they had his peculiar temperament described by two witnesses; and they had this strong testimony, that insanity was inherent in the family. The seed might be said to have been sown in him; and might have rested until the present period, and then might have been all at once developed. These, however, were matters which it was for the jury to decide, and if they had any doubt they ought to lean to the charitable side of the question. The legal principle upon which the judges acted was, that if a man did an act of this sort, knowing the difference between right and wrong, he would be guilty of murder; but, if under the sudden impulse his reason were taken from him, then it would not be murder.—One of the jurors then asked Mr. Harrison whether the symptoms exhibited by Mrs. Novelli would not have been the same if chloroform had been used?—Mr. Harrison said there would be this difference; in cases where prussic acid or chloroform had been used, in addition to the *post mortem* appearances of congestion of the heart and lungs, there would be the smell of the poison; and besides, there would not, in that case, have been the marks over the windpipe corresponding to sub-cutaneous extravasation in the muscular structure. Mr. Harrison further stated, in reply to the coroner, that he still retained the opinion as to the cause of death in both cases, which he expressed at the previous sitting of the inquest.—The room was then cleared, in order that the jury might consider their verdict. After remaining in deliberation for about ten minutes, they returned a verdict, that Mr. A. Novelli had destroyed the lives, first of Mrs. Novelli, and afterwards of himself, being at the time of unsound mind.—The proceedings then terminated.

A further corroboration of the fact proved above, that Mr. Novelli was insane, has been furnished to the coroner by a gentleman residing in Oxford-street, London, from whom Mr. Rutter received a letter on Thursday morning, the day after the adjourned inquest. It contained the information that some years ago Mr. Novelli was on a visit at the house of a mutual friend, Mr. Carl Forster, at Augsburg, and that there he

Figure 6. *Manchester Courier,* 26 January 1850, 45–46. This reproduces the report of the Novelli murder and suicide, and is typical of the reports in the local Victorian press, being closely printed, and without illustrations, but with the text packed with sensational detail.

Appendix 277

WILLING TO WAIT

Officer of the Court: 'Prisoner at the Bar, are you guilty or not guilty?'
Prisoner: 'Sure, it's meself as'll wait'
Officer of the Court: 'Wait for what?'
Prisoner: 'Wait and see fwhat koind ava case me lawyer'll make out for me, sor'

CONSISTENCY
(A study of magisterial method (for corroborative evidence see daily police reports)

Magistrate: 'Eh? What? You say that the prisoner is educated and well-to-do? Dear me – dear me! Why that only constitutes an aggravation of the offence; and I must really make an example of him – ah, I shall fine him one farthing!'

Magistrate: 'Eh? You say the prisoner is ignorant and destitute? Well that certainly is to some extent – ah – a mitigation; and taking that into consideration. I shall only give him penal servitude for life with hard labour and the cat!

Figure 7. *Cassell's Saturday Journal,* 1890. Cartoons illustrating perspectives on court experiences. In "Willing to Wait," the humor to contemporaries would have been largely bound up in the clear indication that the Prisoner was Irish.

MORE UNFAIRNESS

Bill: 'See that cove, Bob! He's a Commissioner for swearing Oaths, he is. Blest if git paid 'arf-a-crown for hevery oath he swears. And look at me an' you. Wy, if we h a tanner, blowed if we wdnt'f ha'bin millinaires.'

PERJURY PROVEN

Magistrate: 'Your husband says you are a regular virago, and that this morning you str him. Is this true?'
Wife (contemptuously): 'Shure, your honour, it's a lie. If I had struck him this mornin wouldn't have been able to be here this afternoon to make the complaint'

Figure 8. *Cassell's Saturday Journal*, 1890. Cartoons illustrating perspectives on class and gender. In "More Unfairness," the attire of the two men in the foreground clearly would indicate to contemporaries that they were likely to be shiftless, drunken, and largely unemployed. Their reproduced accent does not indicate an Irish origin. In "Perjury Proven," the wife is possibly of Irish origin, given the spelling of "Shure."

Figure 9. *Cassell's Saturday Journal*, 1890. Cartoons illustrating perspectives on juvenile delinquency. The Fortune Automaton was an early precursor in machine shape of the modern daily horoscopes in newspapers.

(Frequent Complaints are to be read in the papers of the non-enforcement of the 'Wild Birds-Protection Act!' The close time is quite disregarded and the bird catcher may be seen at any time flying his calling as if now law existed.)

(1) – John Bull paused for a moment in his making laws in favour of his money-grabbing interests. He murmured, 'I must keep up my reputation for superior humaneness to animals in the eyes of the world;' and he posed himself before a glass to practice a humane expression; and passed and Act for the Pretended Protection of Wild Birds.
(2) – It bore fruit. Savage Nations were struck with admiration and decided to accept the protectorate of so humane a person.
(3) – Meanwhile the bird-catcher (and torturer) continued as if nothing had happened; while the executive looked on and smiled.
(4) – 'Wy, Guvner', sniggered the catcher one day 'this ere law don't make no kind o' difference to me!' 'Hist!' whispered John Bull. 'Hold your tongue, can't you? All bunkum dear boy, between you and me. What do I care about cruelty to animals – it's the *look of the thing.*'

Figure 10. *Cassell's Saturday Journal*, 1890. Cartoon illustrating cynical perspectives on the intentions behind legislation, and Victorian interpretations on their global impact. The "close time" is a reference to the closed season for shooting certain kinds of birds, especially game birds. John Bull was the personification of Britain.

THE TIMES, THURSDAY, MARCH 4, 1875.

THE CASE OF MRS. INGRAM.

TO THE EDITOR OF THE TIMES.

Sir,—In reference to the case of Mrs. Ingram, tried at Warwick Assizes, I think it is due to Mr. Maule, Q.C., the Commissioner who tried the case, to say that, although the surgeon in the case was not upon his trial, the learned Commissioner, by the questions which he asked and by his manner in asking them, clearly indicated that the surgeon's conduct was not without blame.

The report of the case in *The Times* of March 1 contains the following:—

"By the Court. I gave the husband no instructions as to what he was to do in case his wife got worse and I could not come. When you have got two cases come on at once you hardly know what to do."

This was an answer to a question asked in the sternest manner, following upon a severe cross-examination by counsel. I enclose a report from the local Press, where the questions and answers are given, but no report can give the full effect of manner and of the general course of a trial. Those who heard the question of the learned Commissioner and observed the emphatic manner in which that question was asked would not fail to be impressed with the feeling that the learned Commissioner had pointed the same moral which the leader in *The Times* has amplified. It is not for me to say one word upon the ability with which the learned Commissioner usually presides in Courts of Justice where he has so large an experience; nor do I suppose that it was intended for one moment to call his conduct as a Judge sitting in a criminal court in question.

I am, Sir, yours truly,

THE REPORTER ON THE MIDLAND CIRCUIT.

Warwick, March 3.

SPRING ASSIZES.

HOME CIRCUIT.

CHELMSFORD, March 3.

The Lord Chief Justice of England arrived from town at 7 o'clock last evening, and proceeded to open the Commission.

The cause list contains ten entries, of which three are marked as special jury cases, two of them being the sea-wall cases, which, it will be recollected, stood for trial at the last Assizes, and were made remanets. Mr. Justice Denman announced that he would only take common jury cases to-day, and would begin the special jury cases to-morrow morning at 10 o'clock, and in the event of his being unable to finish the common jury list to-day he would take the remaining cases on Friday. The Calendar contains the names of 23 prisoners, and some of the cases are of a very heinous character. Of these the most important is that of the Royal Artilleryman, who is charged with killing a little girl at Purfleet. Another Artilleryman is charged with attempting to murder his sergeant at Shoeburyness; there is an indictment for libel against Mr. John Hampden, who has already attained some degree of notoriety in connexion with certain proceedings arising out of a wager that he would prove the earth to be flat. A soldier is charged with committing sacrilege in Brentwood Church, another soldier is charged with burglary at Colchester, a farm labourer is charged with maliciously discharging a loaded gun with intent to do grievous bodily harm, two men are charged with stealing two horses at Barking, a woman is charged with forging a check for £105 12s. upon the Manningtree Branch of the London and County Bank, and the remaining cases included charges of arson, burglary, larceny, and one of wilful and corrupt perjury at the Chelmsford Petty Sessions; there are also two charges of attempting to commit suicide.

WESTERN CIRCUIT.

WINCHESTER, March 2.

The Assizes commenced this morning, when Mr. Justice Lush charged the Grand Jury. There are 57 prisoners in the calendar—not an unusually large number, especially considering that there was no Winter Assize. The majority of the cases, however, are of a heinous character. Putting on one side all the cases which are within the cognizance of justices at Quarter Sessions, there remain 36 prisoners, of whom 17 are charged with offences of violence. Among these charges are one of murder on the high seas, one of child murder, two of attempts to murder, four of wounding or shooting with intent to do grievous bodily harm, one of unlawful assault, and one of criminal assault. Of the charges that do not come within the definition of "crimes of violence," three are of concealment of birth, three of burglary, and three of arson. On the other hand, of the prisoners of good education, three are charged with libel and two with forgery. This almost exhausts the educated class of prisoners, for the other two cases of forgery are charged against persons of very slight education, while the six persons charged with perjury all belong to the same category. Looking at the column of the calendar that gives the degree of education, it appears that out of the whole 57 prisoners only eight are of a higher degree of education than the very moderate one which is described as "imperfect"—a definition which only implies a capacity to read and write imperfectly.

On the Civil side there is a cause list which consists of one cause for trial by a common jury, and cross actions of trial before a special jury. The Lord Chief Baron took his seat at 2 o'clock, and proceeded to try the first mentioned cause.

ASHURST V. MASON. ASHURST V. FOWLER.

These were two contributory suits of some novelty in their facts. Mr. Ashurst, the plaintiff in both suits, was chairman of a company called the English Assurance Company, which was registered under the Companies Act in September, 1867. A Mr. Brossett subscribed to the memorandum of association in respect of 250 shares. He retired from the Board in July, 1869, and applied to be relieved of his shares. The directors agreed that his shares should be placed in the names of nominees for the company, and accordingly a transfer was executed to Mr. Ashurst and Mr. Leyland, the manager of the company. About the same time a Mrs. Elder, who was entitled to 100 shares as executrix of her husband, being dissatisfied, applied to the company to find a transferee, and threatened to take winding-up proceedings in case this was not done. These shares were also transferred to Messrs. Ashurst and Leyland, and £100 paid out of the company's assets as the price of them. The company had no power at that time to invest their funds in their own shares. The company was ultimately wound up voluntarily, under a special resolution passed and confirmed in December, 1870. Messrs. Ashurst and Leyland were settled on the list of contributories in respect of the 250 shares, and Mr. Leyland not being able to pay calls, Mr. Ashurst had to pay a considerable amount in respect of calls and also to recoup the £100 paid on the later transfer out of the funds of the company. He now brought these suits to get contributions from such of his co-directors as approved the transaction. In the suit of "Ashurst v. Fowler" a Mr. Coles was made party. There was no evidence against him of knowledge, except that he had formally approved the transfer of Mrs. Elder's shares. In the suit of "Ashurst v. Mason" one of the directors who had been present at the subsequent meeting, when the minutes of the meeting at which the transfer from Brockett had been approved, was made party.

Mr. Kay, Q.C., and Mr. Locock Webb appeared for the plaintiff; Mr. Bagshawe, Q.C., and Mr. Bagshawe, jun., for four of the directors; Mr. Eddis, Q.C., and Mr. Blakesley for Mr. Banner and Mr. Keyworth, who has become insolvent; and Mr. H. M. Jackson, Q.C., and Mr. North for Mr. Coles. Some of the defendants did not appear.

The Vice-Chancellor said that the case was a singular one but the principle governing it was reasonably plain. A number of persons had to effect a common object come to a common design; in carrying out that design one of them had incurred liability; it was only reasonable that the other parties should contribute their share to the loss and not escape. Mr. Banner had attended a meeting at which the minutes of the previous meeting had been read; he could not be allowed to say that he was not attending, or for some other reason had not notice. He would, therefore, have to contribute in respect of the 250 shares. Mr. Coles was in a different position. No motive could be imputed to him of the reason of the transfer he approved, and he would, therefore, not have to contribute. But against the other defendants a decree was made.

Figure 11. *The Times,* 4 March 1875, 11. Extracts from a full page typically containing Assizes reports, police news, and correspondence.

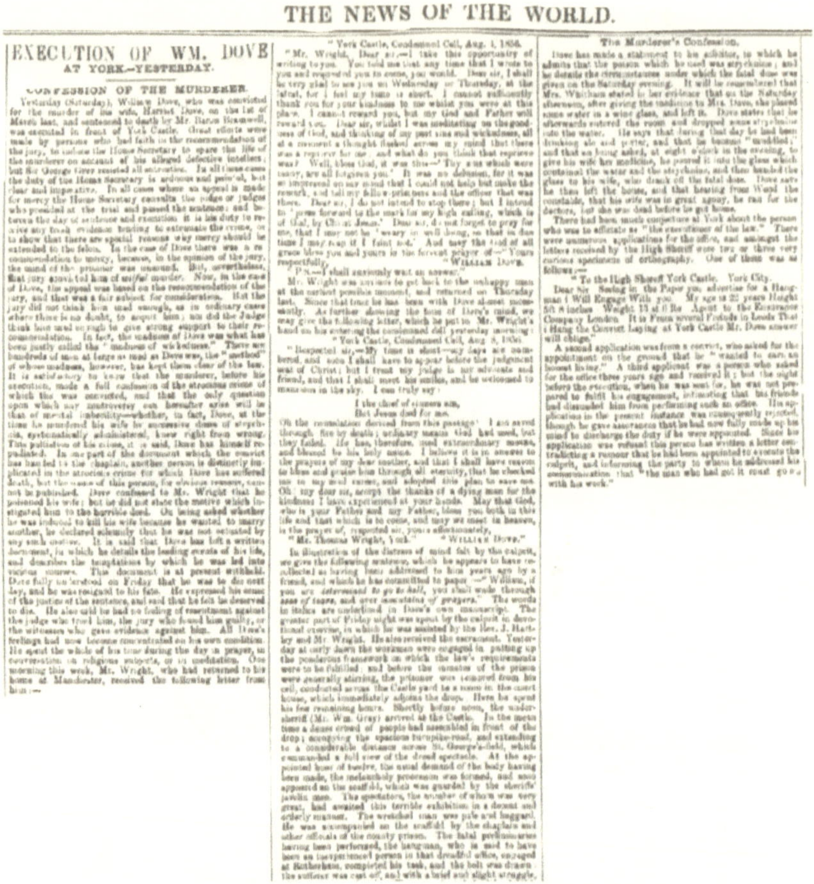

THE NEWS OF THE WORLD.

EXECUTION OF WM. DOVE AT YORK.—YESTERDAY.

CONFESSION OF THE MURDERER.

The Murderer's Confession.

Figure 12. *The News of the World,* 10 August 1856, 5. An extract from the page of police and court reports, featuring the case of William Dove, executed for poisoning his wife with strychnine.

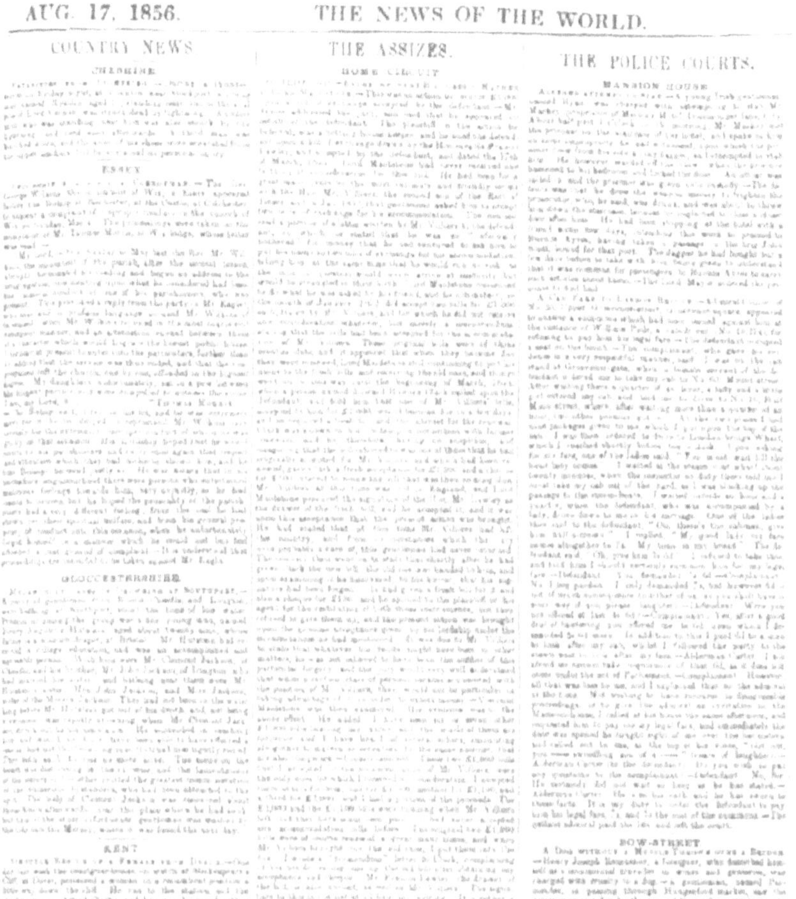
AUG. 17, 1856. THE NEWS OF THE WORLD.

COUNTRY NEWS

CHESHIRE

ESSEX

GLOUCESTERSHIRE

KENT

LANCASHIRE

THE ASSIZES

HOME CIRCUIT

THE POLICE COURTS

MANSION HOUSE

BOW-STREET

MARLBOROUGH-STREET

Figure 13. *The News of the World,* 17 August 1856, 7. Extracts from a typical page containing law court and police news, providing Country News, Assize, and Police Intelligence.

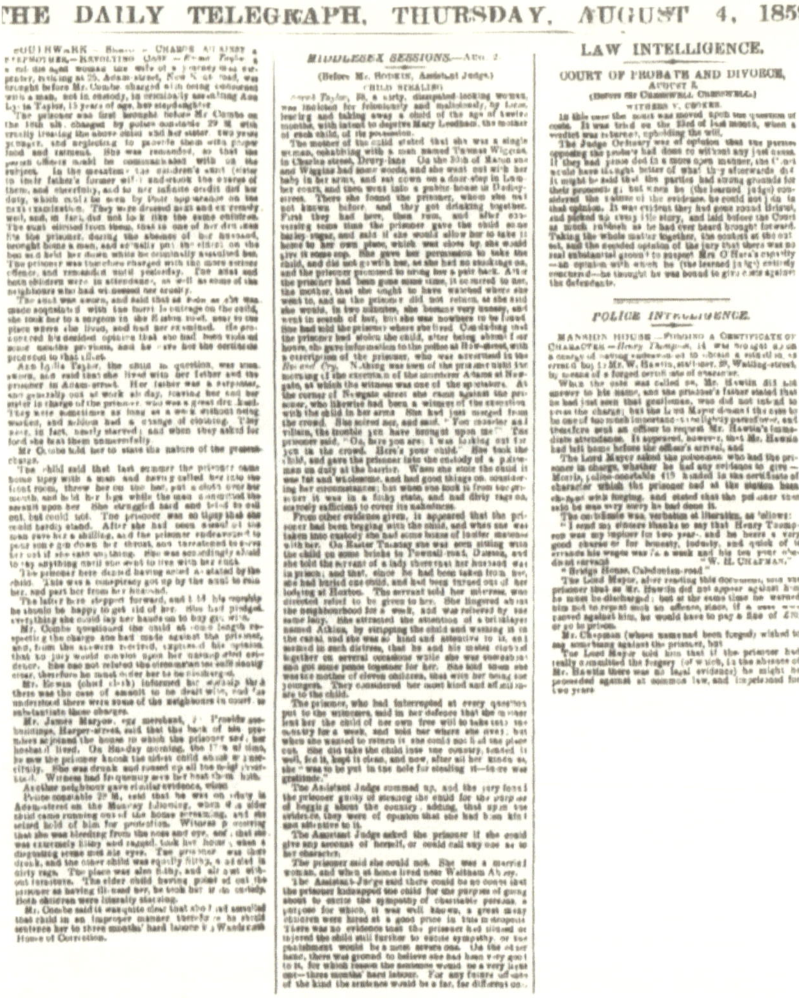

THE DAILY TELEGRAPH, THURSDAY, AUGUST 4, 1859

MIDDLESEX SESSIONS

LAW INTELLIGENCE.

COURT OF PROBATE AND DIVORCE.

POLICE INTELLIGENCE.

Figure 14. *Daily Telegraph*, 4 August 1859, 4. Extracts from a typical page containing Law Intelligence, reports from the Middlesex Sessions, and Police Intelligence.

Daily Telegraph

Starting in 1855, it was the first penny daily. It aimed at a working-class readership, and initially had a radical left inclination, as its early political commentaries in leaders showed. During the 1870s, it began to lose its radical edge, becoming less overtly political and more socially conservative. Its crime reporting was always one of its highlights, and it retained its sensational inclinations throughout the Victorian period, making it appeal more to a working-class and lower-middle-class readership (though actual readership was likely to be larger, especially at times of high-profile cases!).

> Daily Telegraph, *11 August 1859*:
> *Southwark: Extraordinary Case of Crim. Con.*

Harriet Sparks, a middle-aged singular looking female, residing with her husband at 4 Williams-place, Old Kent Road, was charged with stealing an old pair of trousers from the house of Mary Wright, an old lady at 12 Thomas-place, Grange Road, Bermondsey, under the following singular circumstances: The prosecutrix said she was a charwoman and occupied a small two-roomed house in Thomas-place. About 3 o'clock on the previous afternoon she had occasion to go out, when she locked up the house and hid the key at the bottom of the doorway. On her return half an hour afterwards, she was surprised to find the key was gone, and on looking at the door she perceived that it was locked and the key inside. She knocked repeatedly at the door for ten minutes. At last the door was suddenly opened and out rushed a married man residing in the neighbourhood, with his clothes disordered, and he ran away. Immediately afterwards the prisoner ran out with a pair of trousers across her shoulders, very much agitated. She [Sparks] was stopped by a constable who brought her back and she then identified the trousers as her property. On entering the bedroom she [Wright] found it had been recently used, and she found an old cloth cape lying there which did not belong to her. In answer to the magistrate, witness said she knew the prisoner and her husband, but it was not the latter who had been with her in the house. The prisoner must have watched her on leaving her house and by that means discovered where she hid her key. 129M[1] said he stopped the prisoner, and asked her what she had about her shoulders. She said it was her cape. Witness unfolded it, and found it was a pair of trousers, which the prosecutrix had identified as her property. She told him that she had taken them from Mrs Wright's house in mistake for her cape. Witness said they were both of the same colour. The magistrate discharged the prisoner, telling her that there could be no doubt as to her immoral conduct.

Daily Telegraph, *14 May 1856: An Aggravating Wife.*

At Worship-street on Monday, William Miller, a cabinet-maker, was charged with assaulting his wife, a delicate young woman, with an infant in her arms. Complainant said she had been married nearly five years, and her husband was of drunken habits, at times not allowing her more than 2s 6d a week to furnish food for the whole family. She had no desire to hurt his person or feelings by imprisonment, and would be thankful for a separation if he would allow her some little assistance. His cruelty by violence was incessant. Last Saturday night he returned to his home late, and she aggravated him, which caused him to strike her with his fist in the face. Mr. D'Eyncourt: How did you aggravate him? Complainant: Well, Sir, I perceived he was in liquor as usual, and wanted him to go to bed and have his supper there, and then he hit me. Mr. D'Eyncourt: And you call that aggravation! Did the blow pain you much? Wife—Well, Sir, I did scream with pain; and then some lodgers sent for a constable. I certainly have reproached him on previous occasions for keeping his family without food. Cloak, 237G: I found the woman with a lump on her forehead as large as a walnut, and another at the back of her head. She said her husband had knocked her down, and she appeared to me in great anguish. He was drunk. The neighbours complained of his general conduct to her. Mr. D'Eyncourt: She only wishes to separate, but I must punish you for the assault. After three months imprisonment you may perhaps have become a better man, and have some sense of your duty to your wife and family. The defendant, who did not deny the assault, was then removed to the cell, while his wife quitted the court exclaiming, "My children!—oh my poor children!"

Daily Telegraph, *15 July 1856: Riot at Gateshead.*

On Saturday a riot of a serious character took place at the Felling, Gateshead, a body of Ribandmen having attacked some Orangemen. It being the anniversary of the Battle of the Boyne, the Protestant Association of Royal Orangemen went through the streets in procession. Some hundreds of Ribandmen assembled, armed with pistols, swords and bludgeons etc, and attacked the persons in the procession. Great confusion arose, and it is said that between 16 and 20 men were more or less injured in the affray. One man named John Spencer, a tailor, residing in Gateshead, as well as a boy named Edward Badger, were taken to the Infirmary. Spencer had five contused wounds on his head, his front teeth were all knocked out, and his face and body dreadfully bruised; and the boy had a gunshot wound in his thigh, but it was not considered serious. The lad took no part in the affray, and was standing on the side of the road when he was shot. Several pistols were fired, and the Ribandsmen with yells, attacked men, women and children indiscriminately for some time. The names of the ringleaders are known, and measures have been taken for their apprehension. One man named Hannan is in custody, and it is stated that his shoes were studded with iron spikes in order to inflict the greater injury. The road after the occurrence was in many places covered with blood, where the affray was most violent. By the latest accounts received, all further outrage had been prevented by the energetic measures of the police.

Daily Telegraph, *11 May 1870: Bow Street. Masquerading.*

Henry Fletcher and Anne Fletcher, domestic servants, were charged with loitering in Gower-street at half-past two in the morning, and the former defendant with being at the time in female attire. Police Constable 168E deposed that he was on duty in Store-street, and saw the defendants, both dressed as women; but hearing the male prisoner speak to the other, his suspicions were aroused. He accosted them and then took them both into custody. They stated that they had been at a masquerade ball at Highbury. The charge of loitering was not pressed. With regard to the other point, Superintendent Thompson said there had been a masquerade ball at Highbury Barn,[2] and it was very likely the defendants were returning from it. Mr. Ingham told the male defendant it was a piece of great folly on his part to act as he had done. As, however, there was no evidence against them, they would be discharged.

Daily Telegraph, *21 May 1870 (Leader)*

We must be pardoned for reverting to the admired process of "manufacturing" habitual criminals. We have to note the attainment of perhaps the perfection of the fabricated article in a specimen recently labelled by the name of John Bradbury. The raw material of John Bradbury would seem to have been of a "sulky and idle" description. The crude mass, however, was worked up into a manufactured article in an astonishingly short space of time. Before he had obtained the age of nineteen, John Bradbury had contrived to obtain five convictions on serious charges—two being for burglary. He was sentenced not long since to seven years penal servitude, and was duly removed to Chatham Convict Prison. To what further extent the felonious faculties of John Bradbury might have developed—how he might have bloomed in bank robbery, graduated in garrotting, or eventually risen to murder—are matters beyond our ken; but, as it happened, when John Bradbury arrived at the penal servitude stage of manufacture, he was exasperating enough to hang himself by a handkerchief and a hammock strap to the window bars of his cell and was cut down dead. This act of perverse obduracy led to a coroner's inquest; and the jury having sat on John Bradbury's strangled corpse, delivered a verdict of "Temporary Insanity." The "temporary" nature of the wretched creature's lunacy might be questioned; but we have no desire to analyse his character by speculation. He was *prima facie,* a five-times distilled villain; twice had he been in hold for housebreaking; and richly, no doubt had he merited the sentence of seven years penal servitude. Still this wretched burglar and self-murderer was only nineteen years of age; he was, in other words, not a man but a boy. At what age, may we inquire, did the manufacturers take him in hand and put him in the way of becoming a habitual criminal? Perhaps John Bradbury was "born bad" and was a criminal in his cradle. Arguing on that hypothesis would it not have been cheaper and more merciful to poison him with his pap, or brain him with his first peg top, than let him be "manufactured" into a convict destined, ere he arrived at man's estate, to stop the further progress of manufacture by hanging himself in a prison cell?

Daily Telegraph, *9 July 1870: Baby Farming at Brixton.*

An inquest was held yesterday afternoon by Mr. W. Carter at the Lambeth Workhouse, on the body of a female child alleged to have died from the treatment it received from the women Margaret Waters and Sarah Ellis. Serjeant Richard Relf stated that the deceased child was one of those he had found at Frederic-terrace when specially sent there to inquire into this case. When he first saw the child it was lying on the sofa in a state of torpor. Ellen O'Connell, the girl who had given evidence previously, said that she had moved from her former lodging because it had been made too "hot" for her on account of the evidence she had previously given. Witness knew the deceased as having been in Mrs. Waters's house. The child was called Caroline Castle. Mrs Waters had told witness that the deceased came from a street called Castle-street, but witness could not tell where that street was situated. The child was very ill when brought to Mrs. Waters's house. Witness had seen lime water and medicine given to the children, and had procured laudanum by the desire of Mrs Waters. She had never seen anything administered to the deceased, who was sometimes fed with a bottle and sometimes a spoon. Witness was confidant as to the deceased having been one of the children in the house. Witness had to make up the children's food, and put about a dessert-spoonful of lime water in each bottle. Some of the children cried a good deal, but most of them were generally asleep. Dr. Bullen said that the received charge of the deceased child on the 13th ult. It appeared to be from four to six months old, but was very puny and emaciated. It was more lively than the other children, but had evidently been not well-nourished. The muscles were very flabby, and there was an unusual absence of muscular power, and it was not bigger than a newly-born infant, weighing only nine pounds. The child sunk and died on the 5th inst, the immediate cause of death being congestion of the brain. In reply to the coroner the witness further stated that the condition in which he found the brain was not natural. This might have been caused by want of sufficient nourishment, or by the administration of opium. He found no traces of narcotic drugs, but these would soon pass away. Such a condition of brain would be looked for in persons used to taking opium. The coroner regretted that in the interests of justice they could not trace the child's parents, and consequently had no proof that it had ever been entrusted to Mrs. Waters. The jury returned a verdict of "death from congestion of the brain produced by want of sufficient nourishment and the use of narcotic drugs."

Daily Telegraph, *16 July 1870: Westminster. The Liberty of the Subject.*

William Webb, a man having the appearance of an artisan, was charged with knowingly uttering a bad shilling to Mr. Charles Johnson, of the White Horse, Duke-street, Chelsea. The prosecutor stated that the defendant came into his house the previous night, and, having called for half an ounce of tobacco, put down a bad shilling in payment for it. Prisoner said he did not know it was bad, but as prosecutor felt sure that he did he gave him into custody. Mr. Arnold: What makes you feel that he knew it was bad? Prosecutor: I have had several bad pieces of money tendered at my house lately. Mr. Arnold: By the prisoner?—Prosecutor: No, I don't know him. Mr, Arnold: You have charged this man with knowingly uttering this shilling. Why "knowingly." Prosecutor: Why, by his person and appearance. He looked as though he wanted to pass the money when he came in. He asked for tobacco without wanting anything else. Mr. Arnold: Is that the only reason? Prosecutor: Yes. Mr. Arnold: I think it a very bad reason for giving a man in charge. Prisoner is discharged. Inspectors of police should be more cautious how they take these charges.

Daily Telegraph, *23 July 1870 (Leader)*

Whatever opinions may be held as to the policy of the Contagious Diseases Acts, there can be very little difference as to the justice of Lord Henry Lennox's denunciation of the style in which the opposition to them has been carried on. Never, perhaps, during the present century has a mass of literature so utterly obscene been forced upon decent people as the mountains of tracts, memorials, and handbills thrust into the hands of women and unmarried girls by the opponents of the Acts. We cannot soil our pages even to describe or characterise the loathsome stuff which is circulating in the handbills at this moment in London. Suffice it to say, that they contain material which could not otherwise be published for fear of coming under Lord Campbell's Act. Mr. Gladstone having intimated the willingness of the Government to grant an inquiry into the working of these laws, it is difficult to understand in what way the circulation of these handbills and memorials can be justified. It is simply absurd that the abominable broadsides issued by the Anti-Contagious Diseases Acts Association should be thrust into the hands of decent women, and rained upon modest and innocent people, as they now are. The credit or discredit, whichever it may be, of passing these Acts, belongs to no one party or class of persons; and they have indubitable effected some most valuable sanitary and moral effects in the districts where they have been enforced. But the cost of any such reforms may be too great; and if the objections are valid, they can be best urged before the impartial and skilled tribunal of a Royal Commission. The present appeals to fear, or to worse feelings, deserve unqualified condemnation.

Daily Telegraph, *7 September 1870 (Leader)*

Another of those unhappily frequent charges of fraud in connection with the getting up of new companies has just reached the close of the preliminary stage of inquiry. On Monday, six gentlemen, formerly directors of a company called the Commercial Indemnity Corporation of Great Britain were committed by the Lord Mayor for trial at the Central Criminal Court, on the charge of having prepared and issued a false prospectus, and generally of having conspired to deceive and defraud the public. The case so strongly resembles others still fresh in popular recollection that we need hardly recapitulate the evidence. The Corporation seems to have been formed on the ruins of a previous company, then in liquidation; and various individuals were induced to join the board on being assured that the association possessed substantial property and was doing a lucrative business. Some policies seem to have been issued, but there was little or no capital, and there was a difficulty in obtaining the payment of claims. Accordingly, one of the policy-holders invoked the law against the directors, and the Lord Mayor has thought the preliminary evidence sufficient to justify further inquiry at a higher Court. Without at all prejudging the case, we may point out that the admissions made by the accused themselves go far to explain the true causes of such incidents. In self-defence, the directors affirmed that if there had been anything wrong, they were not aware of it, since they had left everything in the hands of the general manager, whose statements as to the promotion and the conduct of the company they implicitly believed. One gentleman, indeed, was frank enough to say, that he had never before been connected with a public company, and was "utterly ignorant of the working of the law on this subject." It is a great pity that such knowledge of the law should be obtained by such a process as a trial at the Old Bailey; but can we really wonder that men should get into difficulties, if they are so heedless of their steps as this confession indicates? Legal points apart, the director who joins a public company and allows his name to be used for its benefit, is morally culpable, if mischief happens, exactly in proportion to his own neglect and to the eminence of his own standing. The plain truth is that, a seat at a ruling board brings honour, it involves distinct responsibility, and it should never be accepted unless with a full knowledge of all the facts, and with an honest determination to perform all the duties. The omission is not fair even to that more active individual who is left without help or advice, to take the whole labour on himself and the whole moral liability. If men have either forgotten such obligations, or have deliberately ignored them, it is no defence to say that they performed the real work of a director by deputy, and therefore washed their hands of the consequences.

Daily Telegraph, *9 April 1875 (Leader)*

Mr. Justice Brett has taken what he rightly describes as a "bold course" in dealing with the principals who were engaged in a fight on Hackney Marshes which ended in the death of one combatant. Seven men, including, of course, the victor, were indicted, and the whole, saving Taylor, the "stakeholder,"[3] who was not present when the battle occurred, pleaded guilty to the charge of manslaughter. We may at once dismiss the case against Taylor, since it involves a curious point of law reserved for decision before the Court of Appeal,[4] to wit, whether stakeholding, under the like circumstances, is a criminal offence. As regards the others, their story is brief. Two men, Tubbs and Dalgar, having quarrelled, it was determined that they should fight it out; and stakes were deposited, as the Judge infers, merely for the purpose of binding the men to the combat. They met, engaged, and Tubbs proved the better man; but Dalgar would not give in until he was so weakened that further efforts were impossible. The injuries he received caused his death, and beyond all doubt the accused were the guilty parties to that painful upshot. What punishment should the Bench inflict? On the preceding day, Mr. Justice Brett had sentenced a pair of ruffians to long terms of penal servitude because, after a quarrel and challenge to fight, they had drawn knives, at a given signal, and had slain a young man—a fearful example of brutal cowardice. In such cases, said the Judge, "I shall punish with the utmost severity." But, "for the sake of laws and good government," he drew a marked distinction "between cases where cowardice and unfairness take place, and those in which in our infirm nature, men sometimes open a quarrel, and upon that a fair fight ensues." He did not mean a "prize-fight" in the ordinary signification of the phrase, a combat solely for money; such encounters, followed by a death, will be punished with the utmost severity. The conflict between Tubbs and Dalgar was not one of that kind. They quarrelled, and, said the Judge, "although it certainly would have been far better if, upon that quarrel, they did nothing more, yet I do not think that we are bound to lay down that when men quarrel it is any great sin that they should fight upon that quarrel, if only they will fight fair and with their natural weapons, their hands." Language more frank and manly has not often been heard on the Bench. Further, the Judge held the opinion that "the fight when it took place, was in all particulars a fair fight; and while he thought the contest was prolonged too far, he threw the blame upon the deceased, being of the opinion that Tubbs committed no grave fault in standing up to his opponent, so long as the latter refused to acknowledge himself vanquished. Nevertheless, the prisoners, said Mr. Justice Brett, were all guilty of a criminal offence—manslaughter. "But desiring, as I do," he continued, "to make a most marked distinction between a fight which occurs upon a quarrel, and which is conducted fairly, and a cowardly fight, whether with knives or kicking, I propose to take what I believe will be considered a bold course." Accordingly 4 men were sentenced to one week's imprisonment, and two onlookers got off with the nominal sentence of 3 days. The remarkable language of the Judge, we trust, will produce a good effect on those classes who are prone to violence. No mercy will be displayed towards the murderous criminal who stabs, kicks, or otherwise behaves like an assassin. Nor will recourse to physical force, as an arbiter of quarrels, be tolerated for an instance without due chastisement. But the Judges, at least one, will not fail to weigh the circumstances in each case, and maintain the distinction between a fair fight, even should it end in manslaughter, and the deadly assaults of dastards who frequently deserve the last penalty of the law.

News of the World

Starting in 1843, as a Sunday paper aimed at a working class readership, it achieved one of the highest circulations of any weekly in the mid-century. It was known for its concentration on the reporting of crime and bad behavior, often lifting its reports directly from the respectable dailies including *The Times* (as did its fellow Sundays).

News of the World, *24 February 1861: Clerkenwell. The Widdy and Her Mites of Children.*

Bridget McGann, a woman who had seen about fifty summers appeared to a summons charging her with unlawfully using threatening language towards Sarah Taylor her landlady. The complainant, a stout woman, with much dignity, said: "Yer 'onner, that woman there, Mistress McGann, is a-lodgin' with me. On Thrusday [sic] she kicked up a row, and threatened to do me bodily 'arm with a broomstick, and I only escapted [sic] her murderous assault by putting up my 'and and ducking it, which was no easy matter for me" (exhibiting her rotundity). The defendant, who had been very restless during complainant's statement, here burst forth: "In me yer wurtchip, ye see a young widdy; me name's Bridget McGann, wid three children an—," Magistrate: "Will you remain quiet; you will have your turn presently. Do you wish to ask the complainant any questions?" Defendant (excited): "I am a young widdy, an' unprotected. I'm put on, I'm trampled on, an' my back has been broken; me orphan children an' meself have been quite suffocated wid me landlady's shmoke (laughter), and I never hit her at all wid the broomstick (a laugh)." Complainant (valiantly): "No, no; 'cause I ducked it (laughter)." Defendant: "Didn't yer hit me black-and-blue, didn't yer kill me and me children wid yer shmoke, and didn't yer—" Magistrate: "Stop! Have you any witnesses?" Defendant: "Yes, yer 'onner. Here Jem Riley, come up wid yer (renewed laughter)." . . . Jem Riley stated that Mishtress McGann's boy had his ears boxed, when a scrimmage took place, and on Mishtress McGann running out, Mrs. Taylor shut the door, and called her an Irish cat, and would not let her in. Mrs. McGann tried to get in through the window. She scrambled in on all fours, and threatened to break Mrs. Taylor's head with a broom handle. He did not see any more. Defendant (exultingly): "There, your wurtchip, I'm a poor widdy woman wid three children (laughter)." Complainant: "I'm in danger of my life, and she's now bound over for three months." Defendant (retractingly): "I'm a poor widdy. I never, be me sowl, insulted nor bate her." Magistrate: "I find you have broken your bond of three months, and I therefore inflict a penalty of 10s or fourteen days." Defendant: "Oh, what'll I do, I've got no money. What'll I do." Turner, the gaoler silently acquainted her, for he at once conducted her to a cell to the laughter and cheers of the spectators.

News of the World, *18 August 1861 Charge of Violation.*

William Slade Bailey, a farmer, aged 40, was charged at the Gloucester Assizes with a rape committed upon Emma Reeves, at Berkeley. The prosecutrix entered into the service of the prisoner on the 23rd of May last, as a domestic servant and the charge which she now made against her late master was, that on the 14th of June following he was alone with her in the house, and the offence was committed. The prosecutrix told him she would go to the magistrates at Berkeley, and he then put a sovereign down upon the dresser,, but she refused to take it, and told him that if he left it there she would give it to her mistress. Subsequently both Mrs Bailey and the prisoner then offered her money to make it up, and Mrs Bailey began to cry and said she could not help her husband's faults, and tried to persuade her not to leave and not to say anything about it. The prosecutrix at length consented to remain, and the prisoner drew up a paper which she signed, to serve Mrs. Bailey from May 23 1861 to October 11. Directly the prosecutrix had signed the document, she went to the Rev Mr. Karr at Berkeley and there charged the prisoner with "pulling her about in an indecent and brutish manner." The prisoner had followed her there and denied the charge and said she only wanted to extort money. She thought the magistrates would understand what she meant by "pulling he about in an indecent and brutish manner." The magistrate told the parties to see if they could settle the matter, and dismissed them till the Friday. The girl had a glass of beer at Berkeley and a glass of ginger wine, and then went back to the prisoner's house, and when she got there Mrs Bailey said she was intoxicated and she did not believe a word about the matter. She asked her master to be allowed to leave but he refused, and said that if she went away he would send a policeman after her. Upon that, the prosecutrix said she did not know what to do, and became so much excited and distressed that she attempted to destroy herself by throwing herself into a pool of water, from which she was taken out in a state of insensibility. The next day, a policeman, Shephard, came, and Mrs. Bailey, in the presence of the policeman and the prisoner offered to give her half a sovereign and a new dress to make it up, and not to have any more ado. The policeman then went away, and on the next Friday, June 21, she went to the petty sessions at Berkeley, and while they were waiting for the case to come on, Shepard said that the prisoner was willing to give her a sovereign and her wages, but she said she would not make it up. The case was then gone into before the magistrates and the prisoner was only committed for an assault with intent to commit a rape. The prosecutrix was subjected to a long and rigid cross-examination, but she answered all the questions put to her with great readiness, even when they seemed to tell against her. The Jury found the prisoner Guilty of an attempt and he was sentenced to 18 months hard labour.

Lloyds Weekly

Founded by Edward Lloyd in 1842, its early editors included Douglas Jerrold. Aimed at a working class readership, with a left-leaning, even radical, orien-

Appendix

Figure 15. *Lloyds News,* 5 June 1870. Personal advertisements, including the baby-farming advertisement which led to the arrest of Margaret Waters.

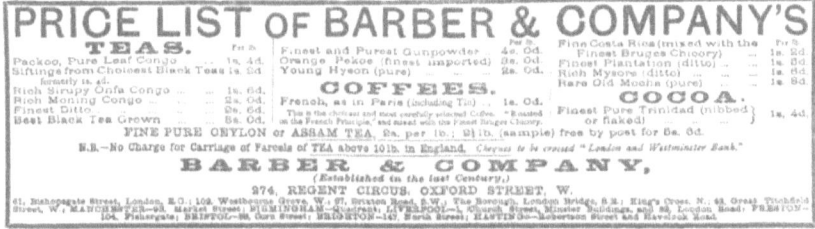

Figure 16. *Cassell's Saturday Journal,* 1890, a typical advertisement for coffee and tea, which appeared throughout that year.

tation, much of its content was actually concerned with crime and scandal (especially that in high life, where possible). It was one of the two most popular of the mid-century Sunday weeklies, and was widely read, as its range of advertisements underlines.

Lloyds News, *27 February 1853: Falsifications of Food*

Mark yonder portly man; he has scarcely passed the period of maturity and yet he incessantly complains of ailments which the art of no physician has yet been enabled to reach; his health is evidently breaking, his system has struggled long against the ravages of an insidious foe. Probably the water with which his domicile is supplied, besides being tainted with all the foulness that a London company can impart, is revived into the leaden cisterns which are fast corroding from the action of carbonic acid and thus hourly tending to bring their victim to the grave by means, slow, but sure, and terrible as sure. At breakfast, his tea, coloured (as it commonly is) with Prussian blue, chromate of lead, or carbonate of copper, adds to the already poisonous nature of the water with which it is combined. His bread, if he resides in London, is certainly adulterated with alum, not improbably with plaster-of-Paris or sand. His beer with *coculus indicus,* grains of paradise, quassia etc. Those girkins of emerald hue, that appear so innocent, and consequently so tempting in their prismatic jar, owe their seductive beauty to use of the deadliest poisons in all the range of chemistry. The verdant apricots in that tart are attractive from the same baneful cause. The anchovy paste produced contemporaneously with the cheese, if analysed, would be found to consist of an amalgam of decayed sprats, Venetian red and red lead; nay, that double-Gloucester itself is not free from contamination; its colour is due to annatto, and that annatto has been compounded of red lead, chrome and ochre. the oil in that salad has possible come from Paris, where incredible quantities are manufactured at the knacker's yard! Whole carcasses of horses being there boiled down, the fat is resolved into its component stearine and elaine; the former being converted into candles and the latter into olive oil.

Reynolds News

Founded by the former Chartist George Reynolds in 1850, it had the reputation of being the most genuinely "working class" of the Sunday papers, partly because of the radical tone taken by its leaders and commentaries, especially during contentious times such as that surrounding the Tichborne Claimant

Case. Like its fellow Sundays, it had a powerful concentration on crime and high-life scandal.

Reynolds News, *13 January 1856. Caution to Jurymen.*

It will be recollected by our readers that at the commencement of the inquest on the body of Mr. Starling, who was so barbarously murdered near Burnfield, that one of the jury, (Mr. Barnett, of Bedford Lodge) who had been summoned, failed to attend, upon which the coroner, J. M. Tavel, Esq., indicted a fine of 40l. A few days ago a writ was received from the Treasury by the Sheriff of Durham to enforce payment of the fine. The writ has since been executed and the money paid. *Durham Advertiser*[5]

Reynolds News, *14 April 1856. Latest Old Bailey Trials. Felonious Assault.*

Robert Pearl, 17, charged with felonious assault upon Sarah Patty, a girl under ten years of age. The jury found the prisoner "guilty" of the attempt only, and he was sentenced to be imprisoned and kept to hard labour for one year.

Reynolds News, *27 October 1861. Bow Street. A Bad Mother and a Good Son.*

On Monday an elderly woman named Hannah Smith was charged with assaulting her son, Thomas Smith. The boy is one of the shoeblacks in the Ragged School Brigade, and out of his scanty earnings in that capacity allowed his mother 2s a week. On Monday morning as he was leaving the office of the Brigade to go to his work, she applied to him for sixpence to go to Epsom for a holiday. As she was drunk, he declined to give it to her. She then began to abuse him, making so much disturbance as to cause a crowd to assemble. Ultimately she knocked his box off his head, spilling the blacking on the ground. The blacking which was the property of the society, was valued at 2s. The inspector of the brigade gave her into custody. The prisoner said that as her son would not give her sixpence to go for a holiday, she determined to give him one by annoying him so that he could not go to his work. She admitted that he was "a good boy" and allowed her 2s a week. Mr. Corrie. "Then you must be a very bad woman to try to prevent him from getting a living. You must pay 5s or go to prison for five days." The prisoner said her son would pay the 5s. Mr. Corrie strongly recommended him to do no such thing, but to let her go to prison.

Pall Mall Gazette

Founded in 1865 as an evening paper with a Liberal inclination, its first editor was Frederick Greenwood, and a major contributor was Sir James Fitzjames Stephen, who established its reputation for reporting of crime, and opinion on the state of the law and the legal process. Later, W. T. Stead succeeded to the editorship, but Stephen never lost interest in the paper, and continued to contribute to and influence its content.

Pall Mall Gazette, *29 July 1865: Dr Pritchard.*

The Times remarks that the crime of poisoning by a medical man in the course of professional attendance goes to the limits of all that we can conceive of wickedness. Treachery of the bases kind is added to the ordinary cruelty and malice which constitute the guilt of murder. Yet, of this most foul, strange and unnatural crime, there have been several instances of late years. The facility of the deed and the improbability of detection seem to suggest it, and men not wanting in talents, in good manners, and in that demeanour which conciliates the goodwill of the world, are transformed until they become morally worse than the most degraded garrotter who is serving his time in gaol. Crimes of poisoning are recorded in every age, but the facilities are now more numerous than at any other time.

Pall Mall Gazette, *23 September 1880: Occasional Notes.*

The juvenile offender is likely to become the absorbing topic of the vacation. It is a relief to turn from the irresponsible correspondence in newspapers to the practical suggestions which have just been published, in the form of a draft bill, by a committee of the magistrates of Manchester. The gist of them is the establishment of "separate places of detention" for criminals under 16 years of age. They are to be as unlike gaols as possible, and no child is under any circumstances to be sent to a common gaol. This seems to be the only solution of the question if "juvenile offenders" are to be confined at all, and are to be protected, as everybody thinks they ought to be, from the contagion of adult criminals. A more questionable suggestion is the prohibition of the casual employment of children under ten years of age, after 7 o'clock at night in winter and 9 in summer. "Casual employment" is defined to mean any sort of employment for gain away from the child's home, the hours of which are not already regulated by Act of Parliament. This proposal, of course, is aimed at the petty merchandise of the streets, by which so many of the most destitute children contrive to pick up some sort of a livelihood. There are grave objections to such legislation. NO law can keep these children out of the streets, and if it could it is difficult to see what moral good would be gained in many cases by driving them to their own wretched homes. And if they are to be left to run about the streets, they may as well be allowed to ply their humble trade as long as they can find customers. It is a misfortune that young children should be driven to this kind of life, but the principle of the Curfew law is not the right one to apply.

Notes

1. The number of the police constable, here a member of the Metropolitan Police Force.

2. A venue associated in the minds of respectable Victorians with drunkenness and immorality.

3. The man in possession of the bets placed on the contest.

4. Popular term for the Court for Crown Cases Reserved.

5. It was common for national titles to "lift" reports from provincial titles, and vice versa, usually acknowledging the source, as here.

Selected Further Reading

Reprinted Primary Texts

Carpenter, Mary. *Juvenile Delinquents: Their Condition and Treatment.* [1851]. Patterson, NJ: Smith, 1970.

Cobbe, Frances Power. "Wife-Torture in England." In *The Sexuality Debates,* edited by Sheila Jeffreys. London: Routledge, 1987.

Doré, Gustave, and B. Jerrold. *London: A Pilgrimage.* [1864–68]. New York: Dover, 1970.

Greenwood, James. *The Seven Curses of London.* [1869]. Oxford: Basil Blackwell, 1981.

Mackay, Charles. *Memoirs of Extraordinary Popular Delusions and the Madness of Crowds.* [1932]. Ware: Wordsworth, 1995.

Mayhew, Henry. *London Street Folk.* Vol. 1, *London Labour and London Poor.* [1851]. London: Frank Cass, 1967.

———. *Selections from London Labour and London Poor.* Edited by J. L. Bradley. London: Oxford University Press, 1965.

———, and J. Binney. *The Criminal Prisons of London and Scenes of Prison Life.* [1862]. London: Frank Cass, 1968.

The Unknown Mayhew. *The Morning Chronicle, 1849–50.* Edited with introductions by E. P. Thompson and Eileen Yeo. Harmondworth: Penguin, 1873.

Waugh, Benjamin. *The Gaol Cradle—Who Rocks It?* [1873]. London: Garland, 1984.

Secondary Texts

Aisenberg, N., ed. *London Crimes.* Boston: Rowan Tree Press, 1982.

Altick, Richard. *Evil Encounters: Two Victorian Sensations.* London: Murray, 1987.

———. *Victorian Studies in Scarlet.* London: Dent, 1972.

Bailey, Victor, ed. *Policing and Punishment in Nineteenth Century Britain.* London: Croom Helm, 1982.

Baker, J. H. *An Introduction to English Legal History.* 4th ed. London: Butterworths, 2002.

Barret-Ducroq, Françoise. *Love in the Time of Victoria.* London: Penguin, 1992.

Behlmer, George K. *Child Abuse and Moral Reform in England, 1870–1908*. Stanford: Stanford University Press, 1982.

Bentley, David. *English Criminal Justice in the Nineteenth Century.* London: Hambledon, 1998.

Brake, Laurel, Aled Jones, and Lionel Madden, eds. *Investigating Victorian Journalism.* Basingstoke: Macmillan, 1990.

Brake, Laurel, Bill Bell, and David Finkelstein, eds. *Nineteenth Century Media and the Construction of Identities.* Basingstoke: Palgrave, 2002.

Brown, Lucy. *Victorian News and Newspapers.* Oxford: Clarendon Press, 1985.

Burnham, Lord. *Peterborough Court: The Story of the* Daily Telegraph. London: Cassell, 1955.

Burnett, John. *Plenty and Want: A Social History of Diet in England from 1815 to the Present Day.* London: Methuen, 1985.

Chibnall, S. *Law and Order News: An Analysis of Crime Reporting in the British Press.* London: Tavistock, 1977.

Cohen, Stanley. *Folk Devils and Moral Panics: The Creation of Mods and Rockers.* London: Routledge, 2002.

Cohen, William. *Sex Scandal: The Private Parts of Victorian Culture.* London: Duke University Press, 1996.

Conley, Carolyn. *The Unwritten Law, Criminal Justice in Victorian Kent.* Oxford: Oxford University Press, 1991.

Crawford, Catherine, and Michael Clarke, eds. *Legal Medicine in History.* Cambridge: Cambridge University Press, 1994.

Cross, Nigel. *The Common Writer: Life in Nineteenth Century Grub Street.* Cambridge: Cambridge University Press, 1985.

Davidoff, Leonore. *Worlds Between: Historical Perspectives on Gender and Class.* Cambridge: Polity, 1995.

D'Cruze, Shani, ed. *Everyday Violence in Britain, c1850–1950: Gender and Class.* Harlow: Longman, 2000.

Emsley, Clive. *Crime and Society in England, 1750–1900.* London: Longman, 1996.

Foucault, Michel. *Discipline and Punish: The Birth of the Prison.* Harmondsworth: Penguin, 1979.

Gatrell, V. A. C., et al., eds. *Crime and the Law: The Social History of Crime in Western Europe since 1500.* London: Europa, 1980.

Goode, Erich, and Nachman Ben-Yehuda. *Moral Panics: The Social Construction of Deviance.* Oxford: Blackwell, 1994.

Harrison, Brian. *Drink and the Victorians: The Temperance Question in England, 1815–1872.* 2nd ed. Keele: Keele University Press, 1994.

Horder, Jeremy. *Provocation and Responsibility.* Oxford: Oxford University Press, 1992.

Howkins, Alun. *Reshaping Rural England.* London: HarperCollins, 1991.

Hunt, Lynn, ed. *The New Cultural History.* Berkeley: University of California Press, 1989.

Inkster, Ian, Colin Griffin, Jeff Hill, and Judith Rowbotham, eds. *The Golden Age: Essays in British Social and Economic History, 1850–1870.* Aldershot: Ashgate, 2000.

Jenkins, Philip. *Intimate Enemies: Moral Panics in Contemporary Great Britain.* New York: Aldine de Gruyter, 1992.

Jones, David. *Crime, Protest, Community, and Police in Nineteenth Century Britain.* London: Routledge and Kegan Paul, 1982.

Jones, Marjorie. *Justice and Journalism.* Chichester: Barry Rose, 1974.
Kidd-Hewitt, David, and Richard Osborn, eds. *Crime and the Media: The Post-modern Spectacle.* London: Pluto Press, 1995.
Kindleberger, Charles P. *Manias, Panics, and Crashes: A History of Financial Crises.* 3rd ed. New York: Wiley, 1996.
Knelman, Judith. *Twisting in the Wind: The Murderess and the English Press.* Toronto: University of Toronto Press, 1998.
Laybourn, Keith, ed. *Social Conditions, Status, and Community, 1860–1920.* Stroud: Alan Sutton, 1997.
Marcus, Steven. *The Other Victorians: A Study of Sexuality and Pornography in Mid-Nineteenth Century England.* New York: Meridian, 1974.
Nead, Lynda. *Victorian Babylon: People, Streets, and Images in Nineteenth Century London.* New Haven: Yale University Press, 2000.
Panayi, Panikos, ed. *Racial Violence in Britain, 1840–1950.* Leicester: Leicester University Press, 1993.
Parsons, Gerald, ed. *Traditions.* Vol. 1, *Religion in Victorian Britain.* Manchester: Manchester University Press, 1988.
Pearsall, Ronald. *The Worm in the Bud.* Harmondsworth: Penguin, 1969.
Pearson, Geoffrey. *Hooligan: A History of Respectable Fears.* London: Macmillan, 1983.
Perkin, Harold. *The Rise of Professional Society: England since 1880.* London: Routledge, 1990.
Poovey, Mary. *Uneven Developments: The Ideological Work of Gender in Mid-Victorian England.* London: Virago, 1989.
Robb, George. "Circe in Crinoline: Domestic Poisonings in Victorian England." *Journal of Family History* 22, 2 (1999).
———. *White Collar Crime in Modern England: Financial Fraud and Business Morality, 1845–1929.* Cambridge: Cambridge University Press, 1992.
Roberts, Nickie. *Whores in History: Prostitution in Western Society.* London: HarperCollins, 1992.
Robson, John M. *Marriage or Celibacy?* The Daily Telegraph *on a Victorian Dilemma.* Toronto: University of Toronto Press, 1995.
Rowbotham, Judith, and Kim Stevenson, eds. *Behaving Badly: Visible Crime, Social Panics, and Legal Responses—Victorian and Modern Parallels.* Aldershot: Ashgate, 2003.
Rowbotham, Judith, Kim Stevenson, and Samantha Pegg. "Children of Misfortune: The Parallel Cases of Thompson and Venables, Bradley and Burgess." *Howard Journal of Criminal Justice* 42, 2 (2003): 107–22.
Schlesinger, Philip, and Howard Tumber. *Reporting Crime: The Media Politics of Criminal Justice.* Oxford: Oxford University Press, 1994.
Segal, Lynne, ed. *New Sexual Agendas.* Basingstoke: Macmillan, 1997.
Sindall, Rob. *Street Violence in the Nineteenth Century: Media Panic or Real Danger?* Leicester: Leicester University Press, 1990.
Springhall, J. O. *Youth, Popular Culture, and Moral Panics: Penny Gaffs to Gangsta-Rap, 1830–1996.* Basingstoke: Macmillan, 1998.
Stebbings, Chantal, ed. *Law Reporting in Britain.* London: Hambledon Press, 1995.
Steedman, Carolyn. *Policing the Victorian Community.* London: Routledge and Kegan Paul, 1984.
Swift, Roger, and Sheridan Gilley, eds. *The Irish in Victorian Britain: The Local Dimension.* Dublin: Irish Academic Press, 1999.

Taylor, David. *Crime, Policing, and Punishment in England, 1750–1914.* Basingstoke: Macmillan, 1998.

———. *The New Police in Nineteenth-Century England: Crime, Conflict, and Control.* Manchester: Manchester University Press, 1997.

Taylor, Howard "Rationing Crime: The Political Economy of Criminal Statistics since the 1850s." *The Economic History Review* 51, 3 (1998).

Thompson, F. M. L. *The Rise of Respectable Society: A Social History of Victorian Britain, 1830–1900.* London: Fontana, 1988.

Tosh, Josh. *A Man's Place: Masculinity and the Middle-Class Home in Victorian England.* New Haven: Yale University Press, 1997.

Walkowitz, Judith. *City of Dreadful Delight: Narratives of Sexual Danger in Late Victorian London.* London: Virago Press, 1992.

Weeks, Jeffrey. *Sex, Politics, and Society: The Regulation of Sexuality since 1800.* London: Longman, 1981.

Wiener, Joel, ed. *Papers for the Millions: The New Journalism in Britain, 1850s to 1914.* Westport, CT: Greenwood Press, 1988.

Wiener, Martin. *Men of Blood, Violence, Manliness and Criminal Justice in Victorian England.* Cambridge: Cambridge University Press, 2004.

———. *Reconstructing the Criminal: Culture, Law, and Policy in England, 1830–1914.* Cambridge: Cambridge University Press, 1994.

Wilson, David, and John Ashton. *What Everyone in Britain Should Know about Crime and Punishment.* London: Blackstone, 1999.

Index

Note that references to specific cases and Statutes are contained in the Table of Cases and Table of Statutes at the front of this volume.

abortion, 199–200
adoption, 200–2, 210
Acton, William, 131
adulteration, food and drink, 89, 127, 157, 158, 159–60, 161–64, 168, 169, 173, 173n 4, 296; alum, 154, 162, 167, 169–70, 171; baking powder, 162; beer and spirits, 161, 167, 168, 296; bottled goods, 162–63, 170–71, 296; bread, 160–61, 167, 169, 175n 77, 176n 98, 296; campaigns against adulteration, 164, coffee, 162, 167; confectionery, 163, 166; dairy products, 161, 164–65, 168, 172; flour, 160–61, 170, 171; food production chain, 160, 163, 164; Food Standards Agency, 173; inspectors, 170; loose and packaged items, 163, 170, 172; meat, 158, 173n 14; medicines, 146–48, 160; sale of adulterated items, 158–60, 163–66; social impacts of, 163, 164; tea, 162, 170, 171, 172, 173n 4, 296; tobacco, 161; water, 160–61, 296. *See also* consumerism; drink and drugs; medical expertise; medical profession; science
adultery. *See* criminal conversation
age, 1, 24, 29, 32, 33–35, 182, 234, 288, 298–99
agriculture, 48, 54n 4; social impacts of changes in, 48–49

Altick, Richard, xxv
Anderson, Sir Robert, 11–14, 15, 16, 19
Armadale (Collins), 140–41
Australia, 101, 211

baby–farming, 198–212, 269, 288–89; contemporary parallels, 198, 269; lying-in houses, 202, 206, 211; regulation of, 205–9
Bailey, Victor, 192
banks, 57, 60, 62, 66, 189; bank crashes, 62, 68n 23; bankers, 39; bank rates, 59–60, 62; Bank of England, 60; Italian bankers, 188. *See also* commerce and the commercial sector; financial crime; financial sector
Bell, John Any Bird, 29, 35–36
Blackstone, William, 247, 251
Blake, Matilda, 247, 248
Booth, Charles, 11
Bordieu, Pierre, 138n 8
Boulton and Park case, 88, 126, 129–31, 135, 137n 4
Brown, Lucy, xxv
Bulger case, 22n 53, 23, 37n 1
Buret, Eugene, 5,
Burgess case, 29–30, 36, 37n 1
Burnett, John, 128–29, 157
Carlyle, Thomas, 107
Campbell's Act, Lord, 290

305

Carpenter, Mary, 5, 10, 25–26, 32, 27
Carter, Sally, 269
Charges. *See* crimes; domestic violence; rape; violence
charities and charity work. *See* philanthropic activity
Charley, Mr., MP for Salford, 205
child murder. *See* murder
children, 5, 24, 26, 32, 202–3, 208; adulteration and, 163; casual employment and, 298–99; child care, 198–200; class and childhood, 24; criminality and, 5, 27–28; cruelty to, 203–5, 208; education and, 25–26, 36–37; employment of, 297, 298–99; gender stereotypes, 28; illegitimate, 198–203, 206; parents and, 8, 27, 31–32; recidivism and, 28, 34–35, 287–88, 298–99. *See also* age; family; juvenile criminality and delinquency; murder; women
Church of England, 1, 45, 47, 48, 50–51, 54nn 45, 50, 96, 100; anti-Catholicism, 112, 115, 117, 119, 121n 37, 182; attendance and support for, 43, 45, 182, 186–87; Church Missionary Society, 92, 95–96, 100; clergymen, 43, 44–45, 47, 49, 51, 121n 37; death and, 183; parochial life, 46, 50–51, 54n 45; popular Protestantism, 112; religious observance and, 43, 45; York Diocesan Board of Education, 42. *See also* civilization; missions; Nonconformity; religion; respectability and respectable society
civilization, standards of, 91–92, 94, 96, 98–99, 100–101, 103, 248, 263, 280; appearance and, 97, 289; "Britishness" and, 92, 94, 96, 98–99, 101, 102, 103–4, 248; class and, 101; law and, 99–100, 248, 263; militant civilization, 97–98; "uncivilized" behavior, 91, 93–94, 96, 101, 103, 248; women as markers of, 92, 100–101, 102, 103, 248
Clarence, Charles, 219–21, 223, 225, 226–27, 230n 29
Clarence, Selina, 215, 216, 219–25. *See also* judges; marriage; rape; sexual offenses; violence
Clark, Anna, 239

class, xxiii, xxiv–xxv, xxx, 1, 4–5, 9–11, 24–25, 35, 50–51, 101, 119, 148, 243–44, 249–50, 275–57, 285; criminality and class, 8–10, 11, 25–26, 117, 277–78; middle-class diversity, 189; middle classes, stereotypes of, 101, 181, 184, 185, 249–50; occupation and social status, 186, 276; working classes, xxiii, 5, 9, 10, 24, 50, 101, 102–3, 109, 113, 117, 119, 171, 187, 241, 249–50, 256. *See also* dangerous classes; criminals; gender; respectability and respectable society
clergymen and ministers. *See* Church of England; Nonconformity
Cleveland Street Scandal, 126
Cobbe, Francis Power, 249–50, 255, 263
Cohen, Stanley, xxvii–xxviii, 42, 44–45, 49, 51, 86n 73
Collins, Wilkie, 140–41, 153n 9
commerce and the commercial sector, 182, 188–90, 269, 290; commercial elites, 185, 188–89, 193; company formation, 56, 62, 63–64; debt, 56, 58–63; economic cycles and, 159, 188, 269; entrepreneurs, 55, 56; export markets in, 189–90; investments and investors, 55, 56, 60; legal protection in, 55–56; Manchester commerce, 185, 188–90,193; Manchester Chamber of Commerce, 189–90; railway firms, 59, 63; retail and retailers, 167, 169, 170; shares and shareholders, 56, 58–63; specialization in, 189–90. *See also* banks; company directors; financial crime; financial sector
common law. *See* law and legislation
company law. *See* companies; law
companies, financial. *See* banks; financial crime; financial sector; limited liability
company directors, 59–60, 61–63; activities, 58, 60, 61, 63; responsibilities of, 64–65. *See also* banks; commerce and the commercial sector; financial crime; financial sector
Conley, Carolyn, 239
consumerism: cheapness, 158–59; co-operative societies, 166, 171; credit systems,

159; *laissez-faire* approaches to, 158, 160, 165; state and, 169; supply and demand issues, 158, 159–60, 163, 169. *See also* adulteration
contagious diseases. *See* legal reform; venereal disease
courts, xxvi, xxx, 30, 73, 98, 277–78; Assizes, 28, 29–30, 70–71, 74–75, 83n 5, 101–2, 109, 252, 253, 261, 281, 283, 293–94; Bankruptcy, 56; Coroners', 183, 185, 209, 288–89, 297; Court of Appeal, 292; Court for Crown Cases Reserved, 72, 74–82, 83nn 11, 14, 84nn 37, 39, 299n 4; Court of Criminal Pleas, 246n 10; Courts of Equity, 251; Divisional Court of the Exchequer, 236; Divorce Court, 181; ecclesiastical courts, xxx; Old Bailey (Central Criminal Court), 12–13, 35, 70–71, 82n 3, 204, 209, 260–61, 290–91; petty sessions/Quarter Sessions, 45, 109, 252, 257, 284, 294; police/summary courts, xxvi, 14, 27, 30–31, 33, 88, 101–2, 109, 168, 207, 236, 247, 252–55, 258–60, 265nn 26, 32, 277–78, 283–84, 285–86, 293, 297; Queen's/King's Bench, xxxi, 215–16, 219–20. *See also* judges; law and legislation; magistrates; trials; violence; women
Cox, Edward, 58, 258–59, 261
Cream, Thomas Neill, 126, 145, 154n 38
crime and bad behavior, xxii–xxiv, xxviii–xxx, 1, 3–5, 7, 23–25, 30–32, 36, 92, 109–10, 141, 268, 274, 285–88; causatory factors of, 5–6, 10–12, 16, 20, 24, 25–26, 31–32, 110, 111–12, 113; detective processes and, 8–13, 157, 182–83, 245n 8, 298; criminal liability, 230n 29, 231n 52; opportunities for, 1, 8, 9–10, 41, 42–43. *See also* crimes; criminal conversations; newspaper and media reportage; social and moral panic
crimes, 6–7, 11, 23–24; assault and disorderly conduct, xxxiv, 29, 89, 108, 109, 110–11, 215, 220–21, 230n 35, 253–55, 257–63, 287, 293; beggars and vagrants, 5, 31–32, 34, 108, 109, 117–18, 279; burglary, 6, 11, 12–13, 14, 15, 237–38, 287–88; Offences Against the Person, 109, 215, 219–21, 223, 230n 29, 251–55, 257–63; theft (including larceny and pickpocketing), 6–7, 11, 23–24, 26–28, 30–31, 70–82, 83n 16, 85nn 47, 50, 86n 72, 108, 115, 243–44, 278. *See also* domestic violence; financial crime; murder; sexual offenses; violent crime and violence
criminal conversation (adultery), xxi, xxx–xxi, xxxi n 2, 199–200, 257, 285–86
criminal conversations, xxi–xxx, 1, 3–19, 23–37, 40, 44–46, 49, 51, 52n 11, 55, 60–61, 63, 82, 99–100, 101–4, 106, 113, 115, 117–20, 131–32, 134–35, 140–48, 149–50, 151–52, 157, 158, 166, 170–72, 179–80, 185, 198–210, 215, 232–33, 238, 248–49, 251–52, 254–61, 264n 24, 267, 292; feminine participation in, 1, 5, 10, 23–26, 27, 35–37, 179–80, 215, 232–33, 236–37, 247, 249–50, 251, 255, 258–61; language of, 7, 8, 19, 117–18, 232–33, 238–40; legal discourse in, 14, 32–33, 233, 235–36, 241, 247–50; press and media reportage of, xix–xx, 10, 11, 12–13, 14, 18, 23–37, 60, 62, 66–67, 81, 91, 93, 200–10, 232, 236–40, 241–42, 248–52, 254, 256–61, 267. *See also* language; newspaper and media reportage
criminal statistics, 11–12, 16, 24, 38–39n 2, 107, 108, 109, 111, 121nn 9–10, 252, 254–56, 261–62, 265n 32; "dark figures of crime," 108; Irish in, 108–9, 114, 121n 9; judicial statistics, 108, 121n 9, 252, 265n 32; women in, 108, 252, 254–55, 261. *See also* criminals; dangerous and criminal classes; newspaper and media reporting
criminality and criminal justice system, 3, 20n 1, 25–26, 32, 35, 71, 107, 113, 198–99, 268, 270
criminals, 4–6, 10, 14–16; appearance, 6, 8, 277–29; as "alien"/other, 4, 6–8, 19, 179, 193; definitions of, 5–20, 24–25;

habitual/professional, xxx, 6, 7–8, 11–12, 14–16, 31, 287–88; location and environment of, 8, 9–10, 13–14, 16–17, 26, 107, 113–14, 117; pathological, insane, feeble-minded, 17; perceptions of, 4, 8, 9, 11–12; recidivists, 11, 12–13, 14–15, 28, 35, 287–88. *See also* crimes; dangerous and criminal classes; sexual offenses; violence
criminology, 5–6, 11–13, 261, eugenics and, 13, 16–18; Lombrosan, 13, 17
Crown Prosecution Service, 264n 8
cyber crime and e-commerce, 55–56, 67

dangerous and criminal classes, xxix–xxx, 3–5, 9, 10–11, 23–26, 117–19
Davidoff, Leonore, 190, 193–94, 218
debates, parliamentary. *See* parliament
defense and defendants, 35, 36, 61, 74–75, 78–80, 142, 147, 149, 150, 158–59, 163–64, 167–68, 204, 220–22, 223, 224–25, 235–36, 237–38, 240, 249–50, 256–57, 259–60, 287, 291, 293, 294; defense council, xxii, 36, 74, 142, 145–46, 151–52, 224, 240. *See also* evidence; judges; juries; law and legislation; prosecutions
Denvir, John, 109, 113
Dickens, Charles, xxvii, 6, 7–8, 9, 19, 21n 14, 96, 245n7. See also *Oliver Twist*; *Our Mutual Friend*
discourse analysis. *See* language
domestic service. *See* service
domestic values. *See* household and home
domestic violence, 98, 247–59, 263, 277, 286; aggravated assaults, 251–58, 262, 265n 26; chastisement 248–49; common assault, 250–52, 262; common law and 247–49; male justification for, 248–49, 257, 259–61, 263; parallels with contemporary law, 248, 263, 264n 24, 265n 67; police response to, 254–55; provocation, 249–50, 258–61, 264n 24, 286; separation orders, 256–57, 266n 63; as uncivilized conduct, 92, 94, 248, 263; underreporting of, 254, 255–56, 261; wife beating, 249–50, 254, 258–59, 264n 12; withdrawal of charges, 254–55, 258–59. *See also* gender; men; marriage; prosecutions; sentencing; violence; women
Doré, Gustave, 9,
Dove, William, 141, 148, 149, 151–52, 282
drink and drugs, 31–32, 42, 89, 98, 103, 109–11, 160, 115, 194, 260–61, 275, 278, 286, 297, 299n 2; drink-related crime, 109, 115, 194, 260–61, 297; gin, 183; illegal production of, 110; Irish and, 109–10; leisure and, 110, 111; spirits and beer consumption, 110, 182–83; teetotalism and temperance, 110, 183. *See also* adulteration; food and drink
Du Cane, Edmund, 13,
Dyer, Mrs. Amelia, 210–12, 214n 55

e-commerce. *See* cyber crime
Ellis, Havelock, 128, 135, 136
Ellis, Sarah, 202–5, 288–89
empire, British, 93, 94–95, 99–100; global dimensions, 94; imperial power, 16; law and, 94–95, 100–101; moral dimensions to, 95, 96
employers and employees, 27, 48–49, 159; theft from employers; 27–28. *See also* prosecutions; service and servants
Emsley, Clive, 7
Entrepreneurs. *See* commerce and the commercial sector
evidence, 1, 74, 82, 127, 129–32, 135–36, 141–50, 167, 171–72, 183–84, 186, 203–5, 214n 58, 235–37, 239–40, 242, 288, 293–94; cross-examinations, 35, 150–51, 294; expert testimony, 127–29, 130, 142–51, 184, 165–68, 203–5; 260, 267–68, 269, 287; scientific, 127, 142–50, 150–51; witnesses, 35, 150, 185–86, 288, 293. *See also* gender; law and legislation; medical expertise; medical profession; police; science; trials; women
Fagin. *See* juvenile criminality and delinquency; *Oliver Twist*
family, 3, 8, 28, 31–32, 79, 181, 185, 190–94, 236, 256, 298–99; the bour-

geois family, 8, 181, 185, 187–88, 190–91, 192; domestic relations, 181, 191; domestic values, 181, 190–91, 256; familial circles and paternalism, 48, 51; friends and neighbors, 182, 183, 254, 259, 286; obligations and duties, 61, 191, 256; property and, 182, 186–87, 191, 195n 20; siblings, 28, 186, 190–91; women's responsibilities within, 193–94, 256. *See also* gender; household and home; women household and home

farming. *See* agriculture

female sexuality. *See* sexuality; sexual offenses

feminists and feminism, 206, 247, 249–52, 261. *See also* gender; language

financial crime, 60–61, 64, 115, 269, 289; "bubble" companies, 60, 65, 68n 32, 290; company directors and, 60–63, 290–91; disclosure of accounts, 64–65; Enron, 66; forgery, 144; fraud, 55, 63–66, 69n 38, 158–59, 166, 167, 224–25, 226, 228, 269, 278, 289, 290–91; Maxwell, Robert, 66; mortgage fraud, 66; press reportage of, 55, 57, 60, 63, 289, 290–91. *See also* banks; commerce

financial sector and markets, 55–56, 60, 62, 63; "boom and bust," 65–66; Minsky's "financial instability hypothesis," 65. *See also* banks; companies; financial crime

Fletcher, G. P., 77–78, 81–82

food, cheapness and availability, 161. *See also* adulteration

Foucault, Michel, xxiv, xxv, 138n 15

forgery and fraud. *See* financial crime

Frégier, M. A., 5

Gaskell, Mrs. Elizabeth, 186

gender, xxx, 28, 35, 181, 190, 191, 244, 248, 269, 275, 287; family and, 181, 185–86, 190, 191, 277; law and, 181, 241, 246n 8, 277–78; stereotypes of masculinity and femininity, xxxi, 1, 28, 35, 92–93, 96, 102, 108, 133, 134, 144, 149, 151, 187, 191, 192–94, 218, 232–34, 237, 238, 240, 244, 261, 277–78, 287. *See also* men and masculinity; women

Gladstone, Herbert (as Home Secretary), 14–16

Goode, 49

Goring, Charles, 4, 17

Great Expectations (Dickens), xxvi

Greenwood, James, 8–9, 201–2, 205

Griffiths, Major Arthur, 13

habitual criminals. *See* criminals

Hassall, Dr. Andrew, 166, 169

hiring fairs, 40, 41, 42–47. *See also* service

Holmes, Sherlock (Conan Doyle, Sir Arthur), xxvi

Home Office, 11, 14, 140–42, 205–7, 208–9, 254–55; petitions to, 169

Homicide. *See* murder

household and home, 144, 181–82, 183, 187, 193–94, 250, 261, 293, 298–99; art in, 187; contents, 182, 191, 261; middle-class homes, 182, 249–50; private and public gaze on, 183. *See also* domestic violence; family; respectability and respectable society; women

human rights, 264n 24

Hunt, Alan, xxviii

Husbands. *See* gender; marriage; women

Immorality. *See* moral order

indecent assault. *See* sexual offenses

Infant Life Preservation Society, 205–7. *See also* Charley, Mr.; legal reform

Infanticide. *See* murder

insanity and feeblemindedness. *See* criminals; medical expertise

infanticide. *See* murder

investments and investors. *See* commercial sector

Ireland, 89, 103, 112–15, 275; Fenian activities, 11, 112–13; Irish diaspora, 119

Irish, 102–3, 105n 41, 114, 124n 69, 180, 249–50, 270, 277–78, 286–87; Anglo-Irish tensions, 107, 112–13, 118; criminality and, 107–8, 113–18, 120; "British"–born, 107–8; disorderly conduct and, 107, 108–9, 110–12,

286–87, 293; Irish-born migrants, 106, 108, 118, 121n 10; Loyalists (Orangeism), 106, 111, 286–87; migration, 106; Murphy Riots, 116; Nationalists, 106, 111, 286–87; poverty and the, 106–7, 109–10; prosecution levels of, 107; Roman Catholicism and, 106, 108, 111–12, 115, 116, 117, 118–19; stereotypes of, 107, 113, 120, 248–49, 270, 276–77; Stockport Riots, 121n 37; women, 108–9, 119, 121n 10, 249–50. *See also* Church of England; religion

Jack the Ripper, Whitechapel serial murders, 126, 215
Jay, Reverend Osborne, 16
Jerrold, Blanchard, 9
joint stock companies, 57–58, 64, 69n 37
journalism, xxx, 4, 71, 83n 6, 182, 185, 250, 267; new journalism, 267; social enquiry, 4–5, 26
journalists, xxv, 4–5, 8, 10, 26, 54n 47, 185–86, 250, 281
judges, 37, 93, 102, 148, 182; as lawmakers, 71–82, 85nn 50, 57, 68, 86n 72, 235–38, 240, 243; powers and limits, 70, 76–77; opinions and comments of, xxiii, 14, 29, 33, 35, 71, 74–75, 78–81, 83n 14, 85nn 50, 57, 68, 86n 72,141, 144, 145–46, 148, 151, 215, 219, 220–27, 237–38, 260, 291–92; women, opinions of, 219–20, 223–29, 230n 38, 234, 238, 240, 243, 261, 263. *See also* crimes; domestic violence; rape; women
judges, individual: Auld, LJ, 84n 36, 264n 8; Blackburn, J, 243; Bramwell, Baron, 78–79, 81, 99, 100–101; Brett, LCJ, 101–2, 291–92; Campbell, LCJ, 146, 150; Cave, J, 84n 29, 34–35; Charles, J, 222; Coleridge, LCJ, 84nn 28–29, 35, 248, 263; Crompton, J, 238; Darby, J, 14; Day, J, 84n 29; Denman, J, 74–75, 78, 80, 81, 83–84n 27, 84nn 29, 33, 85n 68; Esher, Lord (Master of the Rolls), 263; Field, J, 84n 29, 222; Grove, J, 84n 29, 260; Hale, J, 77;

Hale, LJ, 150, 221–22, 225, 228; Hawkins, J, 84nn 29, 37, 210–11, 222–23, 230n 38; Huddleston, Baron, 84n 29; Johnston, J, 85n 64; Kelly, LCB, 204, 214n 58; Lush, J, 100, 214n 37; Manisty, J, 75, 84n 29, 260; Matthew, J, 84nn 29–30; Mellor, J, 261; O'Brien, J, 80; Owen, J, 216; Pollock, Baron, 84n 29, 147, 151, 220, 223; Smith, J, 84nn 29, 43; Stephen, J (New South Wales), 214n 58; Wills, J, 14, 84n 29, 222–27, 231n 53. *See also* newspaper and media reporting; Stephen, Sir James Fitzjames
juries, xxvi, 33, 36, 71, 74, 75–76, 81, 84n 36, 102, 141, 142, 143, 144, 145–46, 147–48, 149–50, 182, 185–86, 204, 208, 237–38, 239, 240, 241, 244–45, 260, 297; coroners, 153n 21, 203, 209, 288–89, 297. *See also* respectability and respectable society
justice and authority, 152; love of, 152, 248
juvenile criminality and delinquency, xxix, 3, 5, 17, 23–37, 118, 279, 298–99; deliberate criminality, 28, 36–37; gangs and hooligans, 17, 27, 30–31, 42, 120; gender and, 28; media reportage of, 23–37, 279; national consciousness of, 23–28; nuisance behavior, 29; parenting and, 3, 19; remedies for, 25–26; stereotypes of, 25–26, 30–31; visibility of, 26–37; social perspectives on, 23–28, 31, 36–37. *See also* Bulger case; Burgess case; children; medical expertise; women

Kerr, Robert Malcolm
Kindleberger, C. P., 65–67

language, xxii, 4–5, 8, 45, 93–94, 101, 103, 183, 232–33, 237–38, 240, 244–45, 245nn 5, 7; coded (including *double entendres*), 91, 93–94, 102, 183, 232–35, 237, 239, 240–42, 244–45; discourse analysis, xxii, 128–29; imperial consciousness in, 93–94, 100–101, 248; inappropriate, 234; masculine, 238–39, 247–50; medicolegal discourses, 184, 217–18, 227, 231n 53; sexually

explicit, 232, 234–35, 240, 241; sexualization/desexualization of, 236, 237, 239, 240, 241–43; written and spoken, 103, 233–34, 239. See also criminal conversations; gender; legal discourse; newspaper and media reporting
laudanum/opium, 203–4, 288–89
law and legislation, 13–14, 72–77, 84n 38, 86n 72, 94–95, 216–17, 253, 268–69, 280; company law, 56, 57–58, 64, 290–91; common law, 94–95, 235, 247–50; customary law, 94–95; enforcement of, 207–9; food safety legislation, 157; masculinity of, 204–5, 247–48, 250–51, 260–61; partnership law, 57–58; poisoning and, 149–50. See also gender; legal reform; women
lawyers. See professionals and professionalism
Lacqueur, Thomas, 184
legal discourse, 70–72, 73, 220–26, 232, 234, 238–39, 248–49; gender in, 181, 241, 246n 8, 261; legal reports, 70–72, 82n 1; sexual violence and, 220–26, 228, 232, 234, 236, 238–39, 241. See also criminal conversations; language
legal reform, 13–15, 32–37, 58, 64, 84n 38, 145, 169–70, 205–6, 250–54, 256–57, 258, 263, 266–9; Anti-Contagious Diseases Acts Association, 290; Contagious Diseases Acts, repeal of, 216–17, 289–90. See also law and legislation
Letheby, Dr., 166, 169
limited liability, 56, 57, 62–67, 67n 4; companies, 55, 56–59, 62, 63, 68n 32
literacy levels, xxvi, 24, 234. See also language; newspaper and media reportage

magistrates, xix, 32, 37, 38n 29, 93, 102, 107, 115, 117, 204, 236, 239, 241, 252, 254, 256–59, 276; comments and opinion, xxiii, 4, 5, 30–34, 99–100, 109, 168, 236, 239, 240, 249–50, 253–54, 258–59, 276, 285–86, 289, 293, 294, 297, 298–99; committals by, 102, 109, 204, 239, 253–54, 259; roles and powers of, 33–34, 38n 29, 236, 253–54, 256–59. See also courts
magistrates, individuals, Arnold, 289; Beadon, 99–100; Carden, Sir Robert, 32, 34, 102; Corrie, 297; D'Eyncourt, 31, 102, 259, 286; Edlin, 257; Newton, 30–31; Paynter, 33–34; Woolrych, Austen, 257
maintenance orders. See marriage
marriage, 151–52, 186, 191, 193, 198–99, 215, 220–27, 228, 247, 255–61; bigamy, 140–41, 144, 147, 260; deceased wife's sister, 190–91; harm of sex within, 220–21, 223, 227–28; husbands and wives, 144, 190–91, 220–22, 224, 226, 247, 249–50, 252, 254, 256–63, 264n 12, 294; legal status of women within, 247, 249, 256, 263; maintenance orders, 256–57; marital contract, 216, 220–24, 227–29, 247; rape within, 220–22, 228; remarriage, 191. See also domestic violence; family; gender; household and home; men and masculinity; women
Maybrick, Florence, 142, 151, 156n 95
Mayhew, Henry, 4, 5–8, 9, 12, 19–20, 26, 27, 110
medical expertise, 17–18, 89, 102, 126–29, 145–48, 269, 296; forensics, 127, 128, 130. 133, 136; law and, 146, 148, 240, 269; insanity/feeble-mindedness, 17–18, 141, 148, 149, 191–94; media reportage of medical evidence, 129, 141, 143–52, 157, 269, 288–89; opinions on insanity and feeble-mindedness, 13, 16–18, 102, 148, 192; phrenology, 182, 193; psychology, 133–34, 136, 138n 16, 192; sexuality and, 128, 130, 131–33, 136, 137n 4, 217, 219, 231n 53; sexology (including European/Continental influences on), 128–31, 134, 136–37; venerology, 128–29, 131, 136, 139n 21, 217. See also adulteration; expert testimony; medical profession; science
medical profession, 126–28, 129, 131, 136–37, 153n 29, 154n 59, 200–1, 298; Analytical Sanitary Commission, 166, 169; authority of, 127, 129; 144,

147–51, 184; law and the, 127–29, 133, 141–45, 148, 240, 138n 16; competence of, 127, 143–52, 269; expert witnesses, 146–52, 184, 204–5, 269; moral authority of, 127, 133, 148, 157, 298; opinions, 184; opinions on women, 102, 219; "quacks," 148. *See also* expert testimony; medical expertise; professionals and professionalism; science

melodrama. *See* language; newspaper and media reportage; social and moral panic; violence

men and masculinity, 106, 190, 192, 193–94, 223–24, 227, 233–34, 247–48, 250, 252, 261, 287, 291–92; masculinity, expectations of, 192–94, 247, 291–92, 298; protectors of women, 247–48, 250–51, 261; sexual proclivities, 217–19, 223–34; as victims, 216–17, 218–19, 223–34, 252, 261. *See also* domestic violence; gender; respectability and respectable society; women

Merritt, Mrs. Ann, 142, 151

Methodism. *See* Nonconformity

missions, foreign, 92, 94–97; heroism and, 92, 97; missionaries, 97; missionary writings, 93–99; women and, 95, 97–98. *See also* Church of England; Nonconformity; philanthropic and charitable activity; religion

moral entrepreneurs, xxviii–xxix, xxx, 42, 49, 51

moral order, xxiv, xxix–xxxi, 1, 9–10, 32, 41–43, 51, 92–93, 94, 96–97, 102, 109, 144, 181, 184, 198–99, 216–18, 223–34, 226–28, 244–45, 257, 268, 289–90, 298; immorality, 8, 42, 43, 44–46, 144, 183, 198–99, 218, 226–27, 227–28, 241, 285, 289–90, 299n 2

moral outrage and moral panics. *See* social and moral panics and moral outrage

murder (homicide), 23, 29–30, 35–36, 140–44, 181, 185, 193–94, 203–5, 208–12, 250, 257, 259, 260–62, 266n 72, 269, 276, 282, 297; child murderers, 17–18, 23, 29–30, 35–36; cot deaths, 269; dialogue of the corpse, 179, 182–85, 192–94; domestic homicides, 181–82, 247, 250, 257, 260–62, 266n 72; infanticide and child murder, 98, 199–200, 204–6, 208–12; manslaughter, 36, 203–4, 208, 247, 250, 261, 291–92; inquests, 143, 145, 183–84, 192, 209, 297; suicide, 182, 192–94, 276, 288, 294. *See also* Bulger case; Burgess case; domestic violence; Novelli family; Novelli, Harriet; violence

nation, health of, 16–18, 92, 268

national identity, xxx, 16, 92, 96, 98–99, 101, 119, 144, 181, 193, 248, 280

newspaper and media reporting, xxii–xxx, xxxinn 1, 12, 1, 10, 20n 1, 23–24, 26–37, 55, 60, 95–96, 97–98, 113, 115, 171–72, 179–80, 185, 198–200, 217–19, 222–28, 232–33, 240, 241–42, 243, 245n 8, 247–50, 256–57, 259–61, 267–71, 289–90; advertisements, 199–203, 207–9, 295; Chartist newspapers, 245n 8; crime reporting, xxiv–xxv, xxvii, 23–25, 26–37, 66, 71, 81–82, 85n 68, 91–92, 93, 100, 120, 140–41, 181, 184–86, 188, 192, 250, 252, 254, 256–57, 259–61, 267, 285, 292, 296, 297, 298; editorial policy, xxiii, xxvii, 45, 94, 285, 296–97; editorials and leaders, 44, 53n 23, 145, 152, 158, 172, 213n 21, 267, 287, 289–91, 298–99; headlines and bylines, xxvi, 30, 232, 236, 242, 267, 285, 286, 287, 288, 289, 293, 296, 297–98; gender and class stereotypes in, 179–80, 232–33, 241, 250, 289–90, 298–99; illustrations in, 274; lawyers and, xxv; letters and, xxvi–xxvii, 14, 33, 44, 140–42, 143, 144, 145, 148, 172, 250, 281; legal system and, xxiii; national press, 26–27, 32, 45, 70–71, 172, 181, 183; print and press conversations, xxii–xxvii, 6–7, 11, 24–30, 32–37, 42, 44, 49, 91, 164, 179–80, 185, 198–200, 217, 232, 234, 247, 250,

257, 268, 285–99; provincial press, 26–27, 32, 44–45, 49, 51, 52n 11, 53n 23, 70–71, 172, 181, 182, 183, 234, 241, 261, 283, 297, 299n 5; readerships, xxii, 182, 274, 285, 292, 294–97; respectable 234, 241, 274; sensationalism, xxi–xxii, xxiv, xxvii, 42, 44, 181, 185, 217, 219, 234, 240, 241, 274, 285, 296, 297; Sunday newspapers, 241, 292, 295, 296–97. *See also* language, literacy levels

newspaper titles: *The Bath Chronicle*, 17; *The Beverley Guardian*, 44; *Chester Chronicle*, 121n 12; *Clerkenwell News*, 200–2; *Daily News*, 142, 150; *Daily Telegraph*, xxii, xxiv, xxvii, 34, 95, 101, 141, 147–48, 152, 205, 215, 220, 257, 266n 72, 267, 284, 285–92; *The Driffield Times*, 44; *Durham Advertiser*, 297; *East London Observer*, 215; *Hull and Eastern Counties Herald*, 44; *Glasgow Herald*, 122n 80; *Illustrated London News* xxiv; *Illustrated Police News*, xvi, xxxiv, 88, 92, 178, 254, 265n 35, 259, 267, 273, 274, 275; *The Leeds Express*, 244; *Leicester Daily Mercury*, 71, 81; *Leicester Journal*, 71, 75, 82, 83nn 26–27, 85n 68; *Lloyds News (Weekly)*, 203, 267, 294–96; *Manchester Courier*, 276; *Manchester Guardian*, 168, 188, 273; *Morning Chronicle*, 26; *Morning Post*, 10; *The Nation*, 113; *News of the World*, 95, 105n 41, 232, 237–38, 239, 240, 241–43, 273, 282, 283, 292–94; *Nottingham Review*, 26–27; *Pall Mall Gazette*, 11, 34, 101, 102–3, 208–9, 229n 7, 240, 250, 298–99; *Reynolds News/Weekly*, xxiii, xxvi, 296–97; *The Spectator*, 242; *The Times*, xxiii, xxvi, 11, 14, 26, 31, 33, 57, 60, 63, 95, 143, 144–45, 153nn 21, 25, 157, 158, 164, 167, 168–69, 172, 203, 204, 213n 21, 215, 219, 220, 252, 257, 267, 273, 281, 292; *The Yorkshire Gazette*, 44, 118; *York Gazette*, 44, 53n 47; *York Herald*, 44, 54n 47. *See also* periodicals

Nonconformity, 50–51; anti-Catholicism, 112; Baptist Missionary Society, 92; London Missionary Society, 92; Popular Protestantism, 112. *See also* Church of England; missions; philanthropic and charitable activity; religion

Novelli Family, 186–89, 192–94, 197n 58; Alexander, 182, 183, 188, 191–94, 195n 10; Lewis, 182, 186–87, 188, 189, 191, 192. *See also* family; household and home; medical expertise; murder; Novelli, Harriet

Novelli, Harriet, 179, 181–87, 191, 193–94, 195n 10, 276. *See also* gender; murder; respectability and respectable society; women

Offences Against the Person. *See* crimes

Oliver Twist (Dickens), 6; Artful Dodger, 27, 35; Bill Sikes, 6, 14, 245n 7; Fagin, 27, 30. *See also* children; Dickens, Charles; juvenile criminality and delinquency

Overend Gurney Ltd., 57, 58–64, 66–67. *See also* banking; financial crime

Our Mutual Friend (Dickens), xxvi

Palmer, William, 141, 144, 145–46, 150–51, 154n 47

parliament, 14–15, 25, 34, 57–58, 64, 77, 209, 261; bills and acts, 57–58; Committees of Inquiry, 64; and the law, 58, 77, 206–7, 252; parliamentary debates, 14–16, 25, 63, 143, 206–7, 209–10, 218, 219, 235, 252. *See also* Home Office; Reports; Select Committees

Patel, Trupti, 269

Paternalism. *See* family

periodical titles: *The Bankers Magazine*, 59, 60; *Blackwoods Magazine*, 149; *British Medical Journal*, 148, 149, 200–1, 207–9; *Cassells Saturday Journal*, xxxin 10, 273, 274, 277–79, 295; *Cornhill Magazine*, 157; *Dublin Review*, 118; *Dublin University Magazine*, 144; *The Economist*, 59; *Journal of Mental Science*, 133; *The Lancet*, 145, 147, 152, 157, 162, 166, 169, 173n 13; *Punch*, 118; *Saturday Review*, 214n 56; *The Spectator*,

144; *Temple Bar*, 63; *Westminster Review*, 248, 264n 6; *Women's Suffrage Journal*, 206, 260–61. *See also* newspaper titles

philanthropic and charitable activity, 14, 25–26, 31–33, 92, 186–87, 198, 258; Girls' Friendly Society, 47; home missions, 92; National Society for the Prevention of Cruelty to Children, 208–9; Ragged School Brigade, 297; Society for the Protection of Women and Children, 258; Toynbee Trust, 14. *See also* Church of England; missions; Nonconformity; religion.

Plint, Thomas, 9–10

Phrenology. *See* medical expertise

poisoners, 260; medical poisoners, 140, 141–43, 145–46, 298; gender issues, 149, 192–93

poisoning, 89, 141–42, 144–50, 153n 9, 193, 194, 260, 282, 298; antimony; 145, arsenic, 142, 143–44, 146–48, 151, 153n 21, 163, 166; *cocculus indicus*, 161, 296; copper sulfate, 162, 296; Prussian blue, 162, 163; strychnine, 145–46, 150, 154n 41, 282. *See also* adulteration; medical profession; poisoners

police, 7, 8, 10, 14, 18, 19–20, 27–28, 30, 45–46, 47, 74, 107, 113, 115–17, 126, 131, 202–3, 206–7, 210–11, 238, 239, 242, 255–56, 258, 275, 285–86, 287, 289, 299n 1; assaults on, 108, 109, 111, 116, 117, 121n 21, 256, 270, 285, 294; Chief Constables, comments, 121n 21, 254; Irish and, 107, 109, 111, 116–17, 287; Metropolitan Police, 7, 8, 202–3, 255, 264n 8; provincial forces, 115–16; Royal Irish Constabulary, 116; Scotland Yard, 11

popular concerns about crime. *See* social and moral panics

popular opinion, 141, 145, 150, 152, 167, 217, 267

Poovey, Mary, 185

poverty and the poor, 5–6, 10, 24, 26–27, 29, 31, 106–7, 109, 113, 115–19, 159, 161, 163, 164–65, 167–68, 169–70,

188, 198–9, 201–2, 208–9

print conversations. *See* newspaper and media reporting

prisons and reformatories, 13–14, 27–28, 31–37, 39n 33, 108, 116–17, 121n 86, 287, 298–99; Carlyle Gaol, 121n 10; Chester Gaol, 108; Holloway Prison, 16; Preston Gaol, 118; role of, 28

Pritchard, Dr., 126, 145, 154n 38, 298

professionals and professionalism, 9, 14, 89, 126–29, 189; doctors, 126–28, 165, 166; lawyers, 126–28, 241. *See also* criminals

prosecution, 27–28, 30–31, 60–61, 74–75, 107–9, 111, 117–18, 119, 127, 143, 159, 164–65, 170, 172, 220–21, 224–25, 230n 29, 236–37, 239–40, 242, 252, 254–60, 269, 289, 293–94; domestic violence and, 251–52, 254–60, 286; victim instigated, 234, 236–37, 239–40, 252, 254, 257–59, 286, 289, 293–94. *See also* crimes; domestic violence; sexual violence; violence.

prostitutes and prostitution, 199–200, 216–18, 220–21, 223–24, 226–27, 228, 244; contagious diseases, 216–17, 289–90; moral fears of, 216–18, 223–24, 226; social evil, 217. *See also* sexuality and sexual practices; venereal disease

public health, 158, 168–69

public opinion. *See* social and moral panic

punishment. *See* sentencing

Quinton, Dr. R. F., 13

race and identity, xxx, 1, 3–4, 95–97, 102, 181, 192–94, 275, 280; Asanti, 93; Australian aboriginals, 96; Britons, 99, 102, 108; Chinese, 103; Germans, 189; Greeks, 189; "Hottentots," 98, 102; Italians, 186–87, 188–89; Jews, 119, 189; Masai, 98; Scots, 108, 109; Spanish, 189; Welsh, 108, 109; Yoruba, 98; Zulus, 98, 99; class and, 102; Englishness, 190, 193, 280; race and criminality, 6, 113–20, racial hierarchies, 96–98, 109; religion and, 92–95, 96; women and, 92–93; xenophobic stereotypes, 89, 92, 96–100, 102, 111–13, 115–16, 119–20, 121n 37, 270, 293. *See also* empire; national identity; Ireland; Irish

Radzinowicz, Leon, 260

railways, 58–59, 63, 200–1, 202–3; 236; assaults on, 236–37, 261; company bylaws, 236–37; navvies, 111; sexual assaults on, 236–37

rape, 220–24, 232, 235–40, 243, 244, 293–94; attempted rape, 236–37, 239, 244, 294, 297; consent, 222–23, 239, 243, 244; definitions of, 235, fraud and, 224; legal opinions and, 220–24, 235–38, 239, 243; marital rape exemption, 220–23; within marriage, 220–24

religion, 25, 43, 50, 106, 108, 110–12, 134; class and, 50–51; influence of, 50, 92, 94, 100, 115, 117, 119, 234; Roman Catholicism, 106, 108, 110–13, 116–20, 186; sectarianism, 111–12, 117, 119

reports, official: Report on the State of the Irish Poor (1836), 107, 109; Report of the Constabulary Commissioners (1839), 107; Board of Health Report on the Sanitary Condition of Wolverhampton (1849), 121, 121n 15; Report of the Select Committee on Criminal and Destitute Juveniles (1852), 39nn 2, 28, 32, 40n 43; First Report from the Commissioners on the Employment of Children, Young Persons and Women in Agriculture (1867–68), 53n 31, 46; Report on the Adulteration of Food and Drink (1856), 169; Report of the Select Committee on Limited Liability Acts (1866), 64; Report of the Select Committee on the Preservation of Infant Life (1871), 206–7; Report of the Select Committee on the Adulteration of Food and Drink Act 1872 (1874), 169; Report to the Secretary of State for the Home Department on the State of the Law Relating to Brutal Assaults (1874), 265n 34; Second Report of the Select Committee on Intemperance (1877), 121n 19; Wolfenden Report, 135

respectability and respectable society, xxiv, xxvii–xxx, 3–5, 8, 9–20, 71, 100–101, 103–4, 140, 144, 147, 181, 184, 185, 233–34, 236–37, 240–44, 257, 299n 2; gender and, 183, 232–33, 238, 240–41; social status and, 242–43; threats to the moral tone of, 9–20, 41, 43, 100–101, 103–4, 109, 184, 216, 241–42, 257; working-class moral condition, 43, 188

retail and retailers. *See* commerce and the commercial sector

Reynolds, George, xiii, 296

Robb, George, 149

Roman Catholicism. *See* religion, Irish; Church of England

Rowbotham, Judith, 263, 273

Royal Commissions, 290; Royal Commission on Penal Servitude (1863), 7; Royal Commission on the Employment of Children, Young Persons and Women in Agriculture, 46

rural society, 50, 113–14

scandals, financial, 55, 57, 60, 679n 4

science and scientific practice, 127, 145–52, 156–57; chemical and biochemical analysis, 127, 142, 143, 147–48, 157, 159, 163–69; public faith in, 142, 145–52. *See also* adulteration; medical expertise; medical profession

sectarianism. *See* religion

Select Committees, 206, 209; Select Committee on Drunkenness (1834), 195; Select Committee on Criminal and Destitute Juveniles (1852), 33–34, 37–38n 2; Select Committee on Food Adulteration (1856), 158, 159, 166–67, 169–70, 172; Select Committee on the Limited Liability Acts (1866), 64; Select Committee on the Preservation of Infant Life (1871), 206; Select Committee, Infant Life Preservation Bill (1896), 210–11; witnesses to, 33–34, 39n 32, 159, 166–67, 172, 206, 209–10, 213n 23, 214n 53. *See also* Reports

Self-Help (Smiles), xxx
sentencing, 12–13, 14–16, 24–32, 35–37, 38nn 22, 29, 75, 82, 84n 41, 100, 108, 114, 116–20, 140–43, 204–5, 208–10, 235, 236–39, 243, 244, 247, 251, 252, 254, 256–62, 266n 72, 276, 286, 287, 292–93, 297; death penalty, xxiv, 35–36, 142–43, 149, 204–5, 208–10, 260–61, 282, 294; deterrence, 33–34, 205, 236–37, 252, 266n 72, 268, 286; practices, 28, 247, 261; preventive detention, 13–16; punishment, 7–8, 28, 33, 36–37, 247–48, 252, 257, 268; transportation, 7–8, 28, 114, 143, 44. *See also* class; crimes; domestic violence; gender; law and legislation; judges; magistrates
service and servants, 236; domestic, 28, 198–99, 239, 241, 243–44, 287, 293–94; contracts of, 40–41, 44, 239, 294; farm, 1, 40, 43, 48–49, 51–52, 52nn 1–3, 54nn 41, 45; hiring practices, 41, 42, 45–47; moral regulation of servants, 1, 43, 45, 51–52, 198–200; references (characters), 41, 44; register (employment) offices, 44, 46; relations with employers, 28, 40, 48, 198, 294; stereotypes of servants, 43, 44–45, 198–200, 294. *See also* employers and employees
sexual intercourse, 184, 193, 220, 222–26, 228; age of consent, 216–19; attraction, 190–91, 193, 233–34; harm of, 216, 220, 223–29; penis, 223, 233–34, 235; promiscuity, 43, 44–45; sexual contract, 216, 223–38; vagina, 233–34; women's agency in, 216, 220, 222–23, 228–29. *See also* rape; sexuality and sexual practices; sexual violence; women
sexual offenses, 219–20, 222–23, 226, 230n 25, 232, 236, 238, 241, 243–44, 251–52, 293–94, 297; aggravated assault, 235–36; child abuse, 152, 230n 35, 297; consent, 216, 222–23, 227–29, 230n 35, 235, 238; criminal assault, 235–36, 244; indecent assault, 220–21, 235–37, 243–44, 251; male culpability, 216, 219, 223, 230n 35, 243–44; sodomy, 127–37, 138n 11, 139n 22. *See also* crimes; marriage; rape; sexual intercourse; sexual violence; sexuality and sexual practices; violence; women
sexual violence, 220, 223, 232, 238, 241–42, 257; language, use of, 238, 241–42; press representations of, 219, 228, 232–33, 238, 241–42, 243–44, 293–94. *See also* crimes; domestic violence; language; rape; violence; women
sexuality and sexual practices, 216–17; difference, xxx; female, 179–80, 216–18, 237, 239, 241; female sexual rights, 179–80, 217, 220, 227–29, 237; history of, 128–29, 131–35, 138n 15; homosexuality, 126, 127–29, 134, 136, 138; law and, 127, 128–29, 135, 136–37, 139n 22; male, 216–18, 226–27; press representations of, 217, 239; sadomasochism, 126; seduction and violation, 223, 226–28, 237–39. *See also* gender; medical expertise; sexual intercourse; sexual offenses; social and moral panic
shareholders, 60, 61, 62, 63–64, 66, 68n 14; Overend Gurney Defence Association, 60–61. *See also* banking; company directors; financial crime; investments and investors
Shipman, Dr. Harold, 145
Smethurst, Dr. Thomas, 140–41, 144, 146–48, 151, 152, 154n 59, 260
Smiles, Samuel. See *Self-Help*
Smith, Madeleine, 141, 153n 33
social control and socialization, xxx, 41, 42–43, 46, 268
social and moral panic and moral outrage, xxii–xxiv, xxvii–xxvii, 1, 3–20, 42–51, 63, 65–67, 82, 126, 128–30, 134, 136–37, 140, 144, 146, 151–52, 157, 159–60, 161, 166, 179–80, 198–212, 216–17, 220–25, 228–29, 232, 233, 236, 268–71, 298; Cohen model, usefulness of, 47–48, 49, 51; counter discourse, 49, 269; media promotions of, xx, xxiii–xxxiv, 1, 3, 4, 23, 44–45, 51, 52n 11, 62–63, 268, 270, 298; public

opinion, attempts to mobilize, 23, 26, 45, 46, 145–46, 205, 236, 268, 270, 298; sexual dimensions to, 128, 134, 137, 217, 228–29; social change and, 48–49. *See also* Cohen, Stanley; criminal conversations; newspaper and media reporting

Social Science Association, 46, 53n 33, 205–6, 213n 10

South Sea Bubble, 56

Stephen, Sir James Fitzjames, 84nn 29, 34, 100, 141–42, 149–50, 156n 95, 214n 58, 220, 224, 226, 241, 248, 298; Indian Criminal Code, 100. *See also* judges, opinions and comments; judges, individual

Stevens, Sir John (Metropolitan Police Commissioner), 20n 2

Stevenson, Kim, 218

Stretton, Hesba, 36–37

Suicide. *See* murder

Sullivan, Dr., 17

Symonds, John Addington, 134–35

Taylor, Dr. Alfred Swaine, 130, 132, 143, 145–48

Taylor, Harriet, 256

Thompson, Keith, 52n 8

Thompson, Robert. *See* Bulger case

Thompson, William (Archbishop of York), 45

Tichbourne trial and Claimant, 5, 296–97

Tomes, Nancy, 252–53, 257

trials, 23, 29–30, 35–36, 61, 71, 74, 99–100, 140–42, 147–49, 210–11, 215, 219–21, 233; "witch" trials, 148–49, 152, 204, 269

urban society, 3–10, 16–17, 24–26, 36–37, 50, 60, 106–7, 111–12, 115–17, 157–58, 165, 200–8, 298–99; London, 5, 10, 12–13, 14, 31, 60, 160, 200–7, 255; Liverpool, 108–9; Manchester, 12–13, 34, 182, 185, 187–89, 298–99; middle-class suburbs, 187–88; Nottingham, 27, 31; religion and, 50; spatial segregation, 5, 8–10, 16–17, 187–88; street life, xxvii, 29, 30–31, 36–37, 188, 298–99; working-class settlements, 187–88. *See also* class; gender; respectability and respectable society

Venables, Jon. *See* Bulger case

venereal disease, 215, 218, 223, 225; contagiousness and, 216; contagious diseases acts, 216–17, 229n 10; gonorrhea, 215, 218–19, 228, 229n 10, 230n 35; syphilis, 229n 10, 235n 10

vice. *See* sexual intercourse; crime and bad behavior; criminal conversation

violence and violent crime, 29–30, 89, 92–93, 113–15, 118–19, 185, 215, 232–33, 245n 8, 256, 263; "acceptable" and "unacceptable" violence, 92, 93, 95, 97, 100, 113–15, 248–52, 256–63, 278, 291–93; decline in crimes of, 114, 118–19, 252, 255–56; interpersonal violence, 115, 221–23, 232–33, 247–48, 254–63; masculine, 248–54, 258–63, 264n 24, 291–92; melodrama and, 181–82, 183, 219; rhetorics of, 93, 94, 97, 232–33, 248–49, 253; sexual violence 92, 221–23, 232–33, 251, 256–57; terrorism, 93; against women, 92, 97, 102, 221–23, 247–63, 286; women and, 92, 97, 100–101, 102, 103, 275, 278, 293; workplace violence, 113. *See also* crimes, domestic violence

Wainewright, Thomas Griffiths, 145, 154n 41

Walkowitz, Judith, 219, 230n 21, 234

war, 16, 93, 97

Waters, Margaret, 202–5, 211, 288–89, 295

Waugh, Reverend Benjamin, 36–37, 208, 210–11, 214nn 53, 56

white collar crime. *See* financial crime

wife-beating. *See* domestic violence

Wilde, Oscar, 126

Winsor, Charlotte, 198, 201–2

witnesses. *See* evidence; medical expertise; Select Committees

women, 190–91, 193, 198–99, 215, 228, 250–51, 256, 263, 289–90; as mothers, 18–19, 198–200, 208, 256, 269, 297;

courts and, 108, 240, 247–48, 252–56; dependence / independence; 215, 217, 225, 242, 247–48, 256; drink and, 32, 236, 237, 239–40, 297; empire and, 95; female testimony, 186, 219, 221, 228, 232–33, 236–37, 241, 245, 254, 258–60, 293–94; feminine stereotypes, 28, 35, 92, 102, 108, 179–80, 184–85, 193–94, 198–99, 218, 220, 237–38, 239–40, 244–45, 245n 5, 252, 259–61, 266n 72, 275, 290, 293, 297; Irish, 108, 249–50, 278, 293; legal status of, 217, 241; madness and, 192–93; male gaze and, 217–18; morals and, 144, 147, 179–80, 183, 193–94, 217–18, 219–20, 256–57, 285; poisoning and, 140, 149; pregnancy and, 198–99, 203; property and, 191, 217, 247, 251; as victims, 179, 215, 218, 232–33, 247–49 252, 254, 257–60, 263; villainesses, 140, 142, 145, 151, 202–5, 297; widows, 182, 191; work and, 198–206. *See also* common law; sexual crime; violent crime

Wood, Mrs. Henry, 67n 1, 68n 32, 83 n5

Woodward, Louise, 198, 269

Wooler, Joseph, 143–44

xenophobia. *See* race and identity

www.ingramcontent.com/pod-product-compliance
Lightning Source LLC
Chambersburg PA
CBHW030105010526
44116CB00005B/108